YOTSUBA&! 7

KIYOHIKO AZUMA

CONTENTS

WITHDRAWN

YOTSUBA&!
KIYOHIKO AZUMA

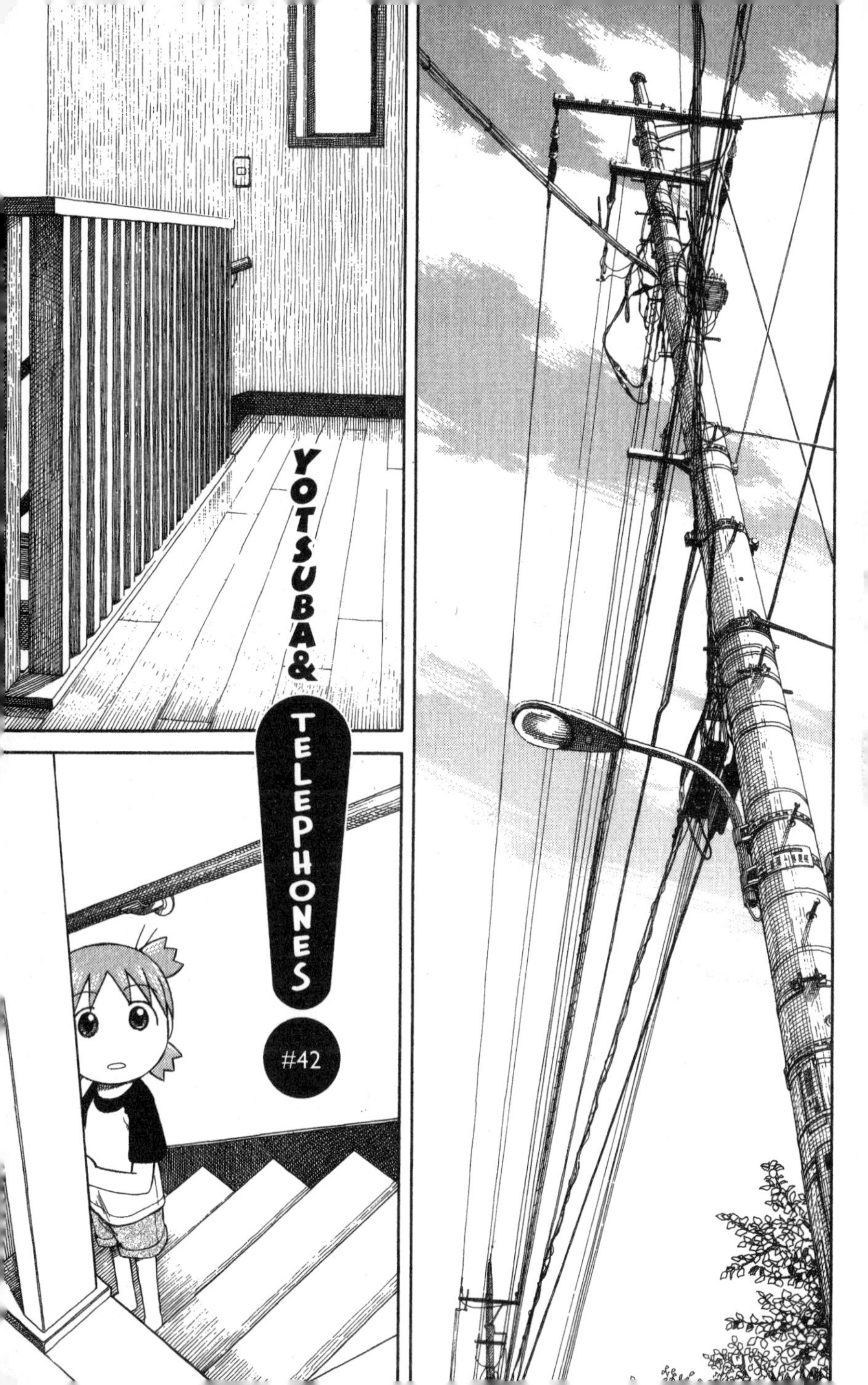
YOTSUBA&
TELEPHONES!
#42

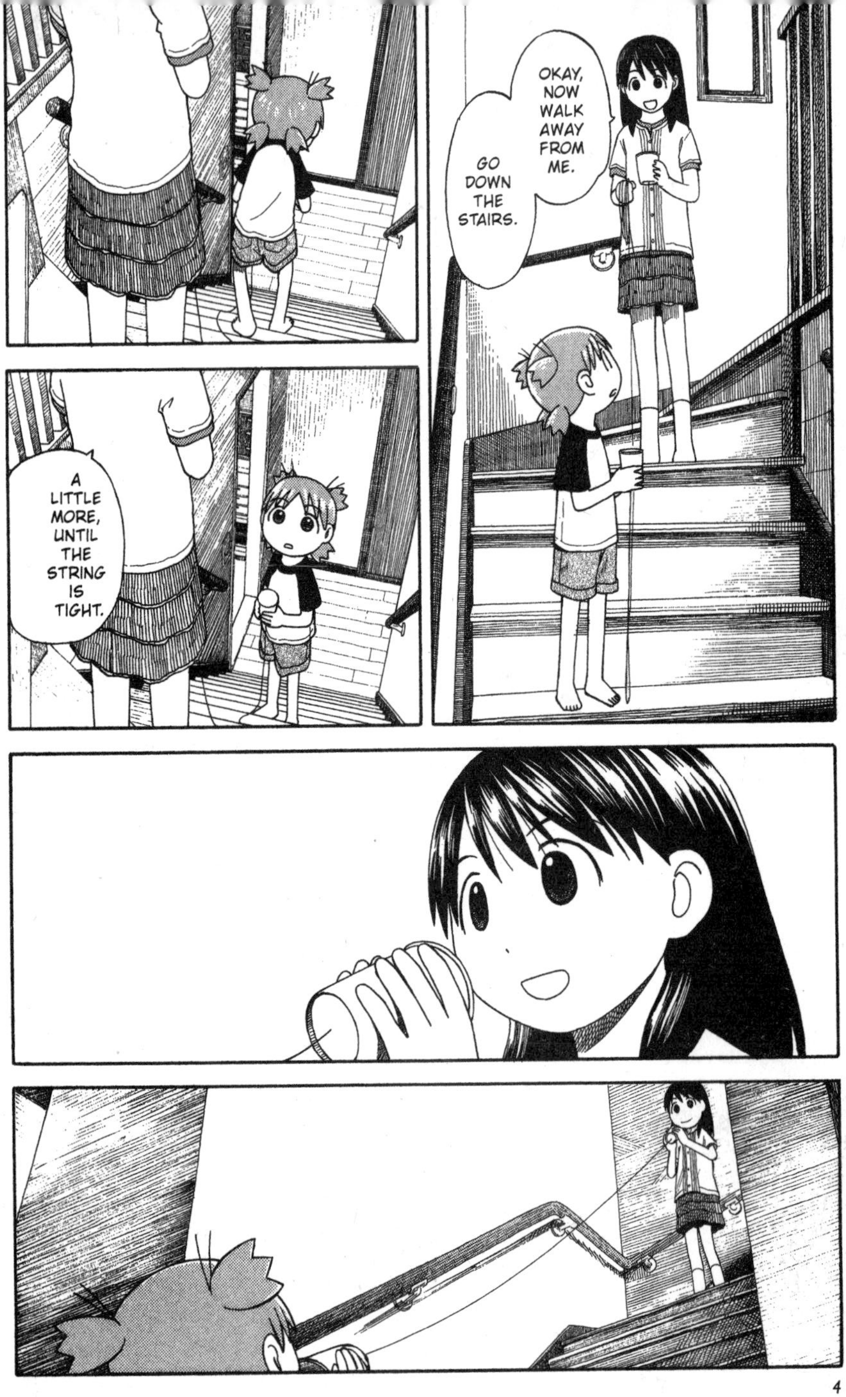
OKAY, NOW WALK AWAY FROM ME.
GO DOWN THE STAIRS.
A LITTLE MORE, UNTIL THE STRING IS TIGHT.

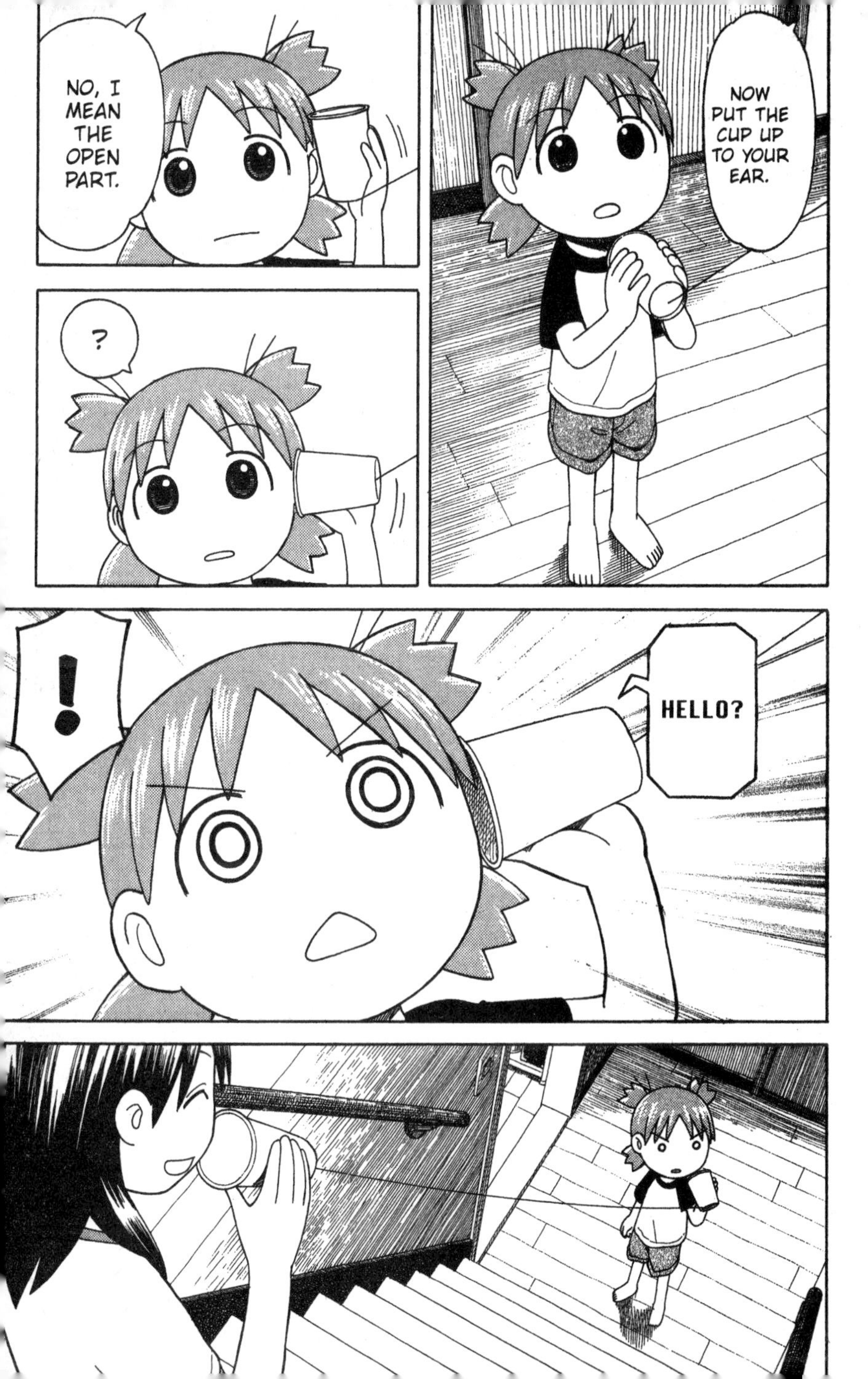
NOW PUT THE CUP UP TO YOUR EAR.
NO, I MEAN THE OPEN PART.
?
HELLO?
!

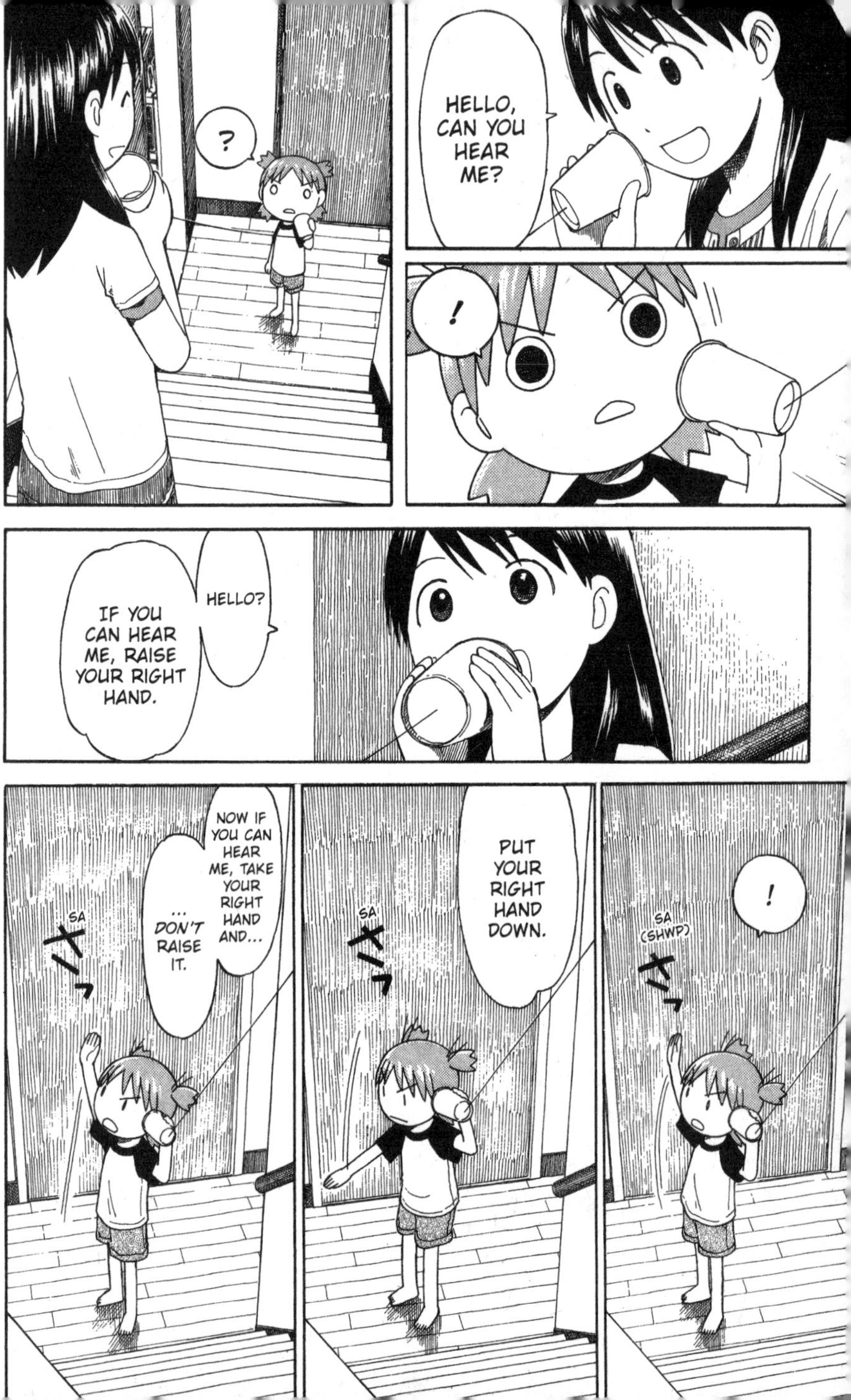
HELLO, CAN YOU HEAR ME?
!
?
HELLO?
IF YOU CAN HEAR ME, RAISE YOUR RIGHT HAND.
!
SA (SHWP)
PUT YOUR RIGHT HAND DOWN.
SA
NOW IF YOU CAN HEAR ME, TAKE YOUR RIGHT HAND AND...
...DON'T RAISE IT.
SA

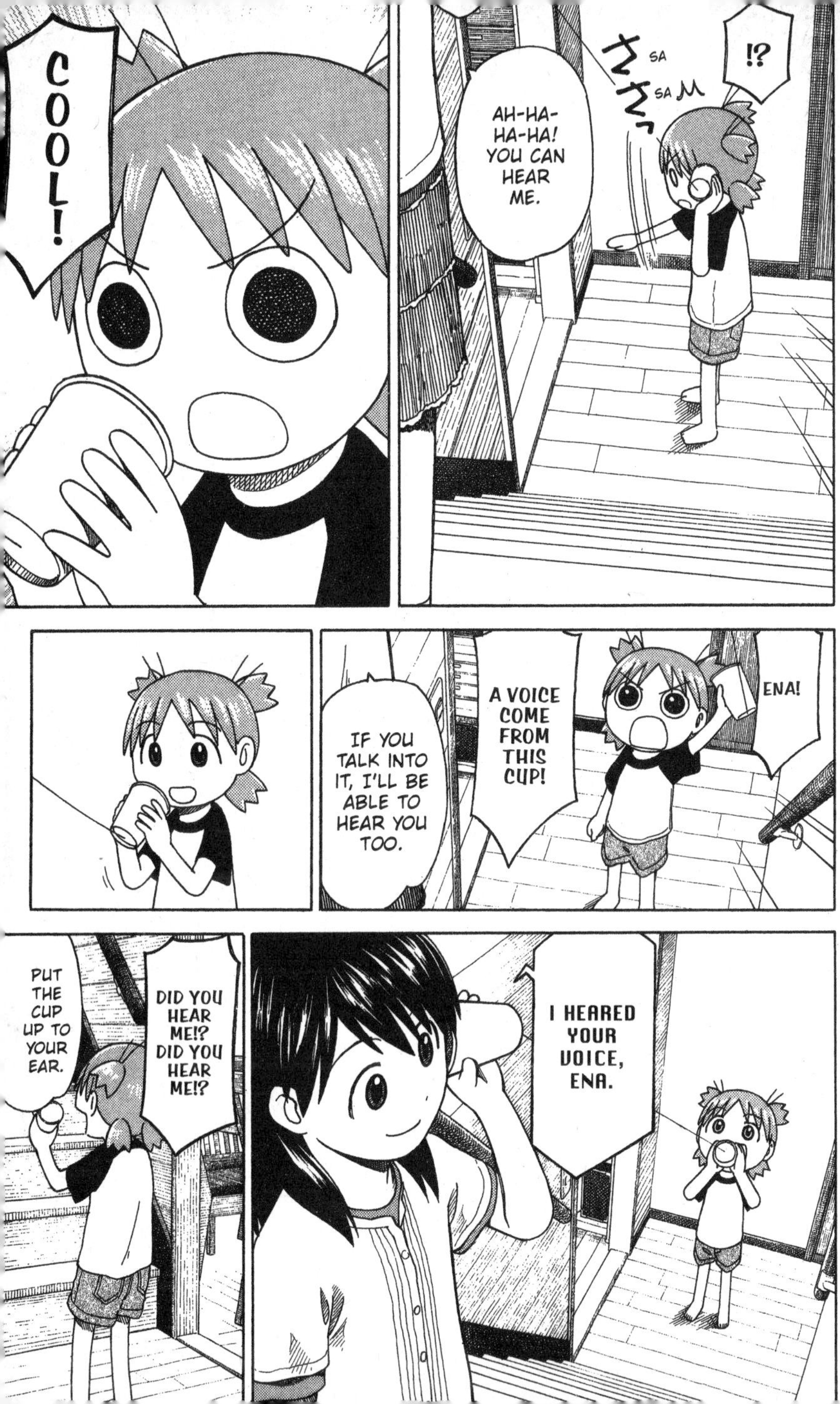
!?
SA SA
AH-HA-HA-HA! YOU CAN HEAR ME.
COOL!
ENA!
A VOICE COME FROM THIS CUP!
IF YOU TALK INTO IT, I'LL BE ABLE TO HEAR YOU TOO.
I HEARED YOUR VOICE, ENA.
DID YOU HEAR ME!? DID YOU HEAR ME!?
PUT THE CUP UP TO YOUR EAR.

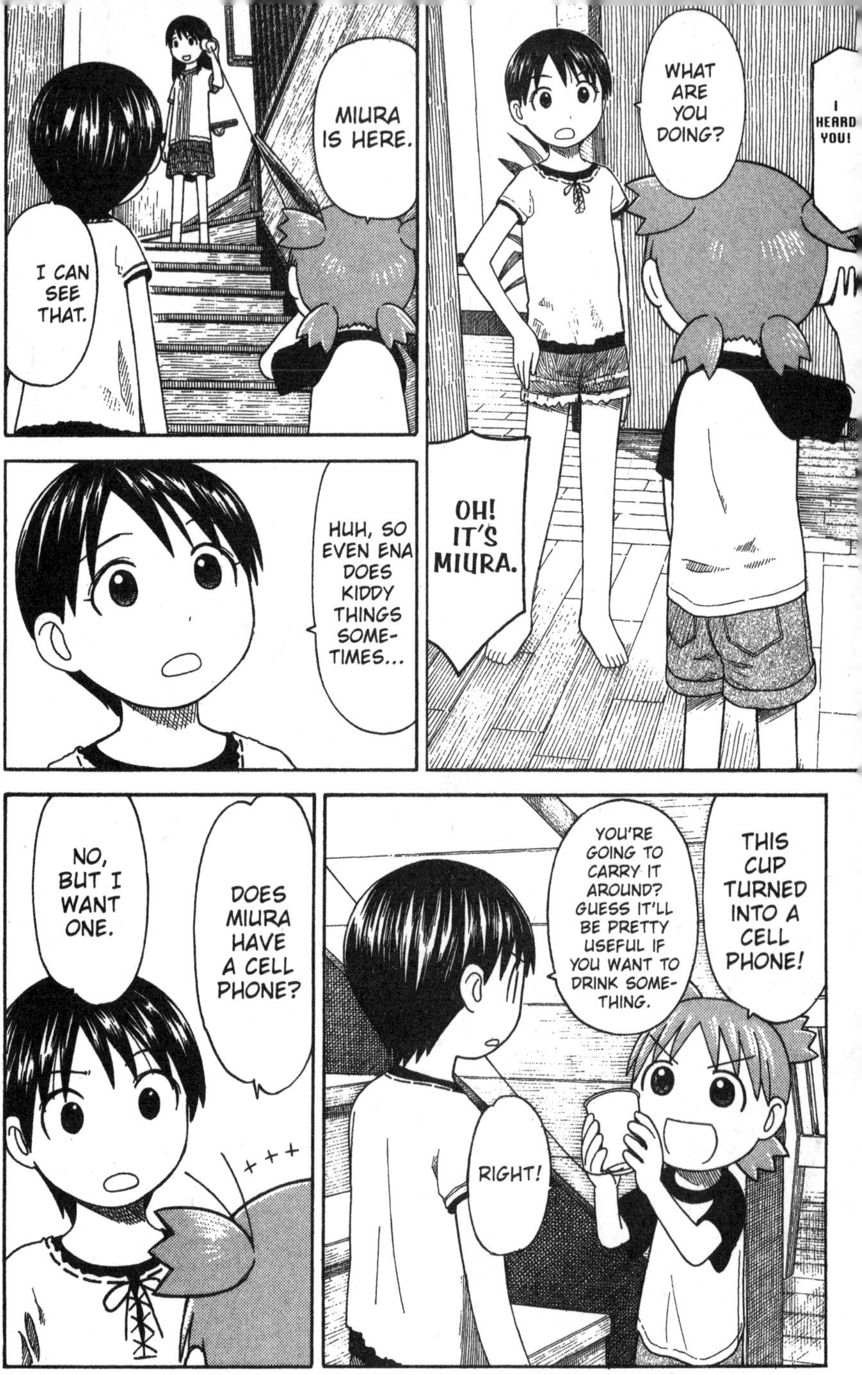
I HEARD YOU!
WHAT ARE YOU DOING?
OH! IT'S MIURA.
MIURA IS HERE.
I CAN SEE THAT.
HUH, SO EVEN ENA DOES KIDDY THINGS SOME-TIMES...
THIS CUP TURNED INTO A CELL PHONE!
YOU'RE GOING TO CARRY IT AROUND? GUESS IT'LL BE PRETTY USEFUL IF YOU WANT TO DRINK SOME-THING.
RIGHT!
DOES MIURA HAVE A CELL PHONE?
NO, BUT I WANT ONE.

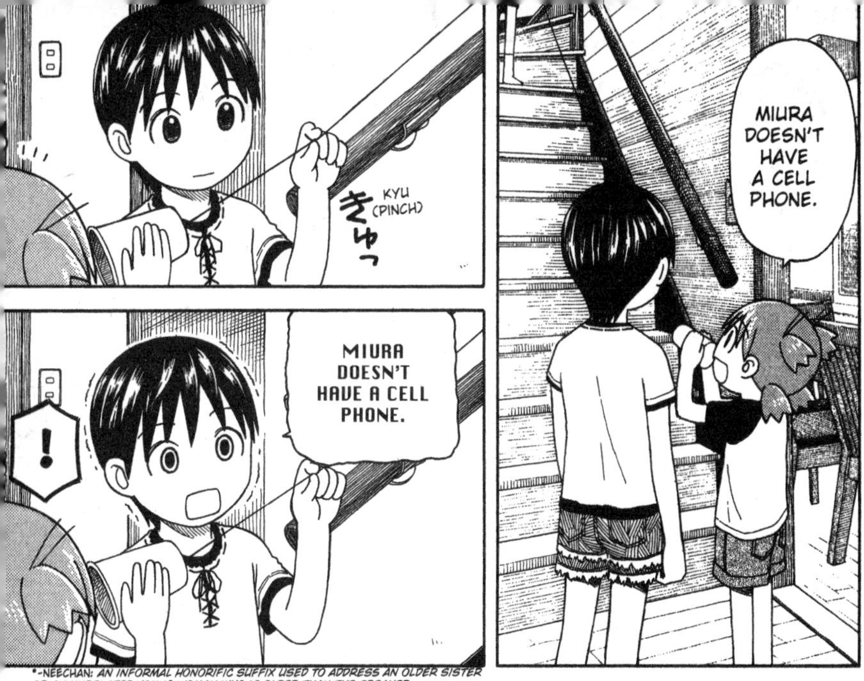
MIURA DOESN'T HAVE A CELL PHONE.
きゅっ
KYU (PINCH)
!
MIURA DOESN'T HAVE A CELL PHONE.

*-NEECHAN: AN INFORMAL HONORIFIC SUFFIX USED TO ADDRESS AN OLDER SISTER OR AN UNRELATED YOUNG WOMAN WHO IS OLDER THAN THE SPEAKER.

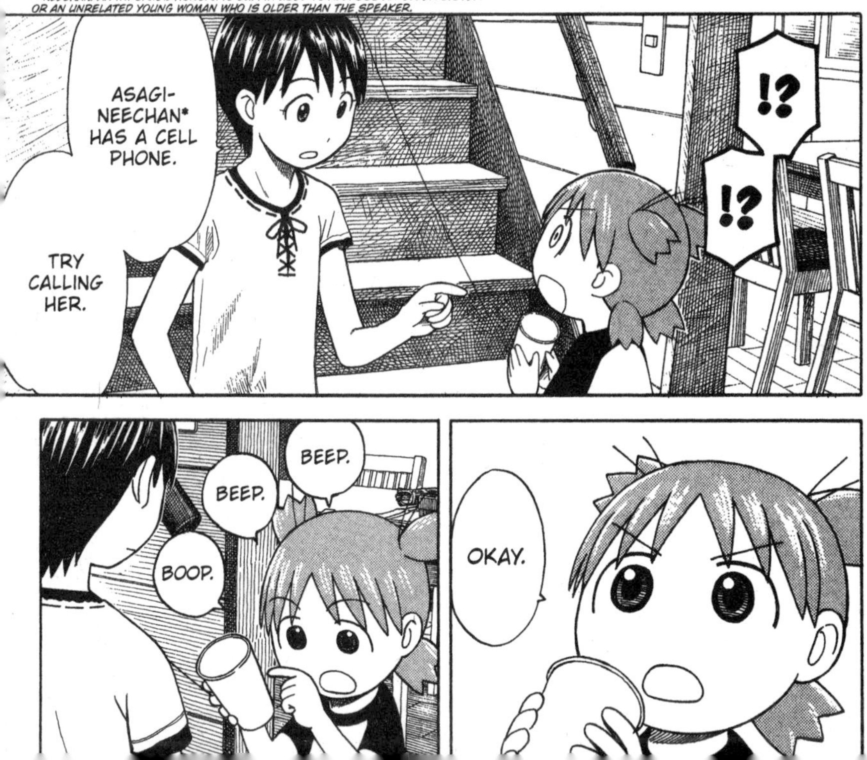
!?
!?
ASAGI-NEECHAN* HAS A CELL PHONE.
TRY CALLING HER.
OKAY.
BEEP.
BEEP.
BOOP.

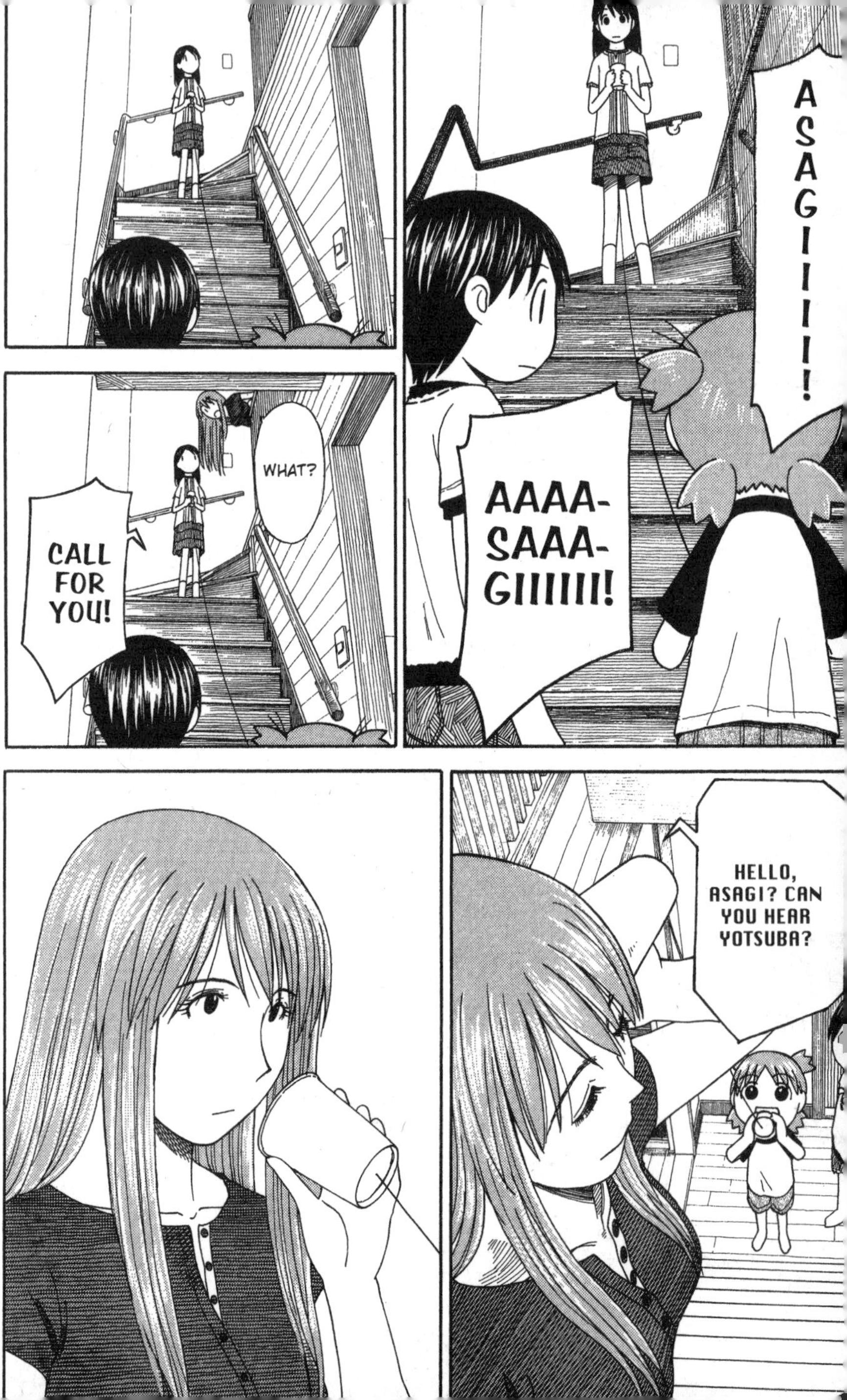
ASAGIIIIII!
AAAA-SAAA-GIIIIII!
WHAT?
CALL FOR YOU!
HELLO, ASAGI? CAN YOU HEAR YOTSUBA?

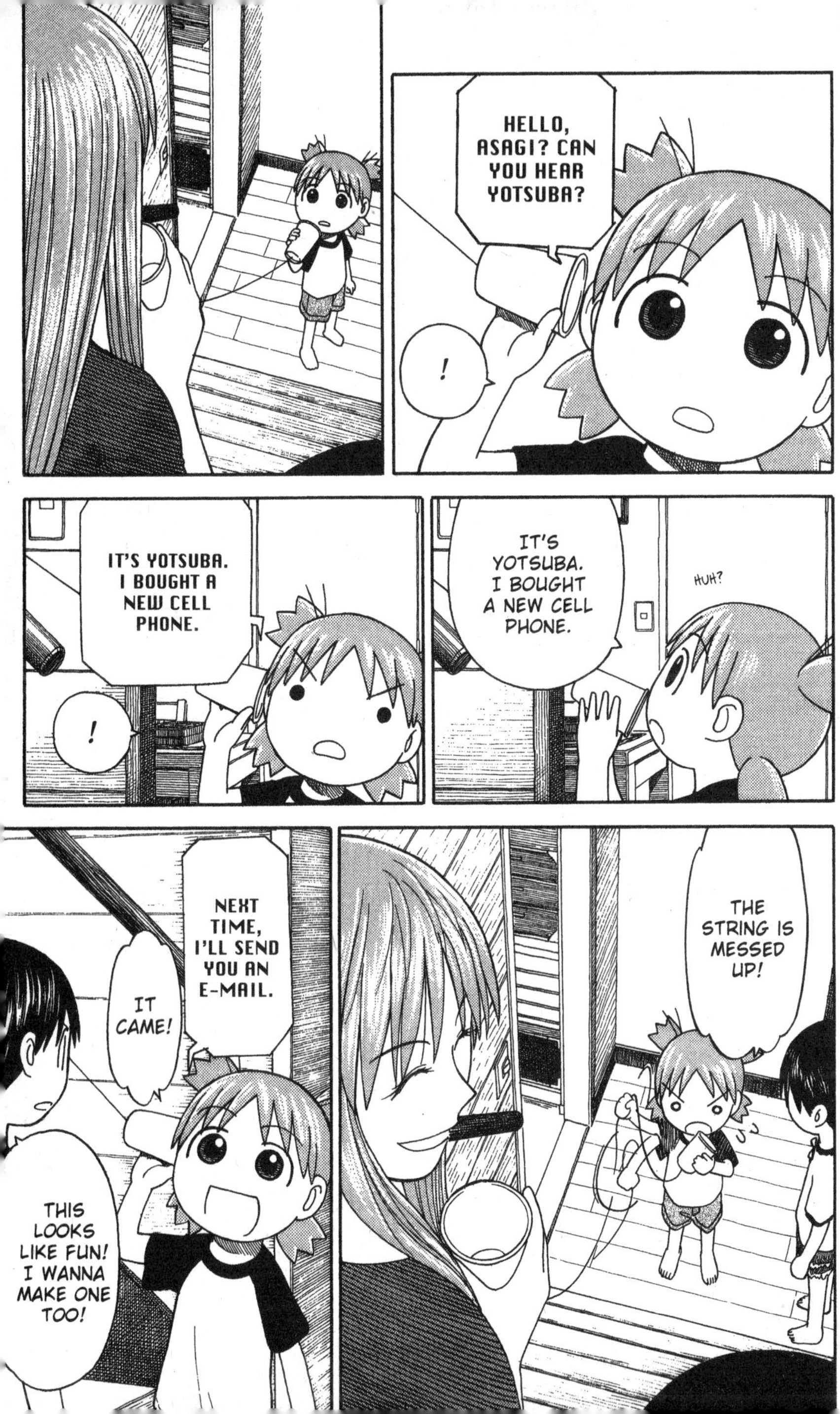
HELLO, ASAGI? CAN YOU HEAR YOTSUBA?
!
IT'S YOTSUBA. I BOUGHT A NEW CELL PHONE.
HUH?
IT'S YOTSUBA. I BOUGHT A NEW CELL PHONE.
!
THE STRING IS MESSED UP!
NEXT TIME, I'LL SEND YOU AN E-MAIL.
IT CAME!
THIS LOOKS LIKE FUN! I WANNA MAKE ONE TOO!

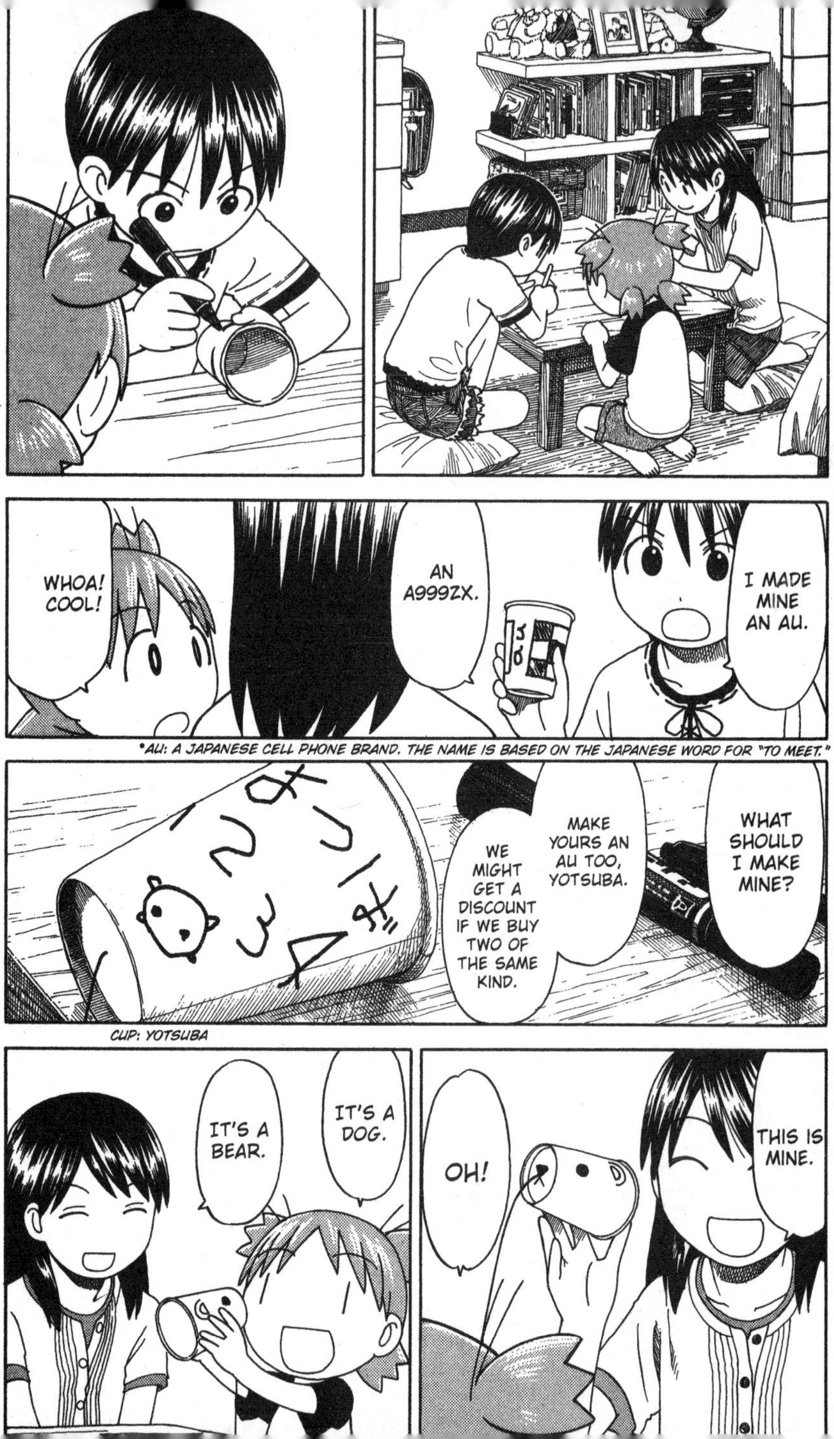
I MADE MINE AN AU.
AN A999ZX.
WHOA! COOL!
*AU: A JAPANESE CELL PHONE BRAND. THE NAME IS BASED ON THE JAPANESE WORD FOR "TO MEET."
WHAT SHOULD I MAKE MINE?
MAKE YOURS AN AU TOO, YOTSUBA.
WE MIGHT GET A DISCOUNT IF WE BUY TWO OF THE SAME KIND.
CUP: YOTSUBA
THIS IS MINE.
OH!
IT'S A DOG.
IT'S A BEAR.

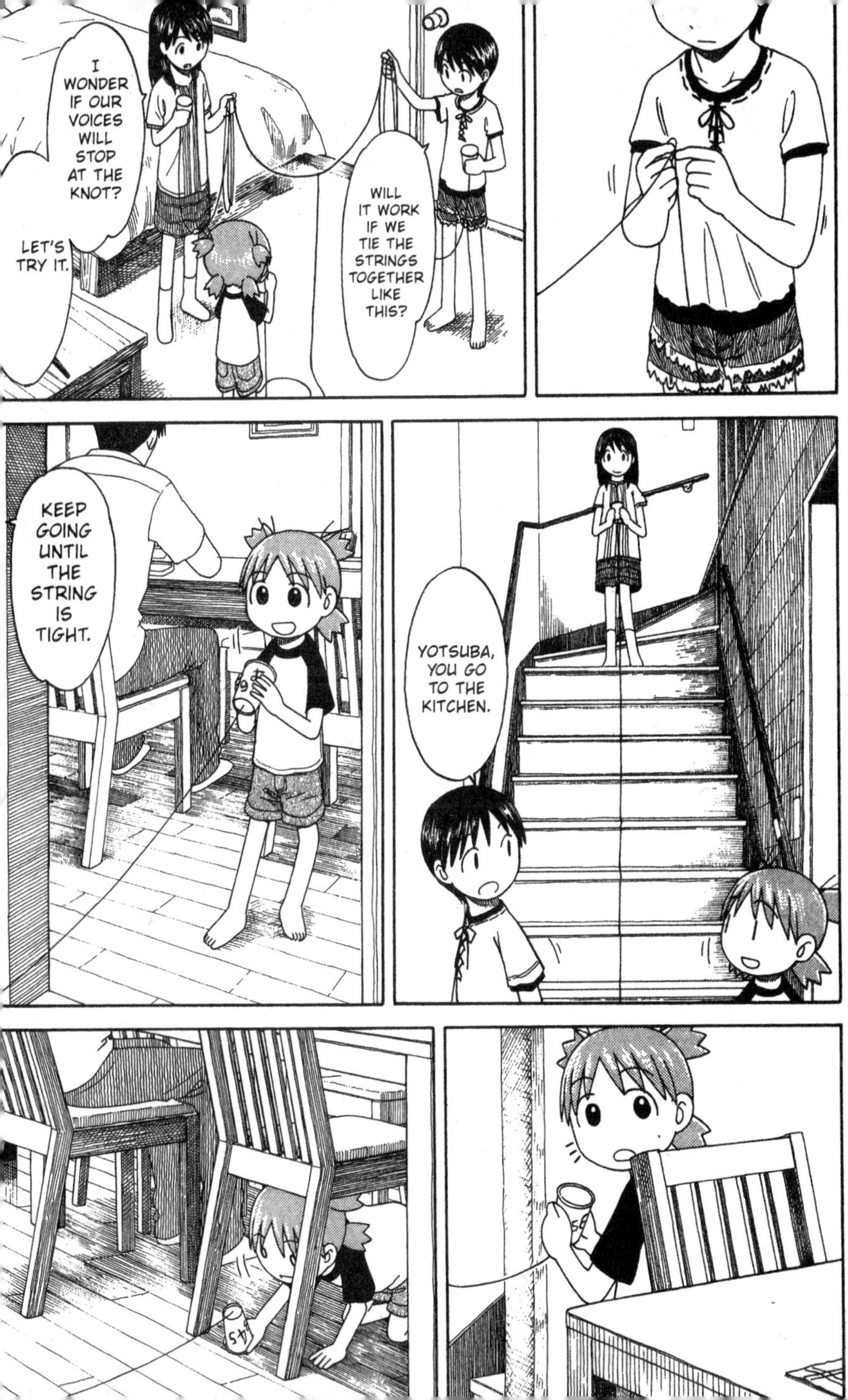
WILL IT WORK IF WE TIE THE STRINGS TOGETHER LIKE THIS?
I WONDER IF OUR VOICES WILL STOP AT THE KNOT?
LET'S TRY IT.
YOTSUBA, YOU GO TO THE KITCHEN.
KEEP GOING UNTIL THE STRING IS TIGHT.

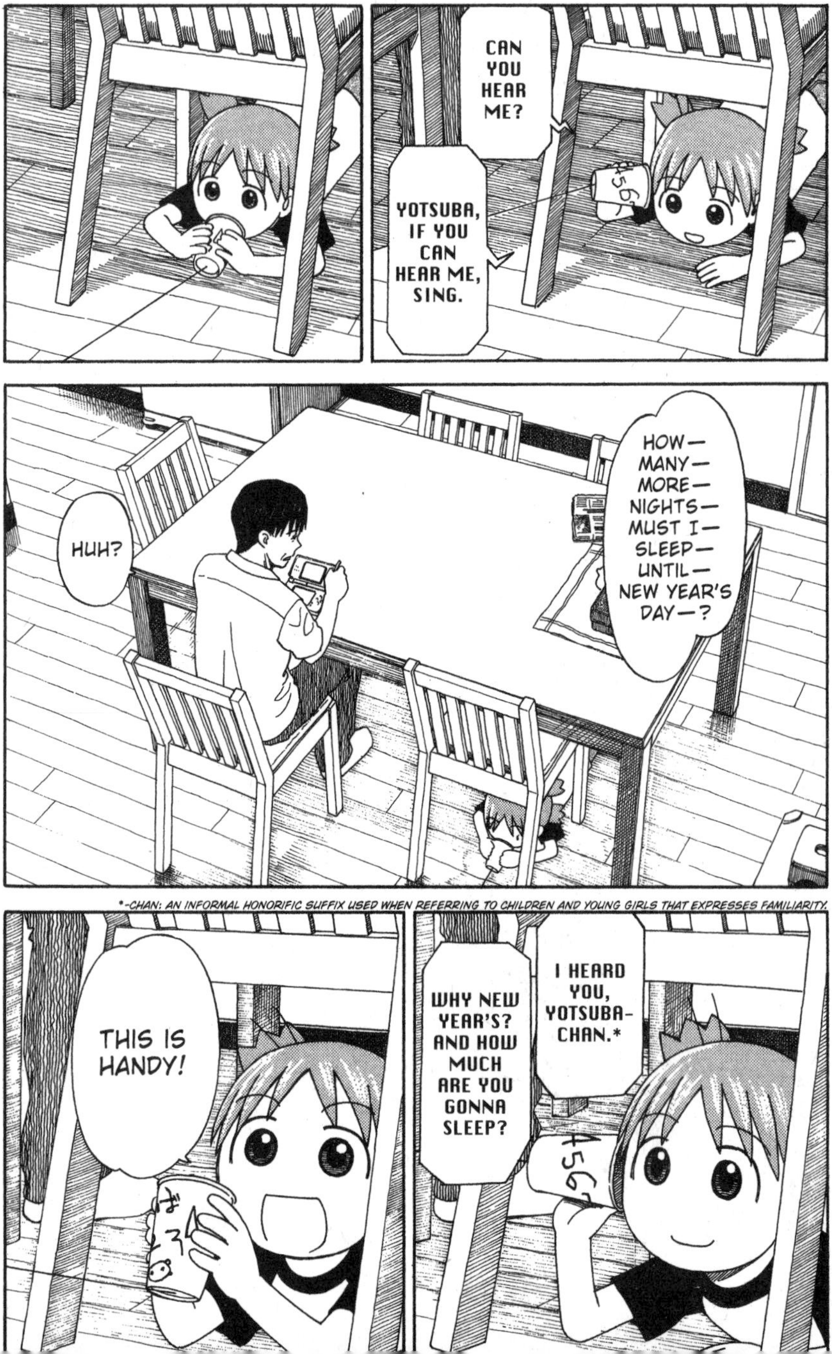
CAN YOU HEAR ME?
YOTSUBA, IF YOU CAN HEAR ME, SING.
HOW—MANY—MORE—NIGHTS—MUST I—SLEEP—UNTIL—NEW YEAR'S DAY—?
HUH?
I HEARD YOU, YOTSUBA-CHAN.*
WHY NEW YEAR'S? AND HOW MUCH ARE YOU GONNA SLEEP?
THIS IS HANDY!

*-CHAN: AN INFORMAL HONORIFIC SUFFIX USED WHEN REFERRING TO CHILDREN AND YOUNG GIRLS THAT EXPRESSES FAMILIARITY.

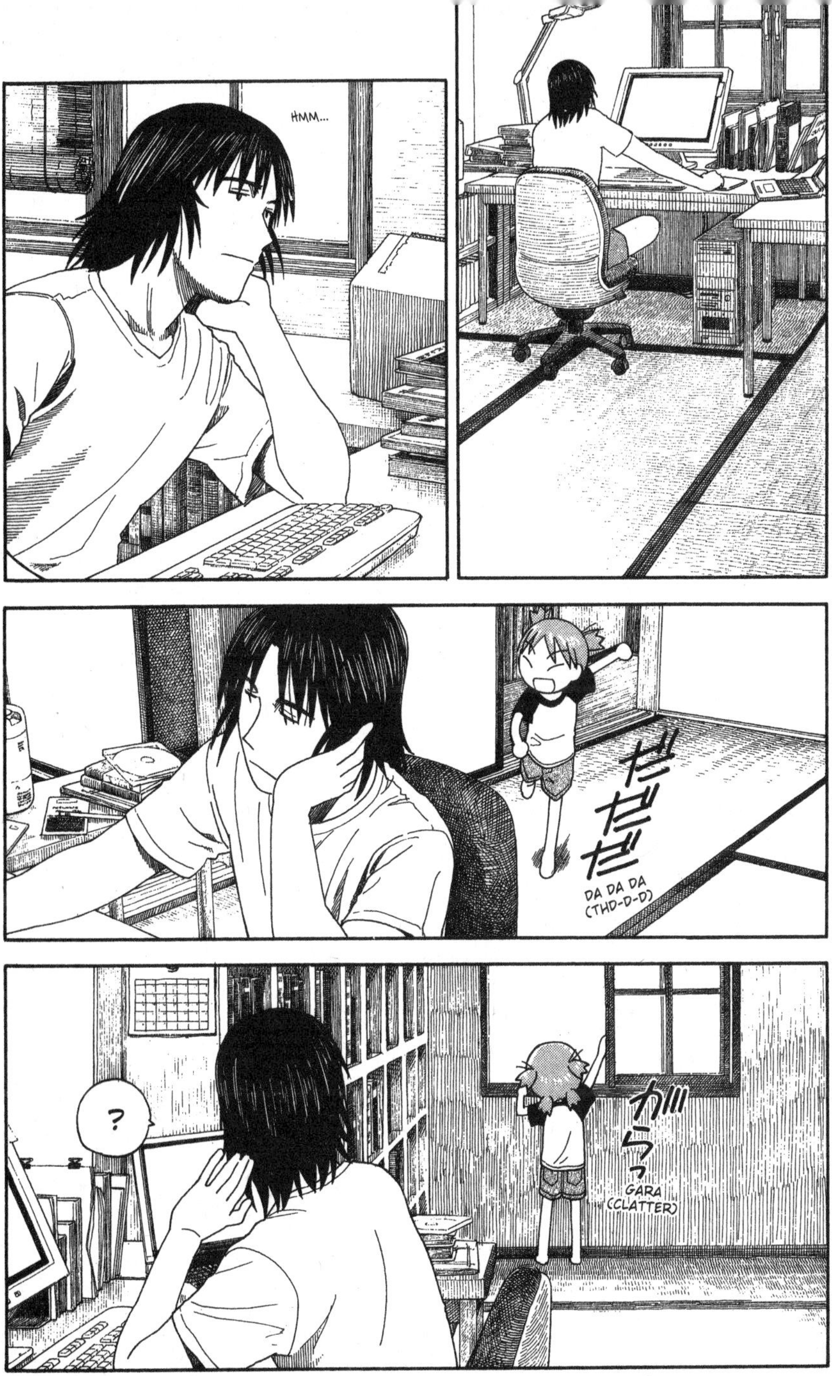
HMM...
だだだ
DA DA DA
(THD-D-D)
がらっ
GARA
(CLATTER)
?

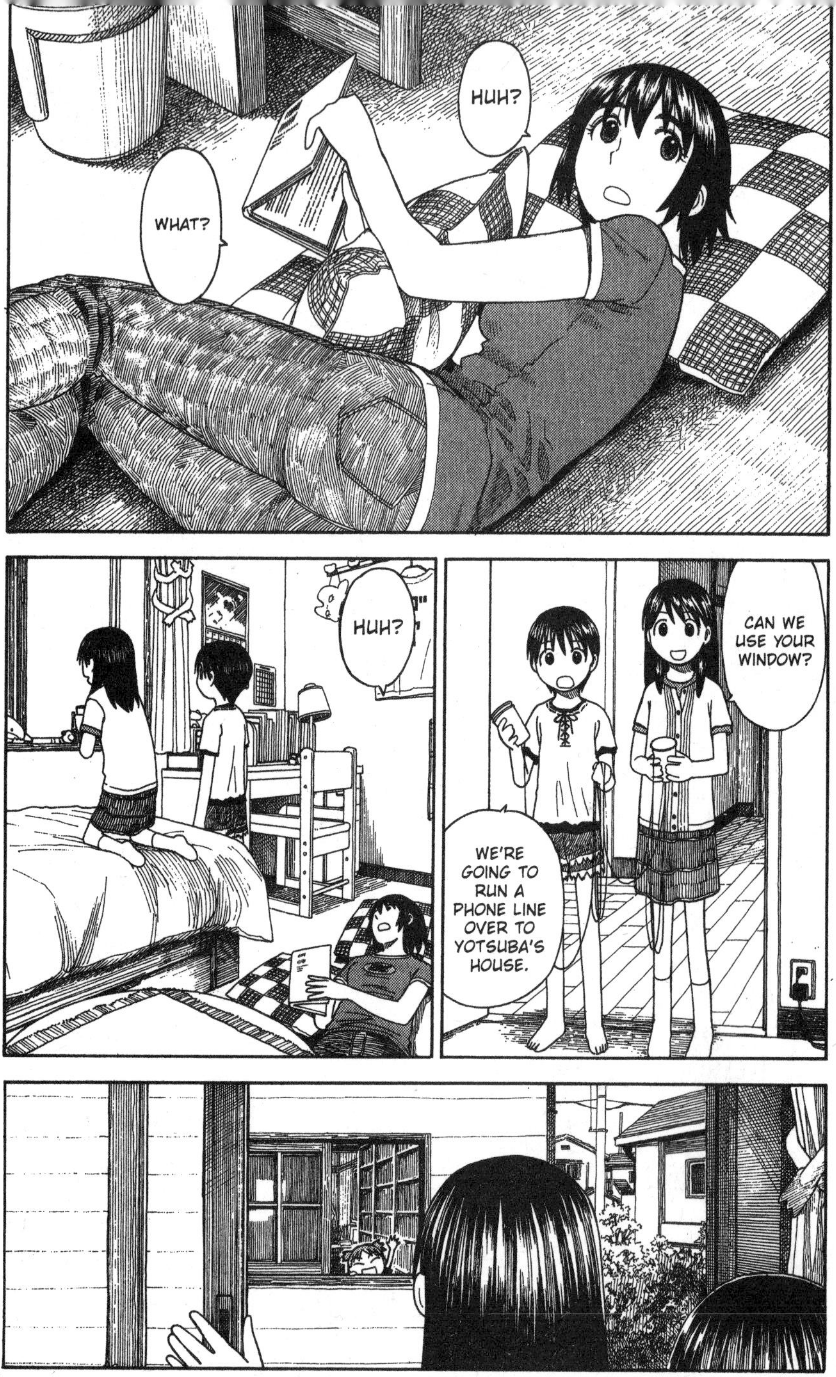
HUH?
WHAT?
CAN WE USE YOUR WINDOW?
WE'RE GOING TO RUN A PHONE LINE OVER TO YOTSUBA'S HOUSE.
HUH?

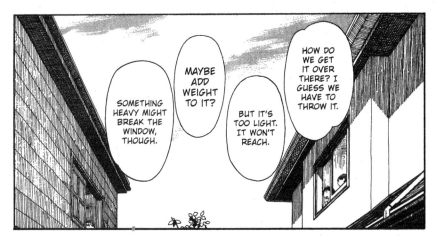

HOW DO WE GET IT OVER THERE? I GUESS WE HAVE TO THROW IT.
BUT IT'S TOO LIGHT. IT WON'T REACH.
MAYBE ADD WEIGHT TO IT?
SOMETHING HEAVY MIGHT BREAK THE WINDOW, THOUGH.
HMM... YOU'RE RIGHT...
FUUKA-NEECHAN, I'M GOING TO BORROW THIS STUFFED ANIMAL.
UM, OKAY?

CUP: YOTSUBA

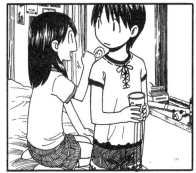

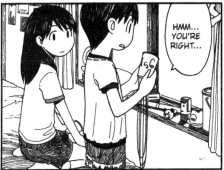

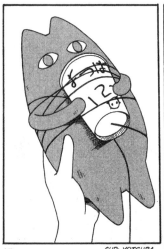

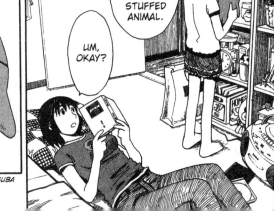

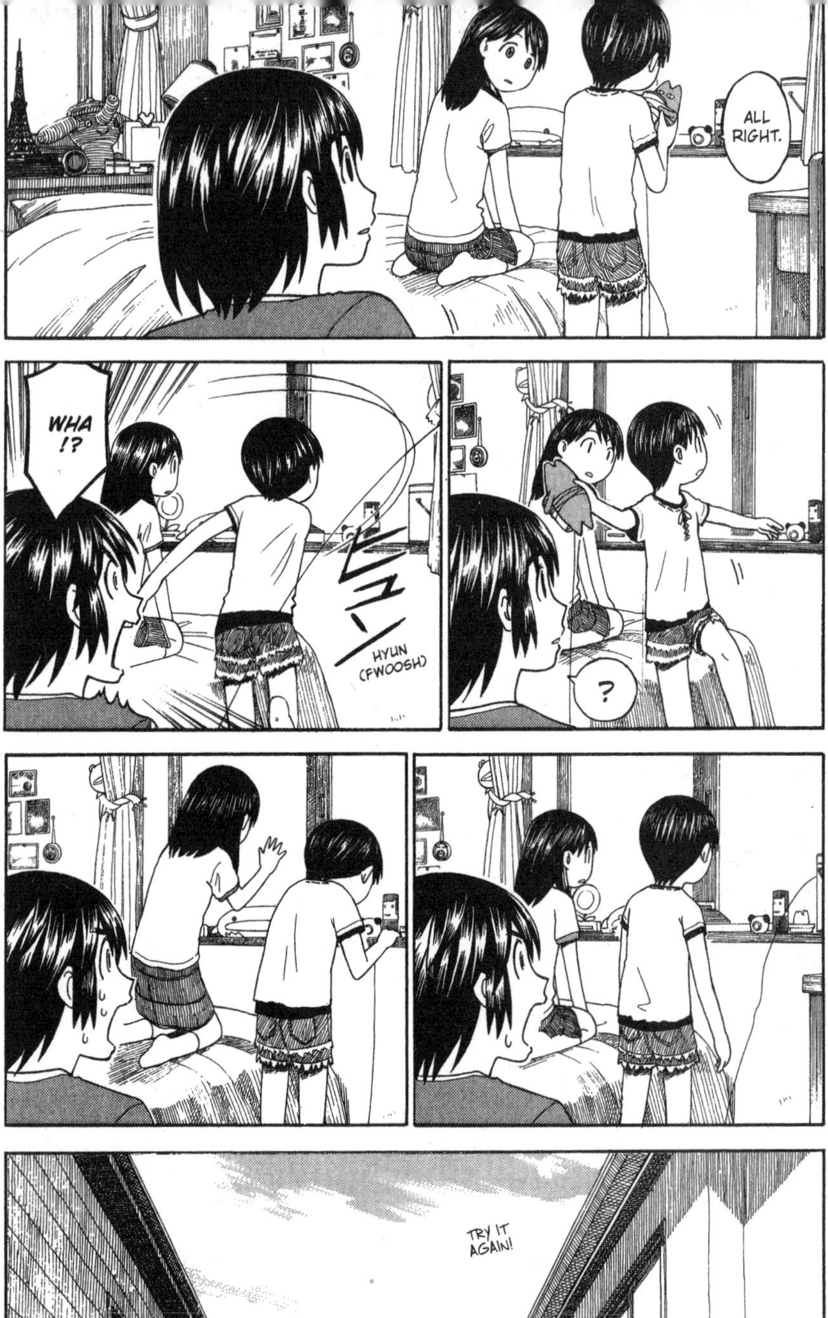
ALL RIGHT.
?
WHA !?
ヒュン
HYUN (FWOOSH)
TRY IT AGAIN!

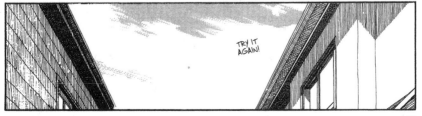

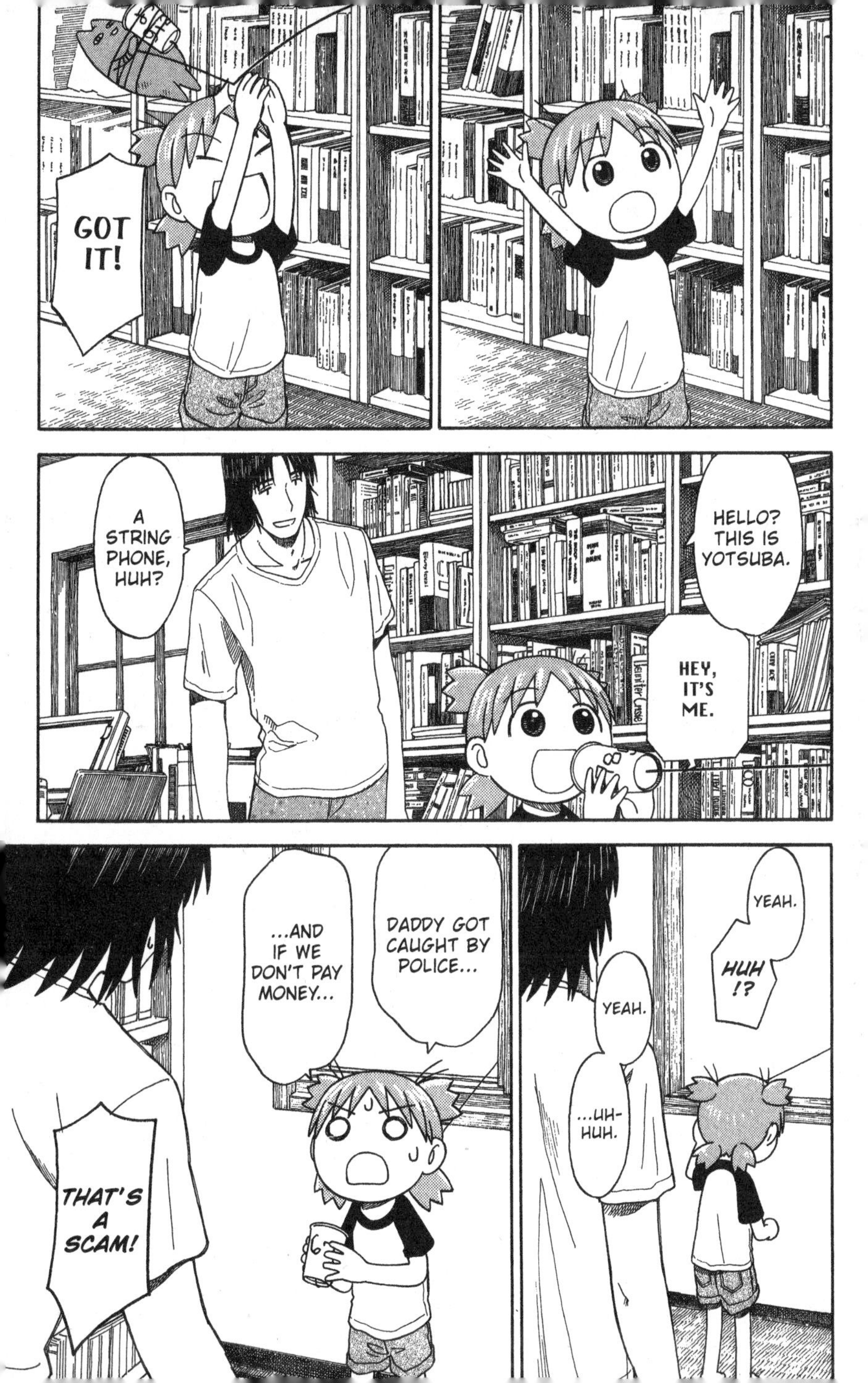
GOT IT!
HELLO? THIS IS YOTSUBA.
HEY, IT'S ME.
A STRING PHONE, HUH?
YEAH.
HUH!?
YEAH.
...UH-HUH.
DADDY GOT CAUGHT BY POLICE...
...AND IF WE DON'T PAY MONEY...
THAT'S A SCAM!

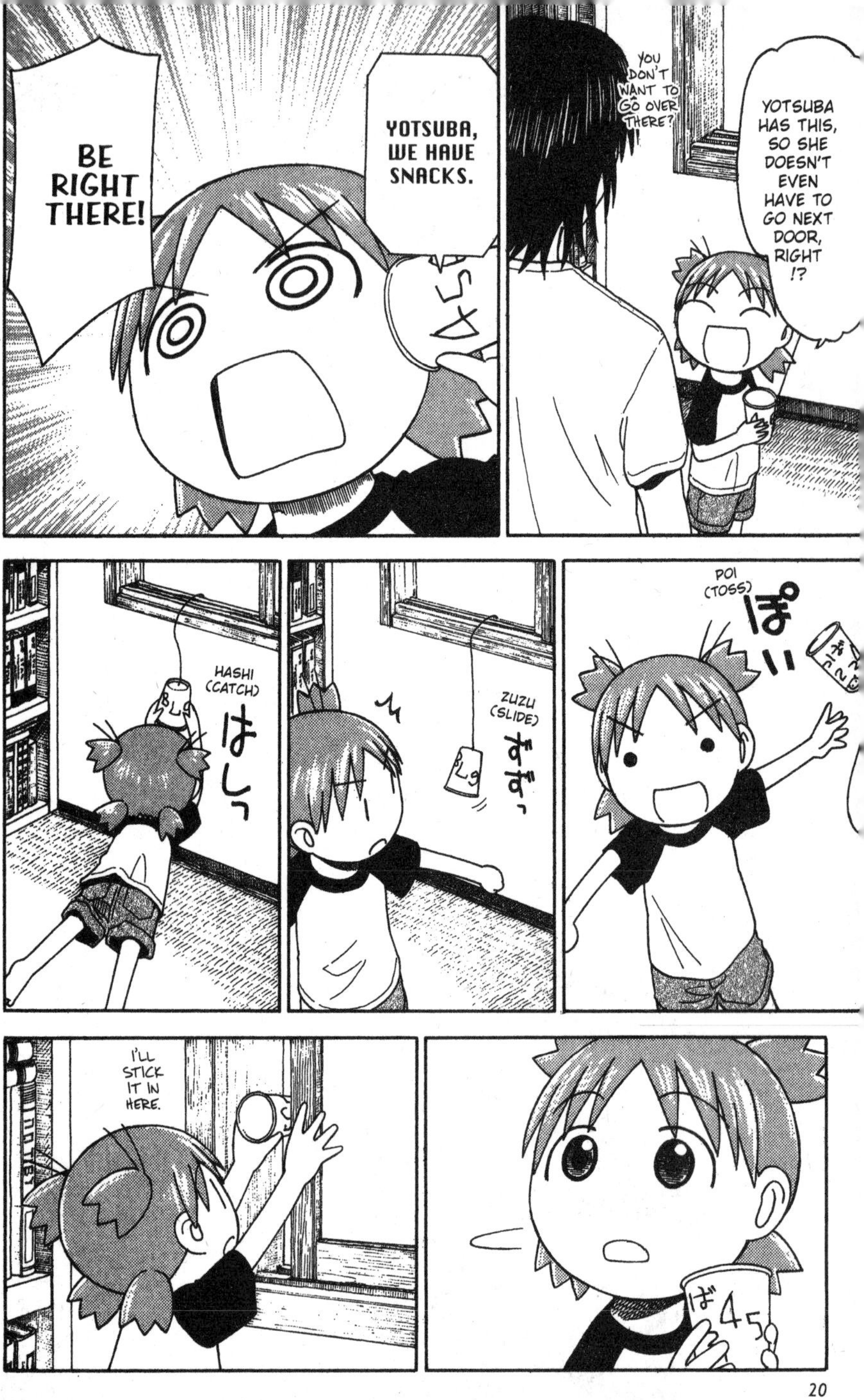
YOTSUBA HAS THIS, SO SHE DOESN'T EVEN HAVE TO GO NEXT DOOR, RIGHT!?
YOU DON'T WANT TO GO OVER THERE?
YOTSUBA, WE HAVE SNACKS.
BE RIGHT THERE!
POI (TOSS)
ぽい
ZUZU (SLIDE)
ずずっ
HASHI (CATCH)
はしっ
ば45
I'LL STICK IT IN HERE.

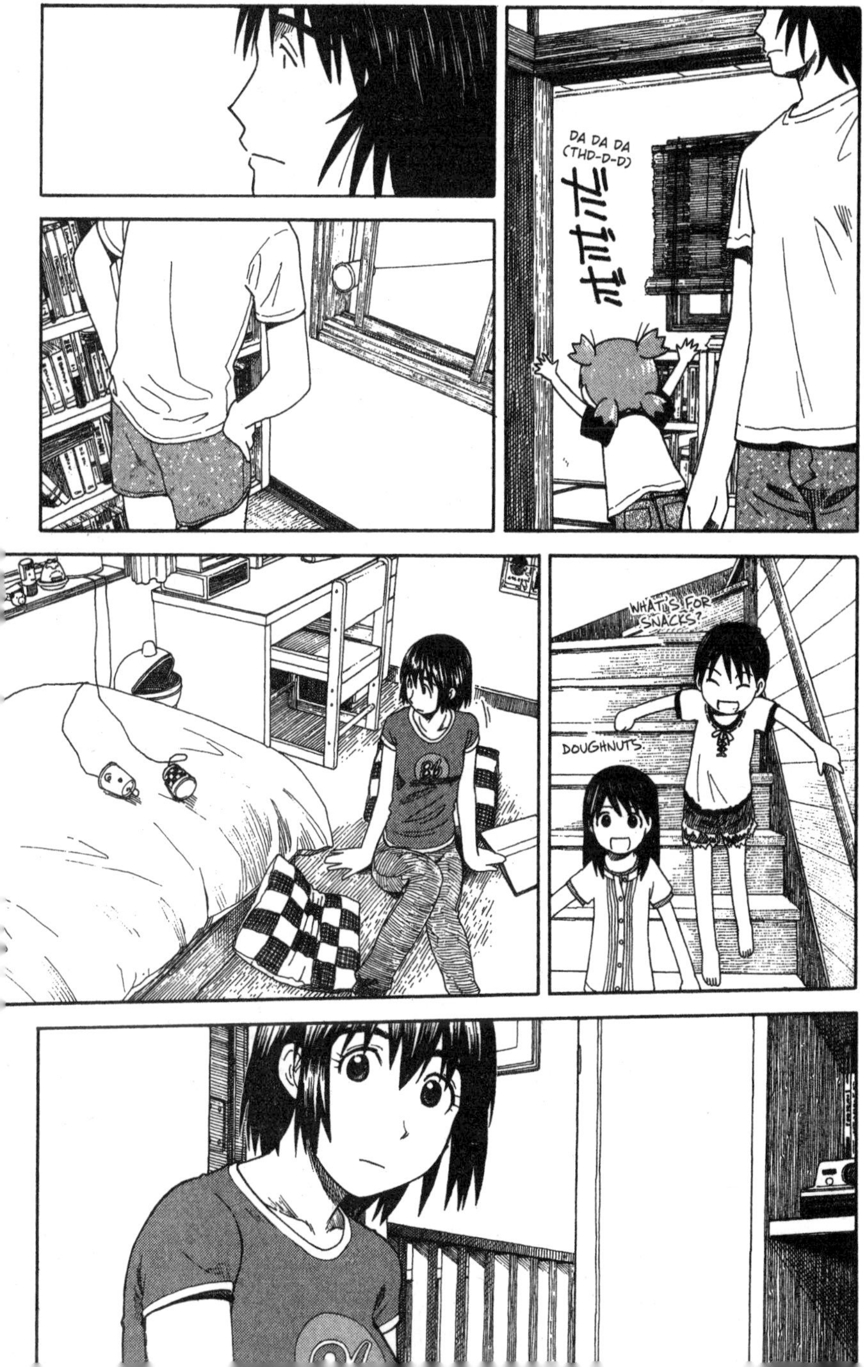
DA DA DA
(THD-D-D)
ダダダ
WHAT'S FOR SNACKS?
DOUGHNUTS.

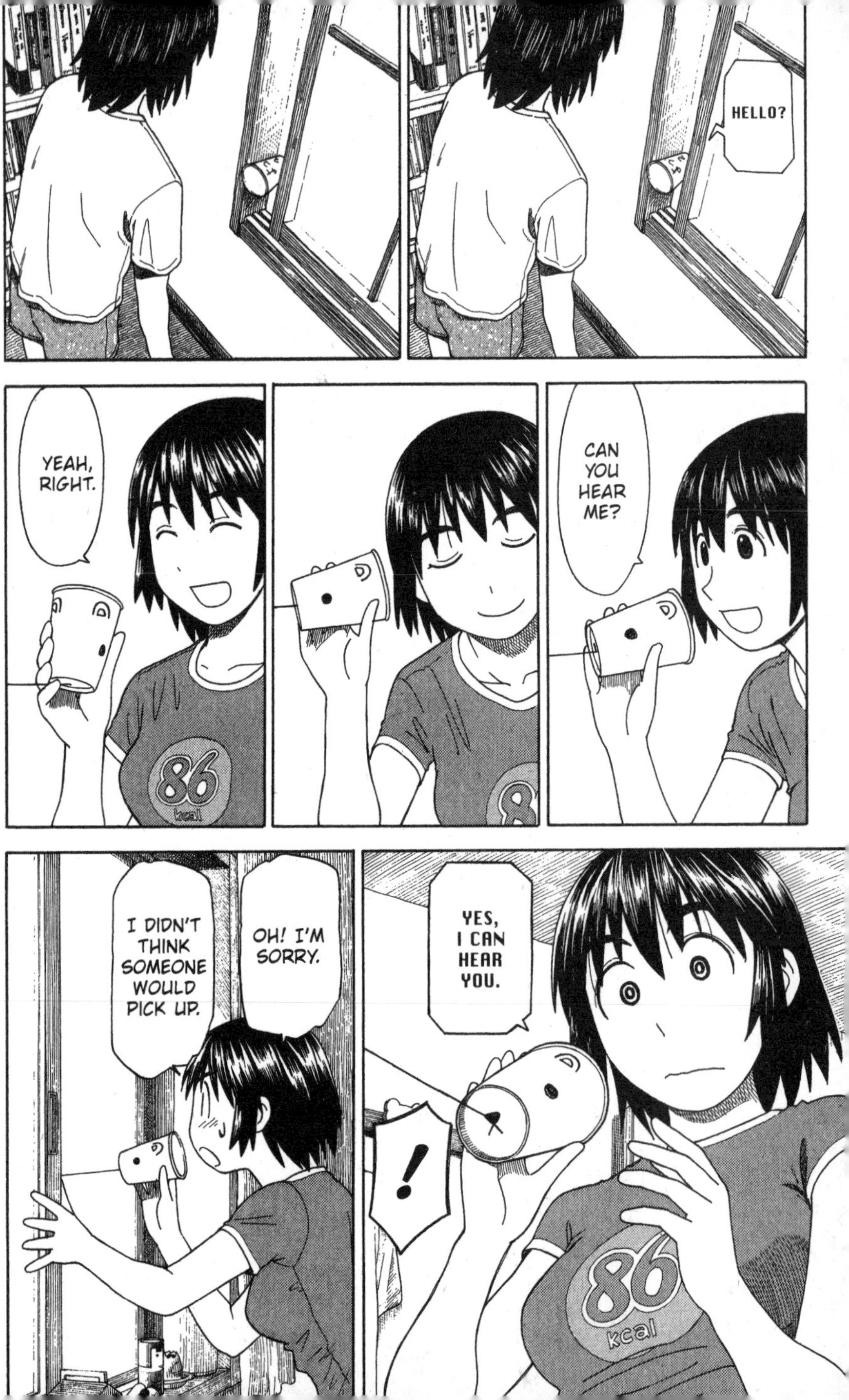
HELLO?
CAN YOU HEAR ME?
YEAH, RIGHT.
YES, I CAN HEAR YOU.
!
OH! I'M SORRY.
I DIDN'T THINK SOMEONE WOULD PICK UP.

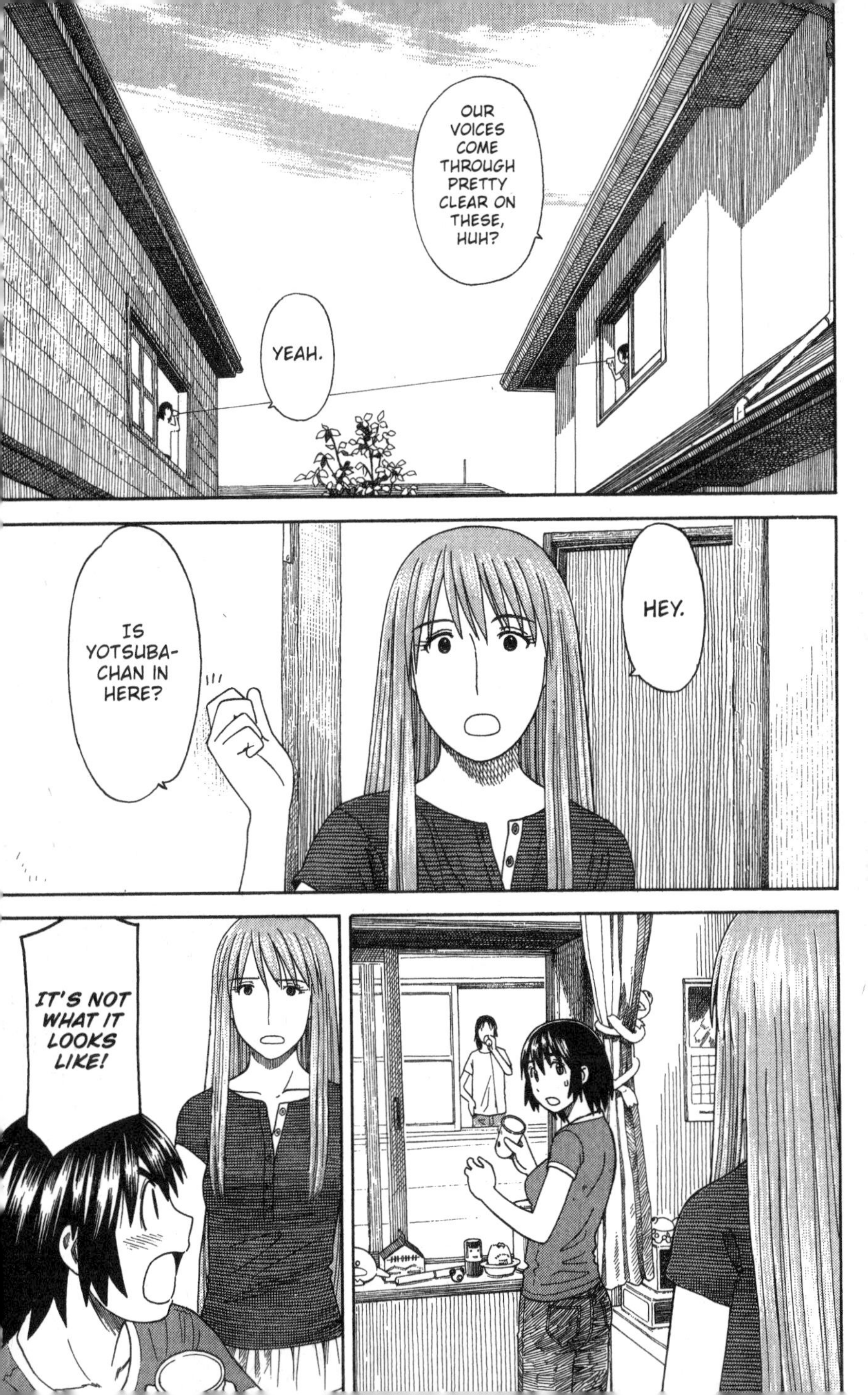
OUR VOICES COME THROUGH PRETTY CLEAR ON THESE, HUH?
YEAH.
HEY.
IS YOTSUBA-CHAN IN HERE?
IT'S NOT WHAT IT LOOKS LIKE!

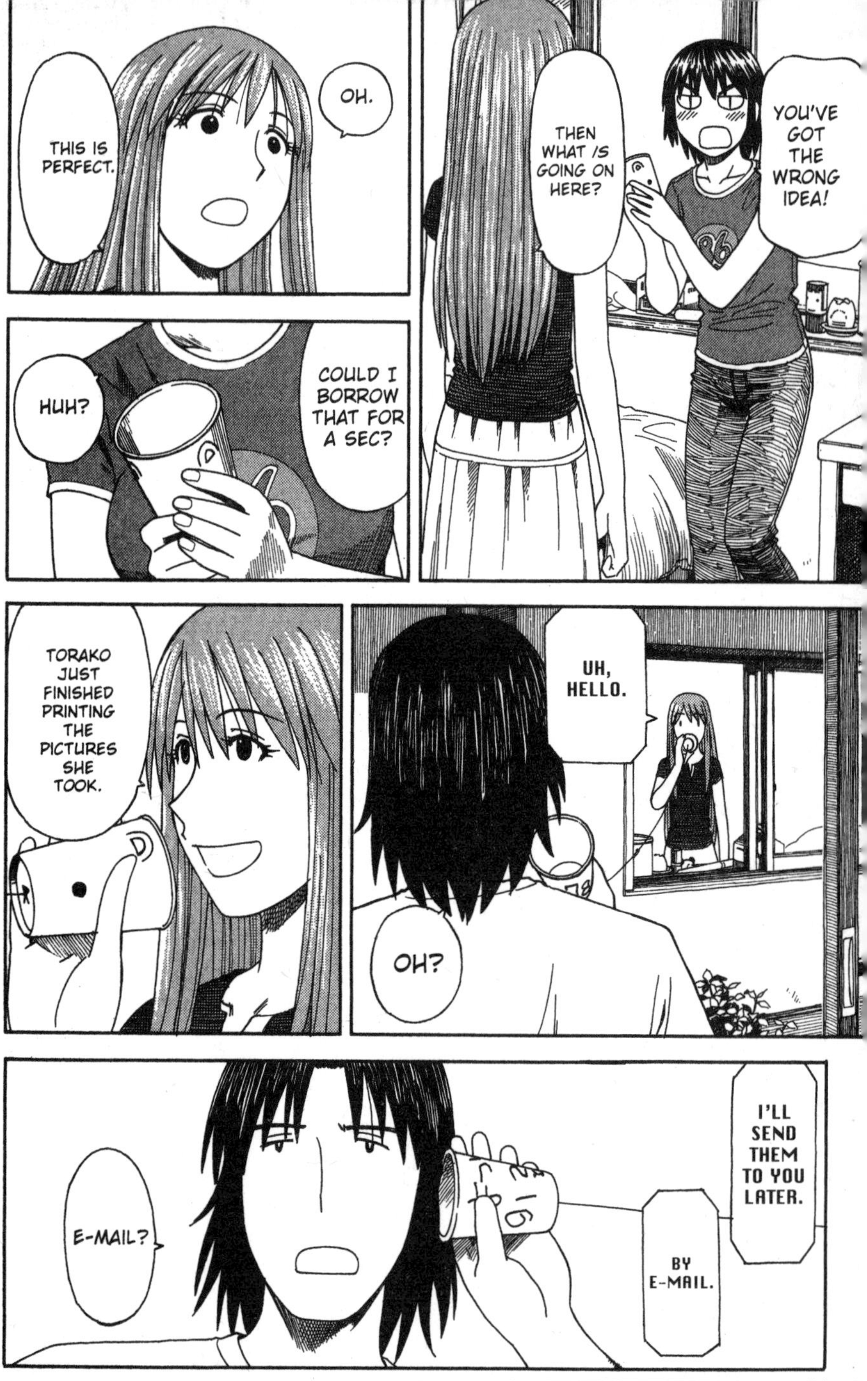
YOU'VE GOT THE WRONG IDEA!
THEN WHAT IS GOING ON HERE?
OH.
THIS IS PERFECT.
COULD I BORROW THAT FOR A SEC?
HUH?
UH, HELLO.
OH?
TORAKO JUST FINISHED PRINTING THE PICTURES SHE TOOK.
I'LL SEND THEM TO YOU LATER.
BY E-MAIL.
E-MAIL?

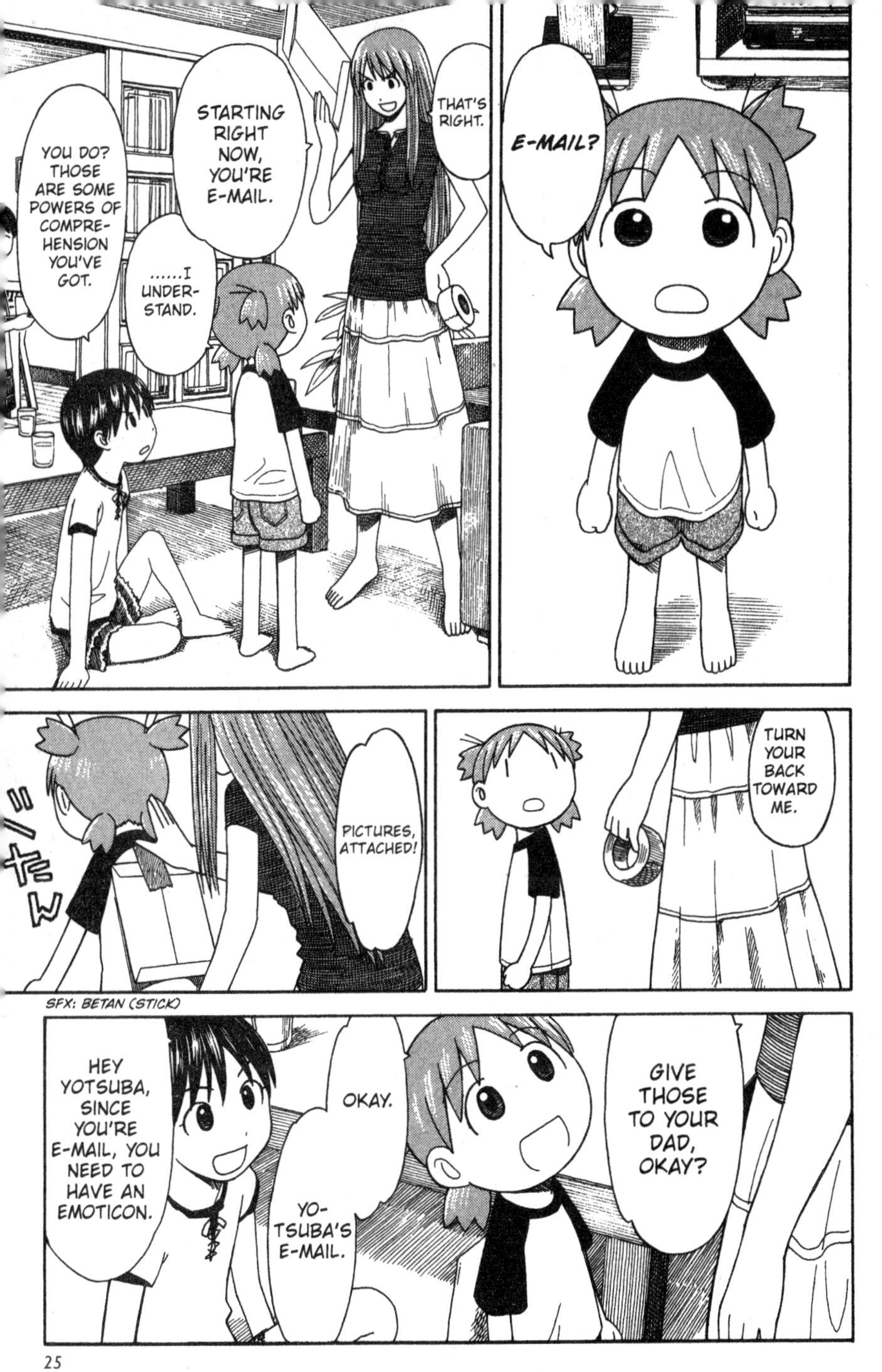
E-MAIL?
THAT'S RIGHT.
STARTING RIGHT NOW, YOU'RE E-MAIL.
......I UNDERSTAND.
YOU DO? THOSE ARE SOME POWERS OF COMPRE-HENSION YOU'VE GOT.
TURN YOUR BACK TOWARD ME.
PICTURES, ATTACHED!
SFX: BETAN (STICK)
GIVE THOSE TO YOUR DAD, OKAY?
OKAY.
YO-TSUBA'S E-MAIL.
HEY YOTSUBA, SINCE YOU'RE E-MAIL, YOU NEED TO HAVE AN EMOTICON.

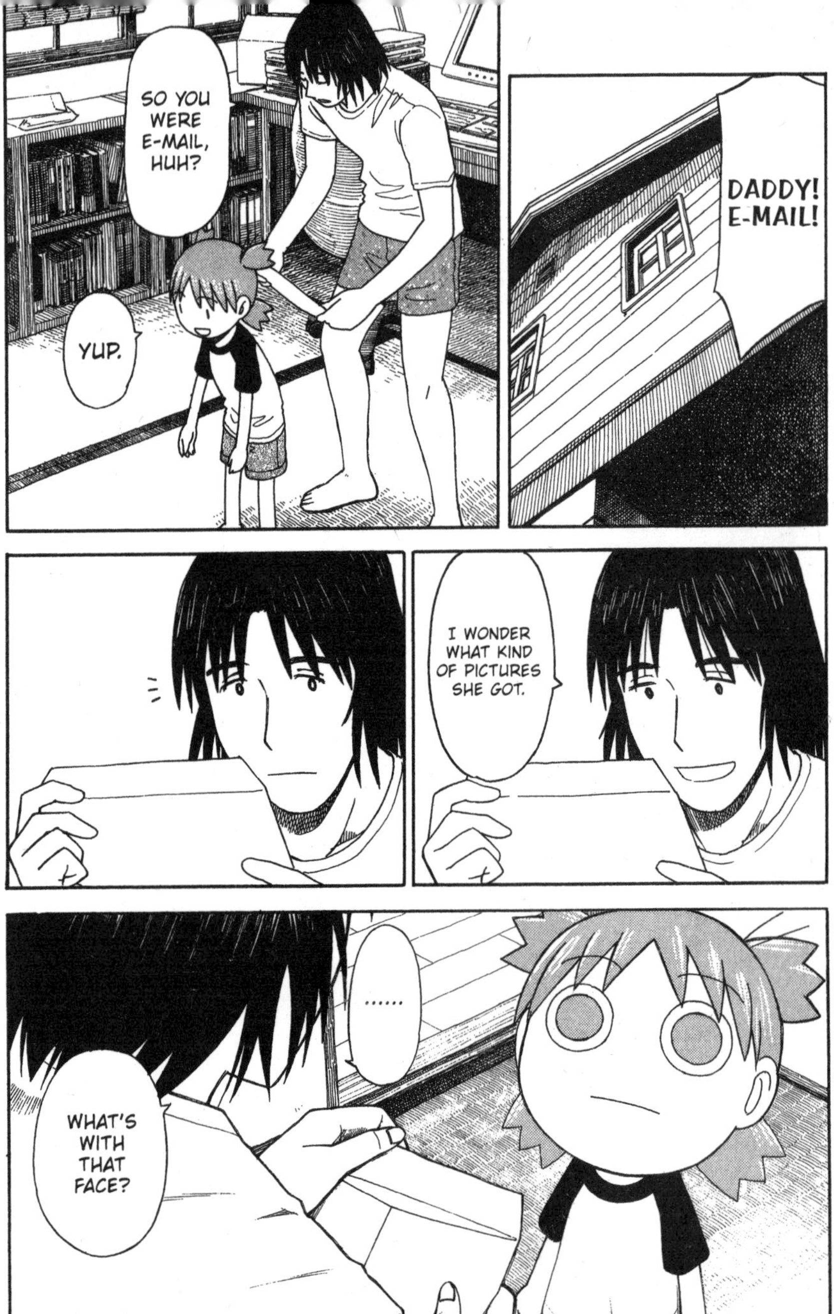
DADDY! E-MAIL!
SO YOU WERE E-MAIL, HUH?
YUP.
I WONDER WHAT KIND OF PICTURES SHE GOT.
......
WHAT'S WITH THAT FACE?

YOTSUBA&!

YOTSUBA&

RESPECT FOR THE AGED DAY

#43

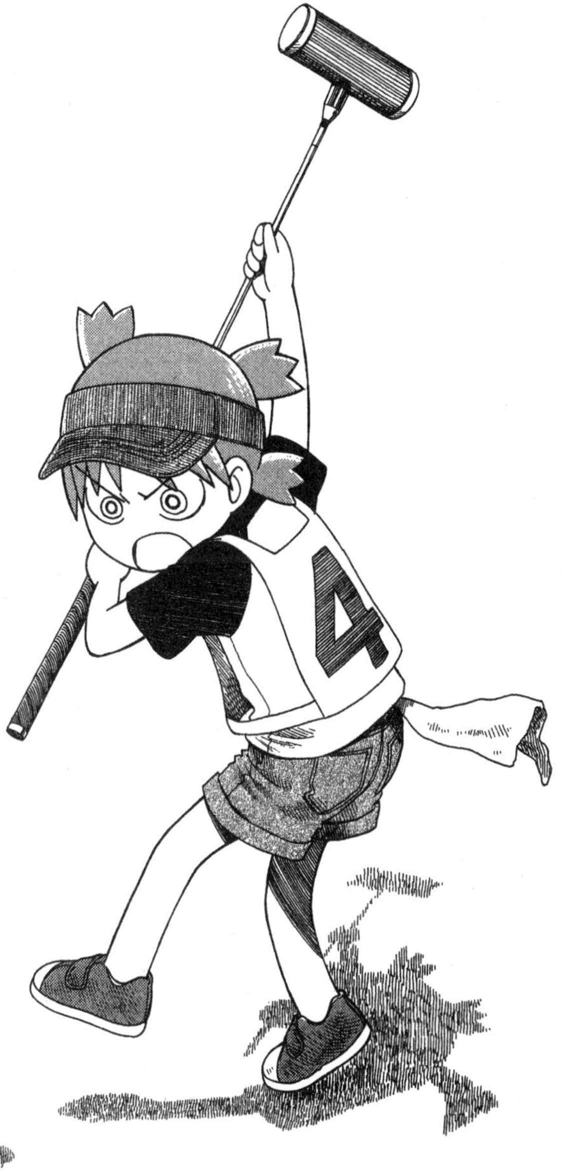

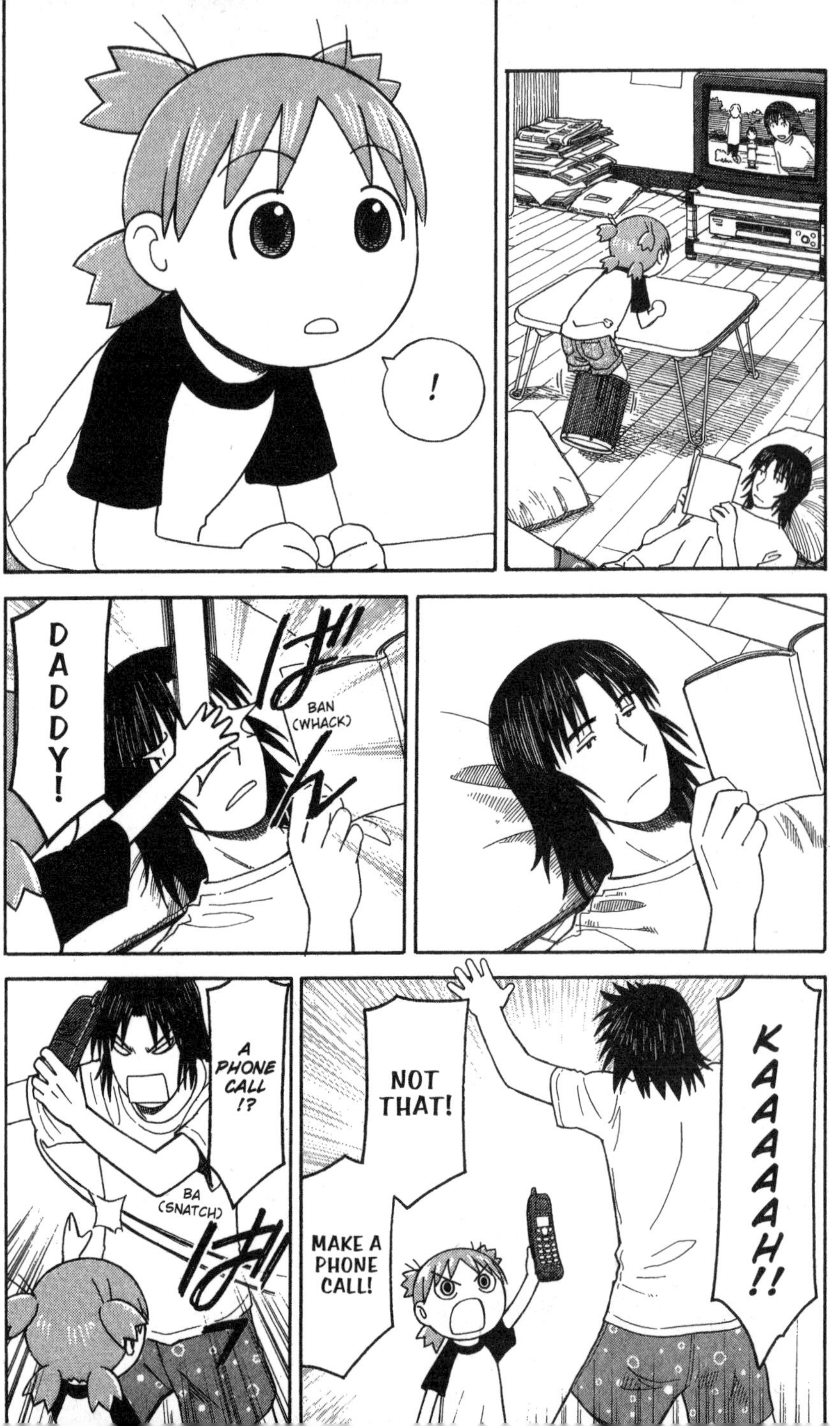
!
DADDY!
ばん
BAN (WHACK)
KAAAAAAH!!
NOT THAT!
MAKE A PHONE CALL!
A PHONE CALL!?
BA (SNATCH)

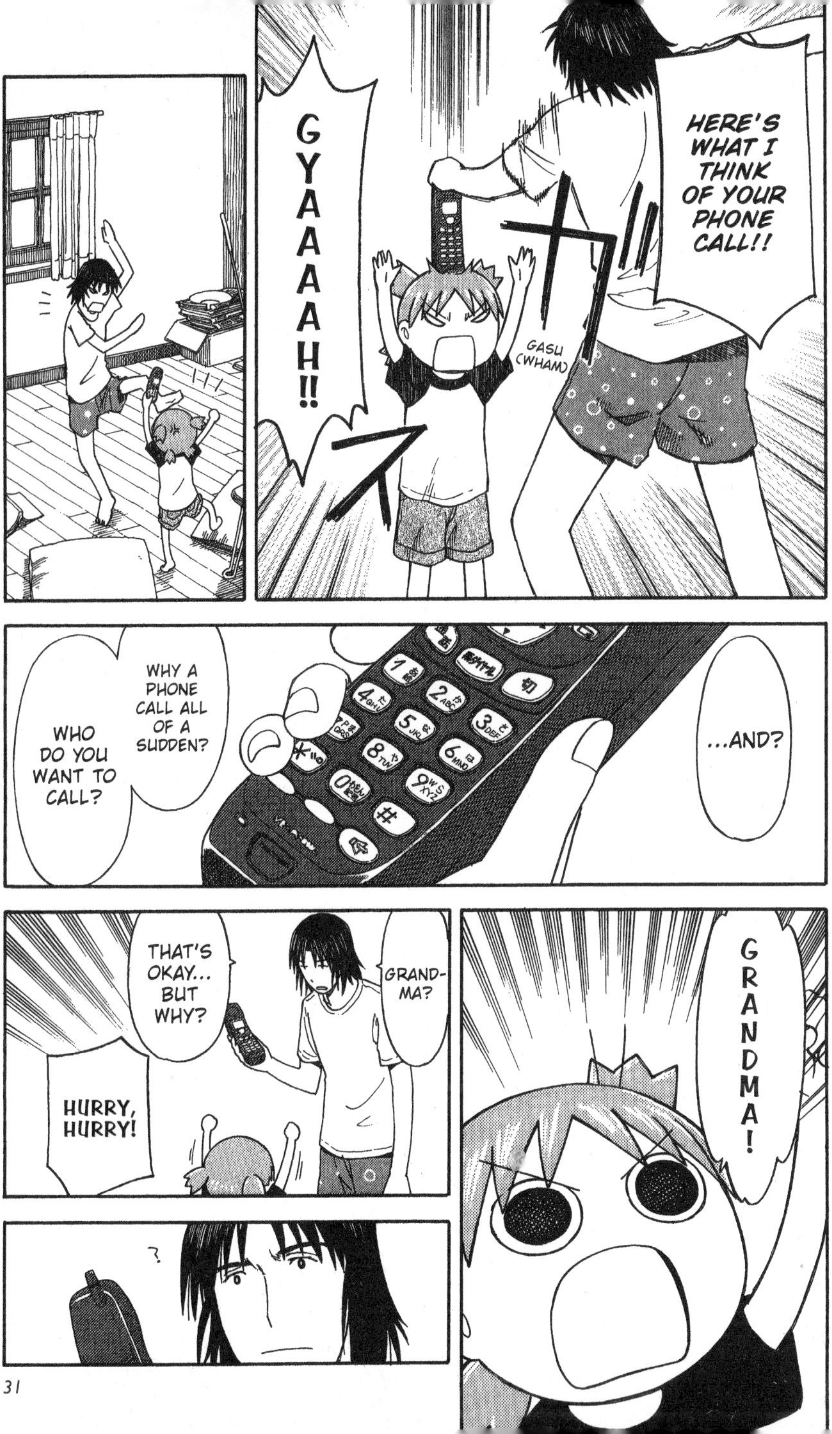
HERE'S WHAT I THINK OF YOUR PHONE CALL!!
GASU (WHAM)
GYAAAAAH!!
...AND?
WHY A PHONE CALL ALL OF A SUDDEN?
WHO DO YOU WANT TO CALL?
GRANDMA!
GRAND-MA?
THAT'S OKAY... BUT WHY?
HURRY, HURRY!
?

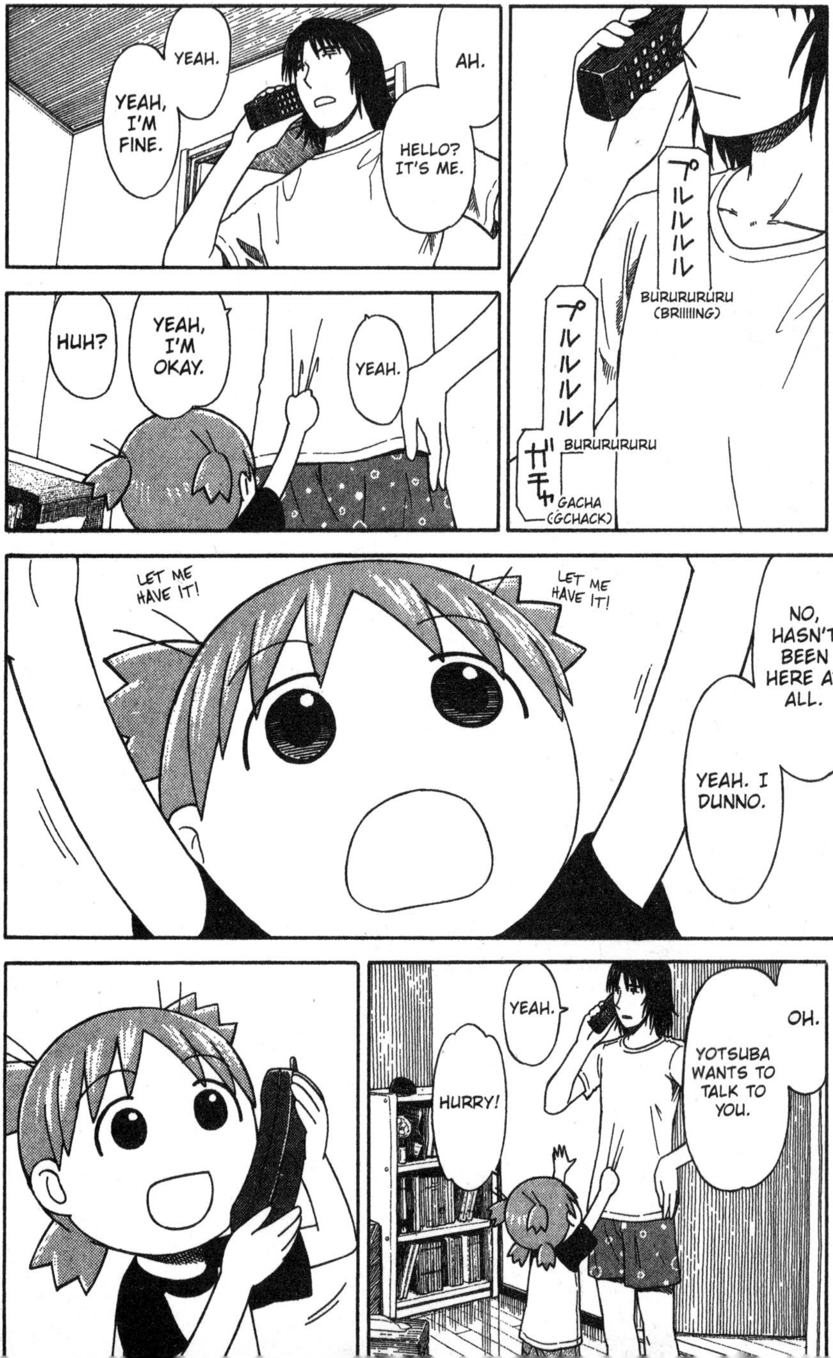
プルルルル
BURURURURU (BRIIIIING)
プルルルル
BURURURURU
ガチャ
GACHA (GCHACK)
AH.
HELLO? IT'S ME.
YEAH.
YEAH, I'M FINE.
YEAH.
YEAH, I'M OKAY.
HUH?
NO, HASN'T BEEN HERE AT ALL.
YEAH. I DUNNO.
LET ME HAVE IT!
LET ME HAVE IT!
OH.
YOTSUBA WANTS TO TALK TO YOU.
YEAH.
HURRY!

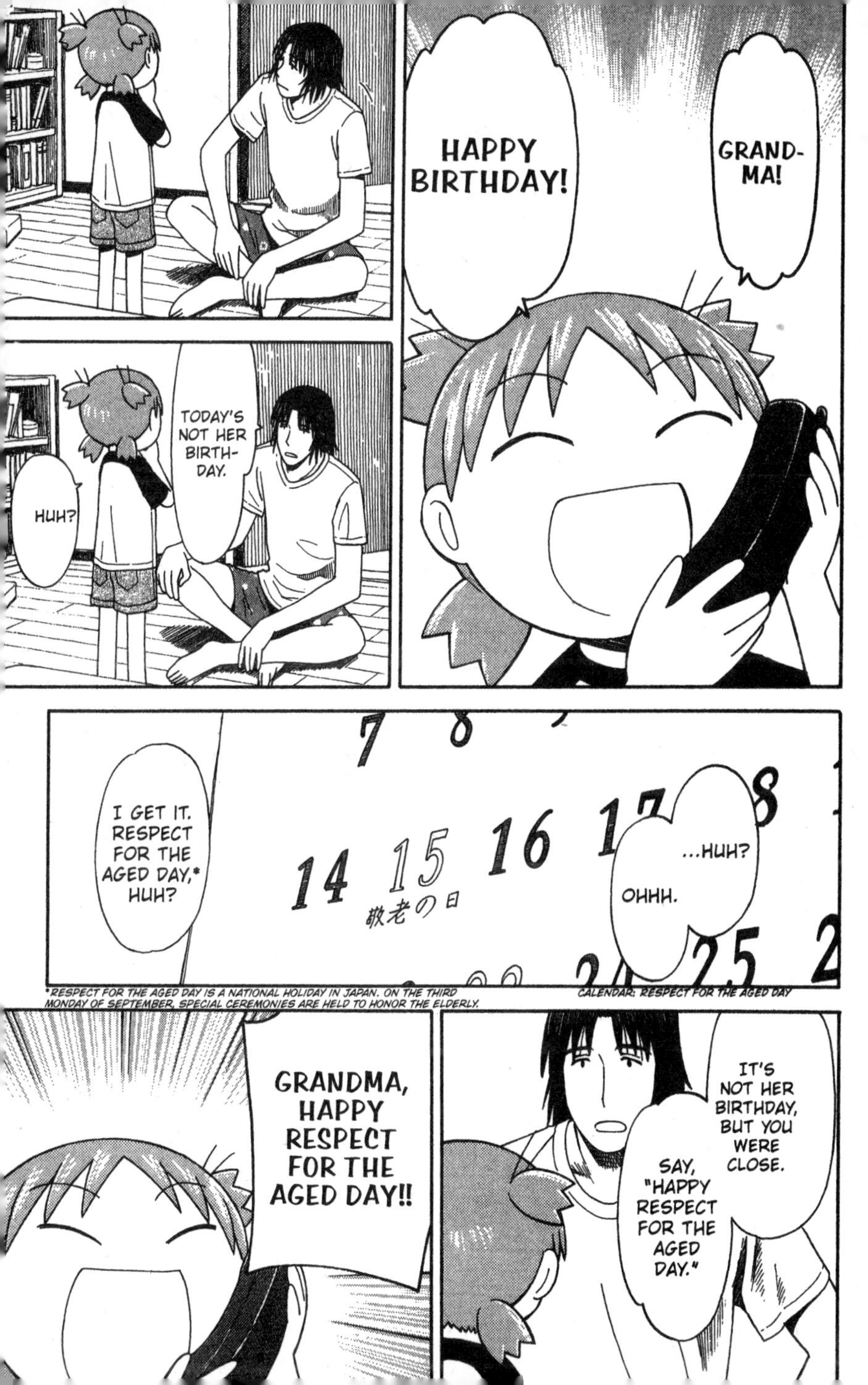
GRAND-MA!
HAPPY BIRTHDAY!
TODAY'S NOT HER BIRTH-DAY.
HUH?
...HUH?
OHHH.
14 15 16 17
敬老の日
I GET IT. RESPECT FOR THE AGED DAY,* HUH?
IT'S NOT HER BIRTHDAY, BUT YOU WERE CLOSE.
SAY, "HAPPY RESPECT FOR THE AGED DAY."
GRANDMA, HAPPY RESPECT FOR THE AGED DAY!!

*RESPECT FOR THE AGED DAY IS A NATIONAL HOLIDAY IN JAPAN. ON THE THIRD MONDAY OF SEPTEMBER, SPECIAL CEREMONIES ARE HELD TO HONOR THE ELDERLY.

CALENDAR: RESPECT FOR THE AGED DAY

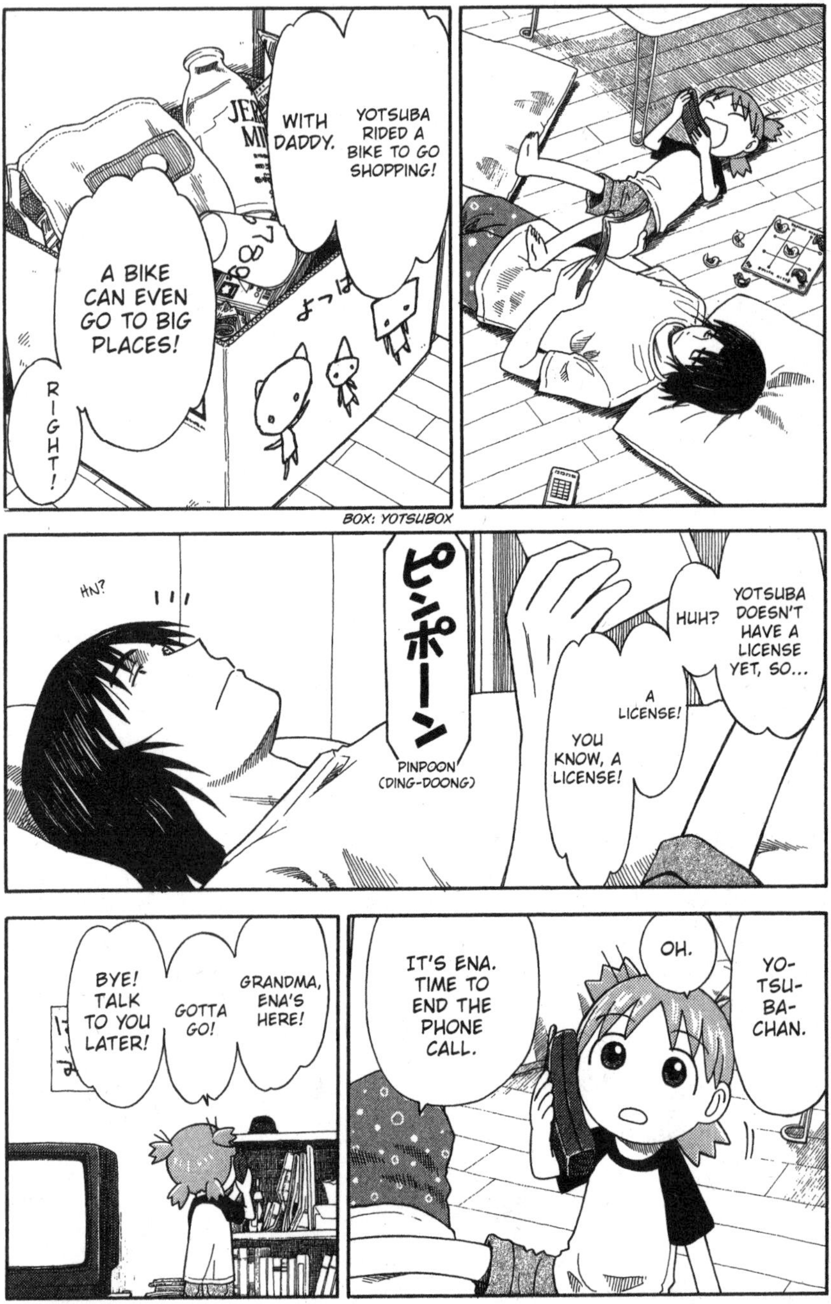
YOTSUBA RIDED A BIKE TO GO SHOPPING!
WITH DADDY.
A BIKE CAN EVEN GO TO BIG PLACES!
RIGHT!
BOX: YOTSUBOX
YOTSUBA DOESN'T HAVE A LICENSE YET, SO...
HUH?
A LICENSE!
YOU KNOW, A LICENSE!
ピンポーン
PINPOON (DING-DOONG)
HN?
YO-TSU-BA-CHAN.
OH.
IT'S ENA. TIME TO END THE PHONE CALL.
GRANDMA, ENA'S HERE!
GOTTA GO!
BYE! TALK TO YOU LATER!

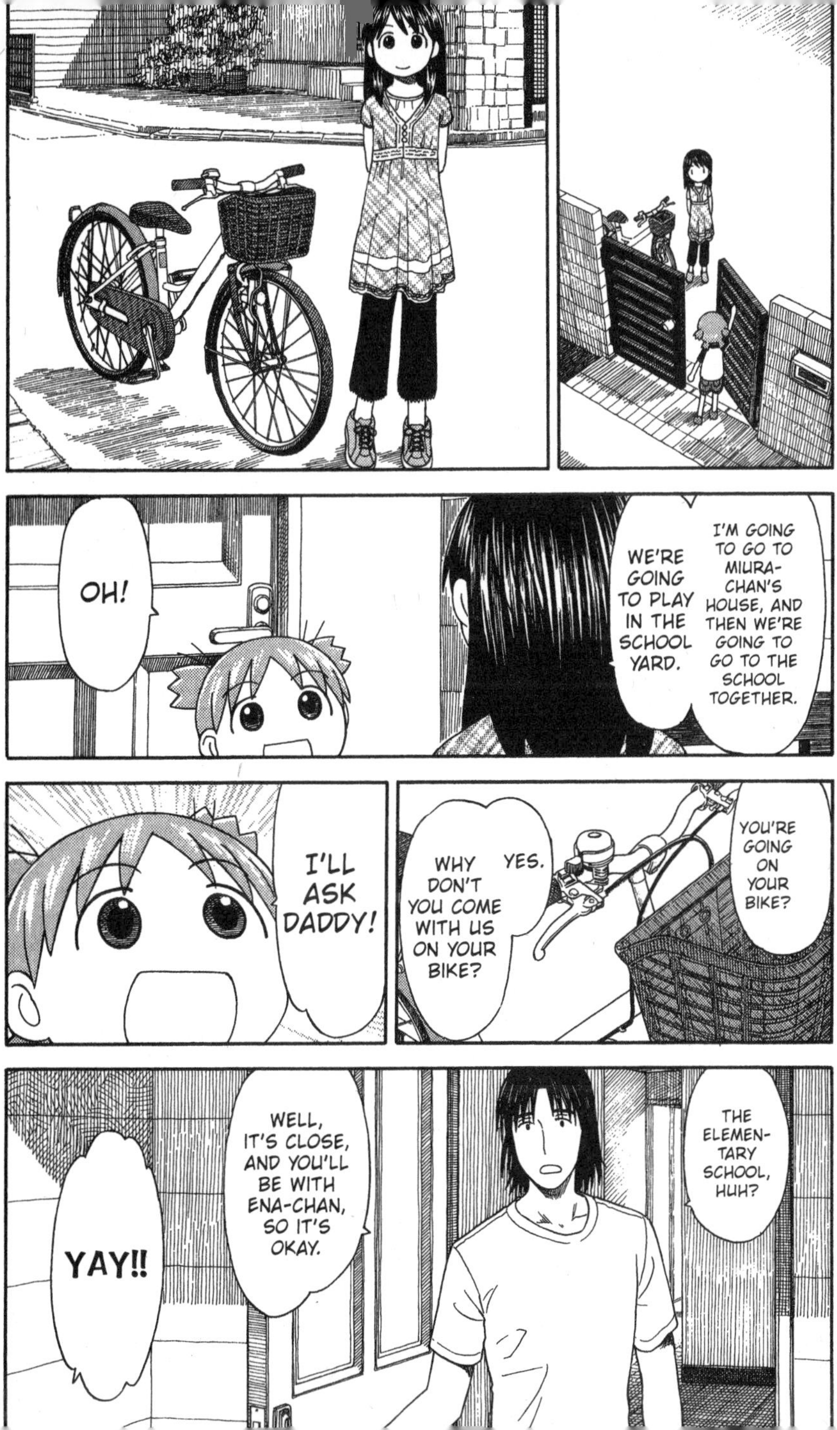
I'M GOING TO GO TO MIURA-CHAN'S HOUSE, AND THEN WE'RE GOING TO GO TO THE SCHOOL TOGETHER.
WE'RE GOING TO PLAY IN THE SCHOOL YARD.
OH!
YOU'RE GOING ON YOUR BIKE?
YES.
WHY DON'T YOU COME WITH US ON YOUR BIKE?
I'LL ASK DADDY!
THE ELEMENTARY SCHOOL, HUH?
WELL, IT'S CLOSE, AND YOU'LL BE WITH ENA-CHAN, SO IT'S OKAY.
YAY!!

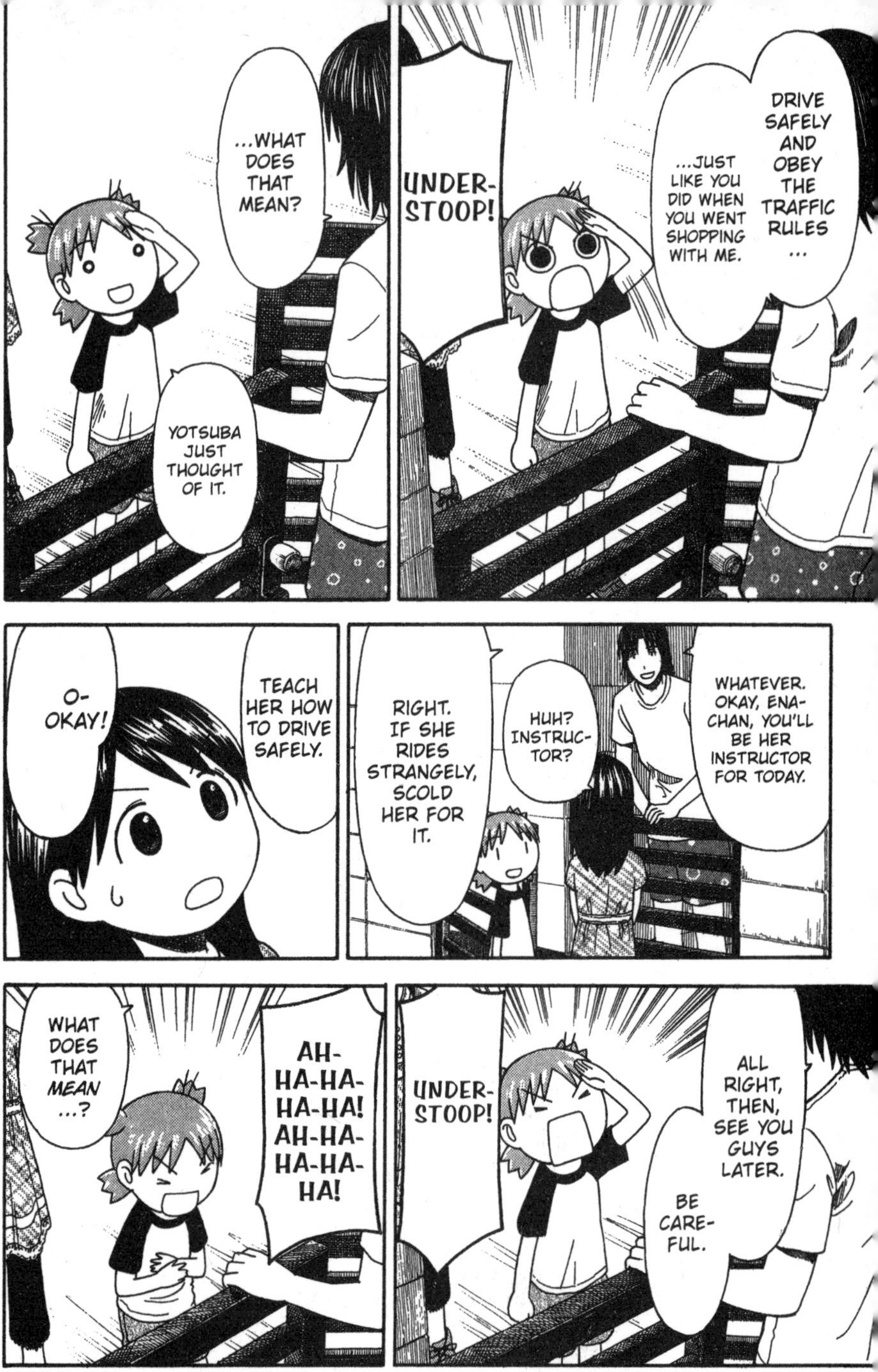
DRIVE SAFELY AND OBEY THE TRAFFIC RULES ...
...JUST LIKE YOU DID WHEN YOU WENT SHOPPING WITH ME.
UNDER-STOOP!
...WHAT DOES THAT MEAN?
YOTSUBA JUST THOUGHT OF IT.
WHATEVER. OKAY, ENA-CHAN, YOU'LL BE HER INSTRUCTOR FOR TODAY.
HUH? INSTRUC-TOR?
RIGHT. IF SHE RIDES STRANGELY, SCOLD HER FOR IT.
TEACH HER HOW TO DRIVE SAFELY.
O-OKAY!
ALL RIGHT, THEN, SEE YOU GUYS LATER.
BE CARE-FUL.
UNDER-STOOP!
AH-HA-HA-HA-HA! AH-HA-HA-HA-HA!
WHAT DOES THAT *MEAN* ...?

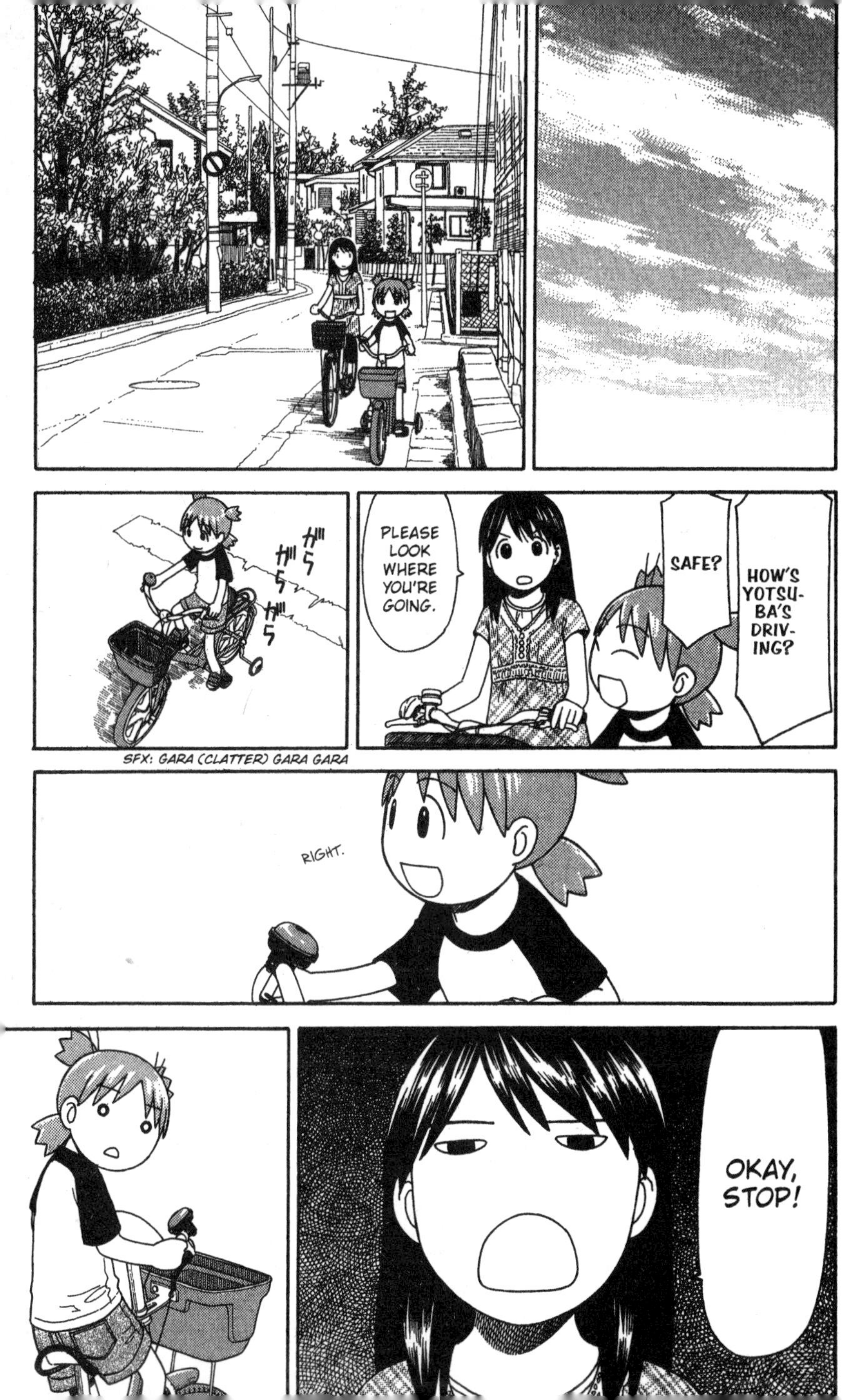
HOW'S YOTSU-BA'S DRIV-ING?
SAFE?
PLEASE LOOK WHERE YOU'RE GOING.
ガラ ガラ ガラ
SFX: GARA (CLATTER) GARA GARA
RIGHT.
OKAY, STOP!

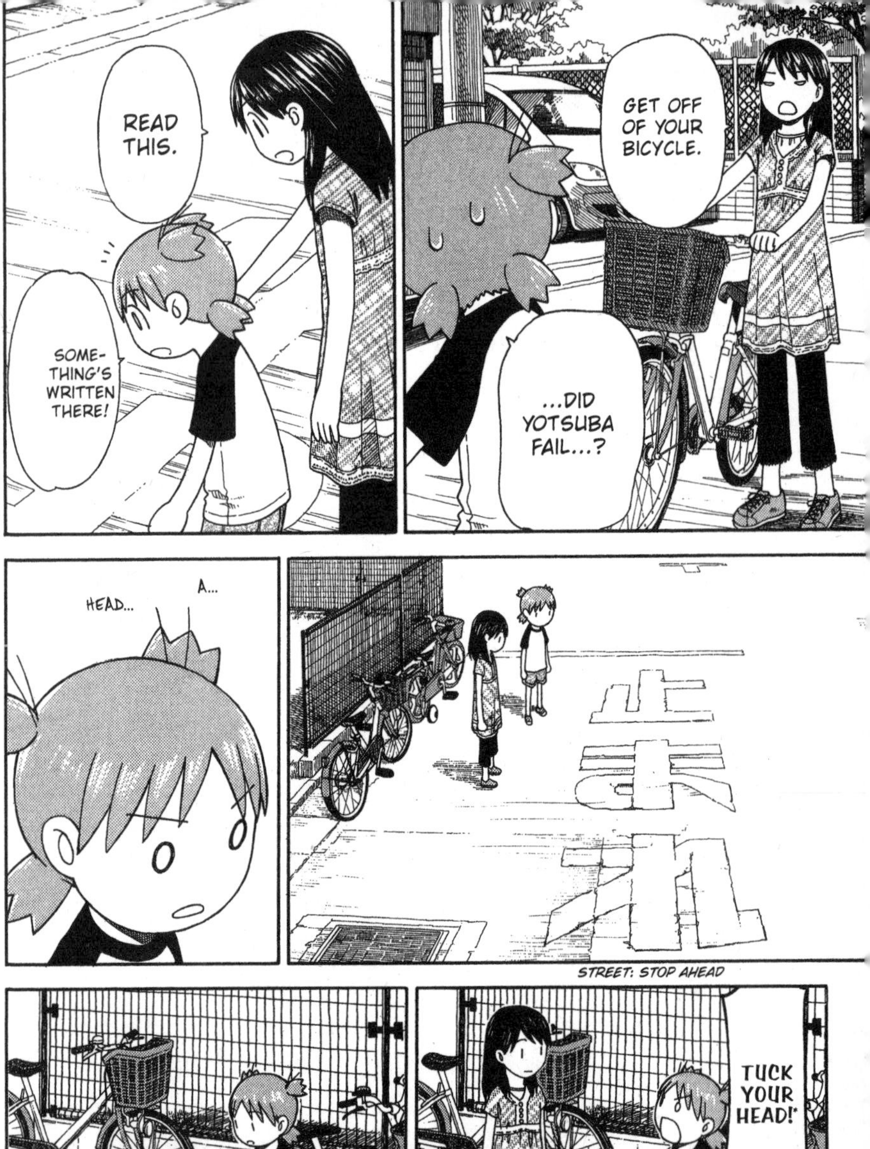
GET OFF OF YOUR BICYCLE.
...DID YOTSUBA FAIL...?
READ THIS.
SOME-THING'S WRITTEN THERE!
STREET: STOP AHEAD
A...
HEAD...
TUCK YOUR HEAD!*

*THE FIRST PART OF THE WORD ON THE STREET IS WRITTEN AS A CHINESE CHARACTER, WHICH CHILDREN LEARN IN SCHOOL, SO YOTSUBA CAN'T READ IT YET. BUT SHE CAN READ THE LAST PART OF THE WORD, WHICH IS WRITTEN IN SIMPLER JAPANESE LETTERS. SHE INCORRECTLY GUESSES THAT IT SAYS, "MARUMARE" (CURL INTO A BALL) INSTEAD OF "TOMARE" (STOP).

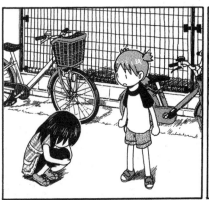

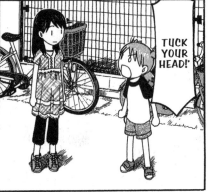

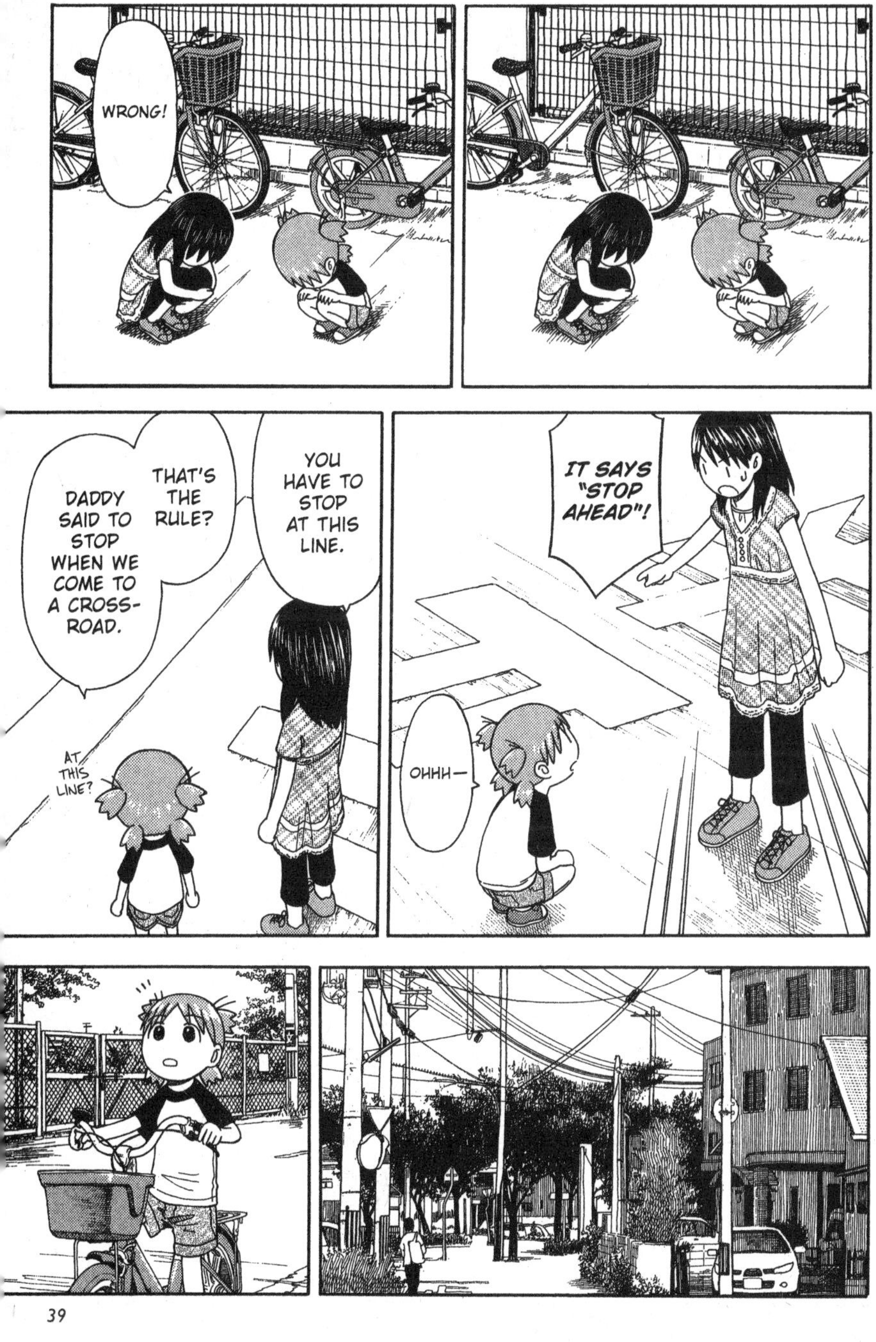
WRONG!
IT SAYS "STOP AHEAD"!
OHHH—
YOU HAVE TO STOP AT THIS LINE.
THAT'S THE RULE?
DADDY SAID TO STOP WHEN WE COME TO A CROSS-ROAD.
AT THIS LINE?

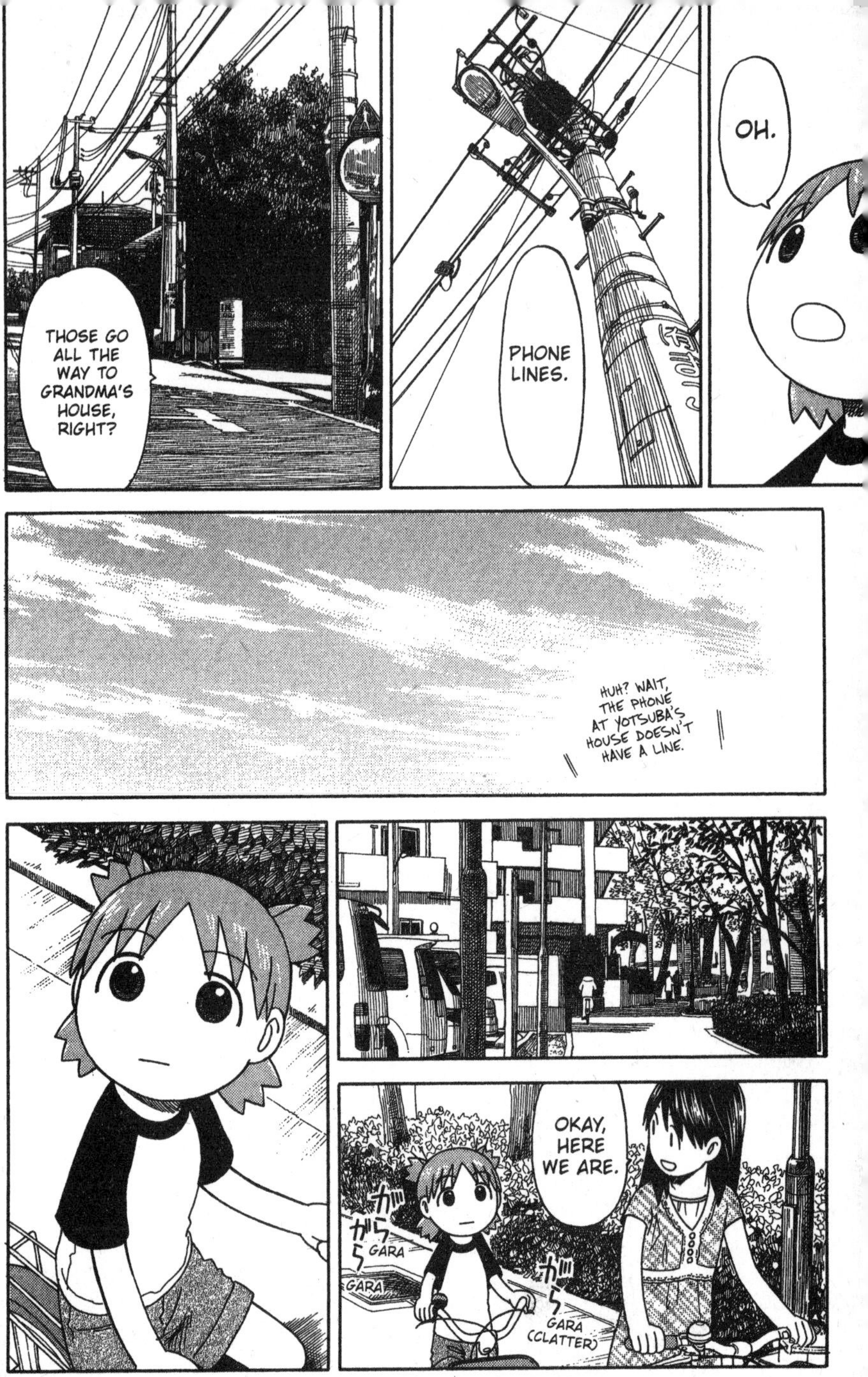
OH.
PHONE LINES.
THOSE GO ALL THE WAY TO GRANDMA'S HOUSE, RIGHT?
HUH? WAIT, THE PHONE AT YOTSUBA'S HOUSE DOESN'T HAVE A LINE.
OKAY, HERE WE ARE.
がら GARA (CLATTER)
がら GARA
がら GARA

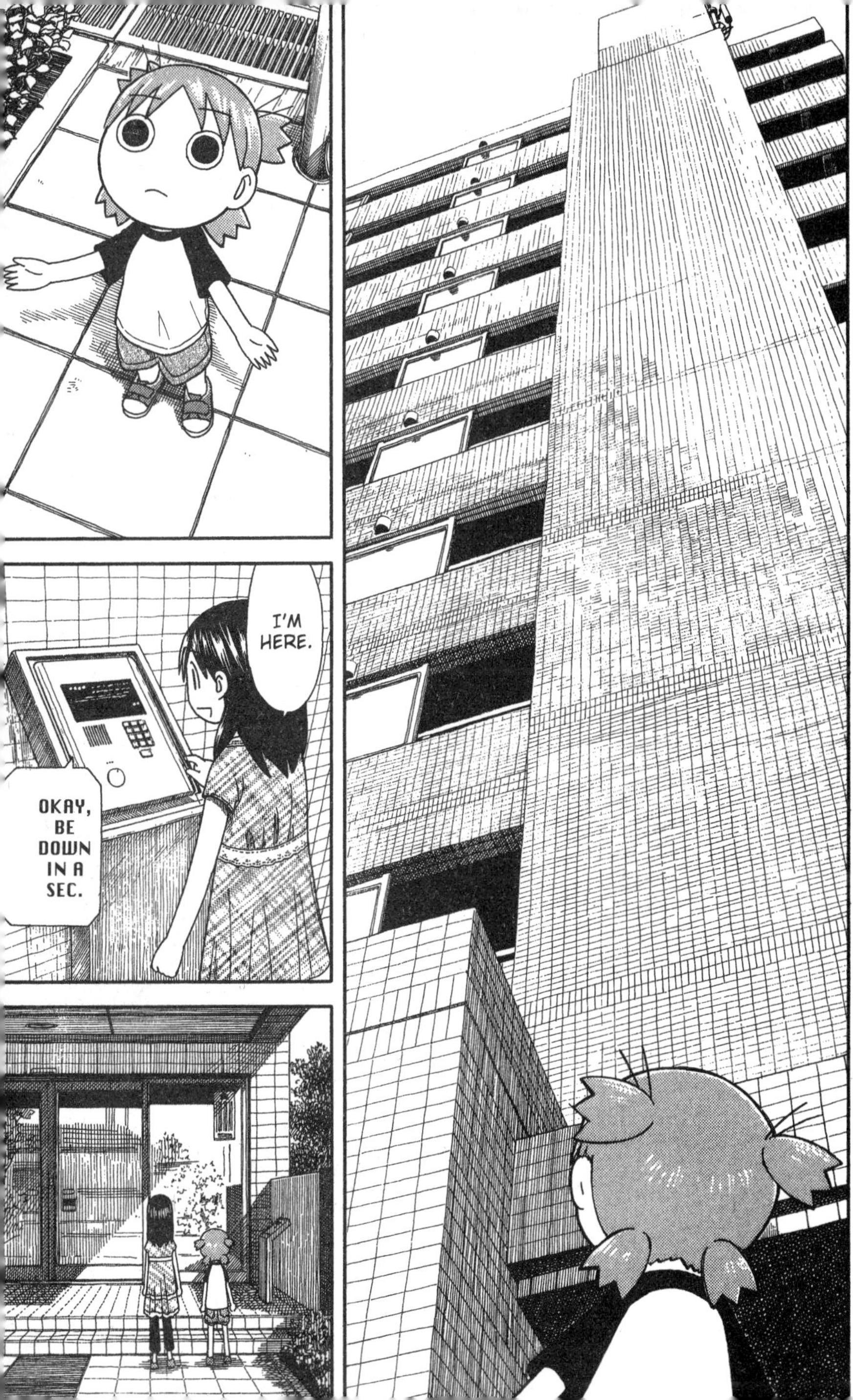
I'M HERE.
OKAY, BE DOWN IN A SEC.

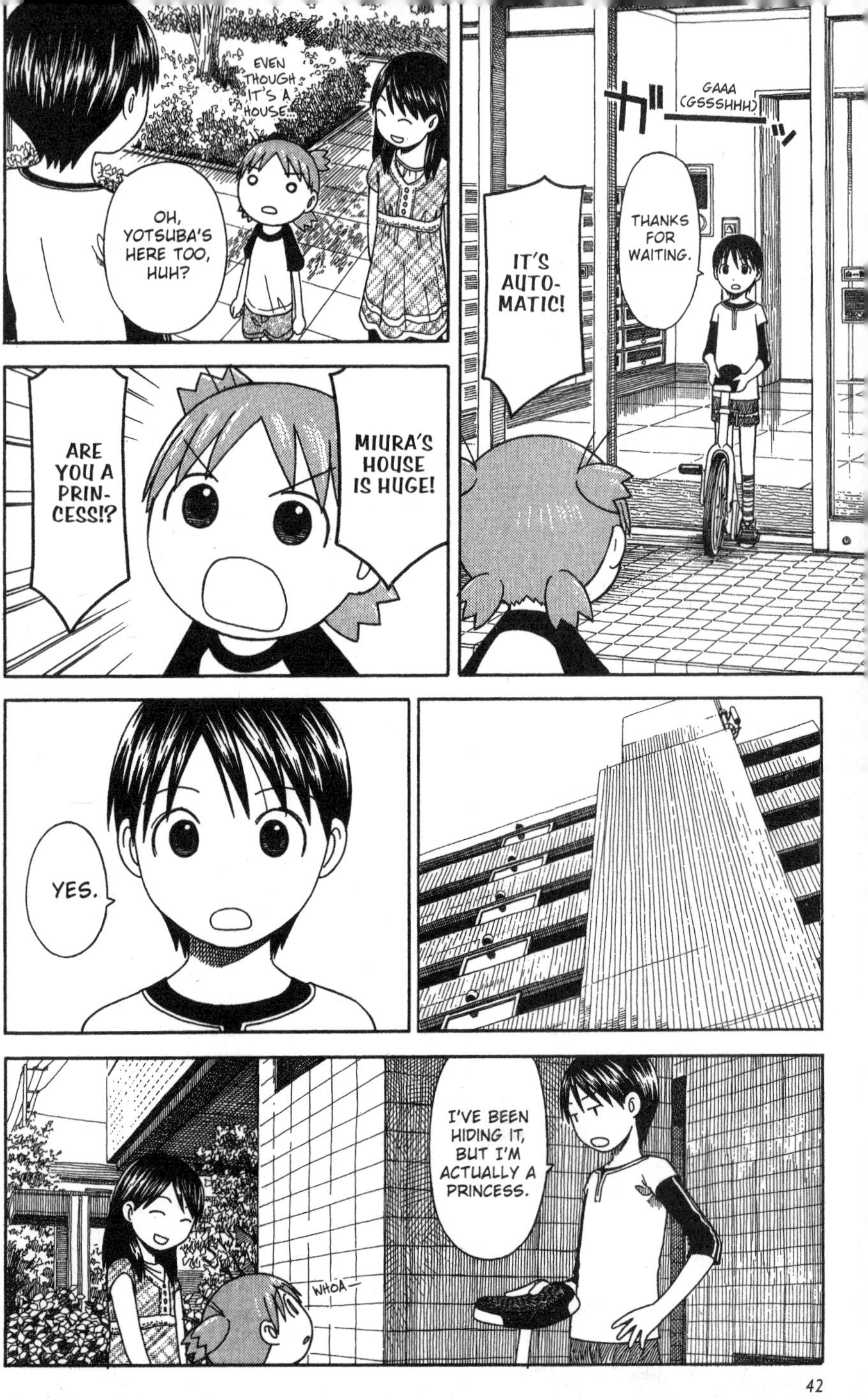
ガーーッ
GAAA (GSSSHHH)
THANKS FOR WAITING.
IT'S AUTOMATIC!
EVEN THOUGH IT'S A HOUSE...
OH, YOTSUBA'S HERE TOO, HUH?
MIURA'S HOUSE IS HUGE!
ARE YOU A PRINCESS!?
YES.
I'VE BEEN HIDING IT, BUT I'M ACTUALLY A PRINCESS.
WHOA—

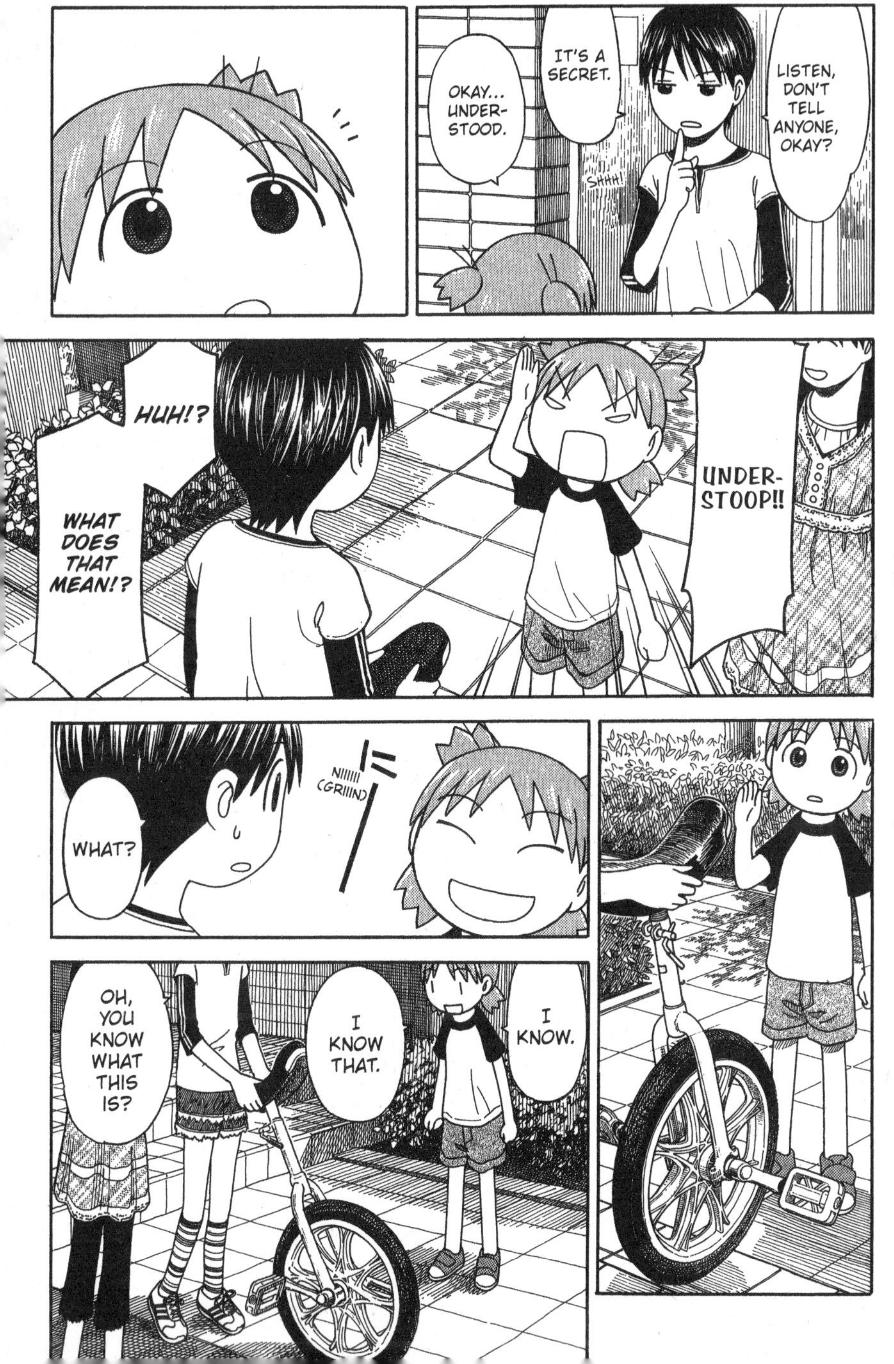
LISTEN, DON'T TELL ANYONE, OKAY?
SHHH!
IT'S A SECRET.
OKAY... UNDER-STOOD.
UNDER-STOOP!!
HUH!?
WHAT DOES THAT MEAN!?
NIIIII (GRIIIN)
WHAT?
I KNOW.
I KNOW THAT.
OH, YOU KNOW WHAT THIS IS?

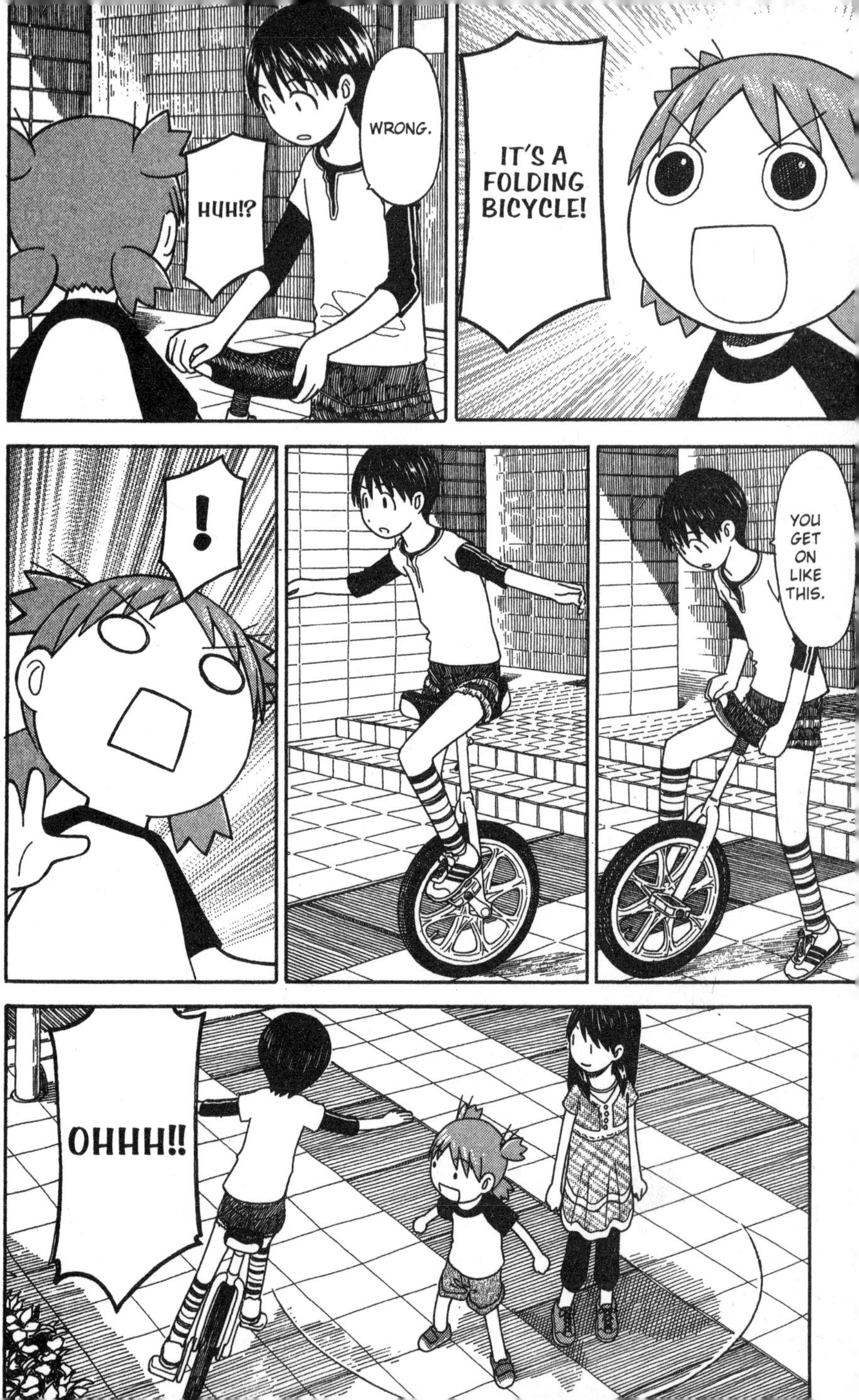
IT'S A FOLDING BICYCLE!
WRONG.
HUH!?
YOU GET ON LIKE THIS.
!
OHHH!!

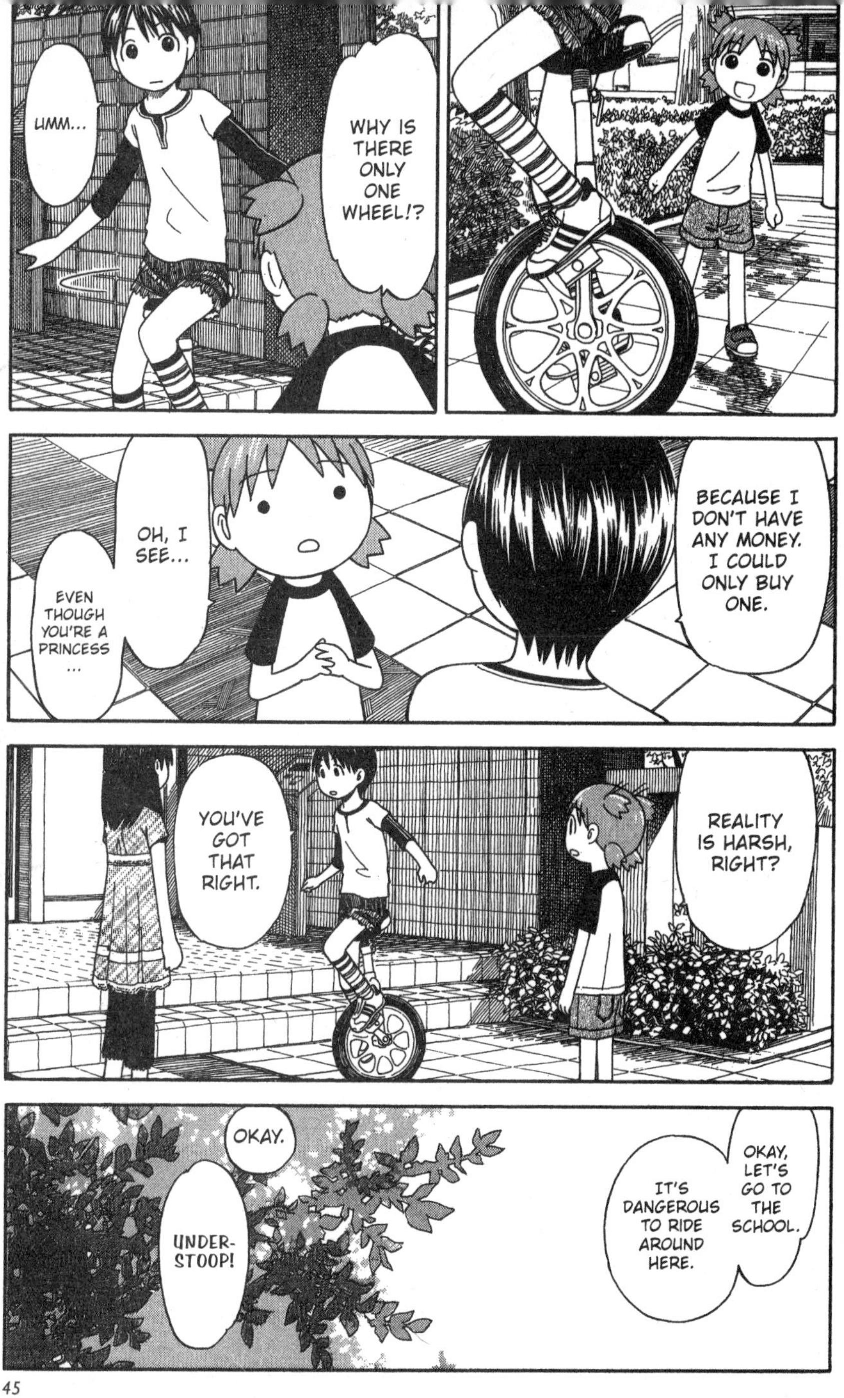
WHY IS THERE ONLY ONE WHEEL!?
UMM...
BECAUSE I DON'T HAVE ANY MONEY. I COULD ONLY BUY ONE.
OH, I SEE...
EVEN THOUGH YOU'RE A PRINCESS...
REALITY IS HARSH, RIGHT?
YOU'VE GOT THAT RIGHT.
OKAY, LET'S GO TO THE SCHOOL.
IT'S DANGEROUS TO RIDE AROUND HERE.
OKAY.
UNDER-STOOP!

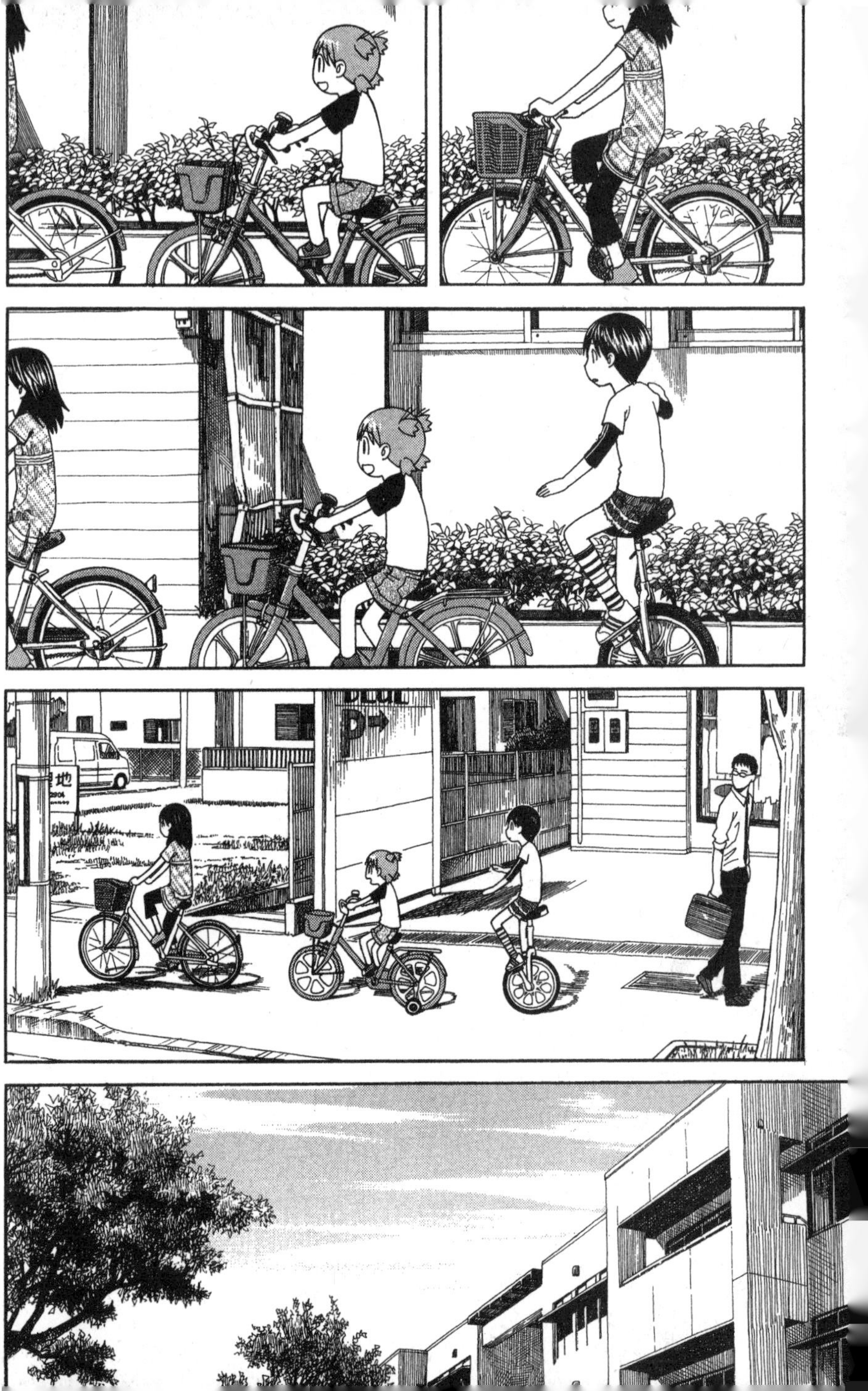

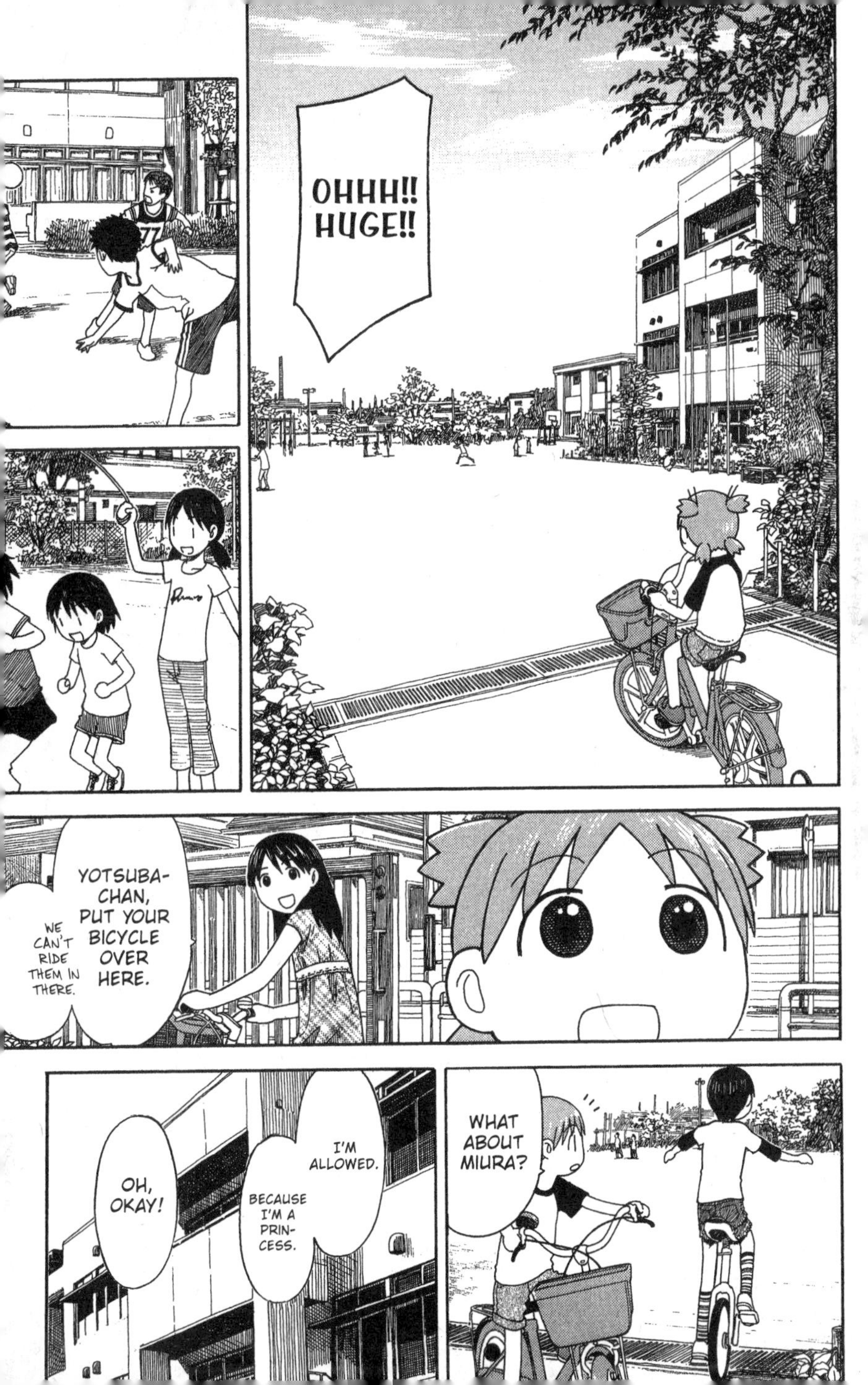
OHHH!! HUGE!!
YOTSUBA-CHAN, PUT YOUR BICYCLE OVER HERE.
WE CAN'T RIDE THEM IN THERE.
WHAT ABOUT MIURA?
I'M ALLOWED.
BECAUSE I'M A PRIN-CESS.
OH, OKAY!

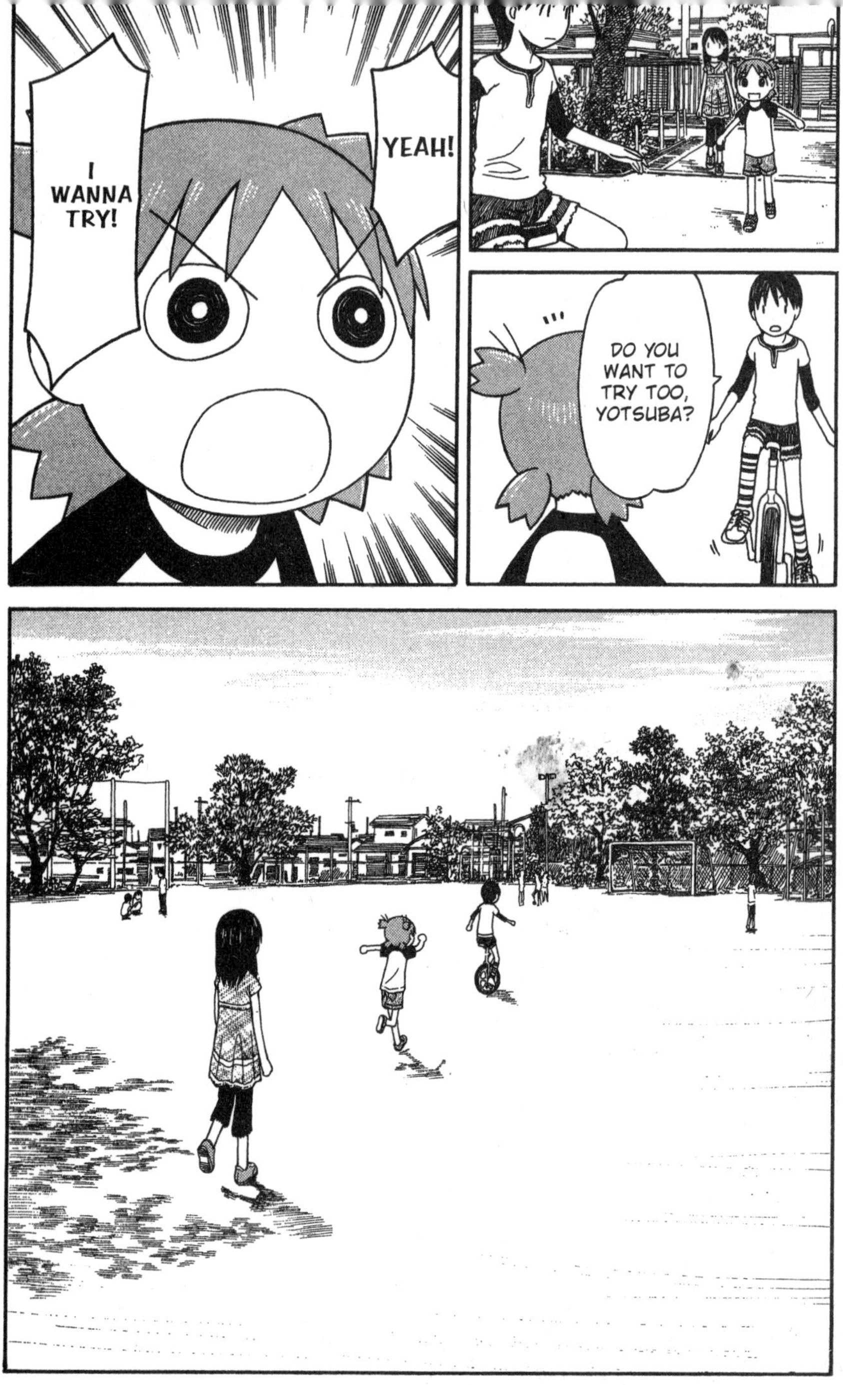
DO YOU WANT TO TRY TOO, YOTSUBA?
...
YEAH!
I WANNA TRY!

YOTSUBA&!

YOTSUBA&!

FEVER

#44

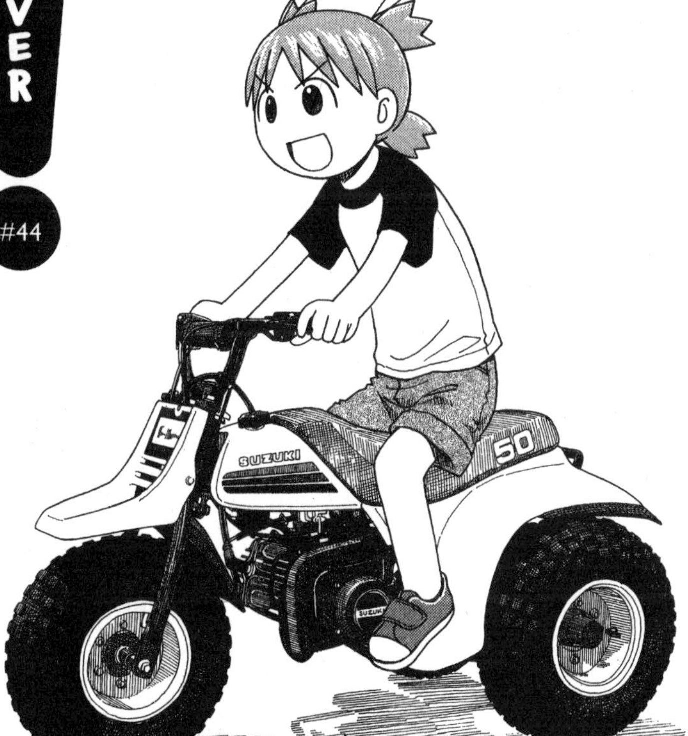
SUZUKI
50

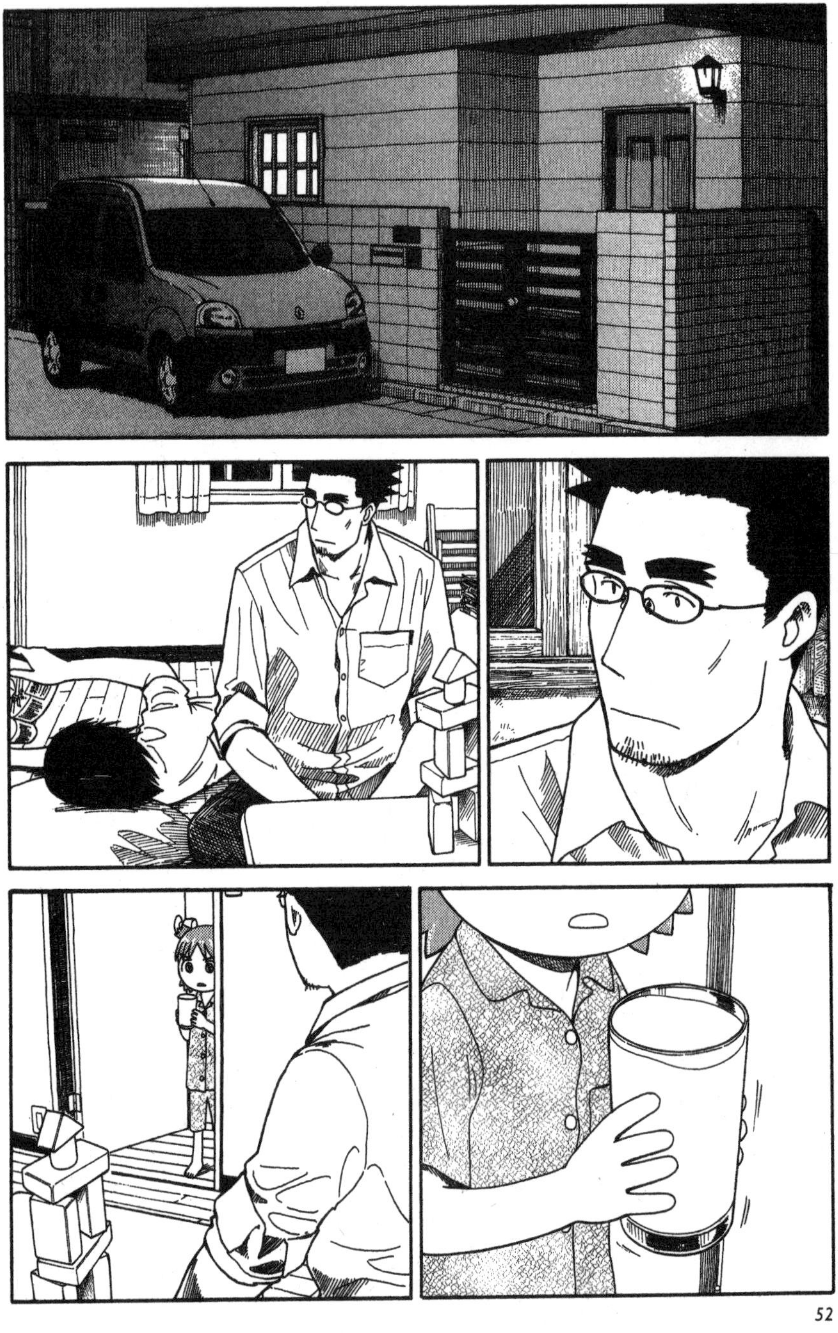

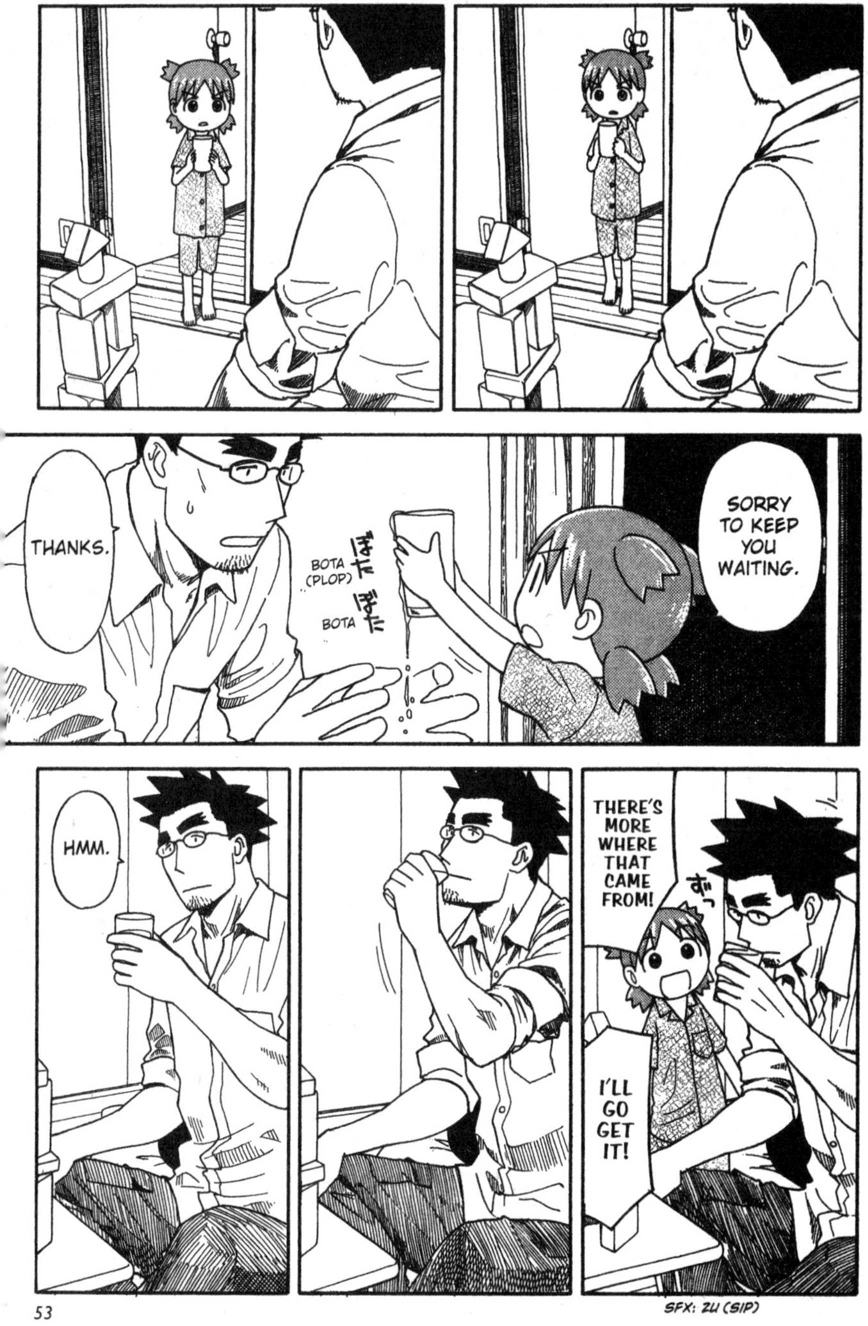
SORRY TO KEEP YOU WAITING.
ぼた ぼた
BOTA (PLOP)
BOTA
THANKS.
THERE'S MORE WHERE THAT CAME FROM!
ずっ
I'LL GO GET IT!
HMM.

SFX: ZU (SIP)

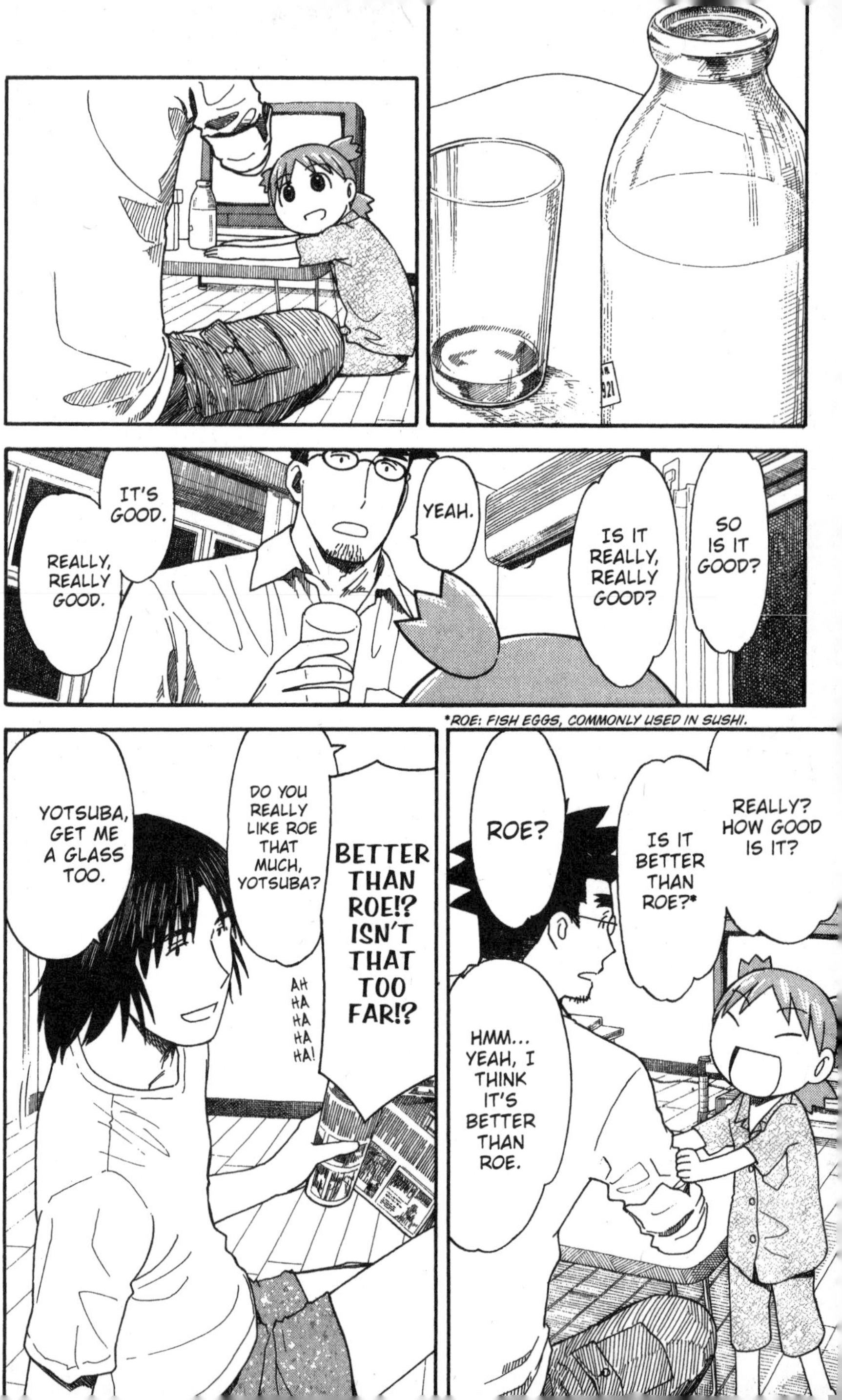
SO IS IT GOOD?
IS IT REALLY, REALLY GOOD?
YEAH.
IT'S GOOD.
REALLY, REALLY GOOD.
REALLY? HOW GOOD IS IT?
IS IT BETTER THAN ROE?*
ROE?
HMM... YEAH, I THINK IT'S BETTER THAN ROE.
BETTER THAN ROE!? ISN'T THAT TOO FAR!?
DO YOU REALLY LIKE ROE THAT MUCH, YOTSUBA?
AH HA HA HA HA!
YOTSUBA, GET ME A GLASS TOO.

*ROE: FISH EGGS, COMMONLY USED IN SUSHI.

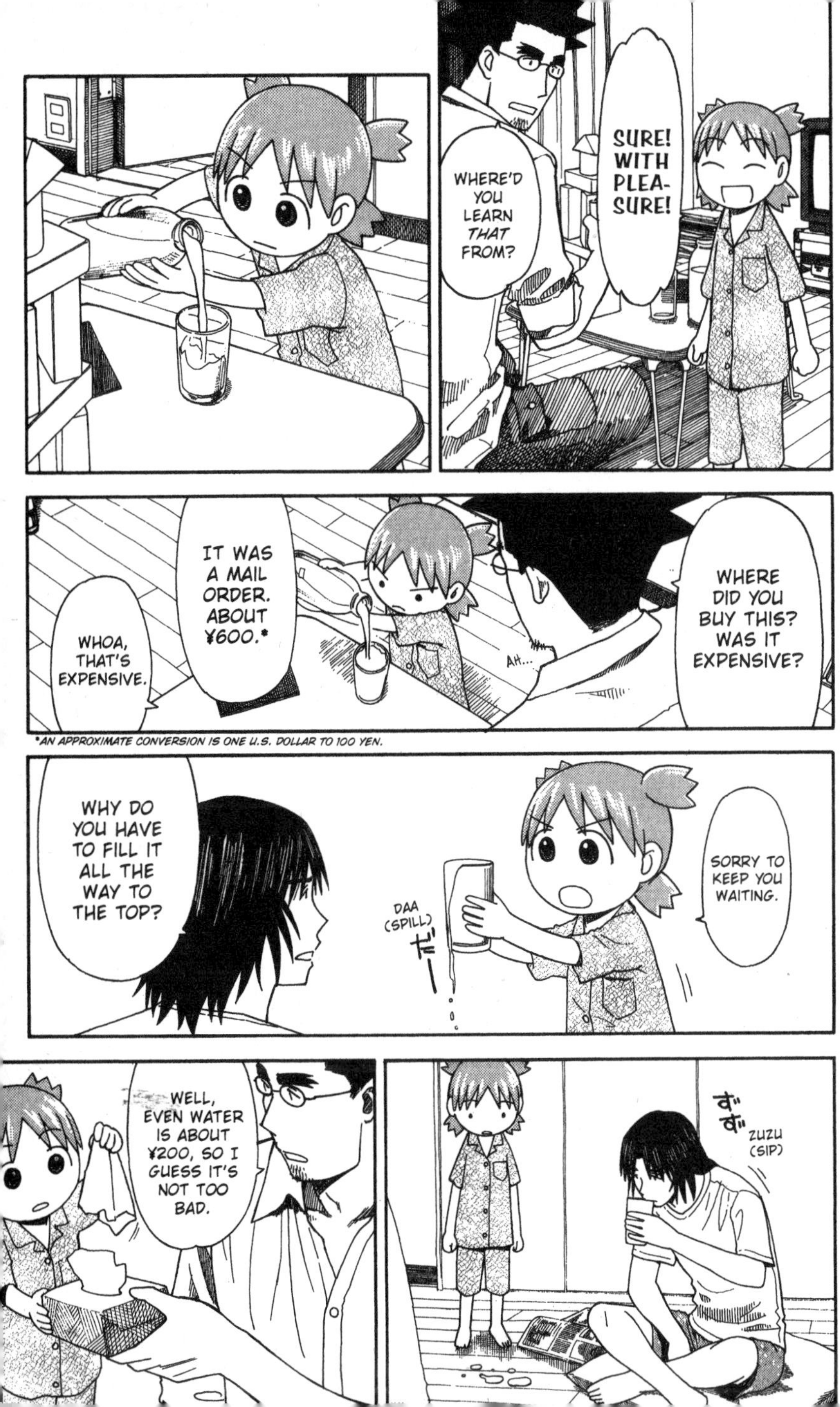
SURE! WITH PLEASURE!
WHERE'D YOU LEARN *THAT* FROM?
WHERE DID YOU BUY THIS? WAS IT EXPENSIVE?
AH...
IT WAS A MAIL ORDER. ABOUT ¥600.*
WHOA, THAT'S EXPENSIVE.
SORRY TO KEEP YOU WAITING.
だー
DAA (SPILL)
WHY DO YOU HAVE TO FILL IT ALL THE WAY TO THE TOP?
ずず
ZUZU (SIP)
WELL, EVEN WATER IS ABOUT ¥200, SO I GUESS IT'S NOT TOO BAD.

*AN APPROXIMATE CONVERSION IS ONE U.S. DOLLAR TO 100 YEN.

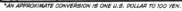

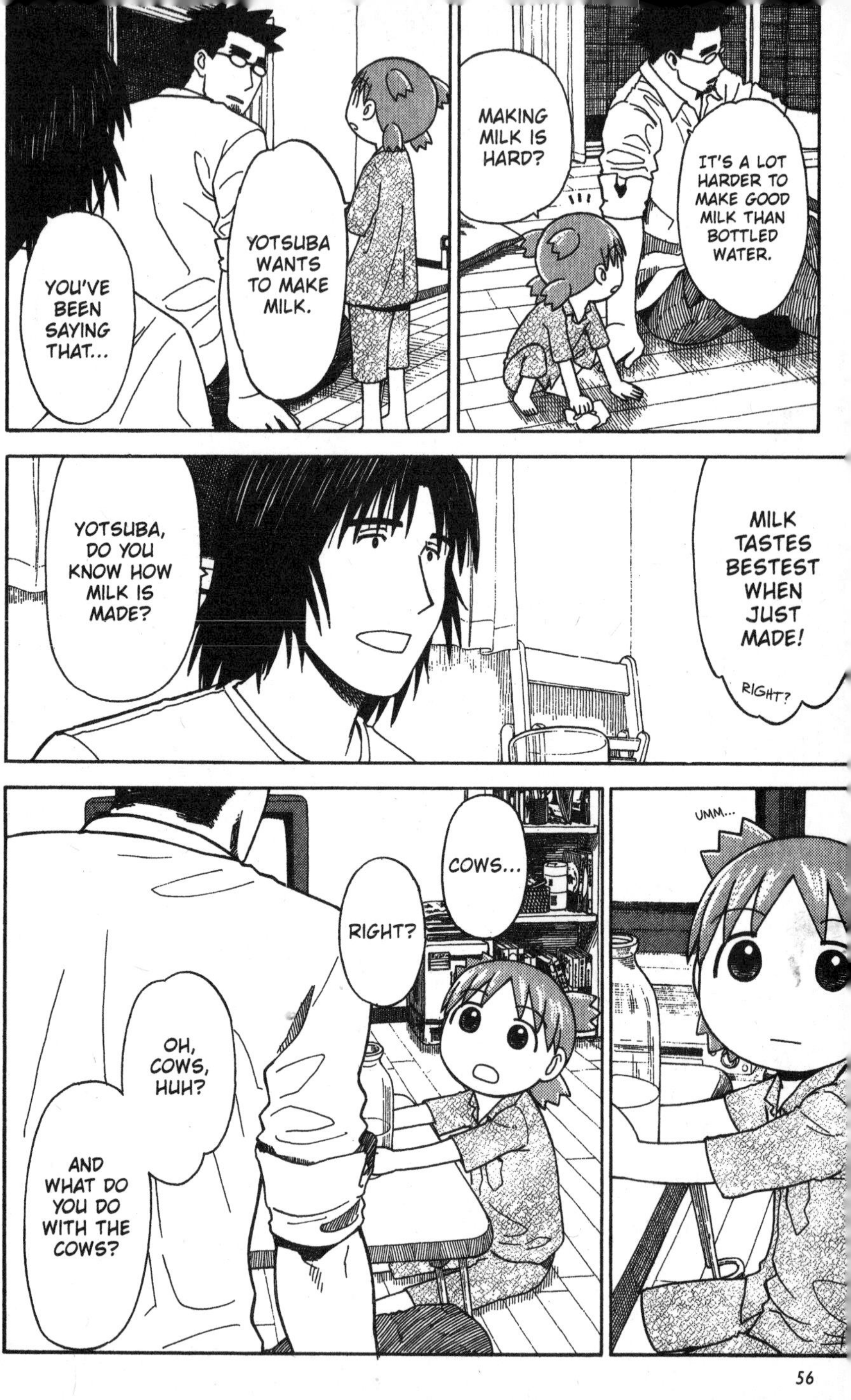
IT'S A LOT HARDER TO MAKE GOOD MILK THAN BOTTLED WATER.
MAKING MILK IS HARD?
YOTSUBA WANTS TO MAKE MILK.
YOU'VE BEEN SAYING THAT...
MILK TASTES BESTEST WHEN JUST MADE!
RIGHT?
YOTSUBA, DO YOU KNOW HOW MILK IS MADE?
UMM...
COWS...
RIGHT?
OH, COWS, HUH?
AND WHAT DO YOU DO WITH THE COWS?

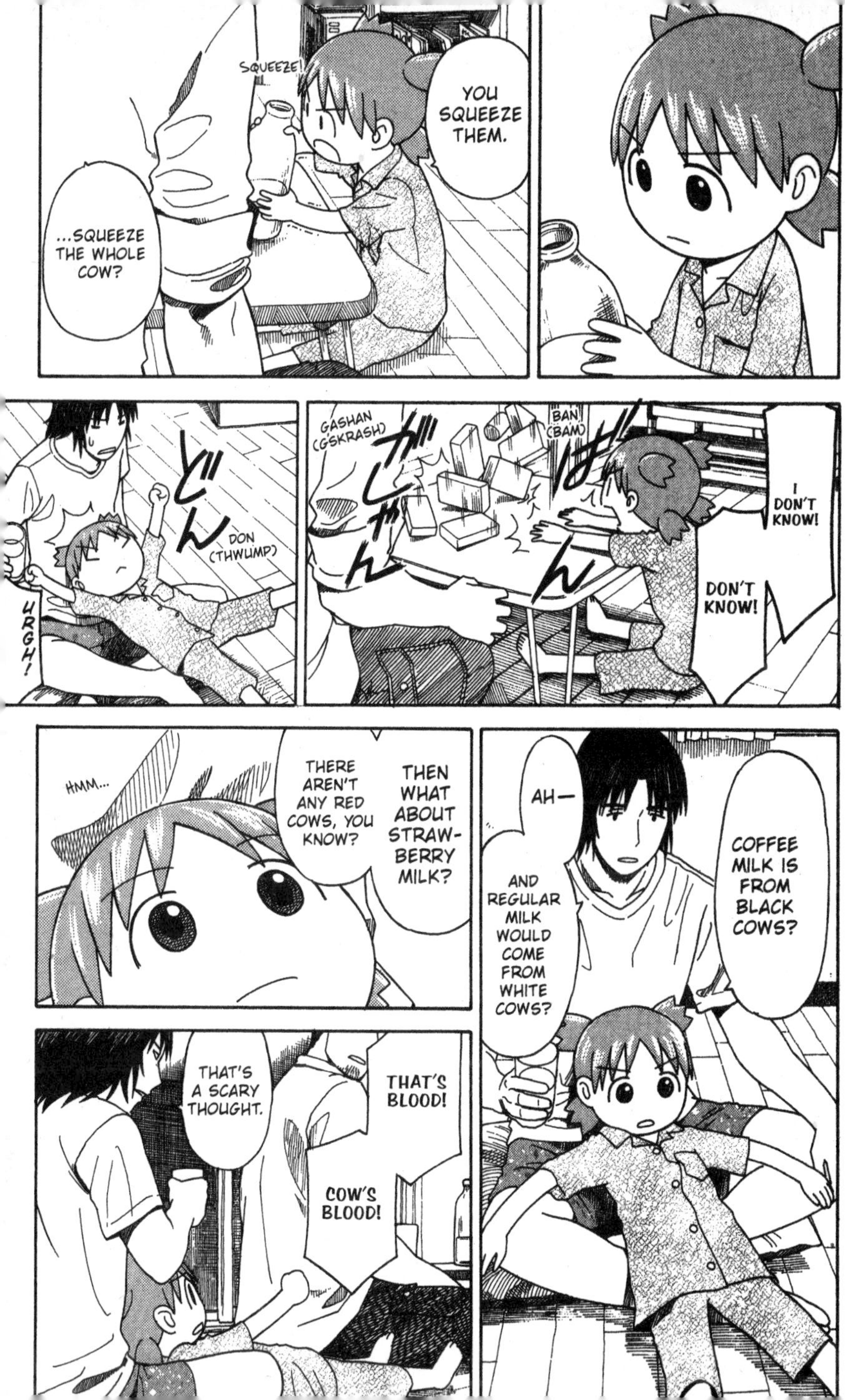
SQUEEZE!
YOU SQUEEZE THEM.
...SQUEEZE THE WHOLE COW?
I DON'T KNOW!
DON'T KNOW!
ばん
BAN (BAM)
がしゃん
GASHAN (G'SKRASH)
どん
DON (THWUMP)
URGH!
COFFEE MILK IS FROM BLACK COWS?
AH—
AND REGULAR MILK WOULD COME FROM WHITE COWS?
THEN WHAT ABOUT STRAW-BERRY MILK?
THERE AREN'T ANY RED COWS, YOU KNOW?
HMM...
THAT'S BLOOD!
COW'S BLOOD!
THAT'S A SCARY THOUGHT.

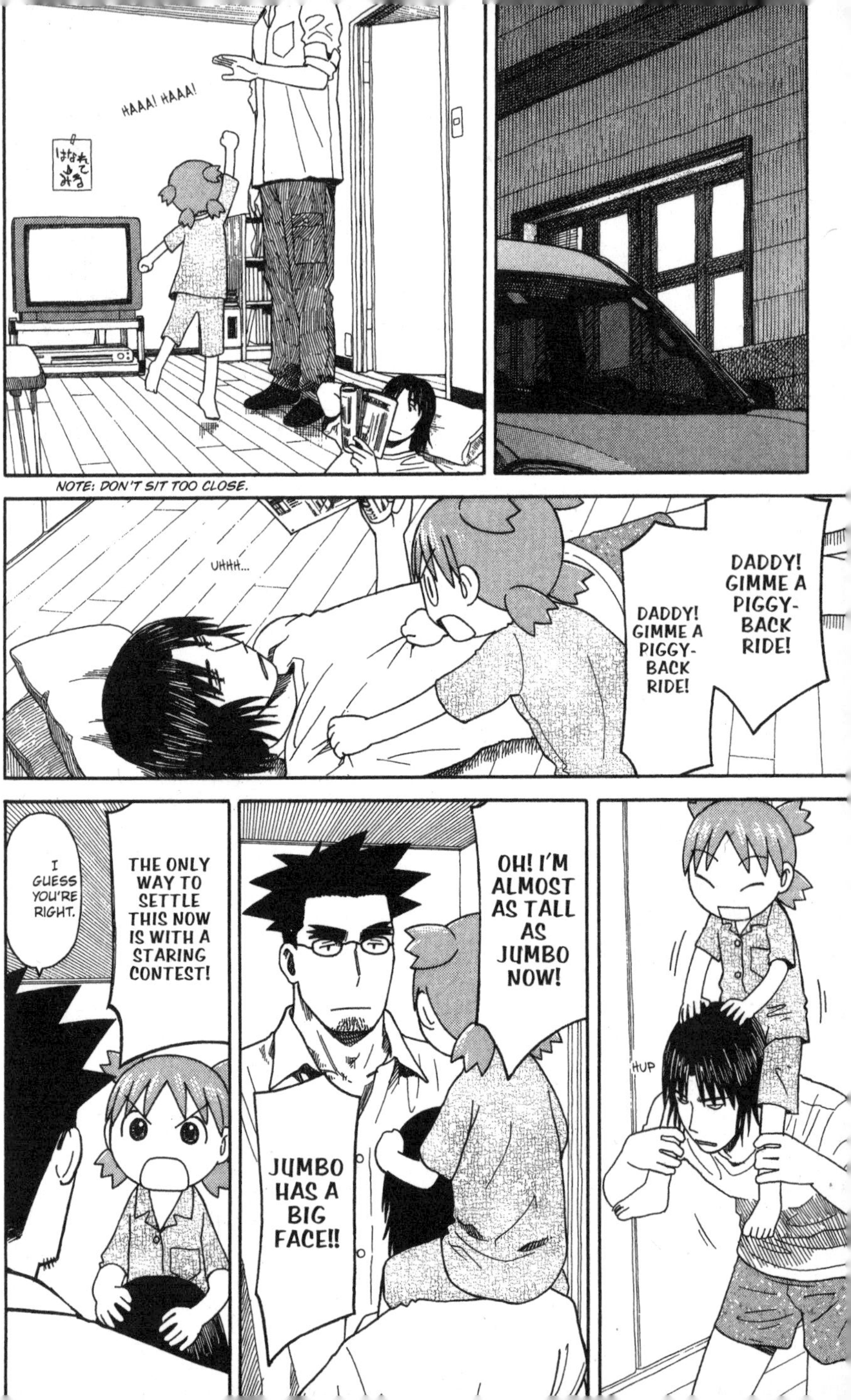
HAAA! HAAA!
はなれてみる
NOTE: DON'T SIT TOO CLOSE.
DADDY! GIMME A PIGGY-BACK RIDE!
DADDY! GIMME A PIGGY-BACK RIDE!
UHHH...
HUP
OH! I'M ALMOST AS TALL AS JUMBO NOW!
JUMBO HAS A BIG FACE!!
THE ONLY WAY TO SETTLE THIS NOW IS WITH A STARING CONTEST!
I GUESS YOU'RE RIGHT.

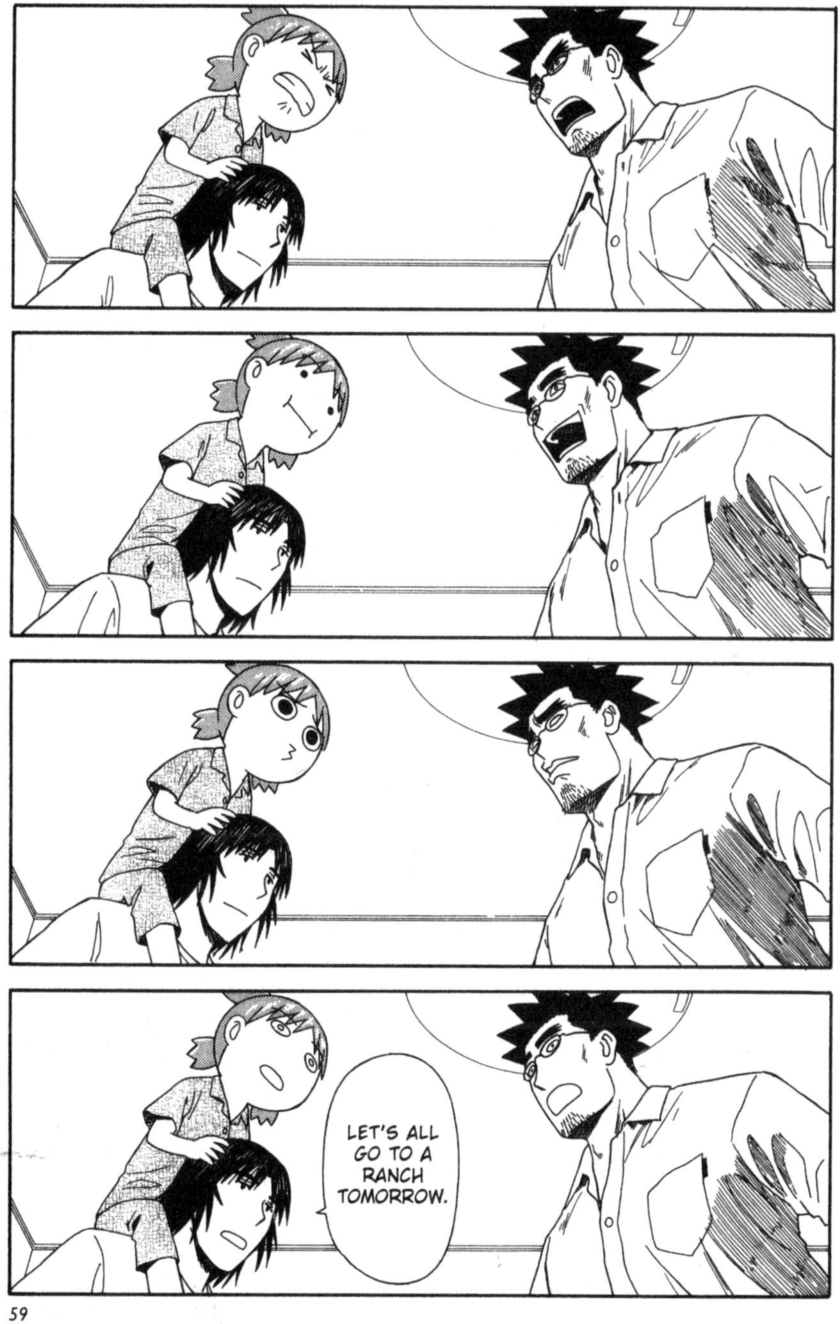
LET'S ALL GO TO A RANCH TOMORROW.

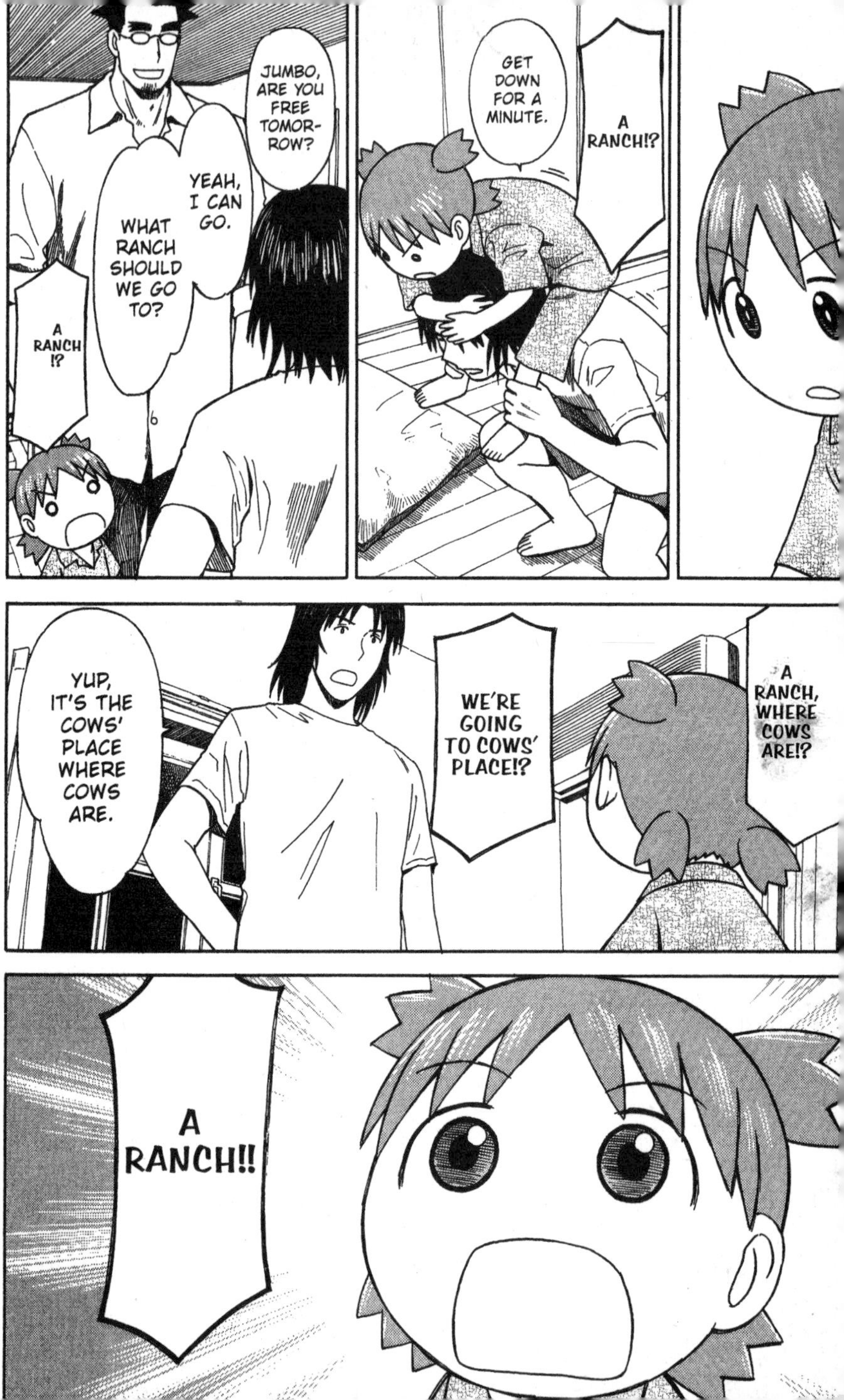
A RANCH!?
GET DOWN FOR A MINUTE.
JUMBO, ARE YOU FREE TOMORROW?
YEAH, I CAN GO.
WHAT RANCH SHOULD WE GO TO?
A RANCH!?
A RANCH, WHERE COWS ARE!?
WE'RE GOING TO COWS' PLACE!?
YUP, IT'S THE COWS' PLACE WHERE COWS ARE.
A RANCH!!

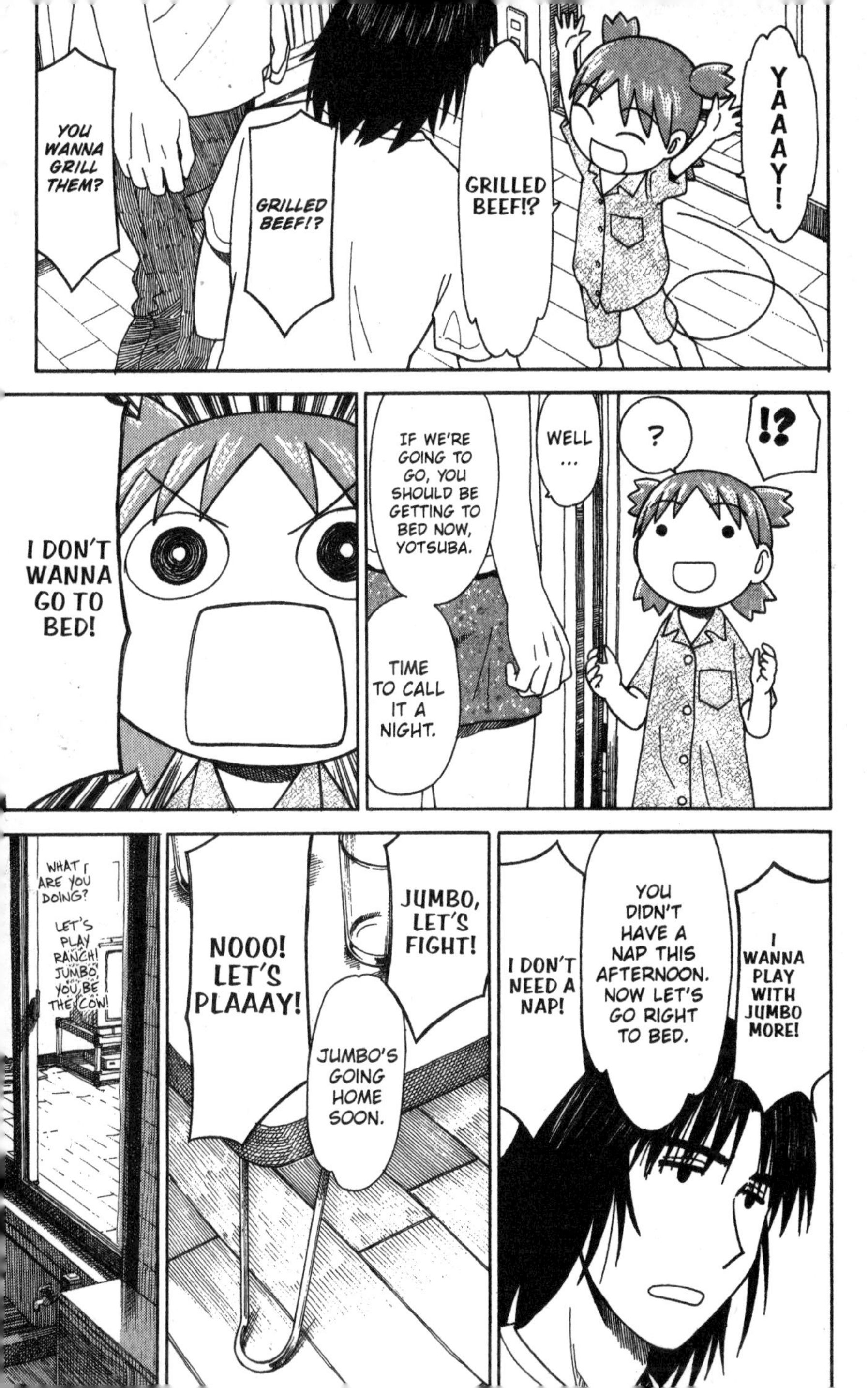
YAAAY!
GRILLED BEEF!?
GRILLED BEEF!?
YOU WANNA GRILL THEM?
!?
?
WELL ...
IF WE'RE GOING TO GO, YOU SHOULD BE GETTING TO BED NOW, YOTSUBA.
TIME TO CALL IT A NIGHT.
I DON'T WANNA GO TO BED!
I WANNA PLAY WITH JUMBO MORE!
YOU DIDN'T HAVE A NAP THIS AFTERNOON. NOW LET'S GO RIGHT TO BED.
I DON'T NEED A NAP!
JUMBO, LET'S FIGHT!
NOOO! LET'S PLAAAY!
JUMBO'S GOING HOME SOON.
WHAT ARE YOU DOING?
LET'S PLAY RANCH! JUMBO, YOU BE THE COW!

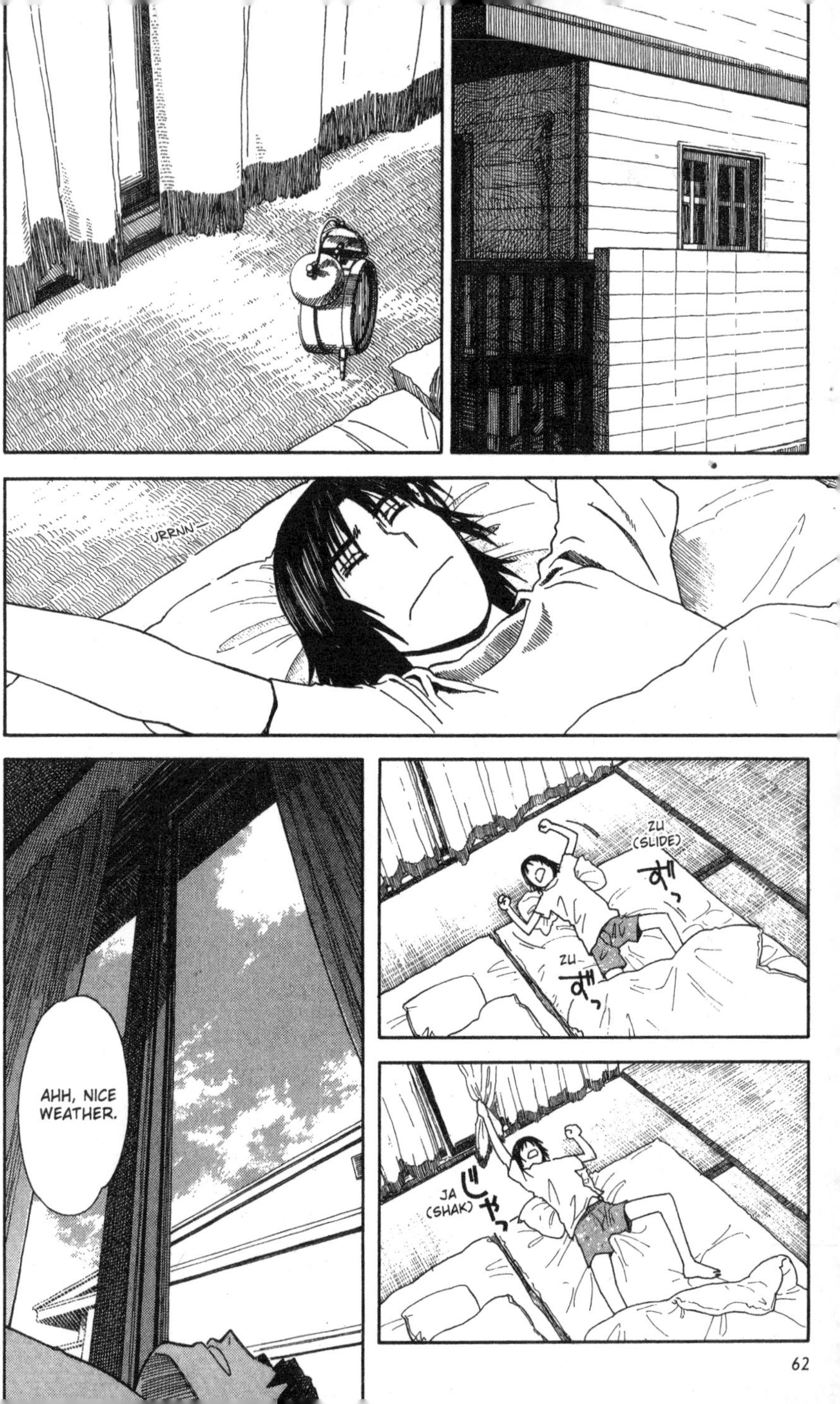
URRNN—
ZU (SLIDE)
ずっ
ZU
ずっ
JA (SHAK)
じゃっ
AHH, NICE WEATHER.

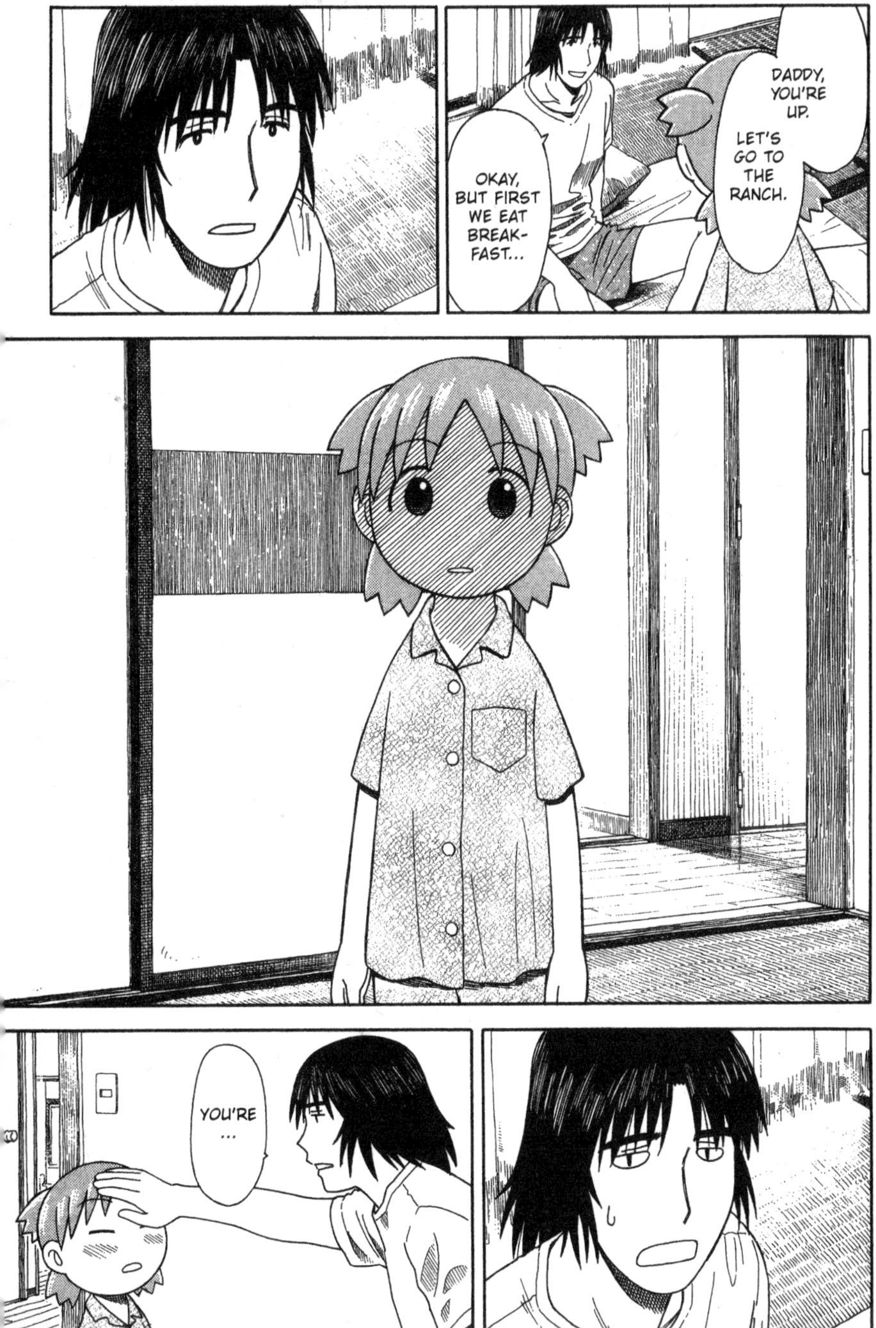
DADDY, YOU'RE UP.
LET'S GO TO THE RANCH.
OKAY, BUT FIRST WE EAT BREAK-FAST...
YOU'RE ...

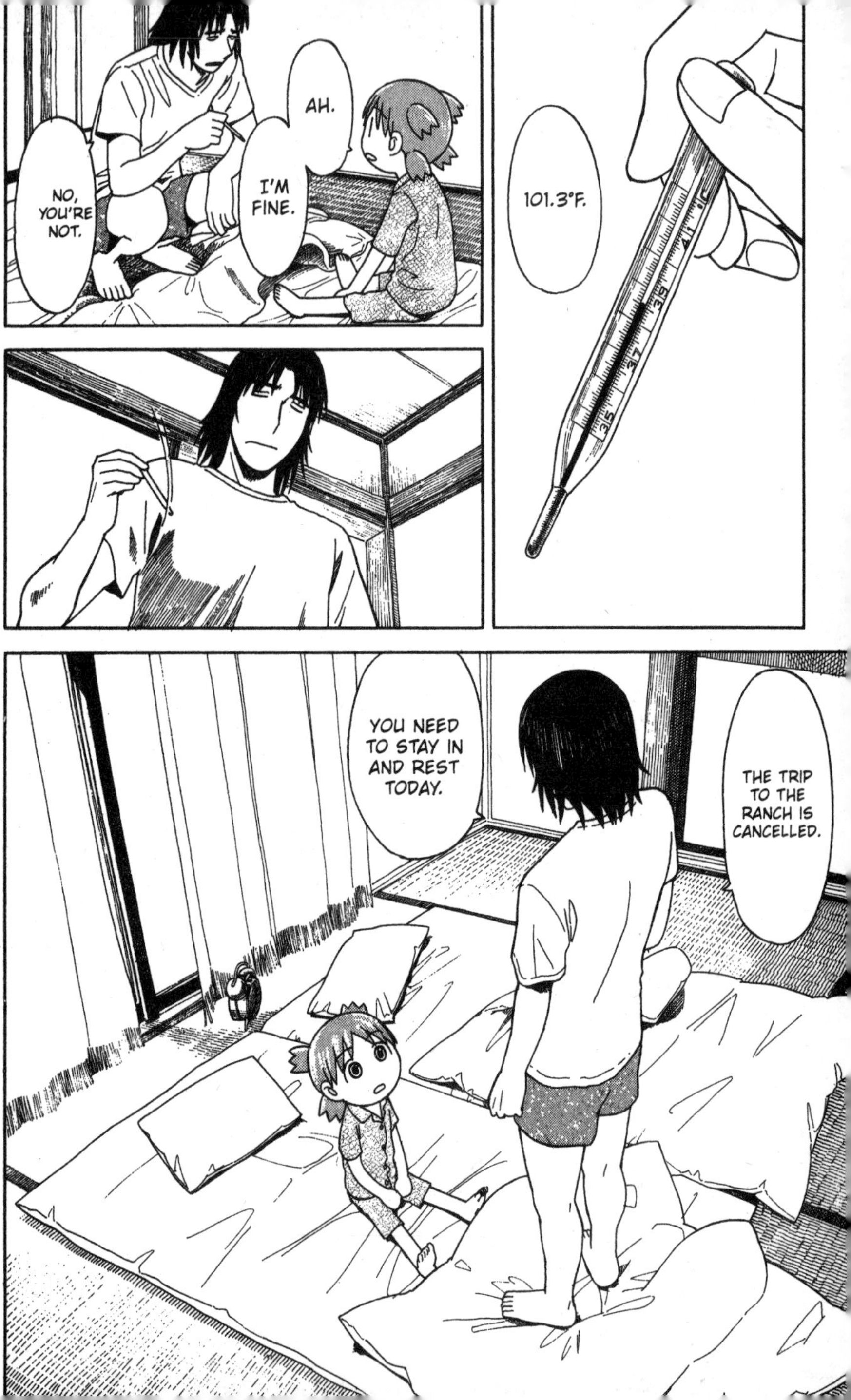
101.3°F.
AH.
I'M FINE.
NO, YOU'RE NOT.
THE TRIP TO THE RANCH IS CANCELLED.
YOU NEED TO STAY IN AND REST TODAY.

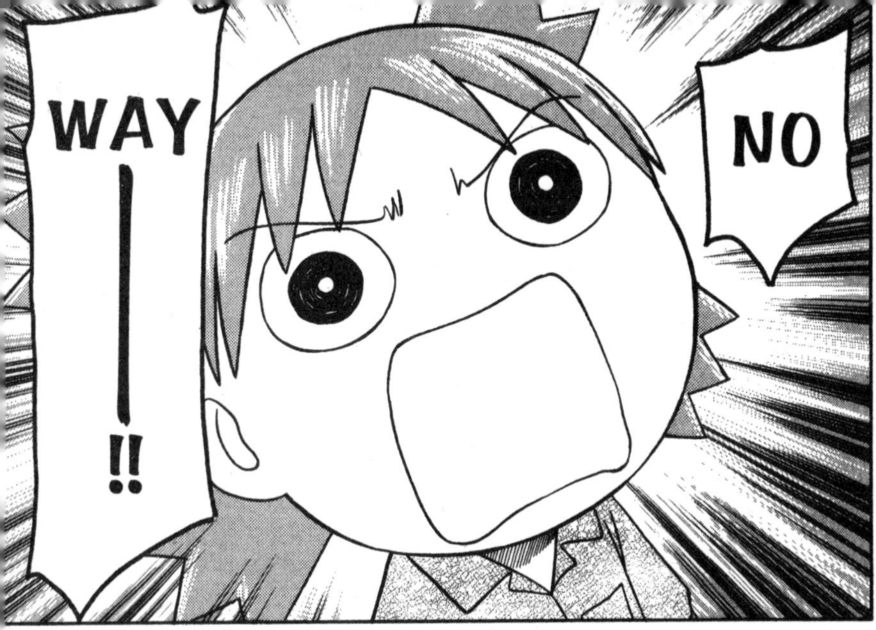
NO
WAY——!!

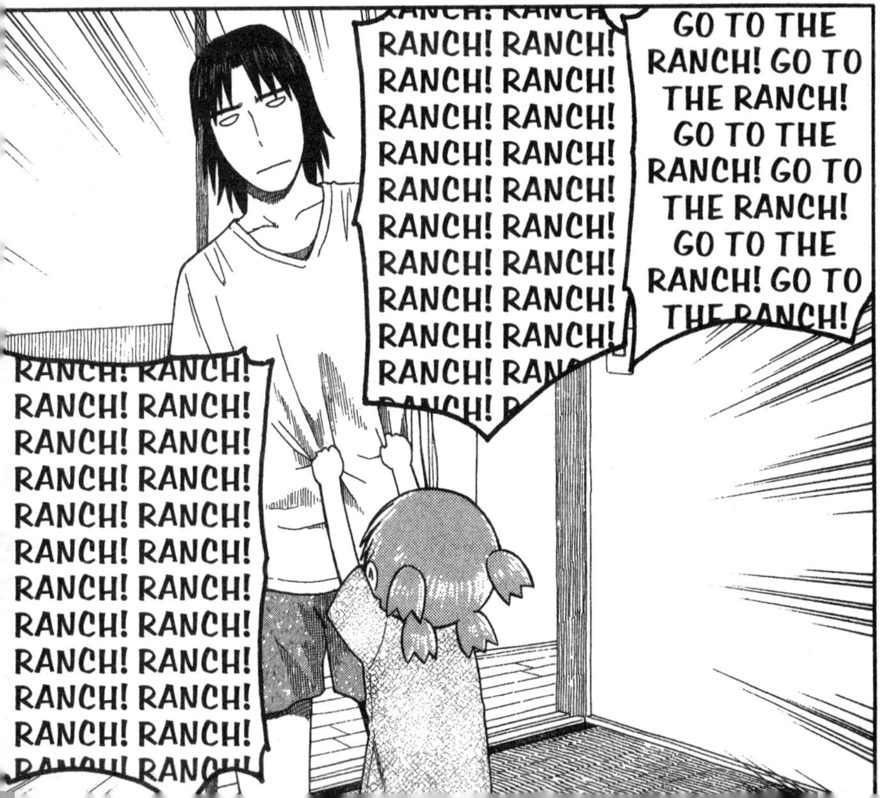
GO TO THE RANCH! GO TO THE RANCH! GO TO THE RANCH! GO TO THE RANCH! GO TO THE RANCH! GO TO THE RANCH!
RANCH! RANCH! RANCH! RANCH! RANCH! RANCH! RANCH! RANCH! RANCH! RANCH! RANCH! RANCH! RANCH! RANCH! RANCH! RANCH! RANCH! RANCH!
RANCH! RANCH! RANCH! RANCH! RANCH! RANCH! RANCH! RANCH! RANCH! RANCH! RANCH! RANCH! RANCH! RANCH! RANCH! RANCH! RANCH! RANCH! RANCH! RANCH!

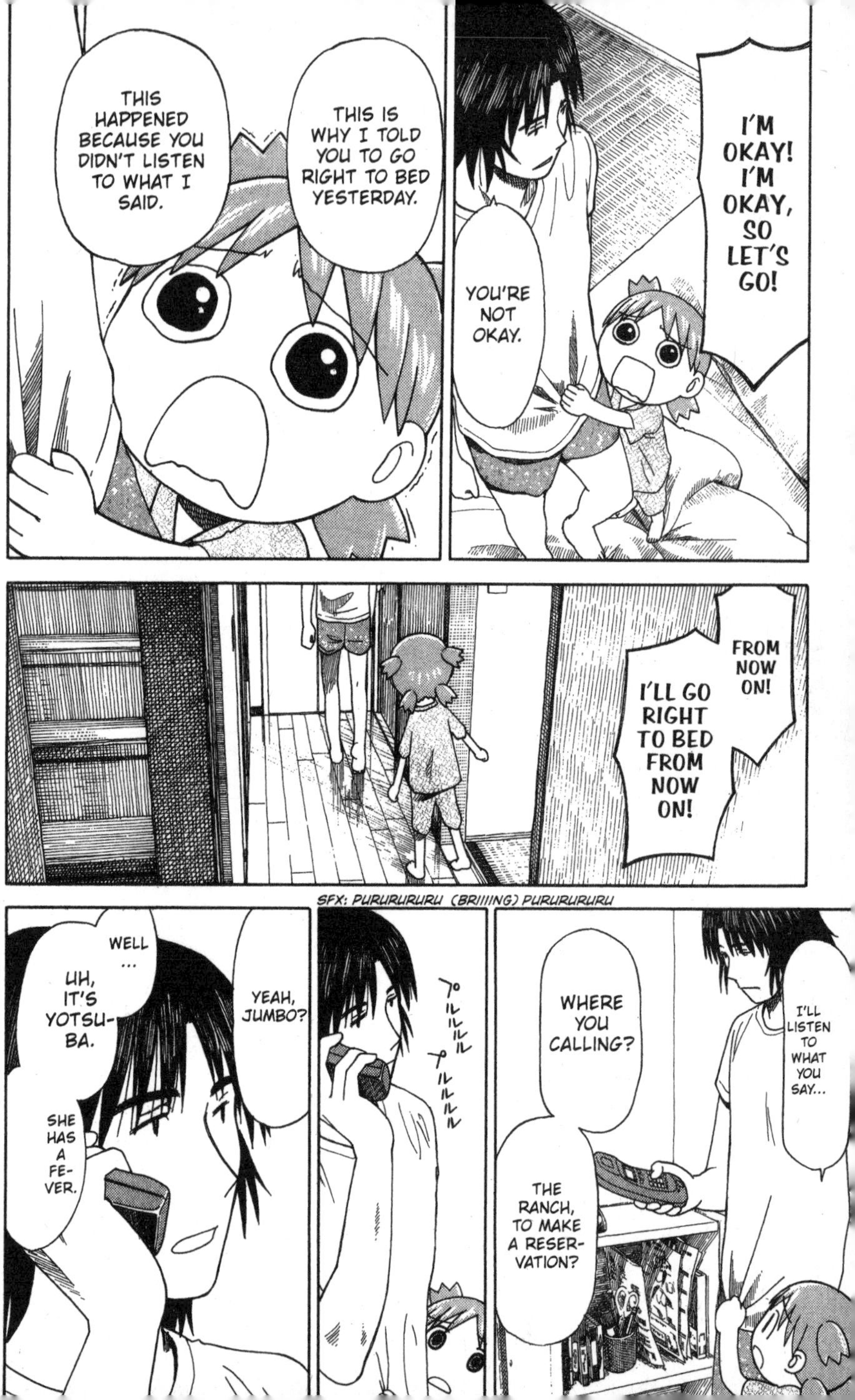
I'M OKAY! I'M OKAY, SO LET'S GO!
YOU'RE NOT OKAY.
THIS IS WHY I TOLD YOU TO GO RIGHT TO BED YESTERDAY.
THIS HAPPENED BECAUSE YOU DIDN'T LISTEN TO WHAT I SAID.
FROM NOW ON!
I'LL GO RIGHT TO BED FROM NOW ON!
SFX: PURURURURU (BRIIING) PURURURURU
I'LL LISTEN TO WHAT YOU SAY...
WHERE YOU CALLING?
THE RANCH, TO MAKE A RESERVATION?
プルルルル
プルルルル
YEAH, JUMBO?
WELL...
UH, IT'S YOTSUBA.
SHE HAS A FEVER.

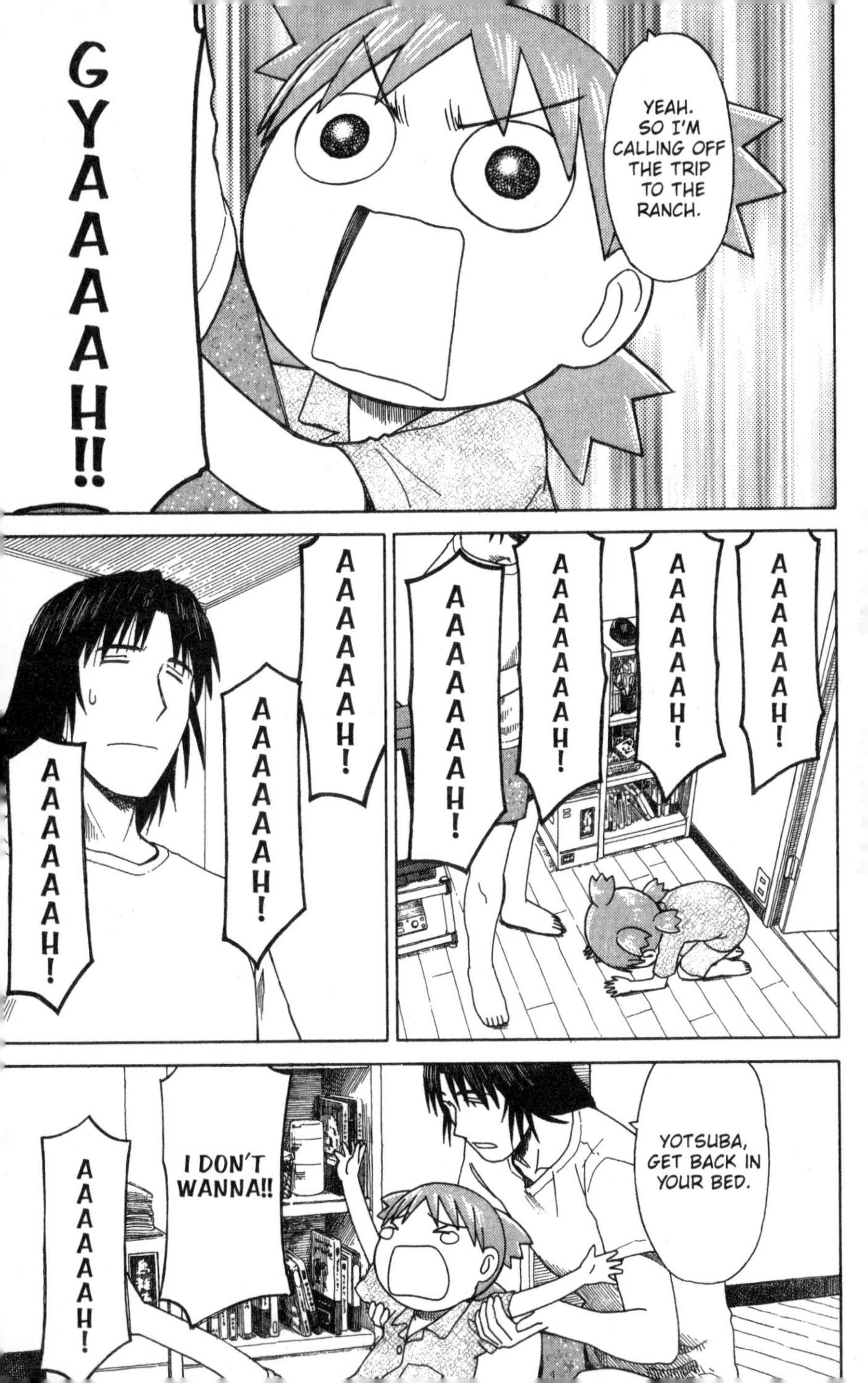
YEAH. SO I'M CALLING OFF THE TRIP TO THE RANCH.
GYAAAAAH!!
AAAAAAAH!
AAAAAAAH!
AAAAAAAAH!
AAAAAAAAAH!
AAAAAAAAH!
AAAAAAAAH!
AAAAAAAAAH!
YOTSUBA, GET BACK IN YOUR BED.
I DON'T WANNA!!
AAAAAAAH!

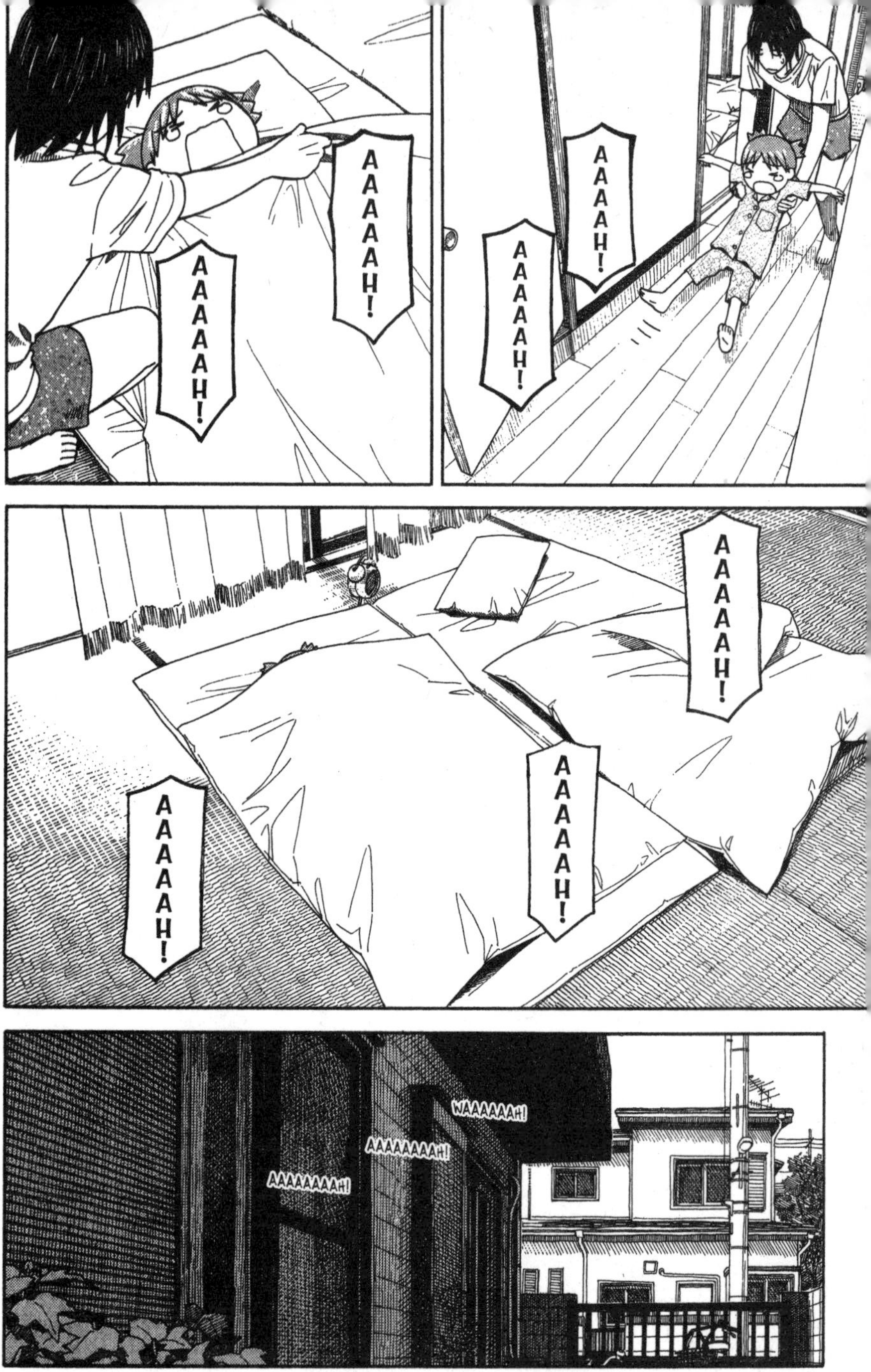
AAAAAH!
AAAAAAH!
AAAAAAH!
AAAAAAH!
AAAAAAH!
AAAAAAH!
AAAAAAH!
WAAAAAAH!
AAAAAAAAH!
AAAAAAAAH!

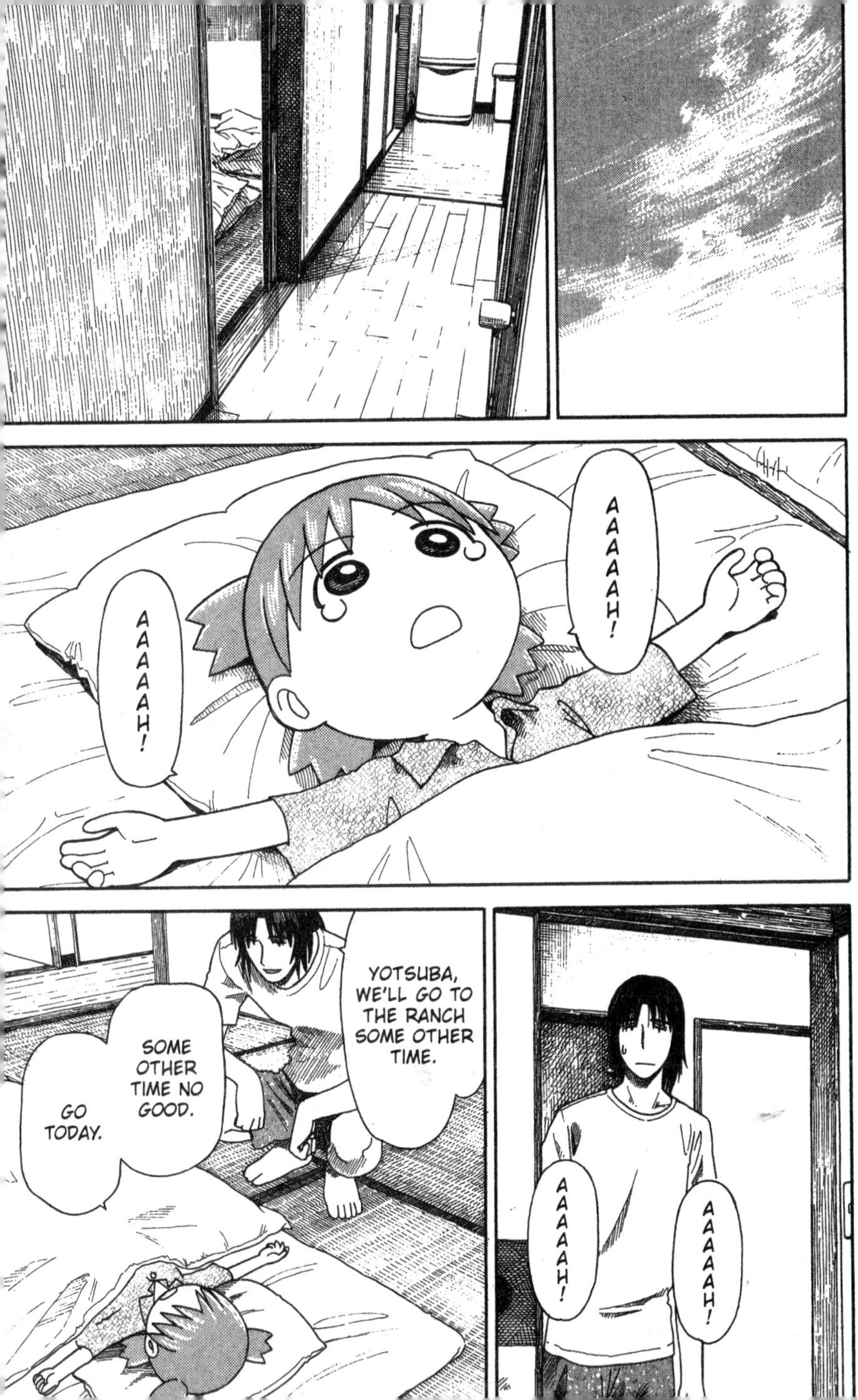
AAAAAAH!
AAAAAAH!
AAAAAAH!
AAAAAAH!
YOTSUBA, WE'LL GO TO THE RANCH SOME OTHER TIME.
SOME OTHER TIME NO GOOD.
GO TODAY.

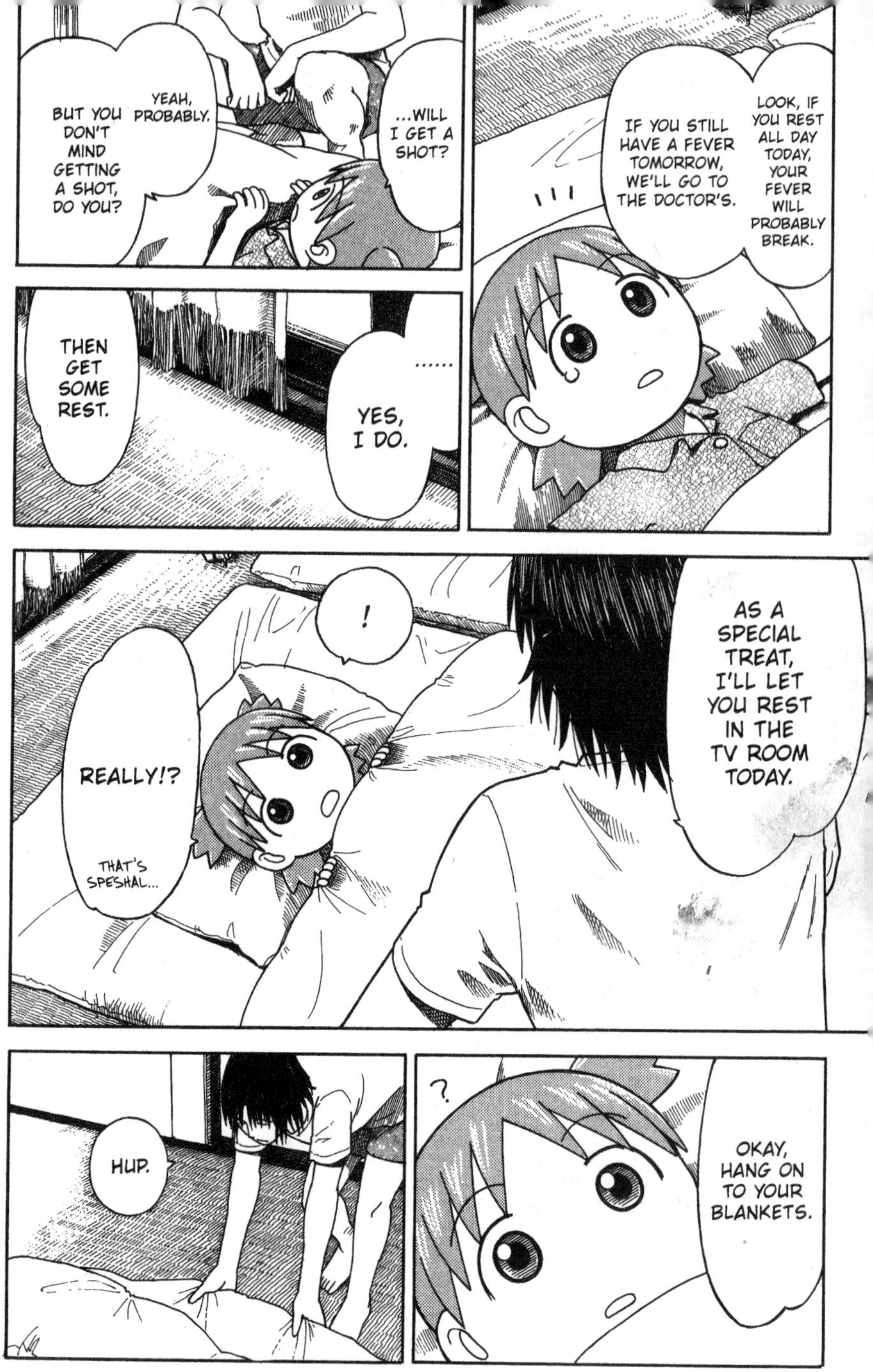
LOOK, IF YOU REST ALL DAY TODAY, YOUR FEVER WILL PROBABLY BREAK.
IF YOU STILL HAVE A FEVER TOMORROW, WE'LL GO TO THE DOCTOR'S.
...WILL I GET A SHOT?
YEAH, PROBABLY.
BUT YOU DON'T MIND GETTING A SHOT, DO YOU?
......
YES, I DO.
THEN GET SOME REST.
AS A SPECIAL TREAT, I'LL LET YOU REST IN THE TV ROOM TODAY.
!
REALLY!?
THAT'S SPESHAL...
?
OKAY, HANG ON TO YOUR BLANKETS.
HUP.

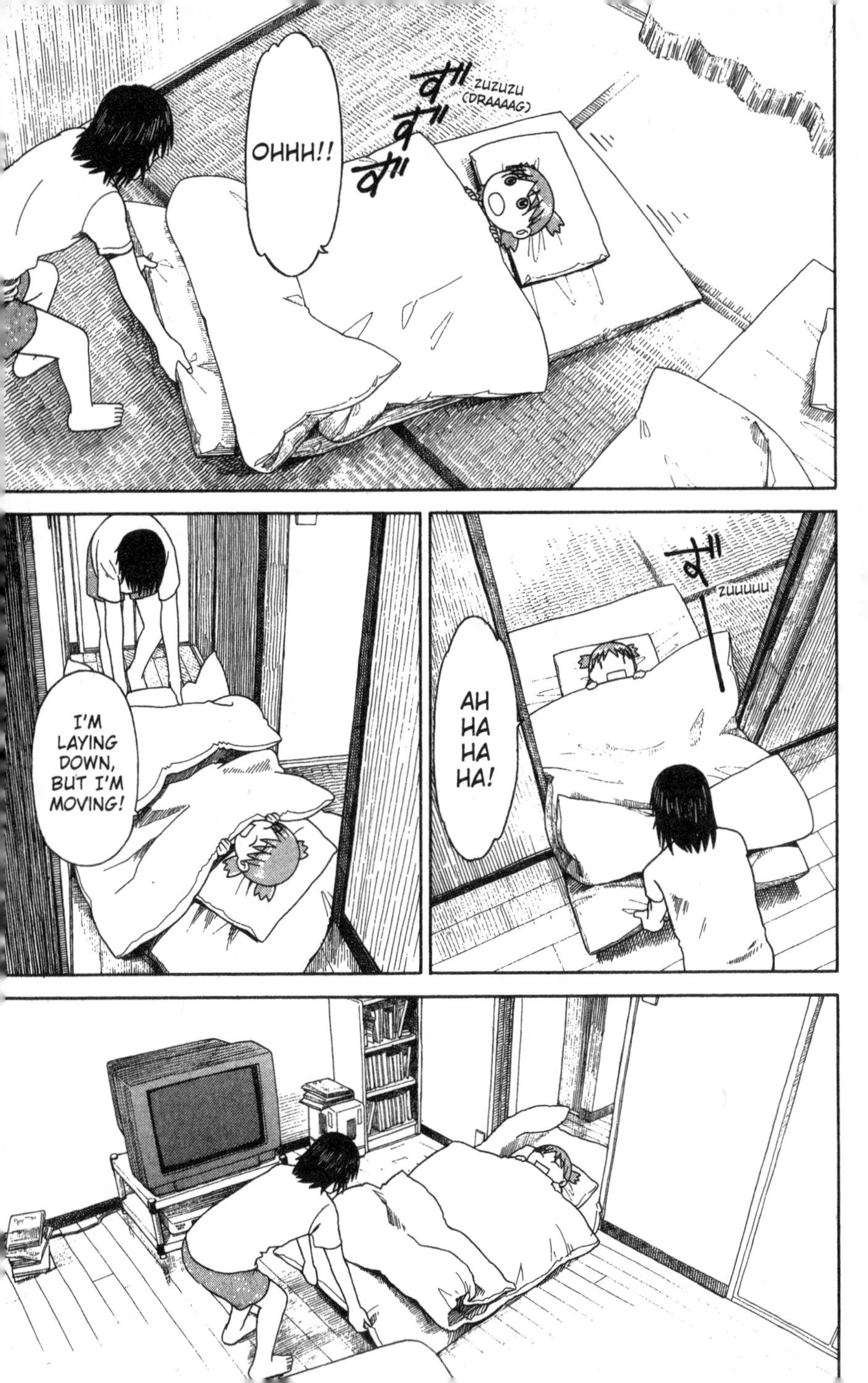
ずずず
ZUZUZU (DRAAAAG)
OHHH!!
ず
ZUUUUU
AH HA HA HA!
I'M LAYING DOWN, BUT I'M MOVING!

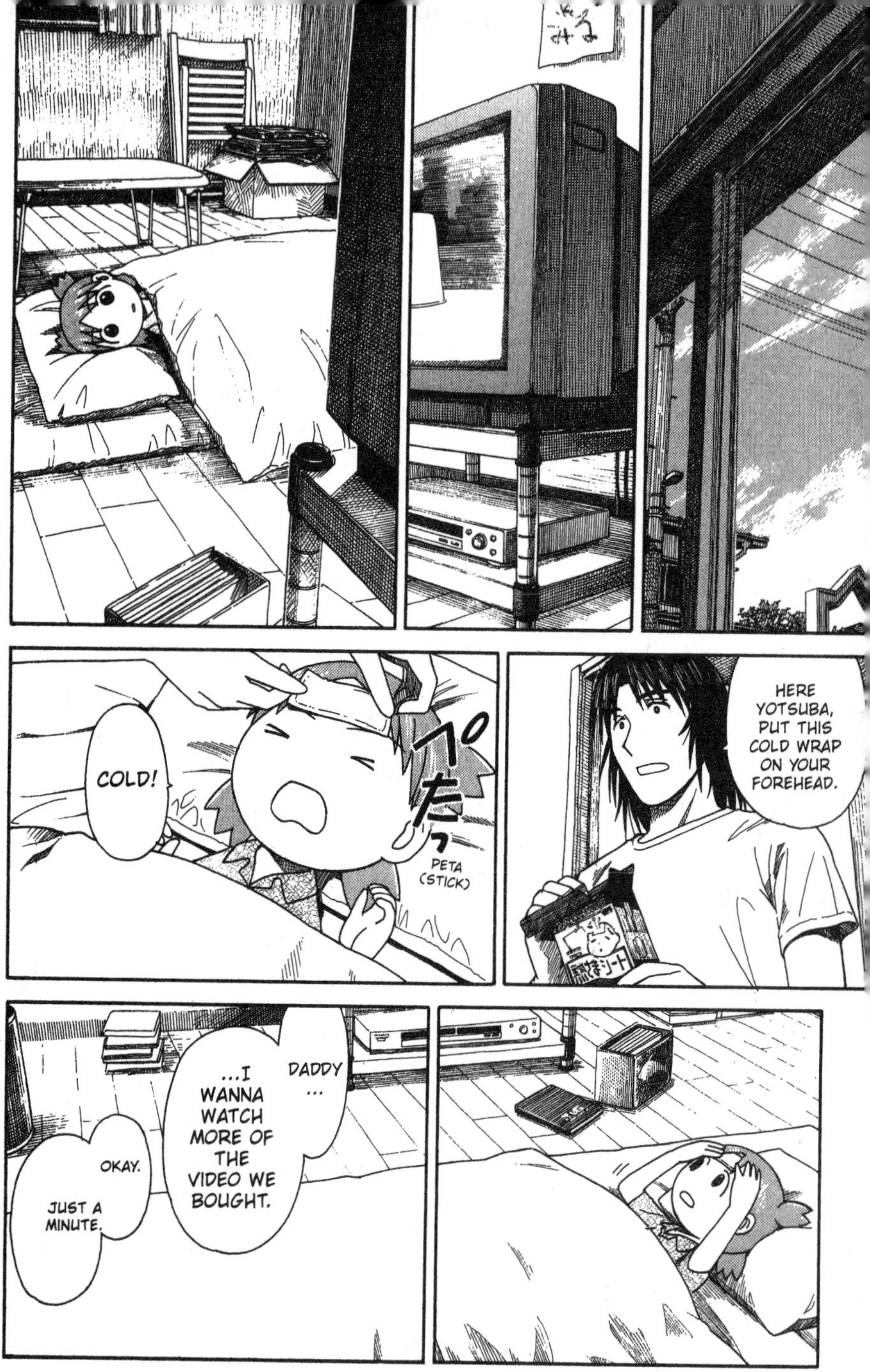
HERE YOTSUBA, PUT THIS COLD WRAP ON YOUR FOREHEAD.
COLD!
ぺたっ
PETA (STICK)
DADDY ...
...I WANNA WATCH MORE OF THE VIDEO WE BOUGHT.
OKAY. JUST A MINUTE.

HN?

YOTSUBA WANTS TO GO THERE WITH DADDY.

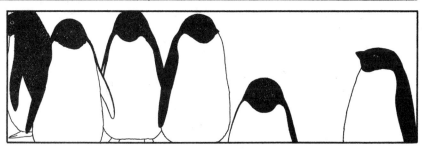

THE SOUTH POLE, HUH?

OKAY.

IT'S COLD THERE. REALLY, REALLY COLD.

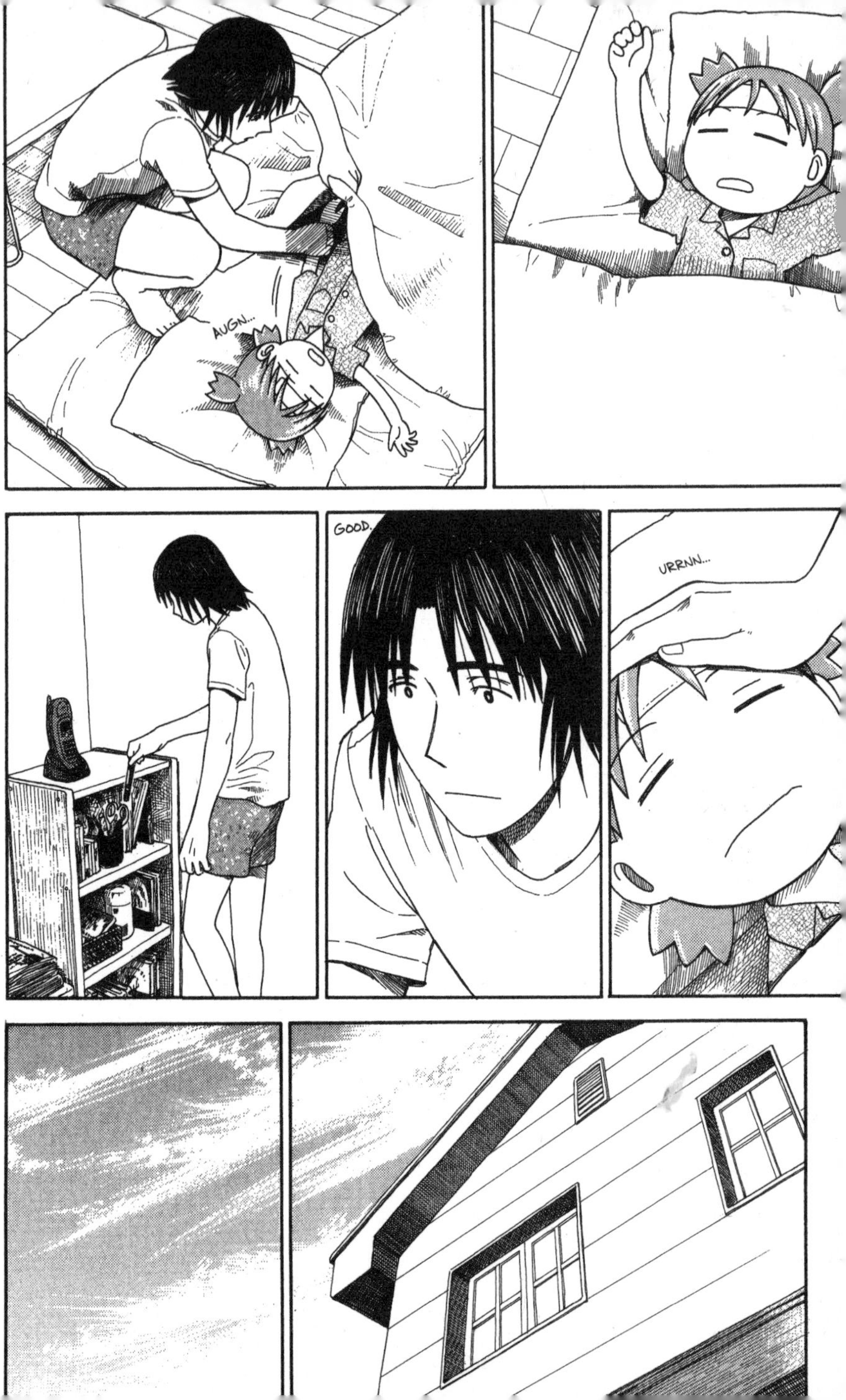
AUGN...
URRNN...
GOOD.

OH, YOU'RE UP?

IT'S OFF.

DADDY, TURN THE TV ON.

HERE, DRINK SOME WATER.

OKAY.

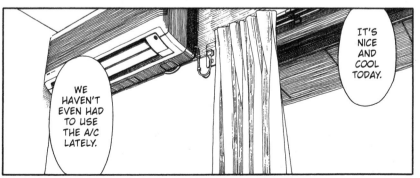

IT'S NICE AND COOL TODAY.

WE HAVEN'T EVEN HAD TO USE THE A/C LATELY.

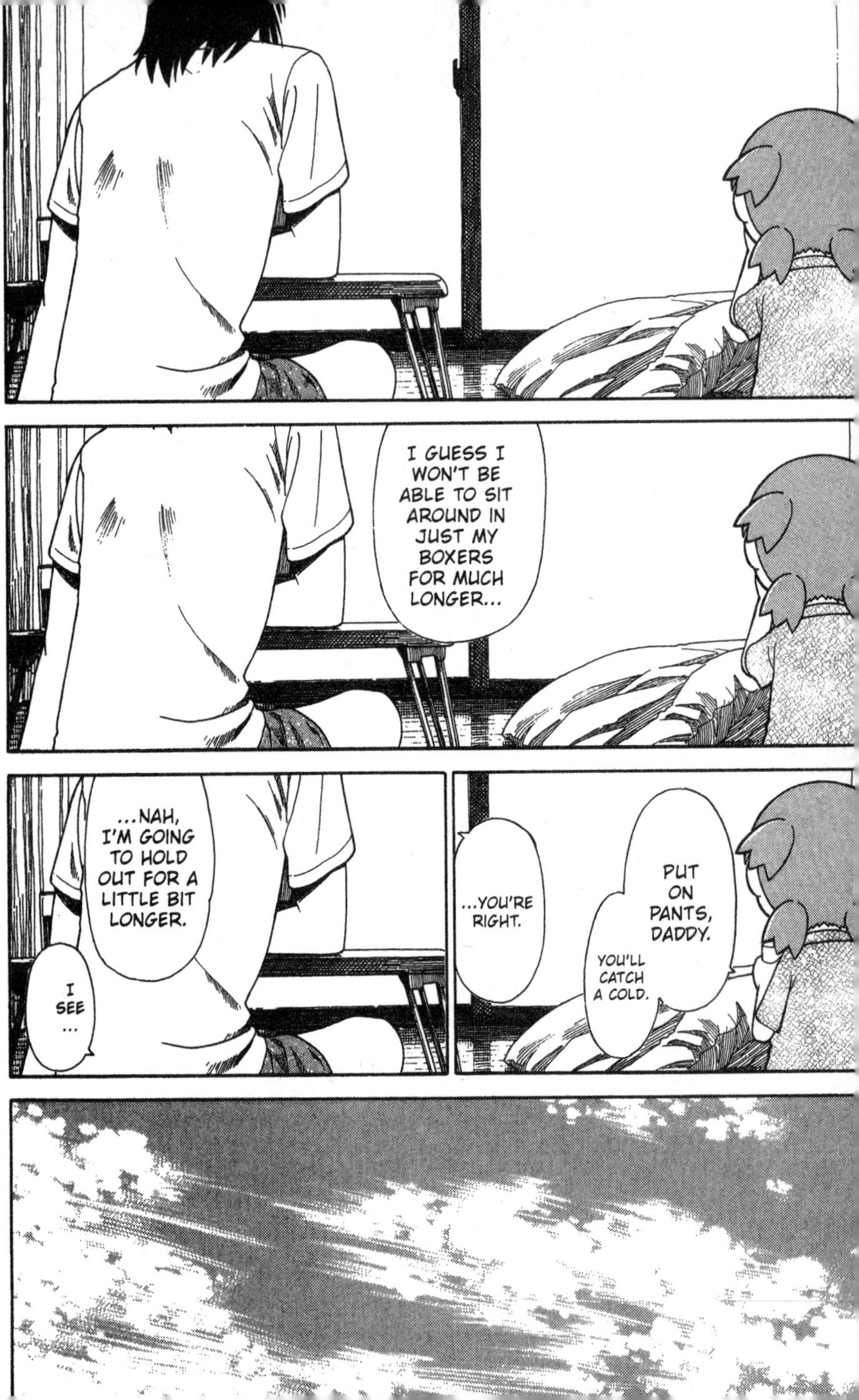
I GUESS I WON'T BE ABLE TO SIT AROUND IN JUST MY BOXERS FOR MUCH LONGER...
PUT ON PANTS, DADDY.
YOU'LL CATCH A COLD.
...YOU'RE RIGHT.
...NAH, I'M GOING TO HOLD OUT FOR A LITTLE BIT LONGER.
I SEE...

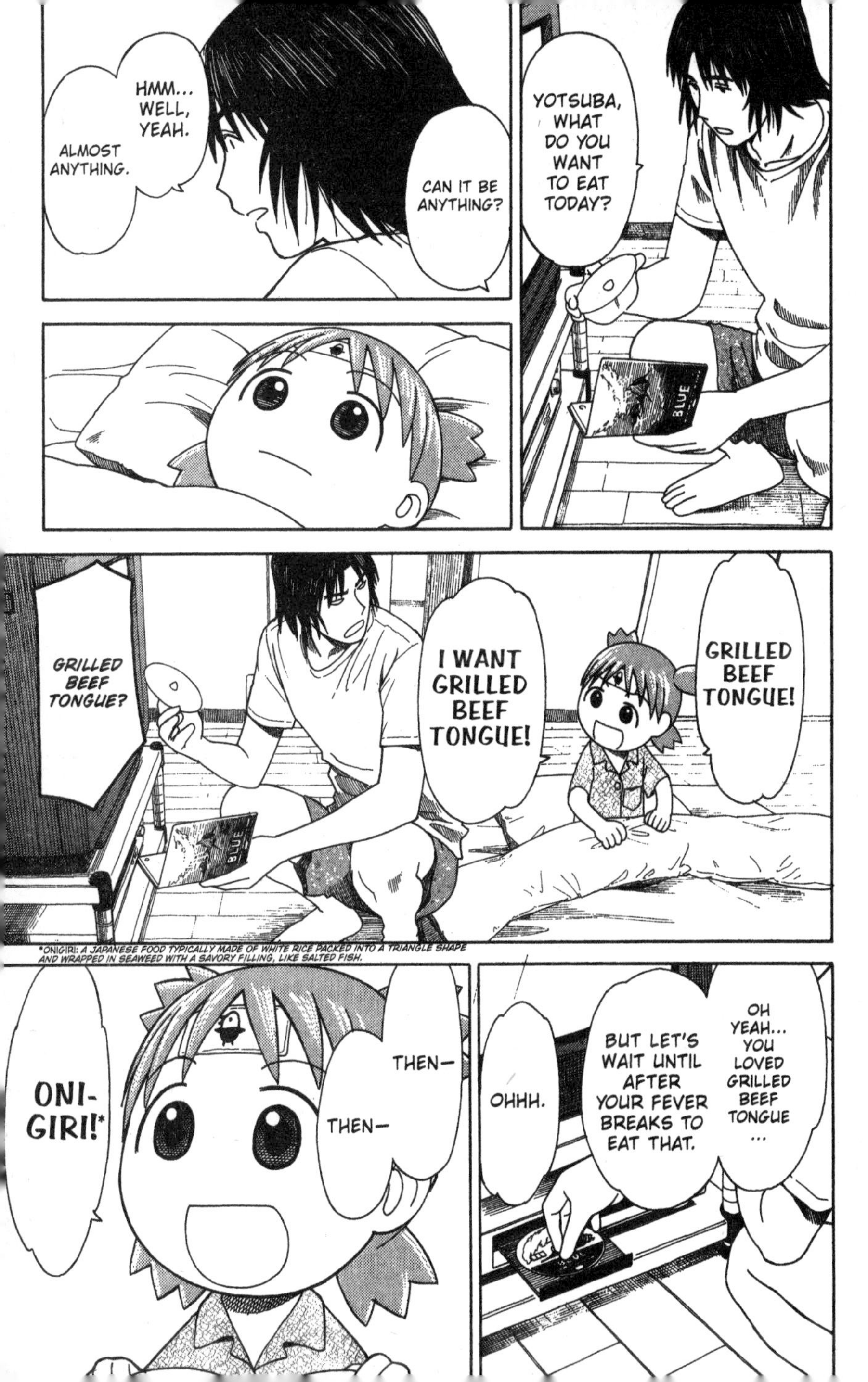
YOTSUBA, WHAT DO YOU WANT TO EAT TODAY?
CAN IT BE ANYTHING?
HMM... WELL, YEAH.
ALMOST ANYTHING.
GRILLED BEEF TONGUE!
I WANT GRILLED BEEF TONGUE!
GRILLED BEEF TONGUE?
OH YEAH... YOU LOVED GRILLED BEEF TONGUE ...
BUT LET'S WAIT UNTIL AFTER YOUR FEVER BREAKS TO EAT THAT.
OHHH.
THEN—
THEN—
ONI-GIRI!*

*ONIGIRI: A JAPANESE FOOD TYPICALLY MADE OF WHITE RICE PACKED INTO A TRIANGLE SHAPE AND WRAPPED IN SEAWEED WITH A SAVORY FILLING, LIKE SALTED FISH.

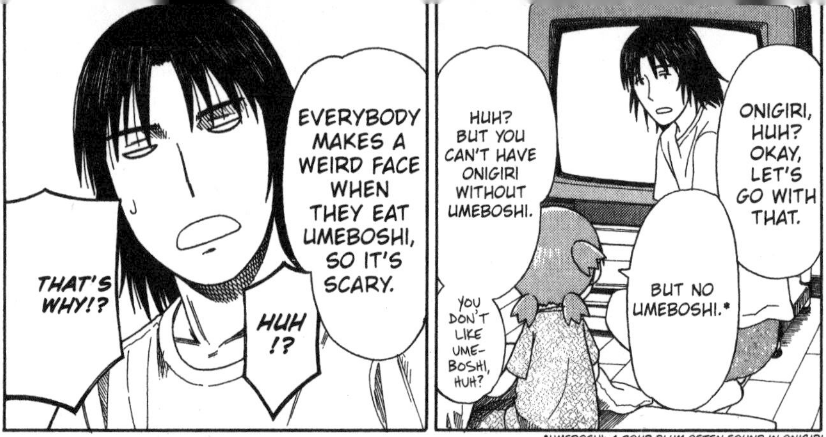
ONIGIRI, HUH? OKAY, LET'S GO WITH THAT.
BUT NO UMEBOSHI.*
HUH? BUT YOU CAN'T HAVE ONIGIRI WITHOUT UMEBOSHI.
YOU DON'T LIKE UME-BOSHI, HUH?
EVERYBODY MAKES A WEIRD FACE WHEN THEY EAT UMEBOSHI, SO IT'S SCARY.
HUH !?
THAT'S WHY!?

*UMEBOSHI: A SOUR PLUM OFTEN FOUND IN ONIGIRI

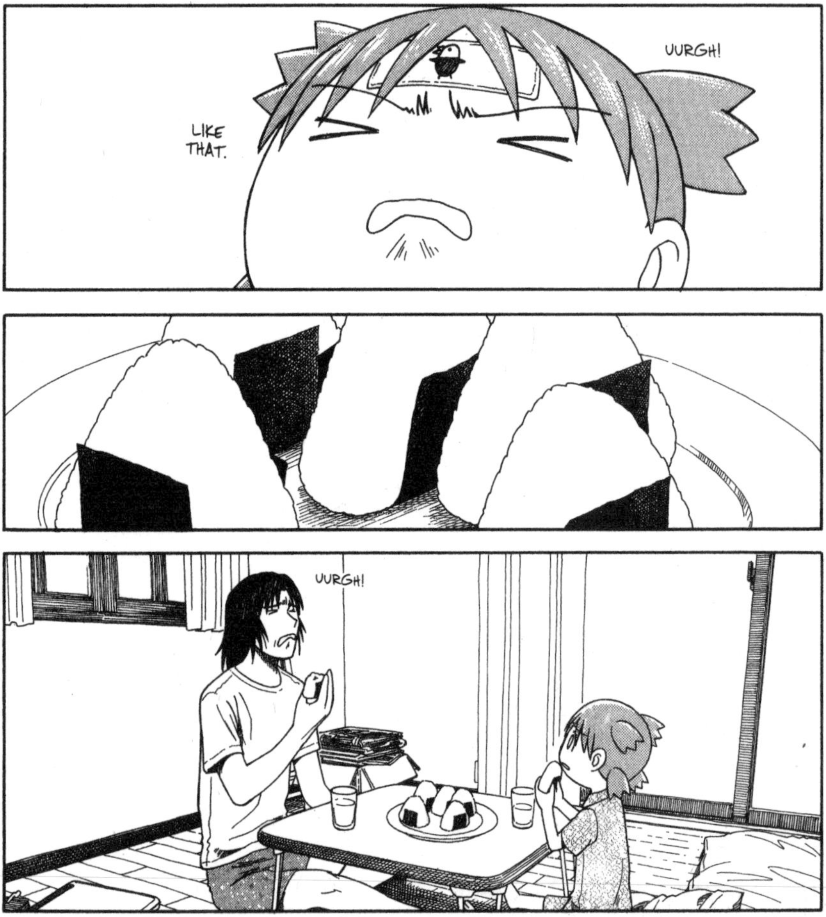
UURGH!
LIKE THAT.
UURGH!

YOTSUBA&!

YOTSUBA& THE PÂTISSIER

#45

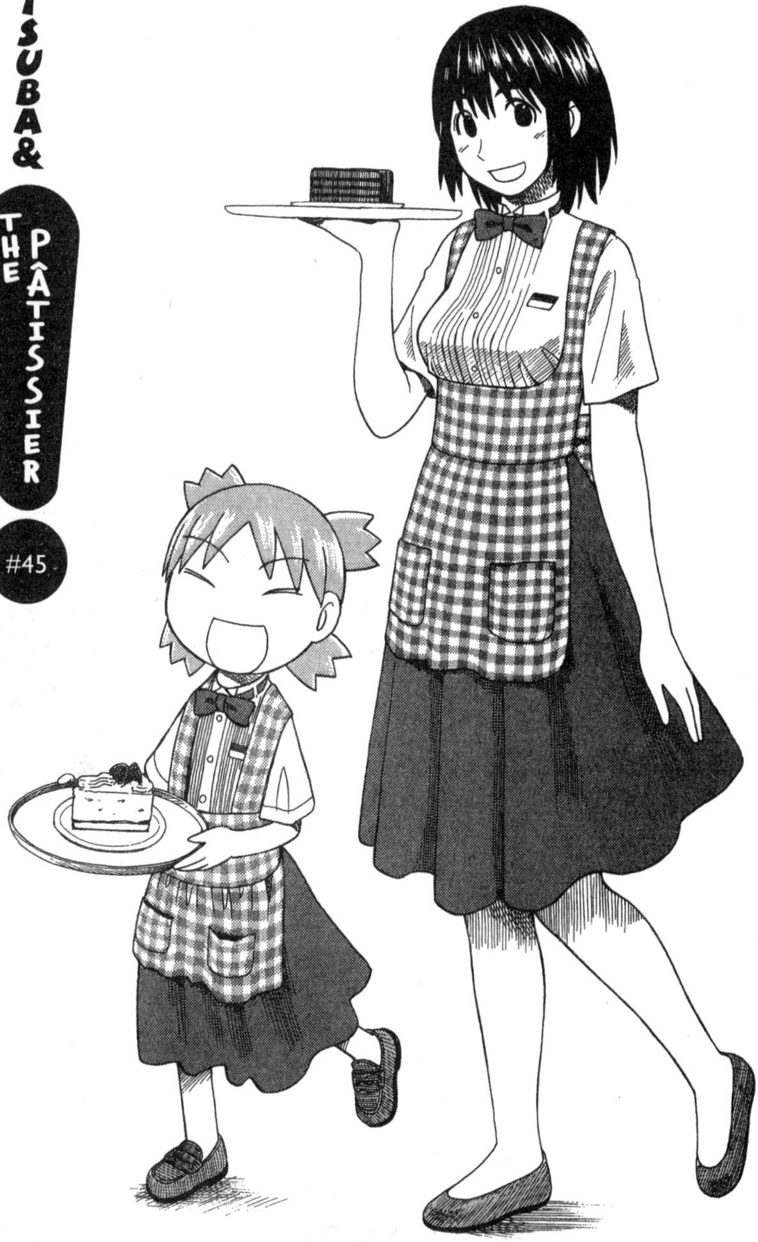

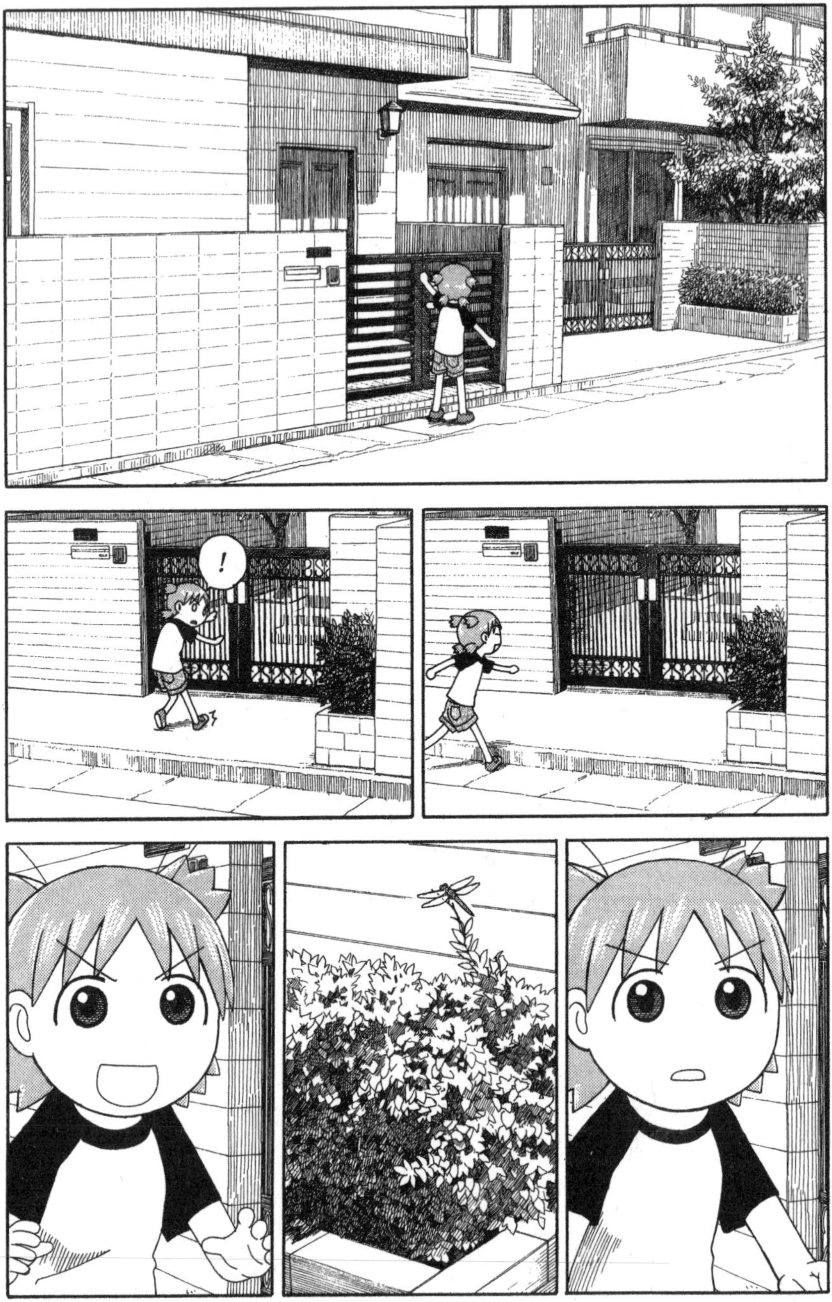
!

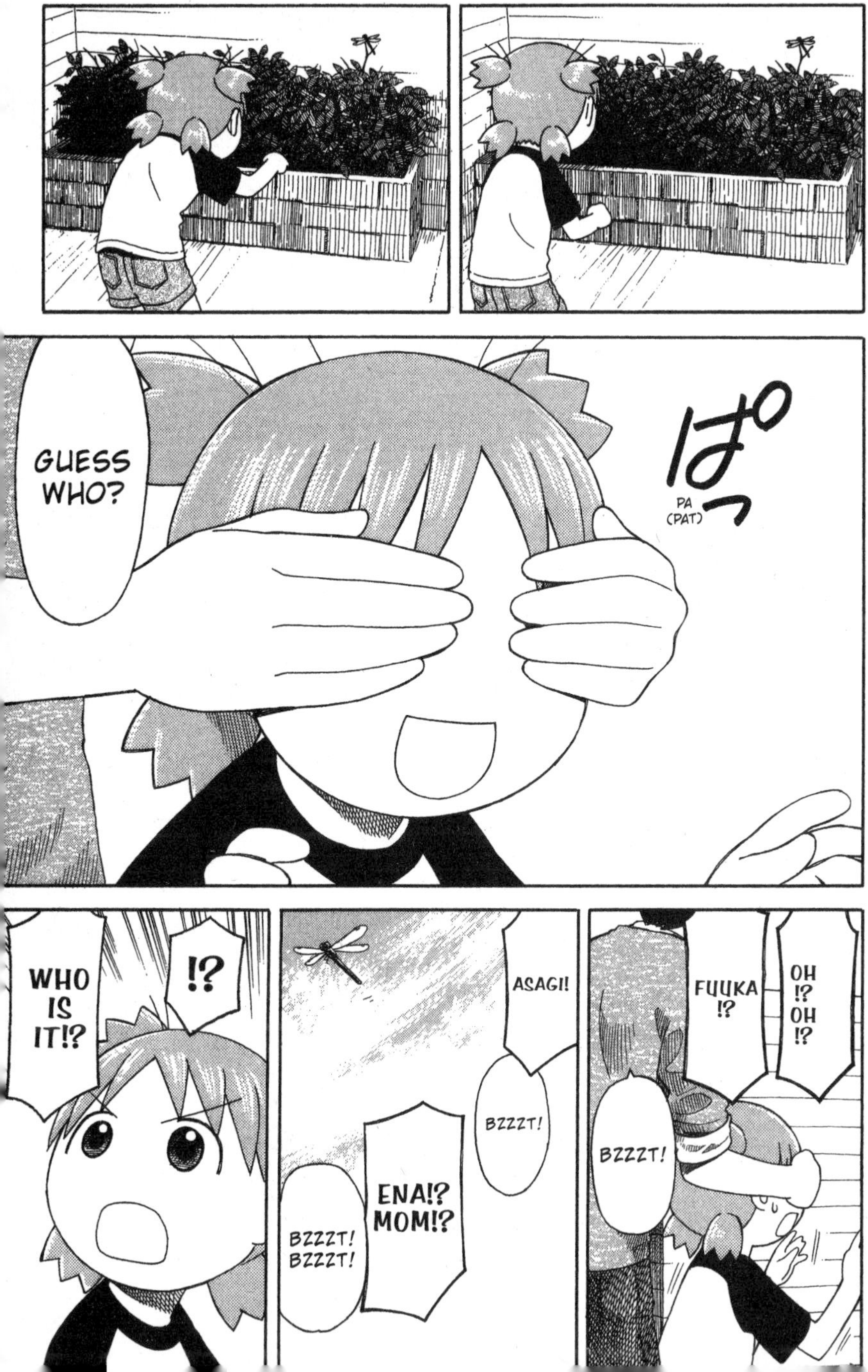

GUESS WHO?
ぱっ
PA (PAT)
OH!? OH!?
FUUKA!?
BZZZT!
ASAGI!
BZZZT!
ENA!? MOM!?
BZZZT! BZZZT!
!?
WHO IS IT!?

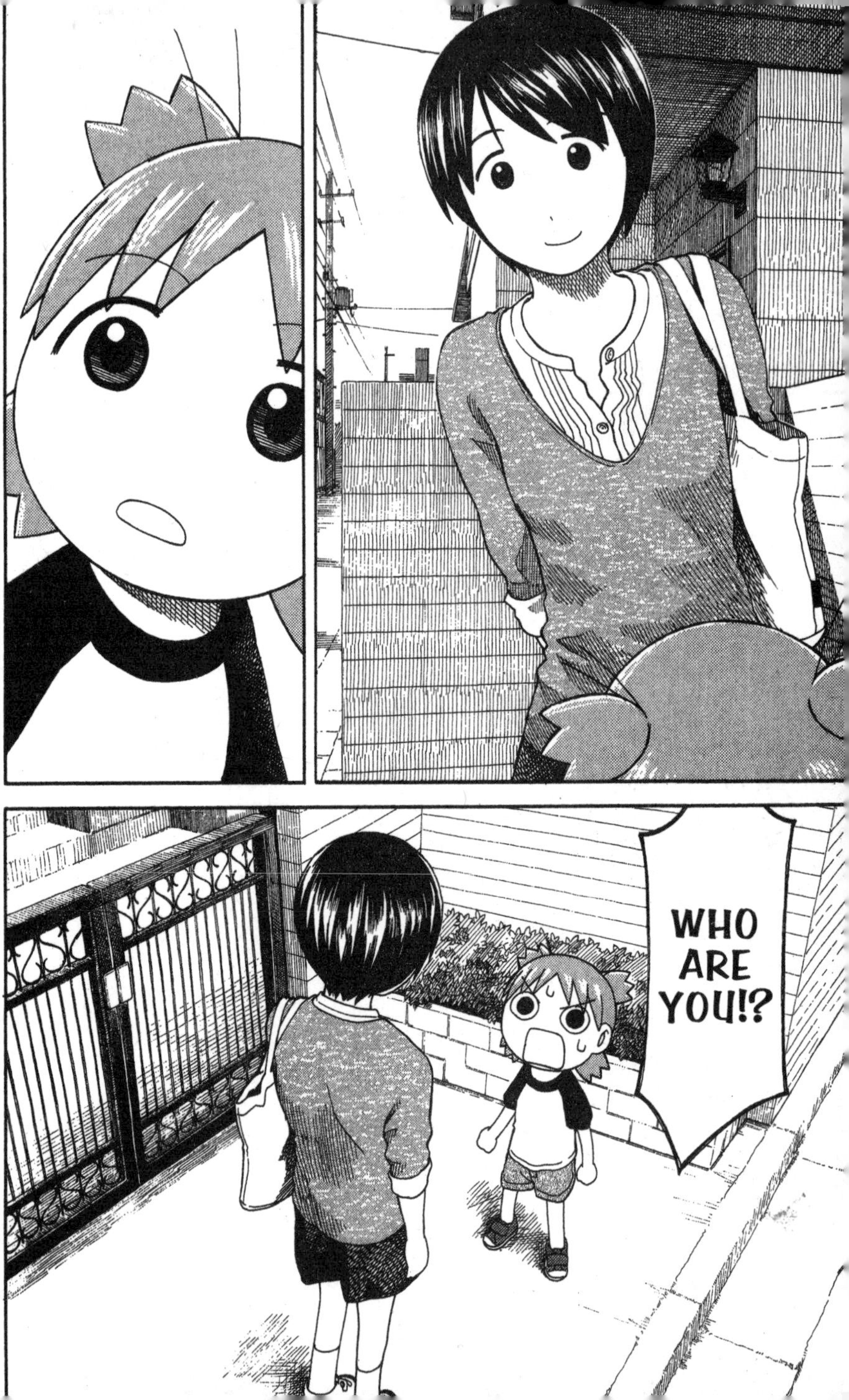
WHO ARE YOU!?

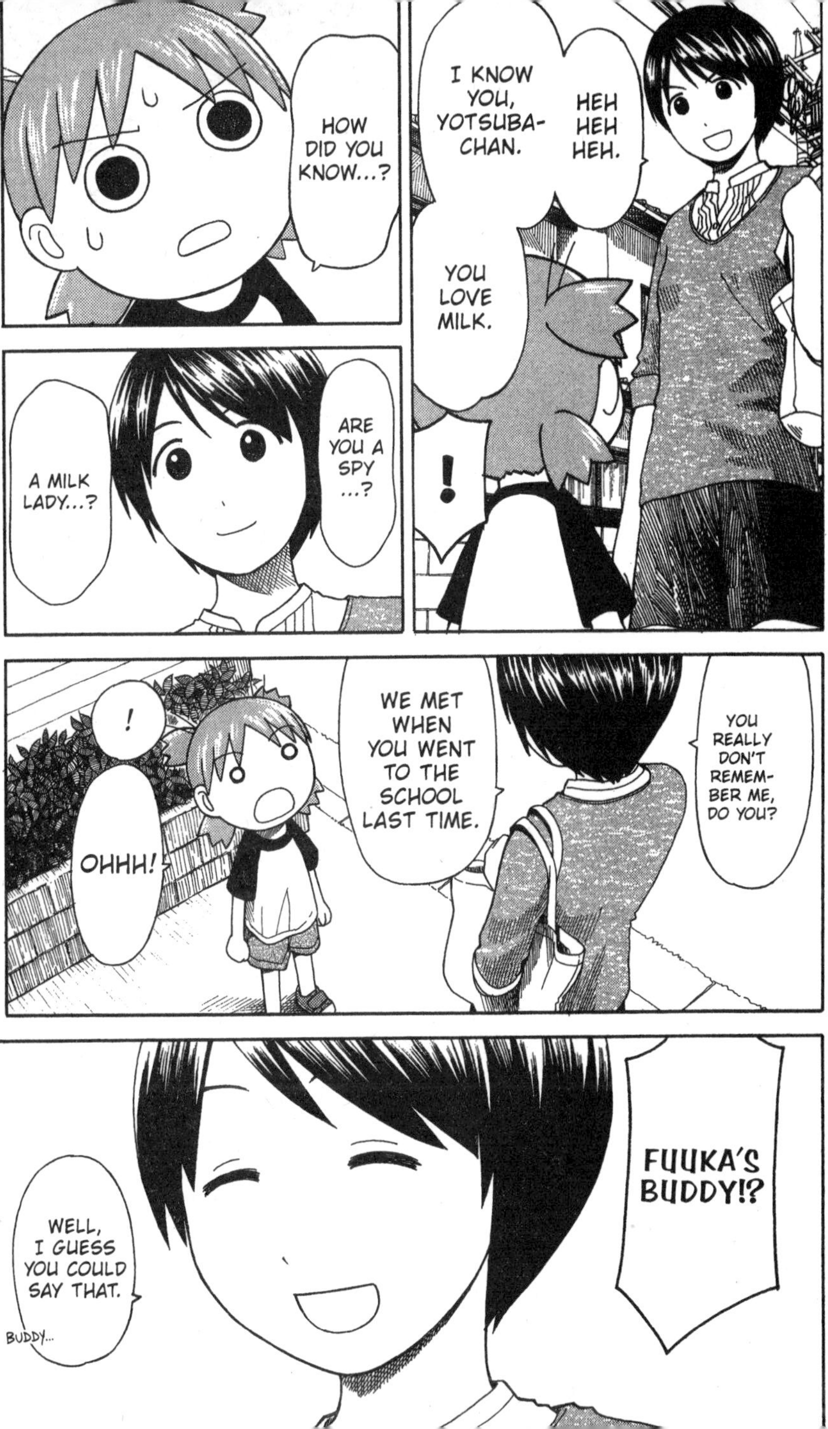

HEH HEH HEH.
I KNOW YOU, YOTSUBA-CHAN.
YOU LOVE MILK.
!
HOW DID YOU KNOW...?
ARE YOU A SPY ...?
A MILK LADY...?
YOU REALLY DON'T REMEM-BER ME, DO YOU?
WE MET WHEN YOU WENT TO THE SCHOOL LAST TIME.
!
OHHH!
FUUKA'S BUDDY!?
WELL, I GUESS YOU COULD SAY THAT.
BUDDY...

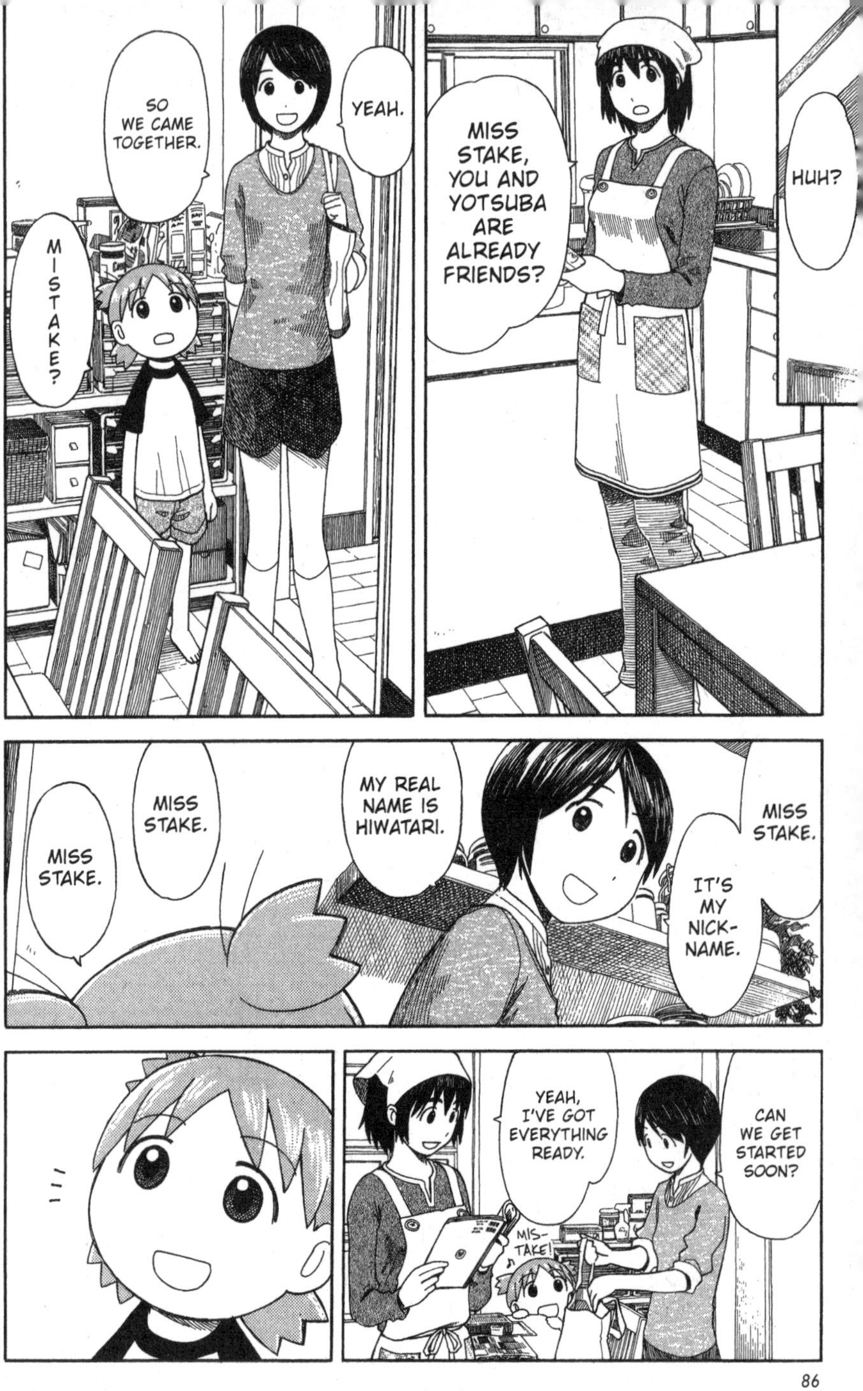
HUH?
MISS STAKE, YOU AND YOTSUBA ARE ALREADY FRIENDS?
YEAH.
SO WE CAME TOGETHER.
MISTAKE?
MISS STAKE.
IT'S MY NICK-NAME.
MY REAL NAME IS HIWATARI.
MISS STAKE.
MISS STAKE.
CAN WE GET STARTED SOON?
YEAH, I'VE GOT EVERYTHING READY.
MIS-TAKE!

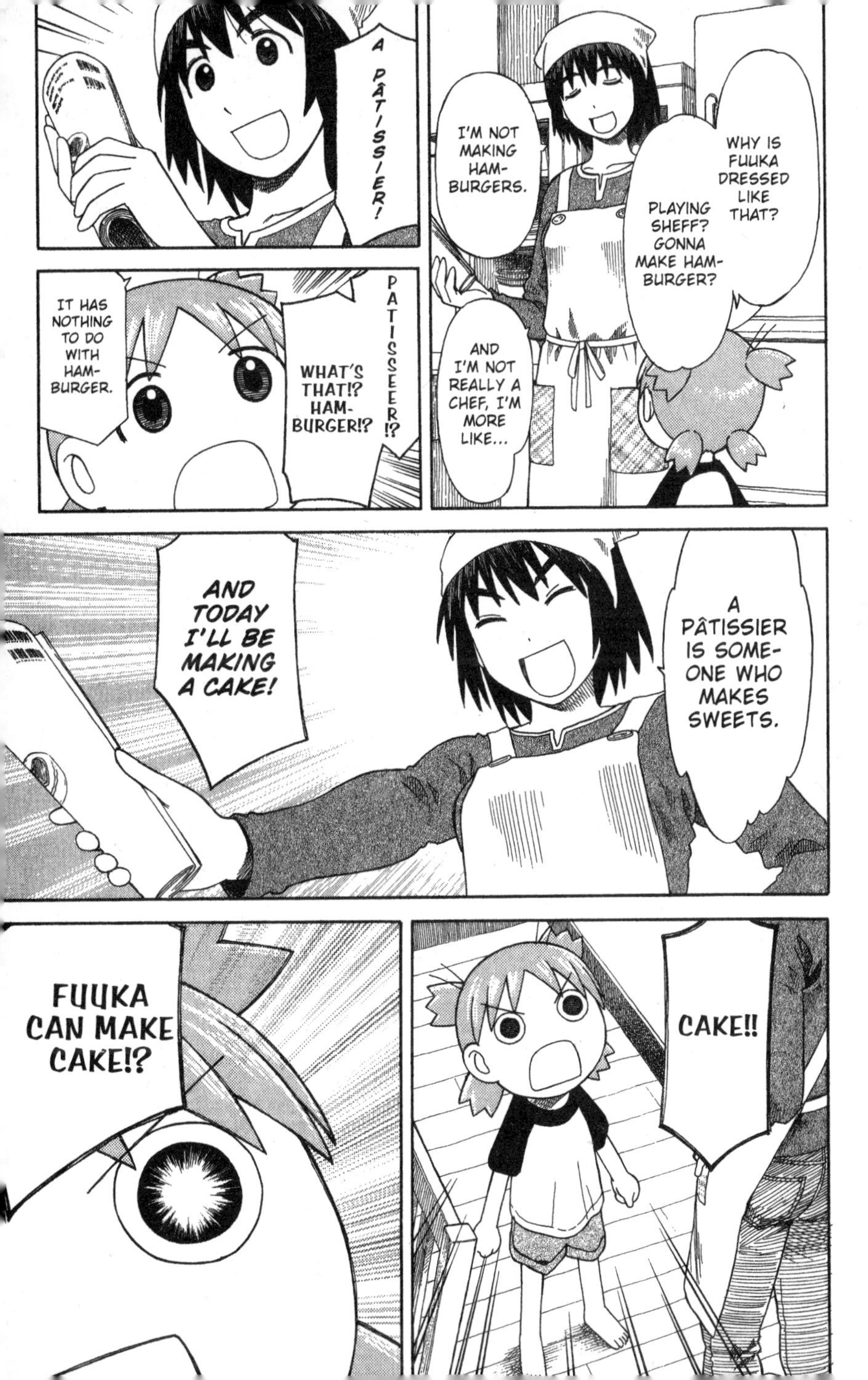
WHY IS FUUKA DRESSED LIKE THAT?
PLAYING SHEFF? GONNA MAKE HAM-BURGER?
I'M NOT MAKING HAM-BURGERS.
AND I'M NOT REALLY A CHEF, I'M MORE LIKE...
A PÂTISSIER!
PATISSEER!?
WHAT'S THAT!? HAM-BURGER!?
IT HAS NOTHING TO DO WITH HAM-BURGER.
A PÂTISSIER IS SOME-ONE WHO MAKES SWEETS.
AND TODAY I'LL BE MAKING A CAKE!
CAKE!!
FUUKA CAN MAKE CAKE!?

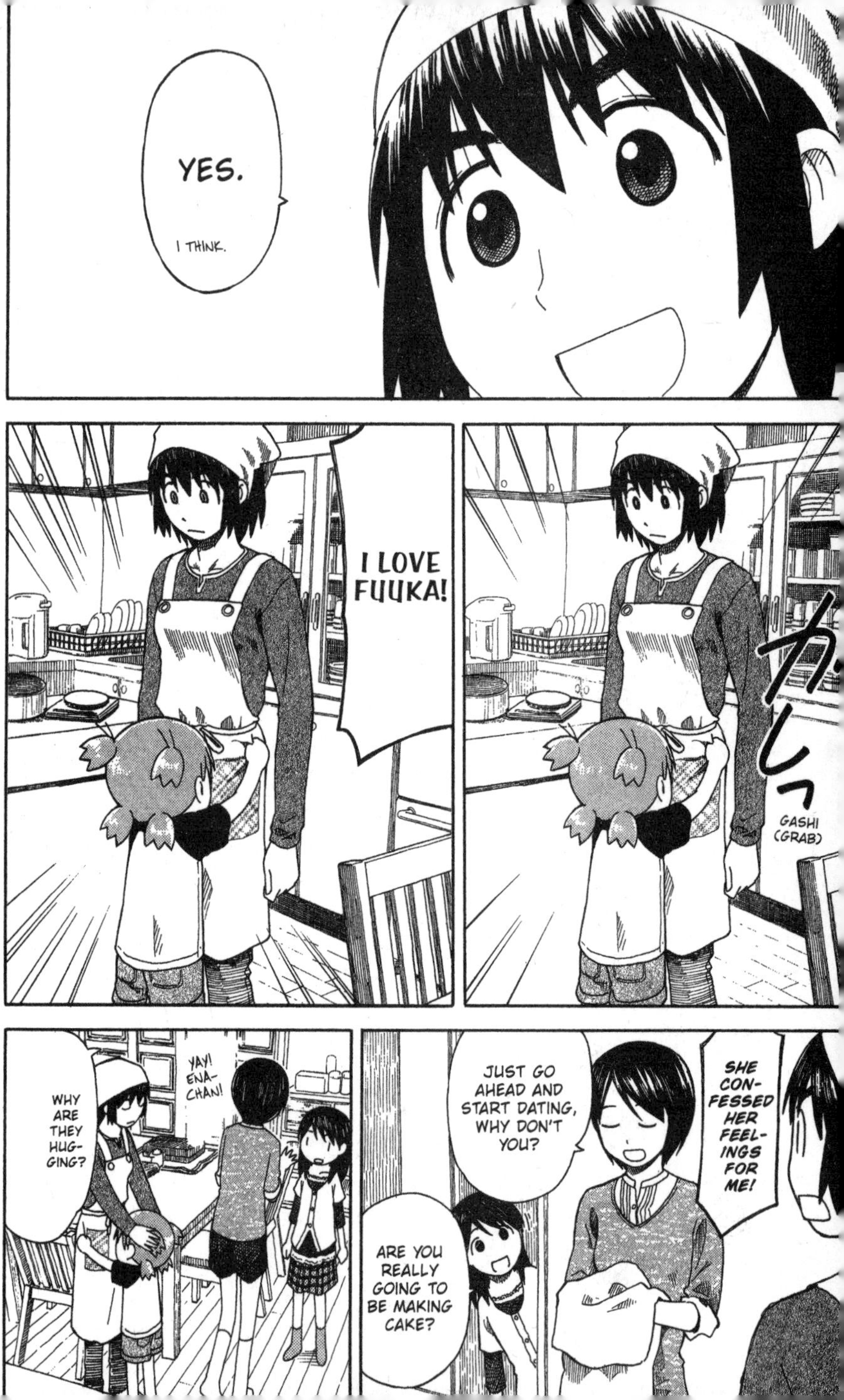

YES.
I THINK.
がしっ
GASHI (GRAB)
I LOVE FUUKA!
SHE CONFESSED HER FEELINGS FOR ME!
JUST GO AHEAD AND START DATING, WHY DON'T YOU?
ARE YOU REALLY GOING TO BE MAKING CAKE?
YAY! ENA-CHAN!
WHY ARE THEY HUGGING?

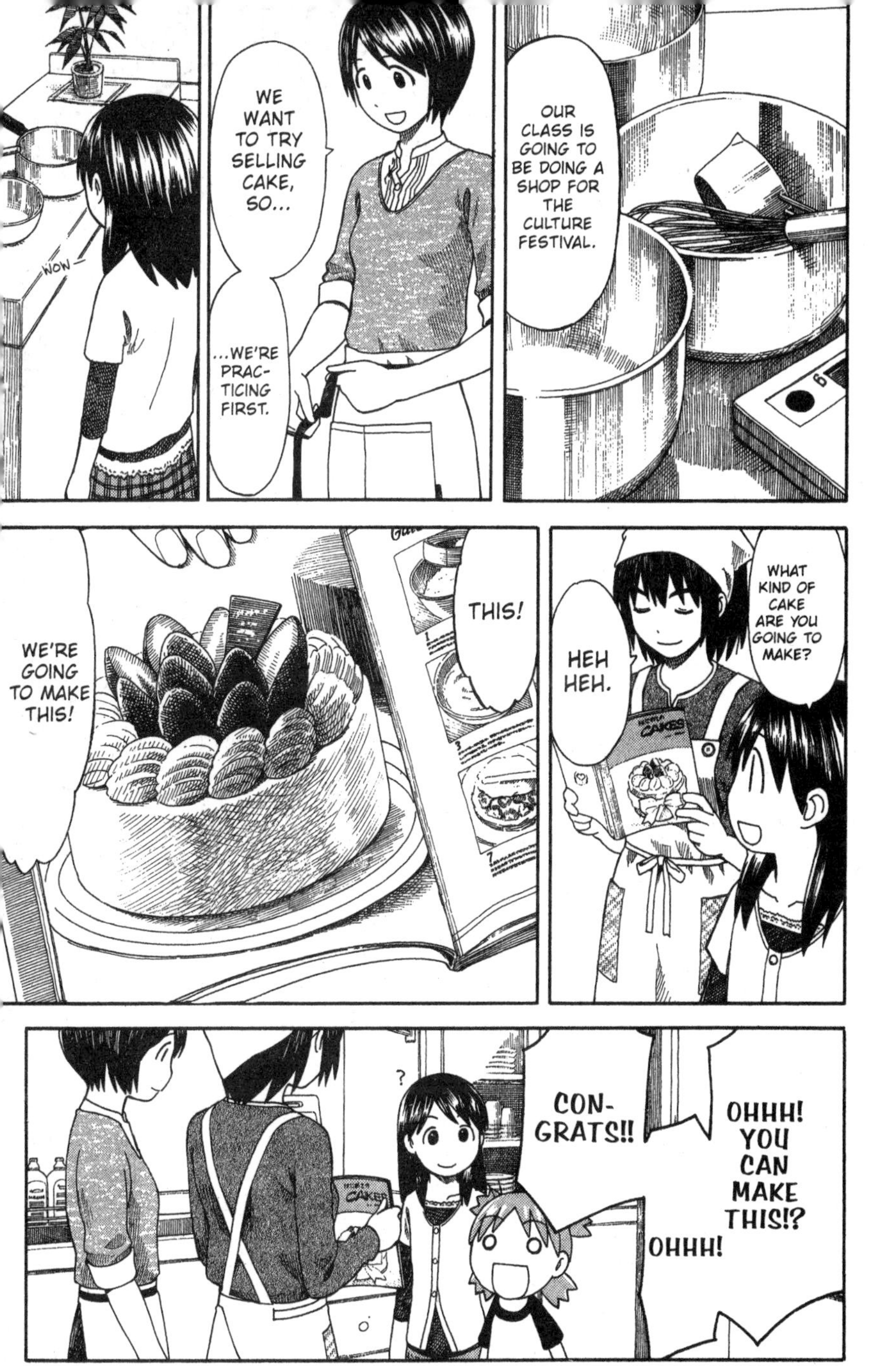
OUR CLASS IS GOING TO BE DOING A SHOP FOR THE CULTURE FESTIVAL.
WE WANT TO TRY SELLING CAKE, SO...
...WE'RE PRAC-TICING FIRST.
WOW
WHAT KIND OF CAKE ARE YOU GOING TO MAKE?
HEH HEH.
THIS!
WE'RE GOING TO MAKE THIS!
OHHH! YOU CAN MAKE THIS!?
OHHH!
CON-GRATS!!
?

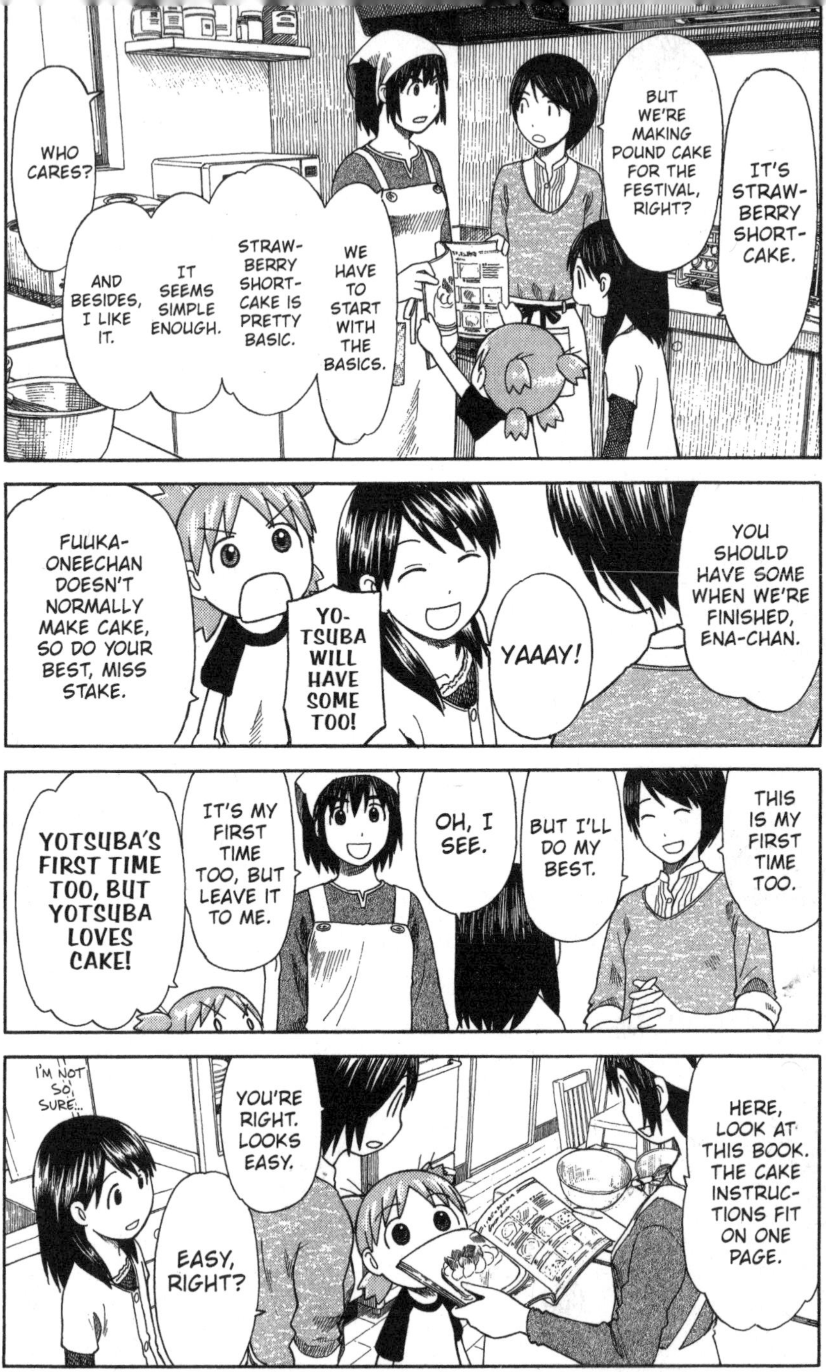
IT'S STRAWBERRY SHORTCAKE.
BUT WE'RE MAKING POUND CAKE FOR THE FESTIVAL, RIGHT?
WHO CARES?
WE HAVE TO START WITH THE BASICS.
STRAWBERRY SHORTCAKE IS PRETTY BASIC.
IT SEEMS SIMPLE ENOUGH.
AND BESIDES, I LIKE IT.
YOU SHOULD HAVE SOME WHEN WE'RE FINISHED, ENA-CHAN.
YAAAY!
YOTSUBA WILL HAVE SOME TOO!
FUUKA-ONEECHAN DOESN'T NORMALLY MAKE CAKE, SO DO YOUR BEST, MISS STAKE.
THIS IS MY FIRST TIME TOO.
BUT I'LL DO MY BEST.
OH, I SEE.
IT'S MY FIRST TIME TOO, BUT LEAVE IT TO ME.
YOTSUBA'S FIRST TIME TOO, BUT YOTSUBA LOVES CAKE!
HERE, LOOK AT THIS BOOK. THE CAKE INSTRUCTIONS FIT ON ONE PAGE.
YOU'RE RIGHT. LOOKS EASY.
EASY, RIGHT?
I'M NOT SO SURE...

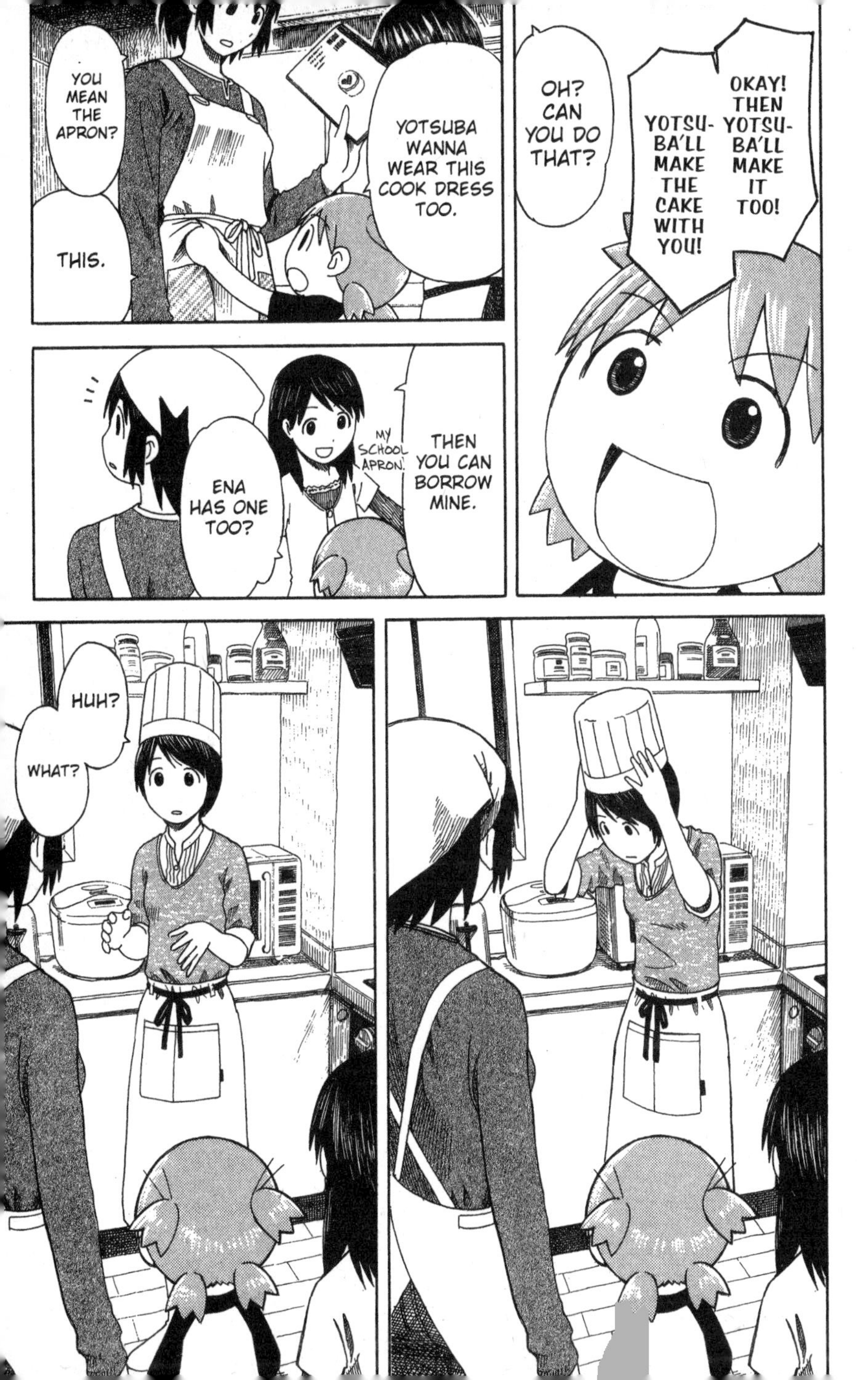
OKAY! THEN YOTSU-BA'LL MAKE IT TOO! YOTSU-BA'LL MAKE THE CAKE WITH YOU!
OH? CAN YOU DO THAT?
YOTSUBA WANNA WEAR THIS COOK DRESS TOO.
YOU MEAN THE APRON?
THIS.
THEN YOU CAN BORROW MINE.
MY SCHOOL APRON!
ENA HAS ONE TOO?
HUH?
WHAT?

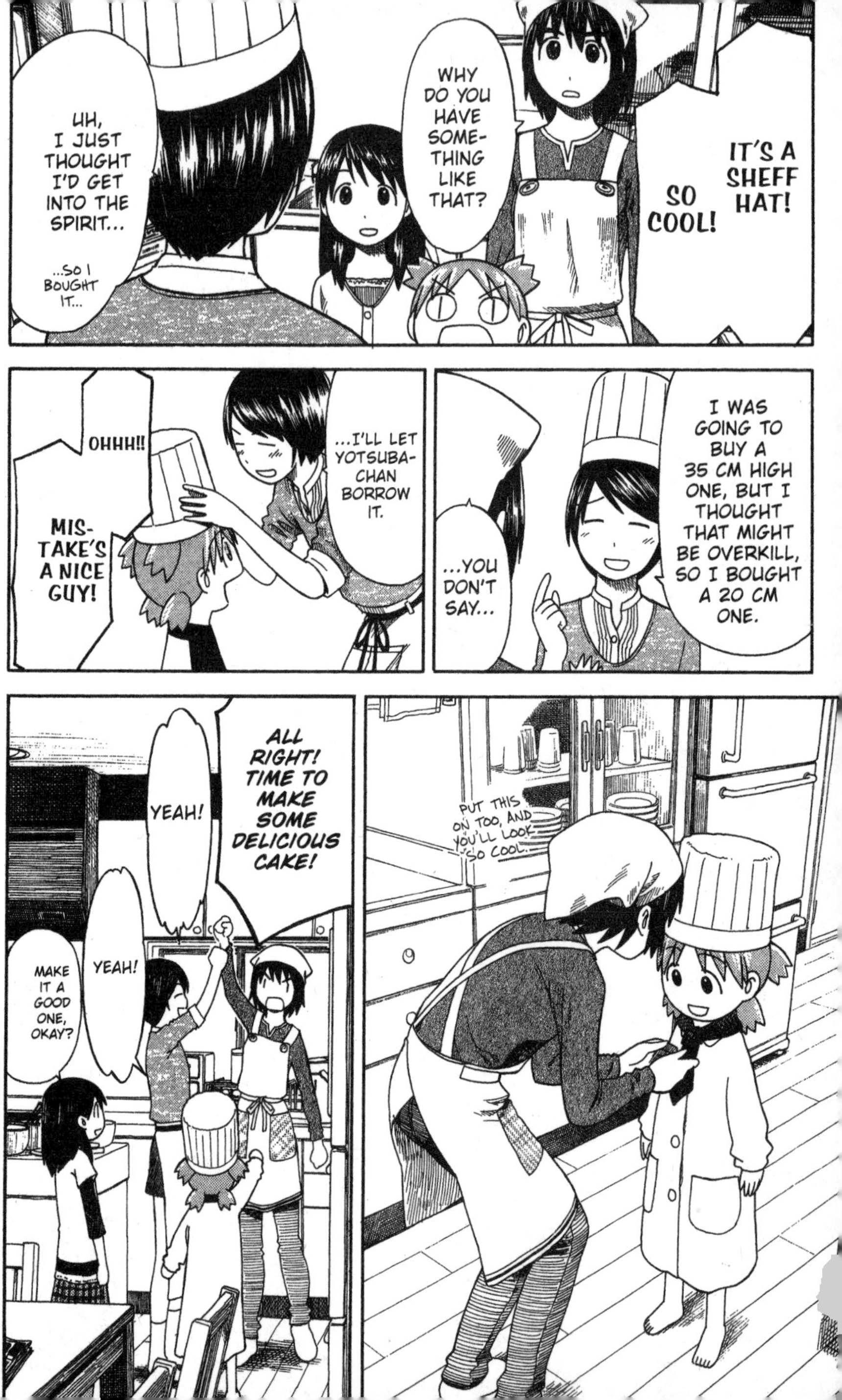
IT'S A SHEFF HAT!
SO COOL!
WHY DO YOU HAVE SOME-THING LIKE THAT?
UH, I JUST THOUGHT I'D GET INTO THE SPIRIT...
...SO I BOUGHT IT...
I WAS GOING TO BUY A 35 CM HIGH ONE, BUT I THOUGHT THAT MIGHT BE OVERKILL, SO I BOUGHT A 20 CM ONE.
...YOU DON'T SAY...
...I'LL LET YOTSUBA-CHAN BORROW IT.
OHHH!!
MIS-TAKE'S A NICE GUY!
PUT THIS ON TOO, AND YOU'LL LOOK SO COOL.
ALL RIGHT! TIME TO MAKE SOME DELICIOUS CAKE!
YEAH!
YEAH!
MAKE IT A GOOD ONE, OKAY?

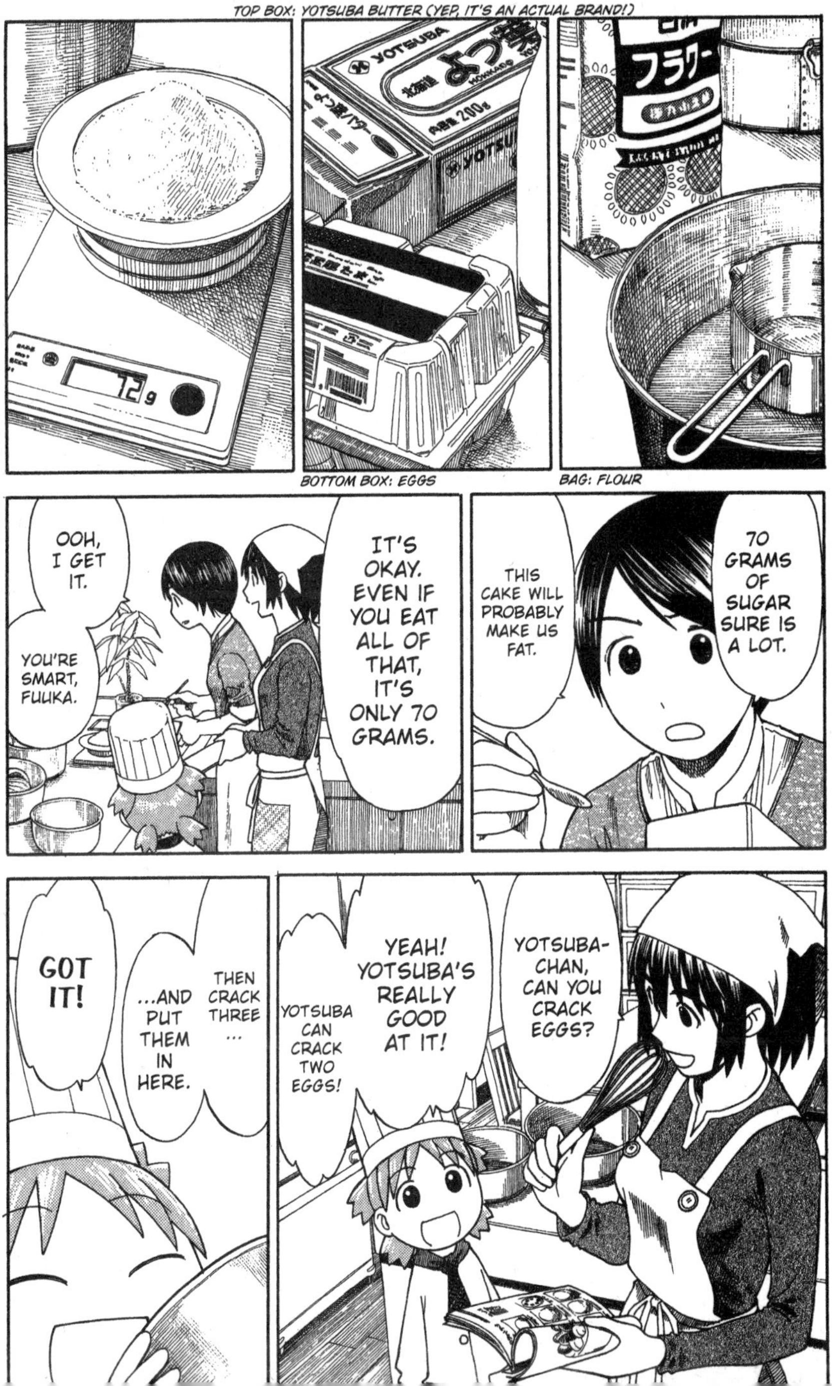
BAG: FLOUR
TOP BOX: YOTSUBA BUTTER (YEP, IT'S AN ACTUAL BRAND!)
BOTTOM BOX: EGGS
72g
70 GRAMS OF SUGAR SURE IS A LOT.
THIS CAKE WILL PROBABLY MAKE US FAT.
IT'S OKAY. EVEN IF YOU EAT ALL OF THAT, IT'S ONLY 70 GRAMS.
OOH, I GET IT.
YOU'RE SMART, FUUKA.
YOTSUBA-CHAN, CAN YOU CRACK EGGS?
YEAH! YOTSUBA'S REALLY GOOD AT IT!
YOTSUBA CAN CRACK TWO EGGS!
THEN CRACK THREE ...
...AND PUT THEM IN HERE.
GOT IT!

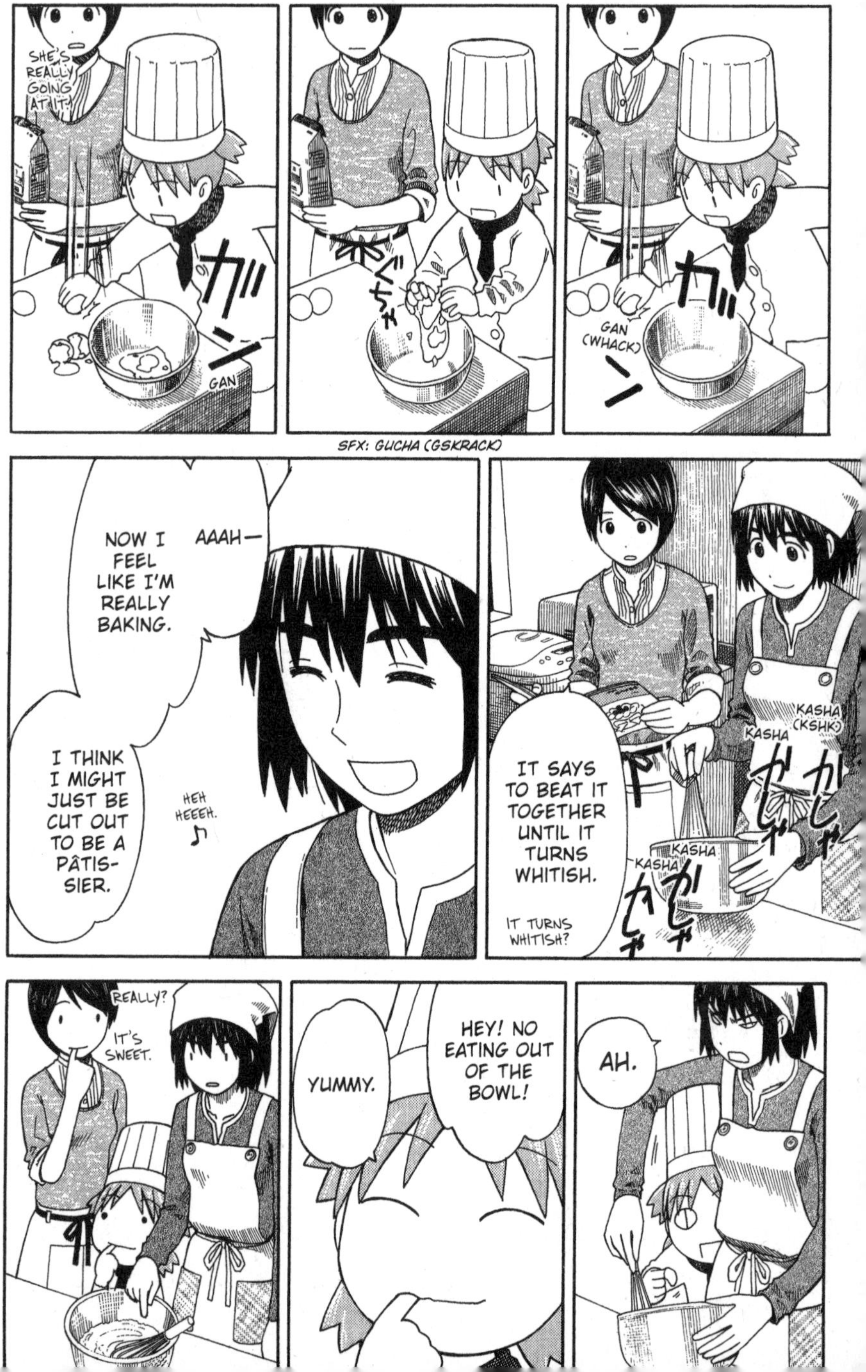
ガン
GAN (WHACK)
ぐちゃ
SHE'S REALLY GOING AT IT!
ガン
GAN
SFX: GUCHA (GSKRACK)
IT SAYS TO BEAT IT TOGETHER UNTIL IT TURNS WHITISH.
かしゃ
KASHA (KSHK)
KASHA
かしゃ
KASHA
KASHA
IT TURNS WHITISH?
AAAH—
NOW I FEEL LIKE I'M REALLY BAKING.
I THINK I MIGHT JUST BE CUT OUT TO BE A PÂTISSIER.
HEH HEEEH. ♪
AH.
HEY! NO EATING OUT OF THE BOWL!
YUMMY.
REALLY?
IT'S SWEET.

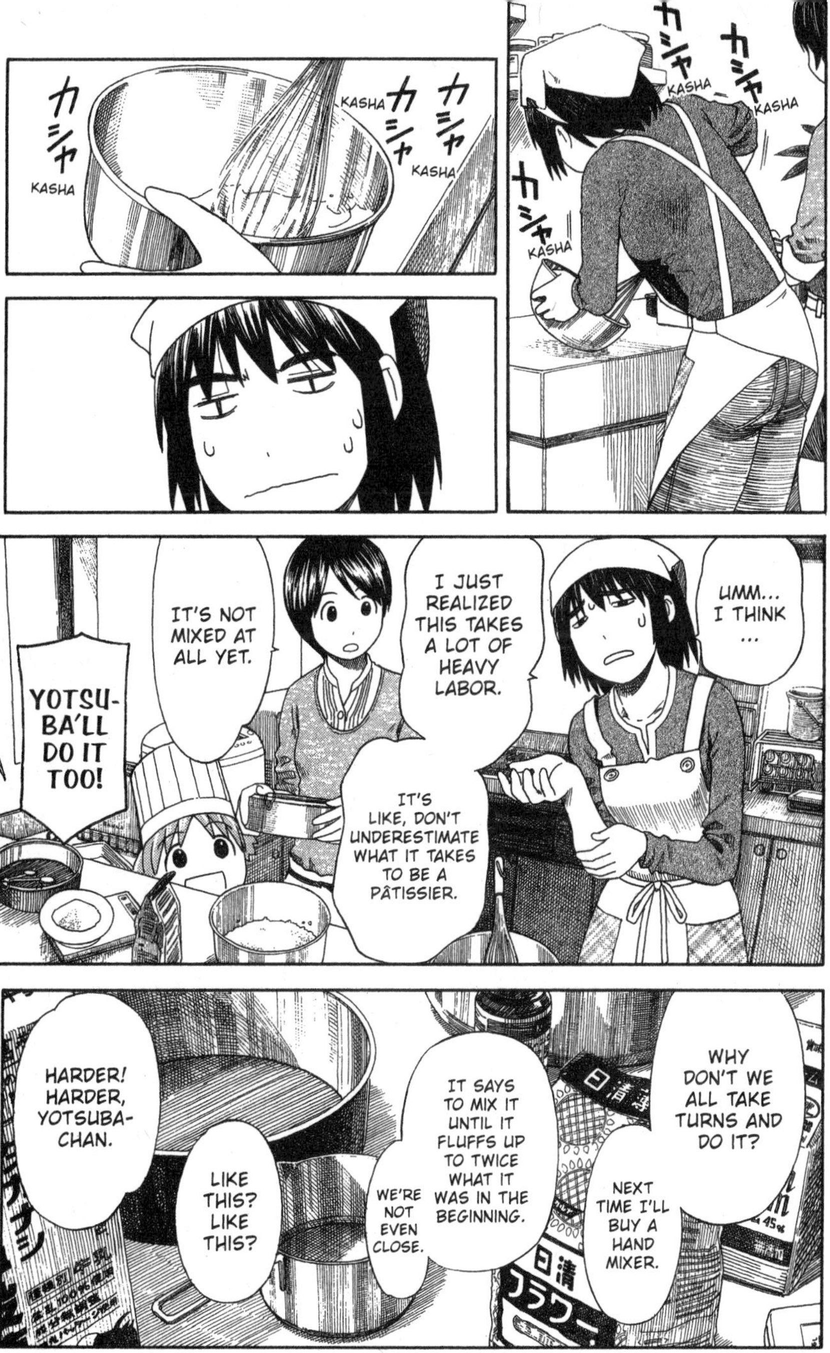
カシャ KASHA
カシャ KASHA
カシャ KASHA
カシャ KASHA
カシャ KASHA
カシャ KASHA
UMM... I THINK ...
I JUST REALIZED THIS TAKES A LOT OF HEAVY LABOR.
IT'S LIKE, DON'T UNDERESTIMATE WHAT IT TAKES TO BE A PÂTISSIER.
IT'S NOT MIXED AT ALL YET.
YOTSUBA'LL DO IT TOO!
WHY DON'T WE ALL TAKE TURNS AND DO IT?
NEXT TIME I'LL BUY A HAND MIXER.
IT SAYS TO MIX IT UNTIL IT FLUFFS UP TO TWICE WHAT IT WAS IN THE BEGINNING.
WE'RE NOT EVEN CLOSE.
HARDER! HARDER, YOTSUBA-CHAN.
LIKE THIS? LIKE THIS?

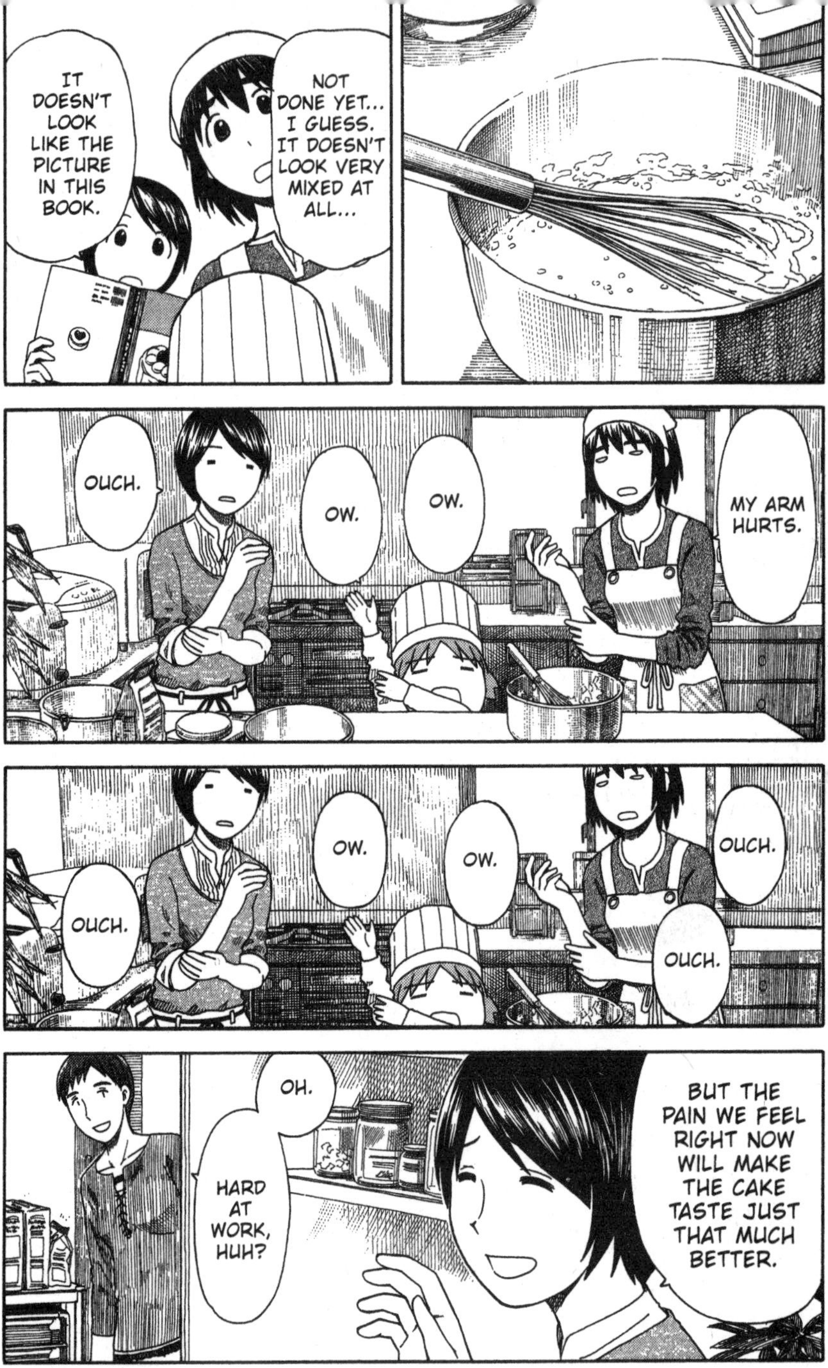
NOT DONE YET... I GUESS. IT DOESN'T LOOK VERY MIXED AT ALL...
IT DOESN'T LOOK LIKE THE PICTURE IN THIS BOOK.
MY ARM HURTS.
OW.
OW.
OUCH.
OUCH.
OUCH.
OW.
OW.
OUCH.
BUT THE PAIN WE FEEL RIGHT NOW WILL MAKE THE CAKE TASTE JUST THAT MUCH BETTER.
OH.
HARD AT WORK, HUH?

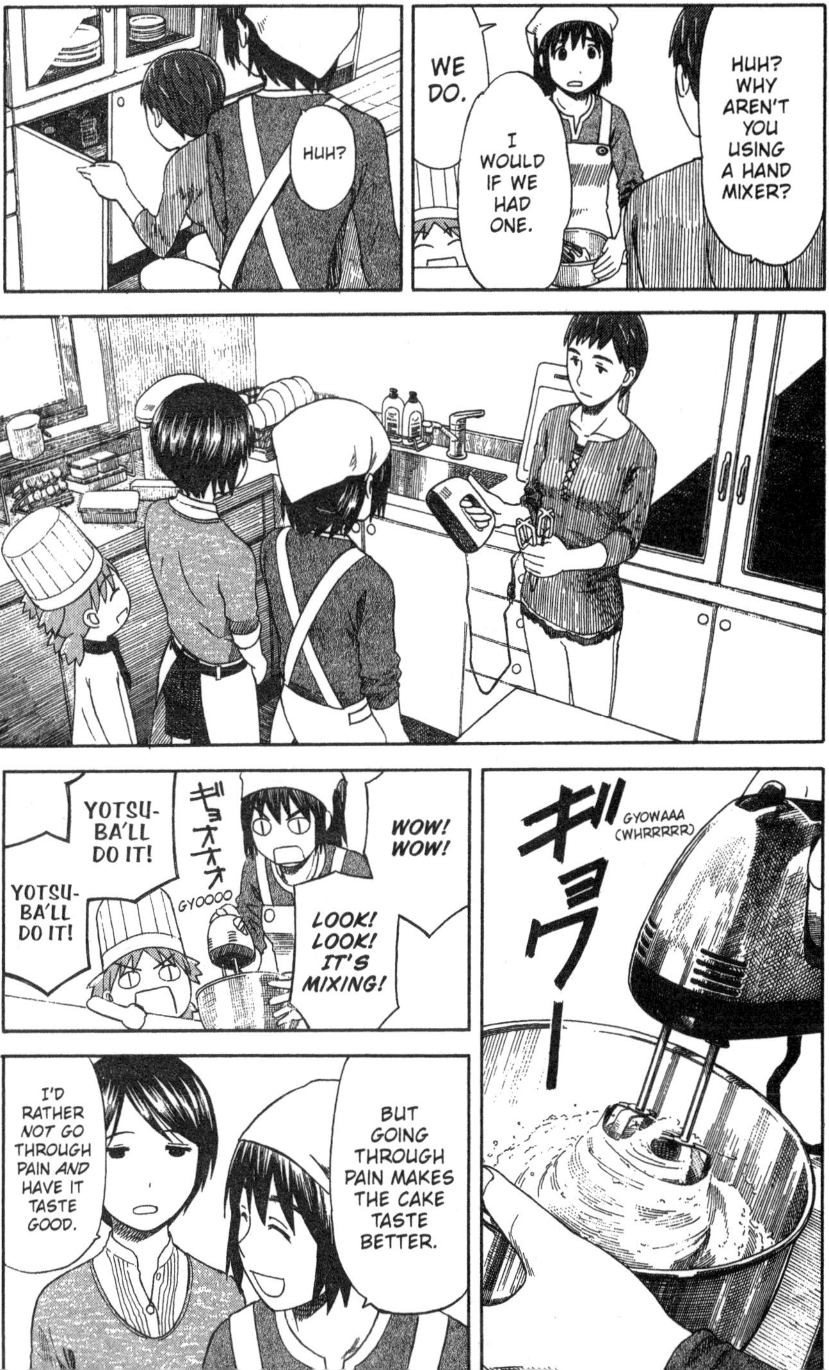
HUH? WHY AREN'T YOU USING A HAND MIXER?
I WOULD IF WE HAD ONE.
WE DO.
HUH?
ギョワー
GYOWAAA (WHRRRRR)
WOW! WOW!
LOOK! LOOK! IT'S MIXING!
ギョオオオ
GYOOOO
YOTSU-BA'LL DO IT!
YOTSU-BA'LL DO IT!
BUT GOING THROUGH PAIN MAKES THE CAKE TASTE BETTER.
I'D RATHER NOT GO THROUGH PAIN AND HAVE IT TASTE GOOD.

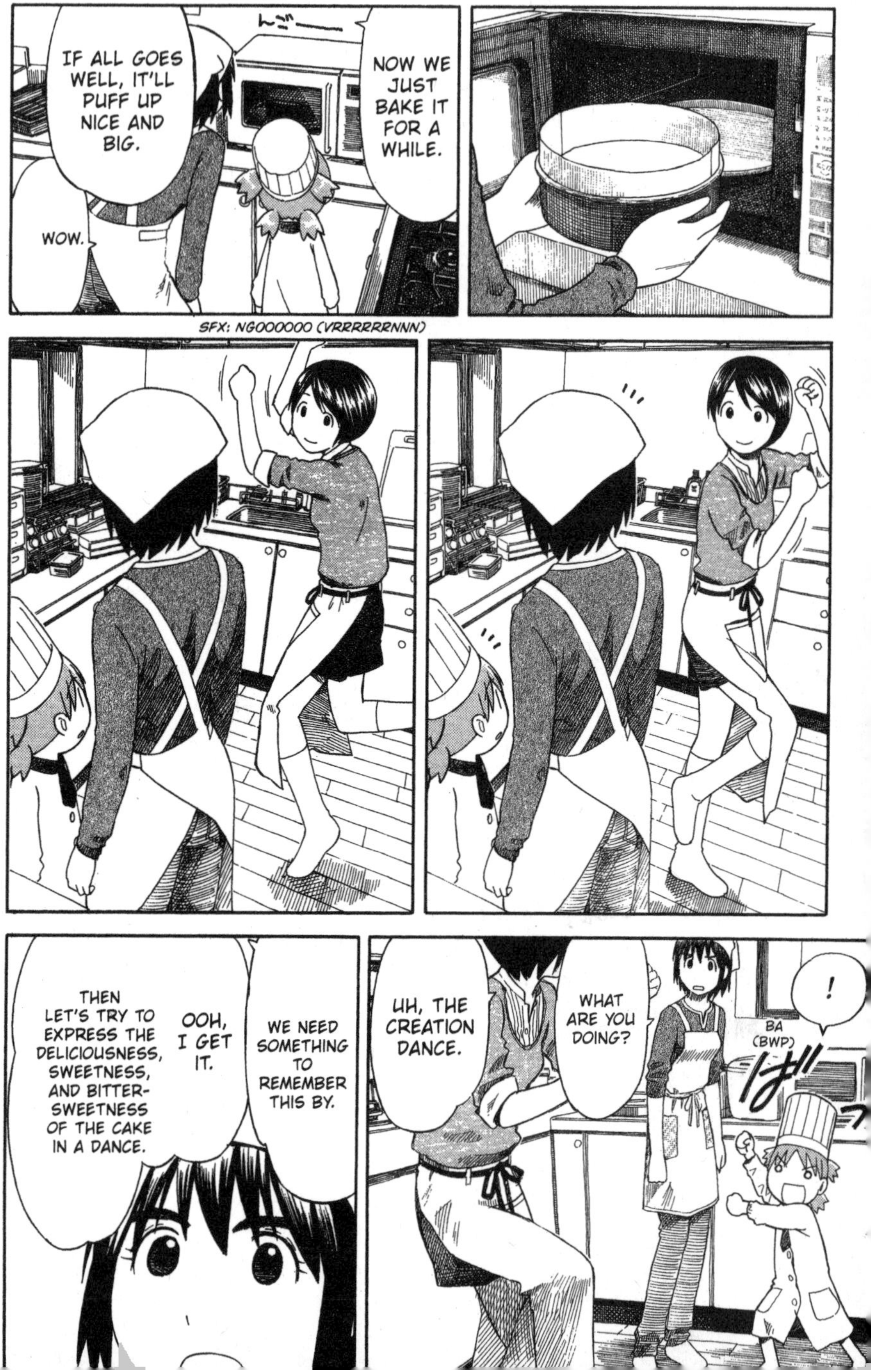
NOW WE JUST BAKE IT FOR A WHILE.
IF ALL GOES WELL, IT'LL PUFF UP NICE AND BIG.
WOW.
SFX: NGOOOOOO (VRRRRRRNNN)
!
BA (BWP)
WHAT ARE YOU DOING?
UH, THE CREATION DANCE.
WE NEED SOMETHING TO REMEMBER THIS BY.
OOH, I GET IT.
THEN LET'S TRY TO EXPRESS THE DELICIOUSNESS, SWEETNESS, AND BITTER-SWEETNESS OF THE CAKE IN A DANCE.

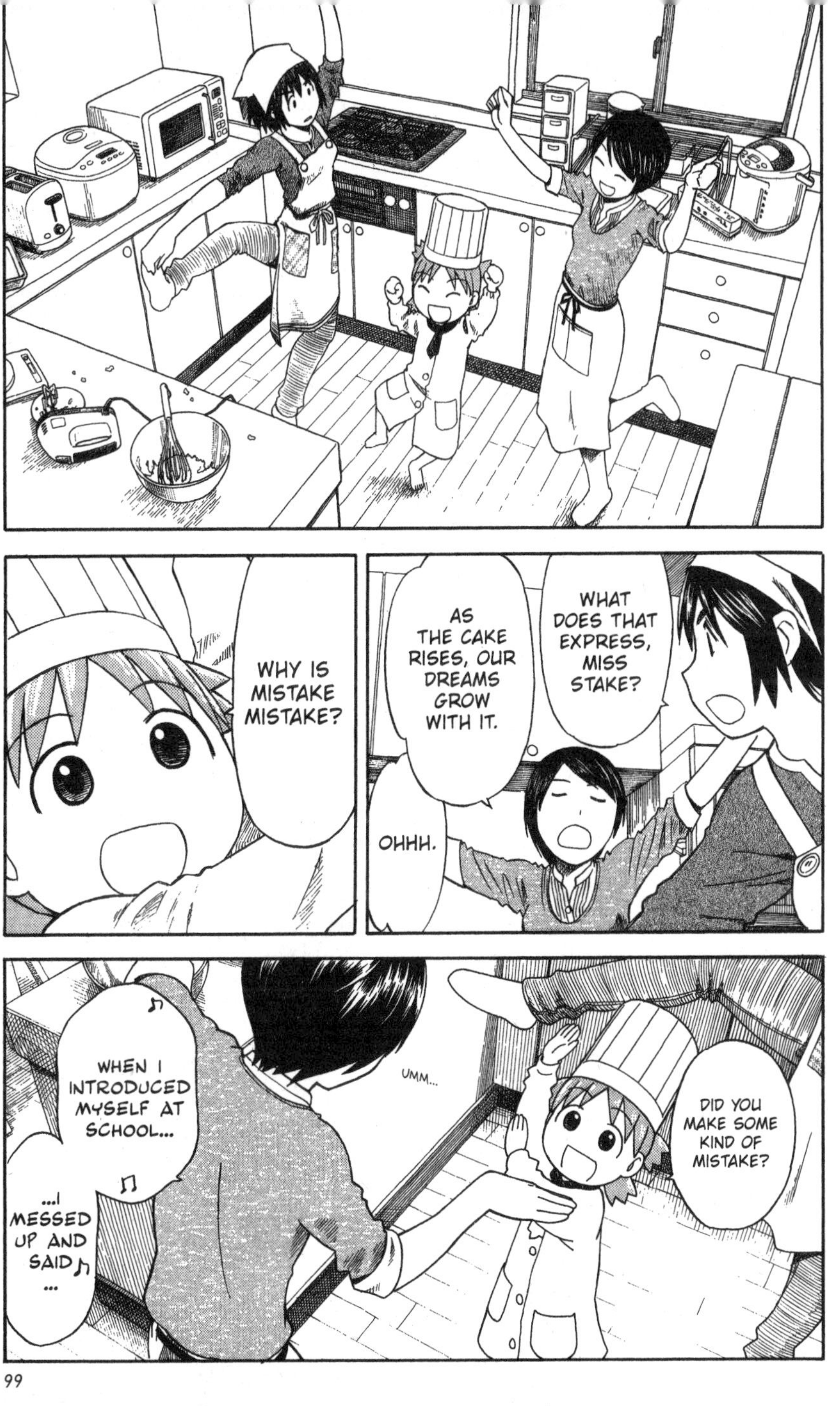
WHAT DOES THAT EXPRESS, MISS STAKE?
AS THE CAKE RISES, OUR DREAMS GROW WITH IT.
OHHH.
WHY IS MISTAKE MISTAKE?
DID YOU MAKE SOME KIND OF MISTAKE?
UMM...
WHEN I INTRODUCED MYSELF AT SCHOOL...
...I MESSED UP AND SAID ♫ ...

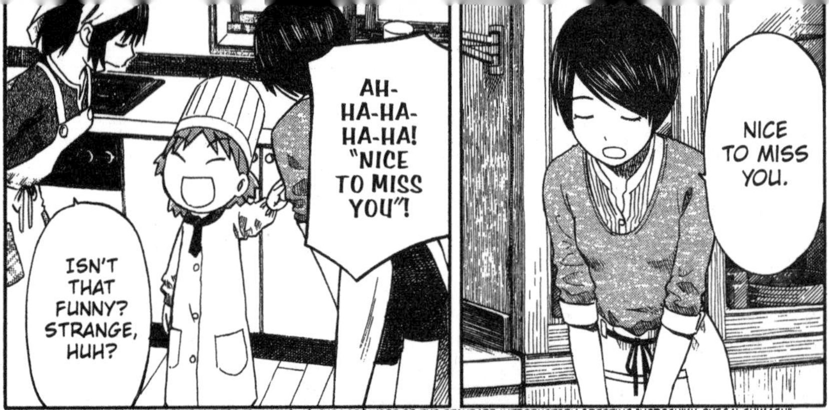
NICE TO MISS YOU.
AH-HA-HA-HA-HA! "NICE TO MISS YOU"!
ISN'T THAT FUNNY? STRANGE, HUH?

*IN JAPANESE, MISS STAKE MISSPOKE, CHANGING THE LAST WORD OF THE STANDARD INTRODUCTORY GREETING "YOROSHIKU ONEGAI SHIMASU" TO "SHIMAU." ADDING "SHIMAU" TO THE END INDICATES SOMETHING WAS DONE BY MISTAKE, WHICH IS WHERE SHE GETS HER NICKNAME FROM.

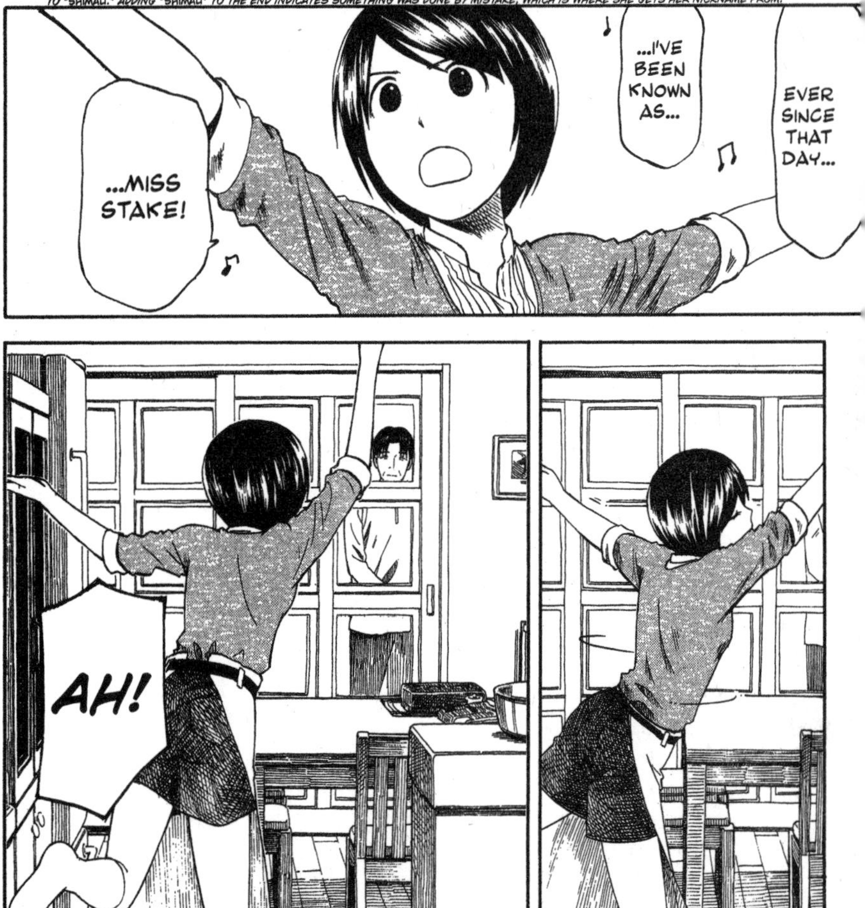
EVER SINCE THAT DAY...
...I'VE BEEN KNOWN AS...
...MISS STAKE!
AH!

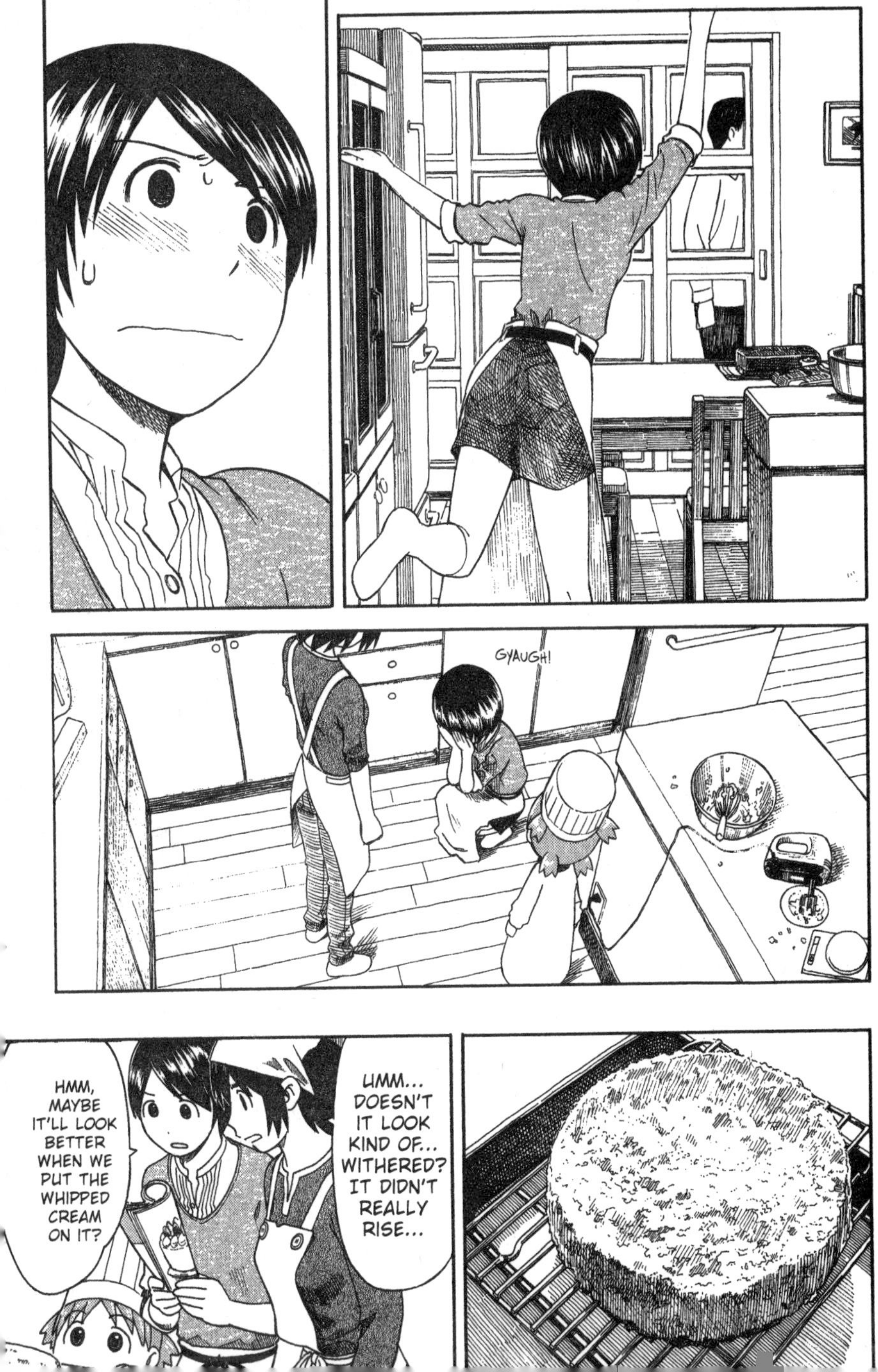
GYAUGH!
UMM... DOESN'T IT LOOK KIND OF... WITHERED? IT DIDN'T REALLY RISE...
HMM, MAYBE IT'LL LOOK BETTER WHEN WE PUT THE WHIPPED CREAM ON IT?

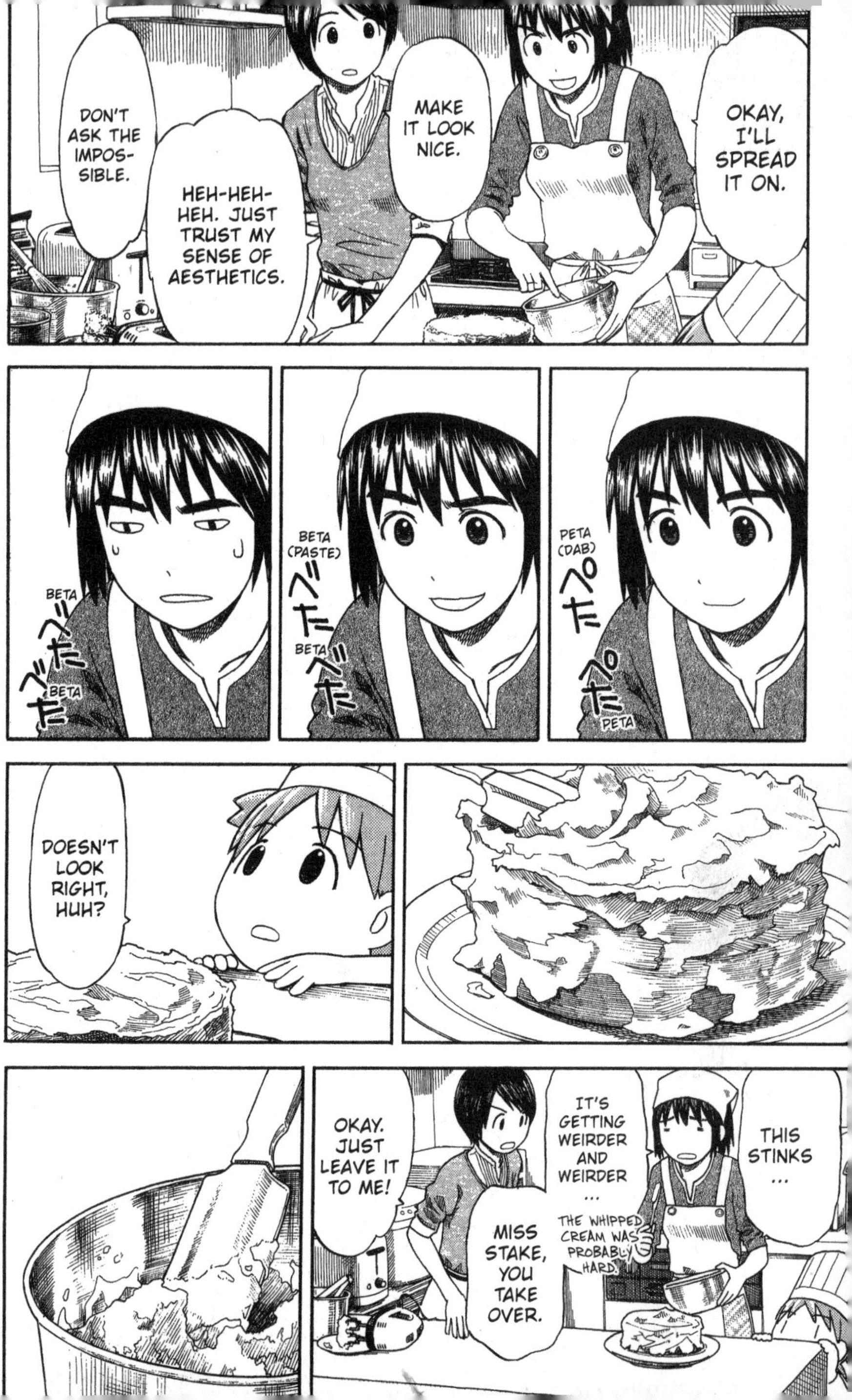
OKAY, I'LL SPREAD IT ON.
MAKE IT LOOK NICE.
HEH-HEH-HEH. JUST TRUST MY SENSE OF AESTHETICS.
DON'T ASK THE IMPOSSIBLE.
PETA (DAB)
ぺた
PETA
ぺた
BETA (PASTE)
べた
BETA
べた
BETA
べた
BETA
べた
DOESN'T LOOK RIGHT, HUH?
THIS STINKS...
IT'S GETTING WEIRDER AND WEIRDER...
THE WHIPPED CREAM WAS PROBABLY HARD.
MISS STAKE, YOU TAKE OVER.
OKAY. JUST LEAVE IT TO ME!

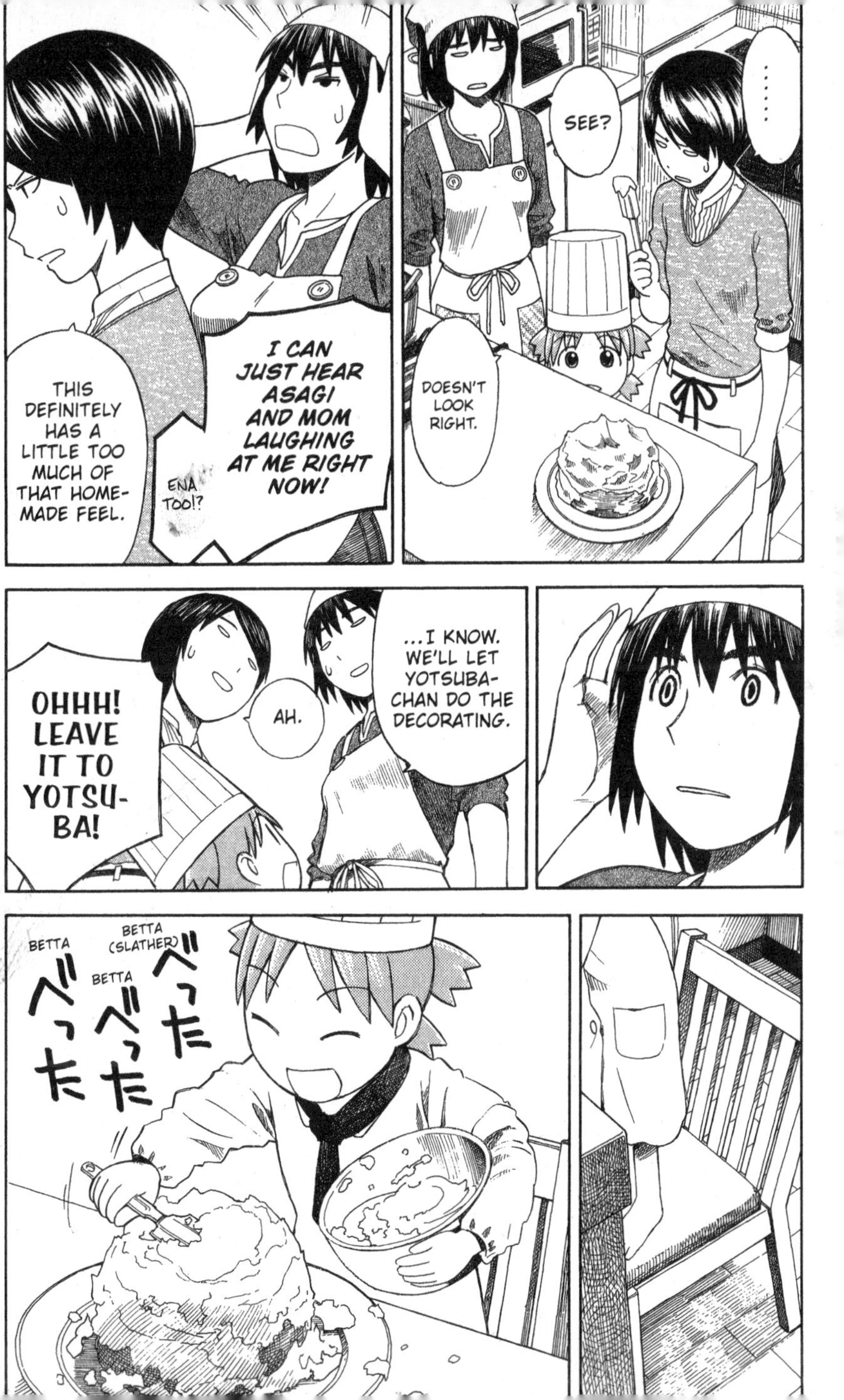
......
SEE?
DOESN'T LOOK RIGHT.
I CAN JUST HEAR ASAGI AND MOM LAUGHING AT ME RIGHT NOW!
ENA TOO!?
THIS DEFINITELY HAS A LITTLE TOO MUCH OF THAT HOME-MADE FEEL.
...I KNOW. WE'LL LET YOTSUBA-CHAN DO THE DECORATING.
AH.
OHHH! LEAVE IT TO YOTSUBA!
べった
BETTA (SLATHER)
べった
BETTA
べった
BETTA

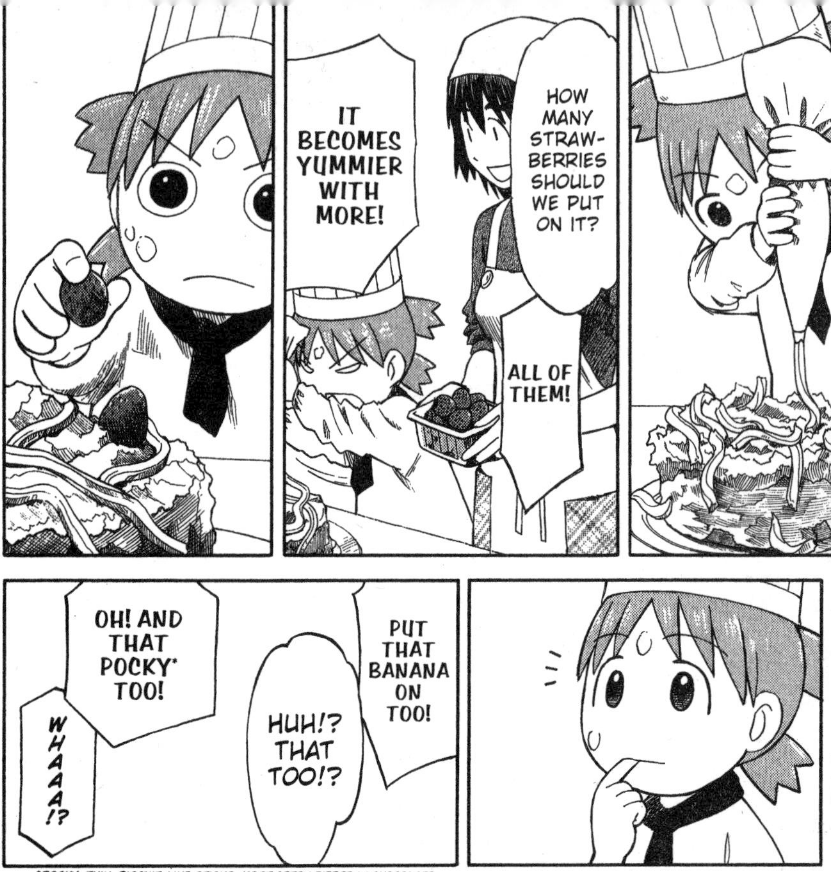
HOW MANY STRAW-BERRIES SHOULD WE PUT ON IT?
IT BECOMES YUMMIER WITH MORE!
ALL OF THEM!
PUT THAT BANANA ON TOO!
HUH!? THAT TOO!?
OH! AND THAT POCKY* TOO!
WHAAAA!?

*POCKY: THIN, BISCUIT-LIKE STICKS, MOST OFTEN DIPPED IN CHOCOLATE.

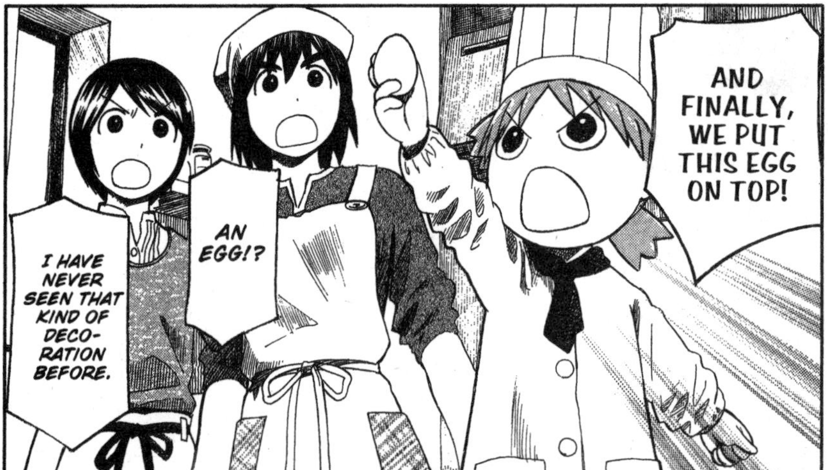
AND FINALLY, WE PUT THIS EGG ON TOP!
AN EGG!?
I HAVE NEVER SEEN THAT KIND OF DECO-RATION BEFORE.

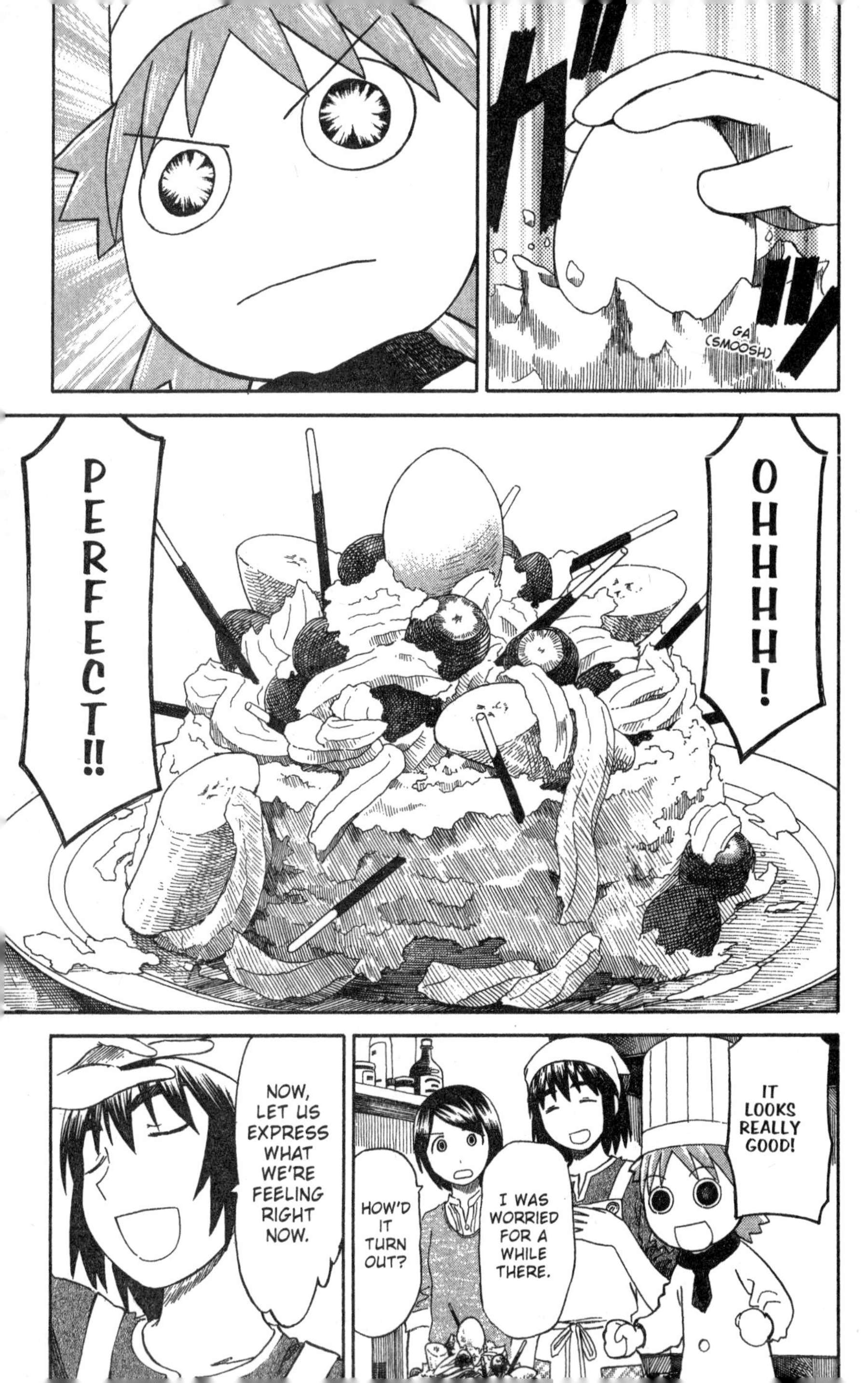
GA (SMOOSH)
OHHHH!
PERFECT!!
IT LOOKS REALLY GOOD!
I WAS WORRIED FOR A WHILE THERE.
HOW'D IT TURN OUT?
NOW, LET US EXPRESS WHAT WE'RE FEELING RIGHT NOW.

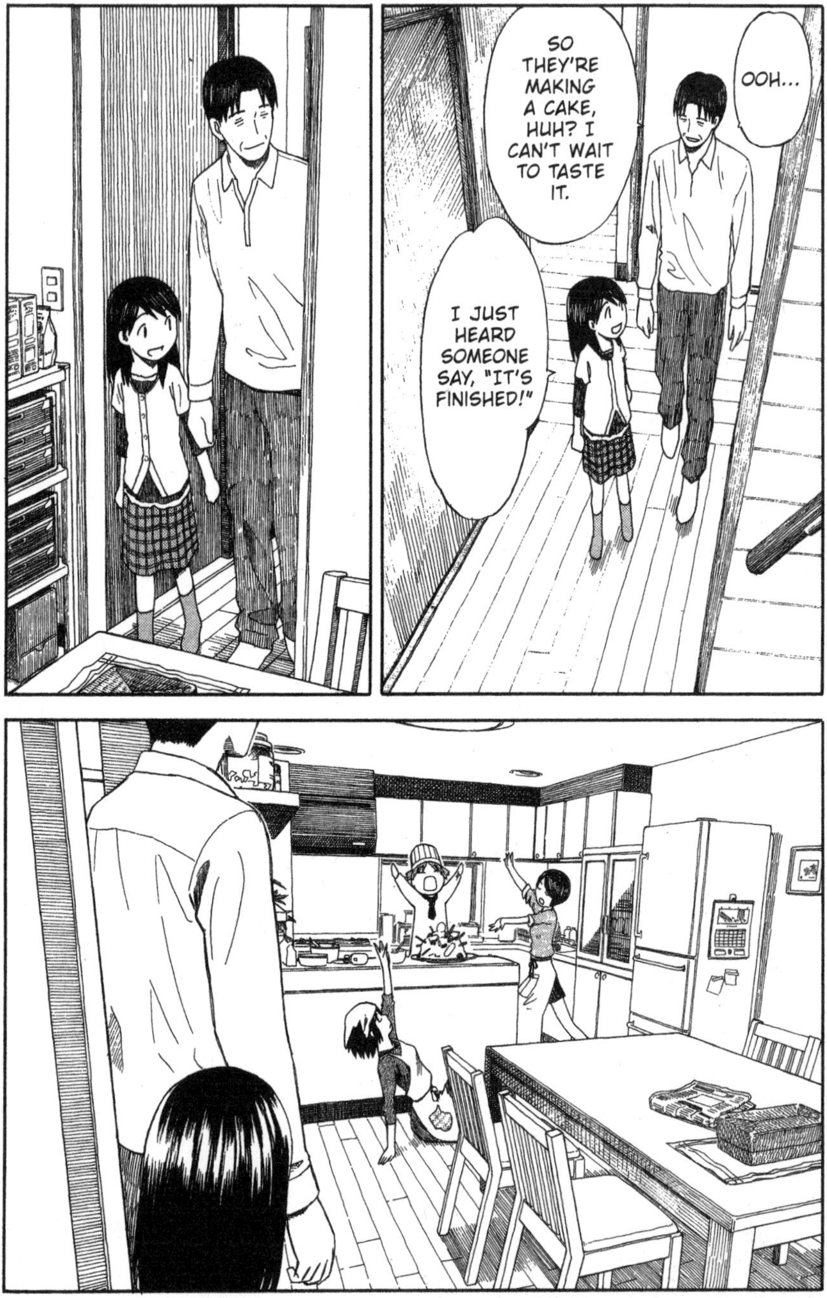
OOH...
SO THEY'RE MAKING A CAKE, HUH? I CAN'T WAIT TO TASTE IT.
I JUST HEARD SOMEONE SAY, "IT'S FINISHED!"

YOTSUBA&!

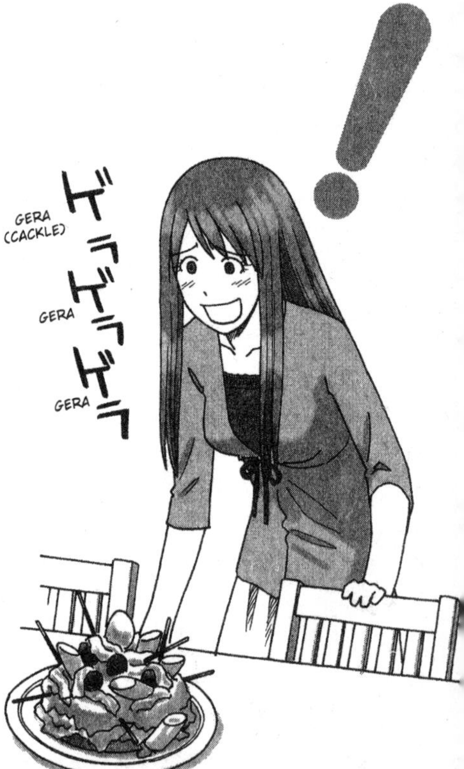

!
ゲラ
GERA (CACKLE)
ゲラ
GERA
ゲラ
GERA

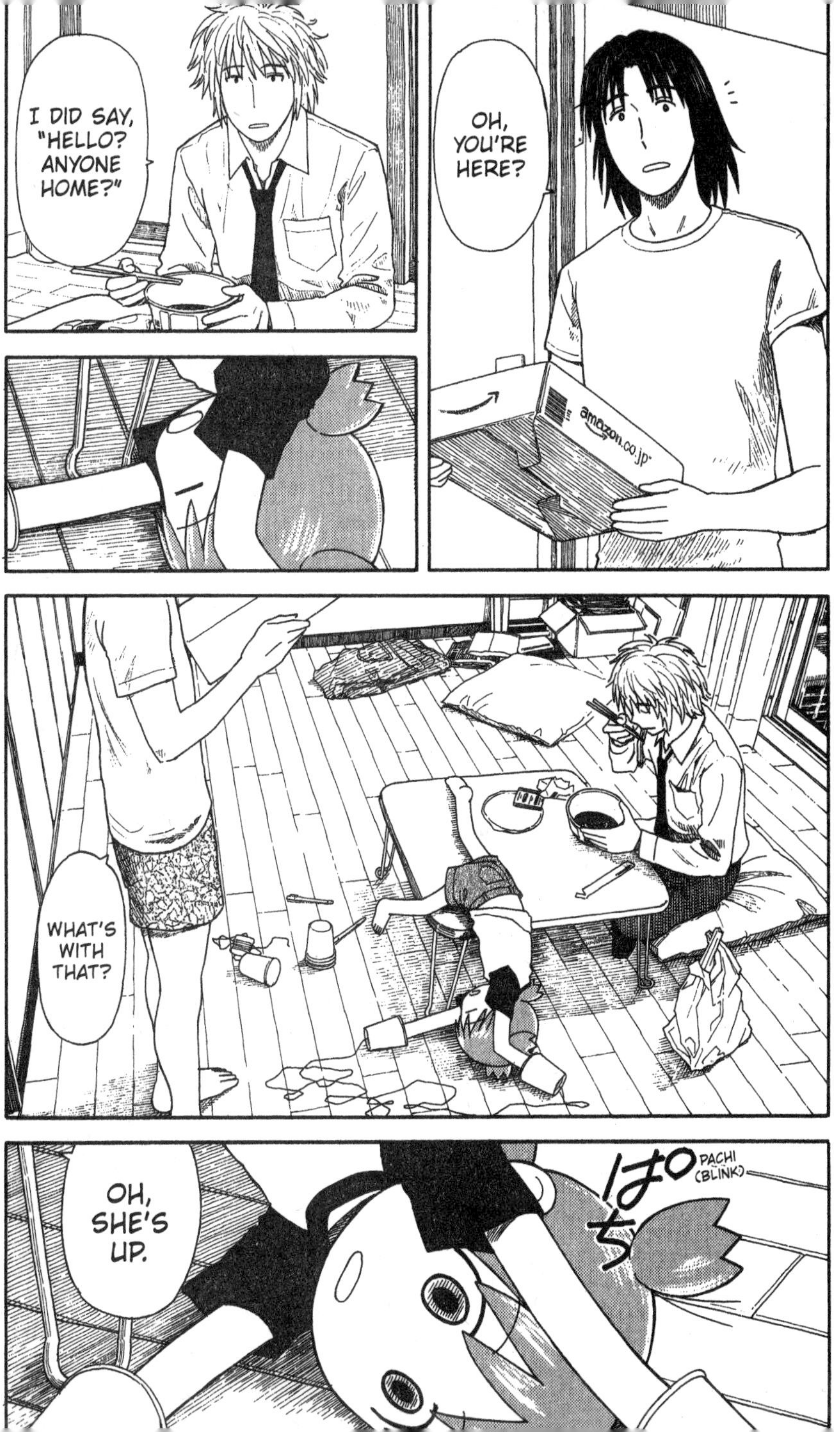
OH, YOU'RE HERE?
I DID SAY, "HELLO? ANYONE HOME?"
WHAT'S WITH THAT?
ぱち
PACHI (BLINK)
OH, SHE'S UP.

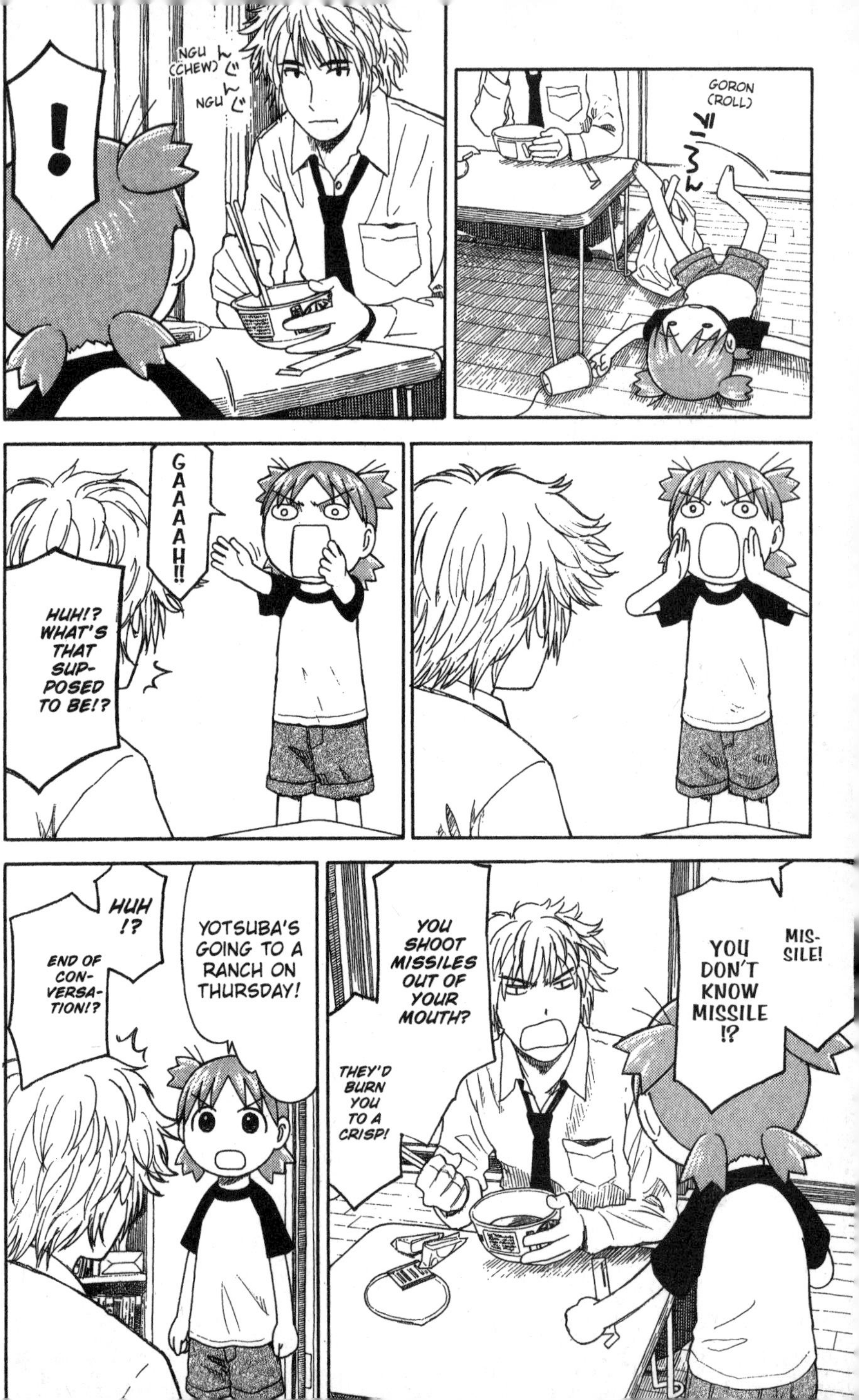
GORON (ROLL)
NGU (CHEW) NGU
!
GAAAAAH!!
HUH!? WHAT'S THAT SUP-POSED TO BE!?
MIS-SILE!
YOU DON'T KNOW MISSILE!?
YOU SHOOT MISSILES OUT OF YOUR MOUTH?
THEY'D BURN YOU TO A CRISP!
YOTSUBA'S GOING TO A RANCH ON THURSDAY!
HUH!?
END OF CON-VERSA-TION!?

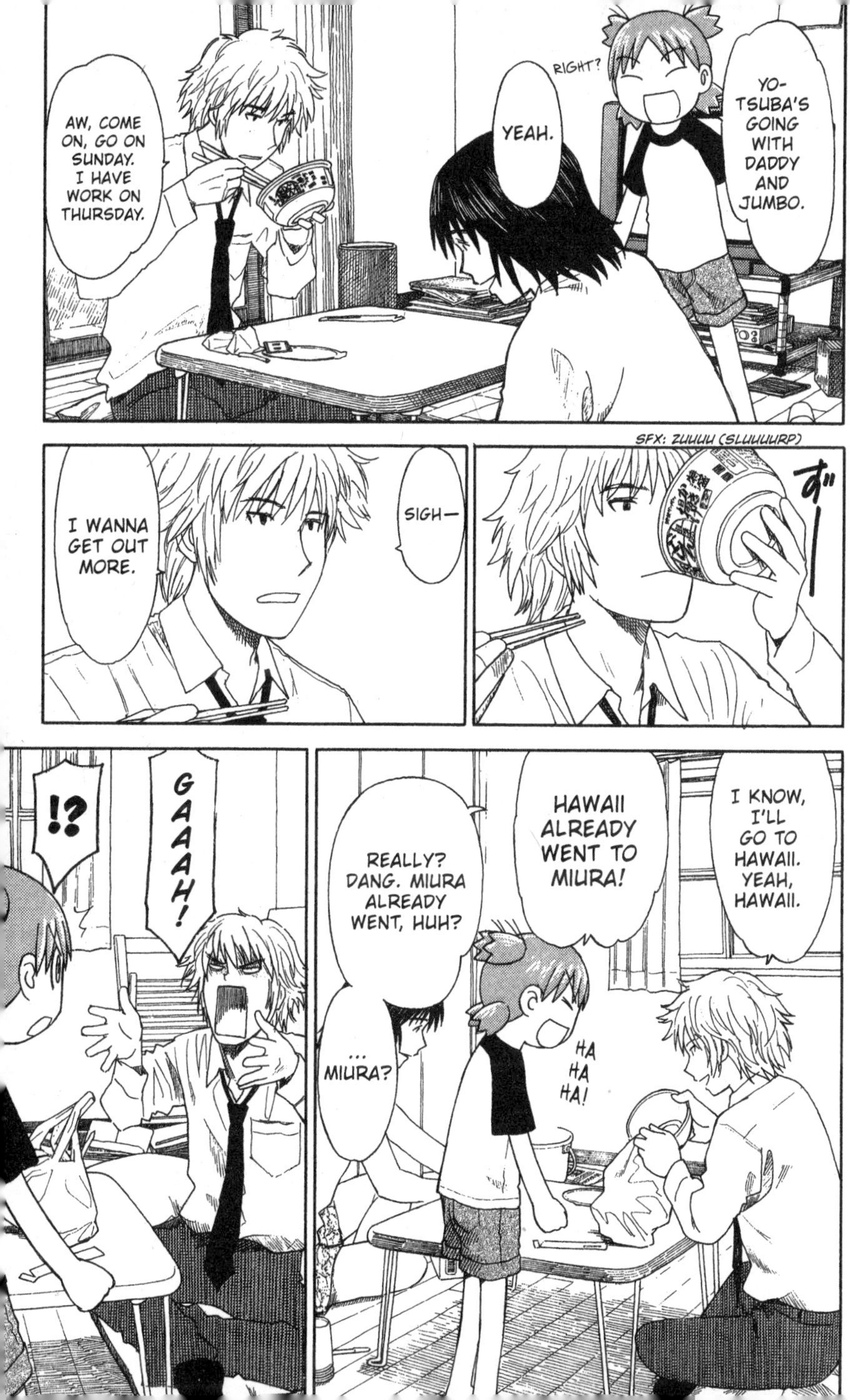
YO-TSUBA'S GOING WITH DADDY AND JUMBO.
RIGHT?
YEAH.
AW, COME ON, GO ON SUNDAY. I HAVE WORK ON THURSDAY.
SFX: ZUUUU (SLUUUURP)
ずー
SIGH—
I WANNA GET OUT MORE.
I KNOW, I'LL GO TO HAWAII. YEAH, HAWAII.
HAWAII ALREADY WENT TO MIURA!
HA HA HA HA!
REALLY? DANG. MIURA ALREADY WENT, HUH?
... MIURA?
GAAAAH!
!?

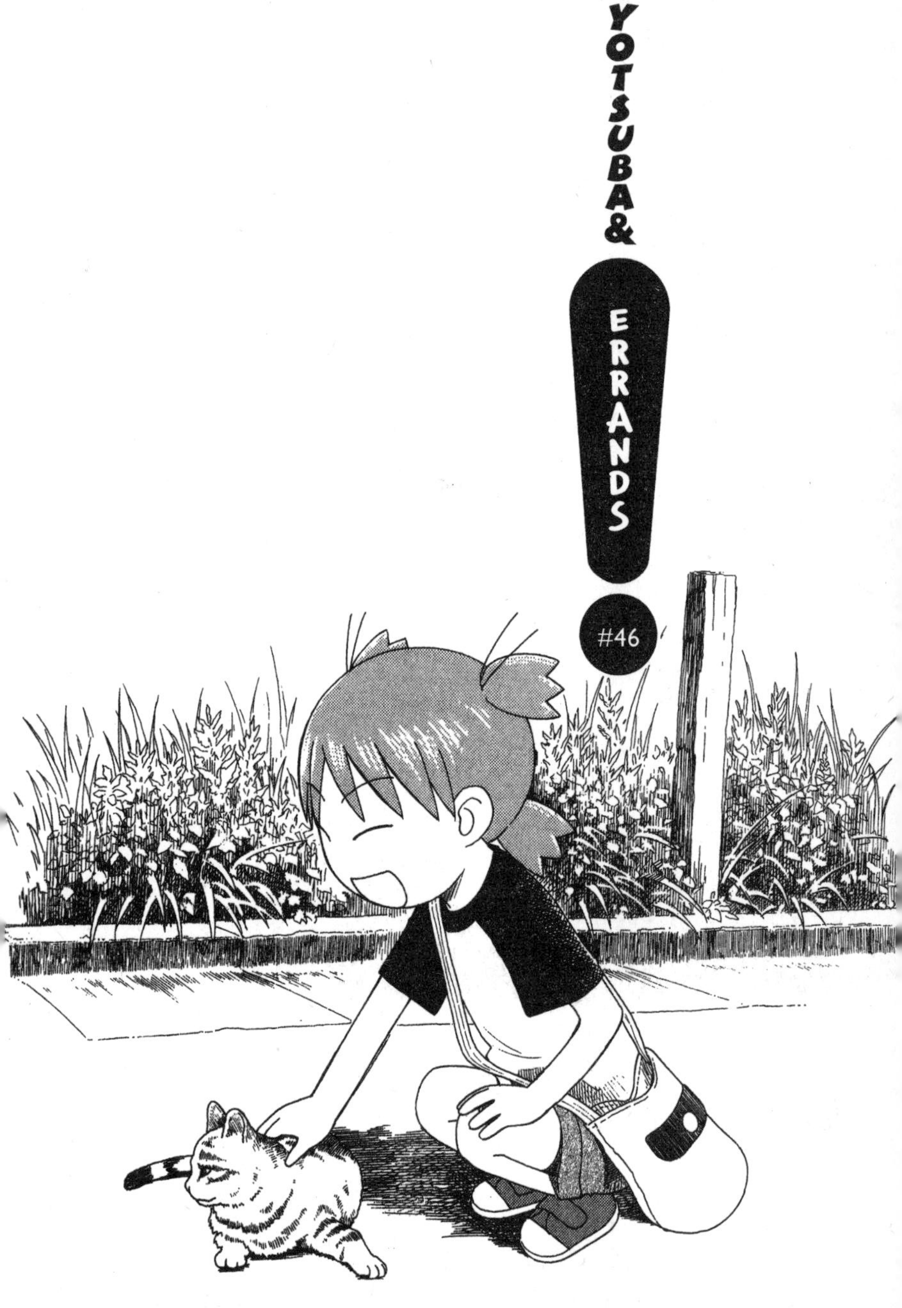
YOTSUBA&
ERRANDS
#46

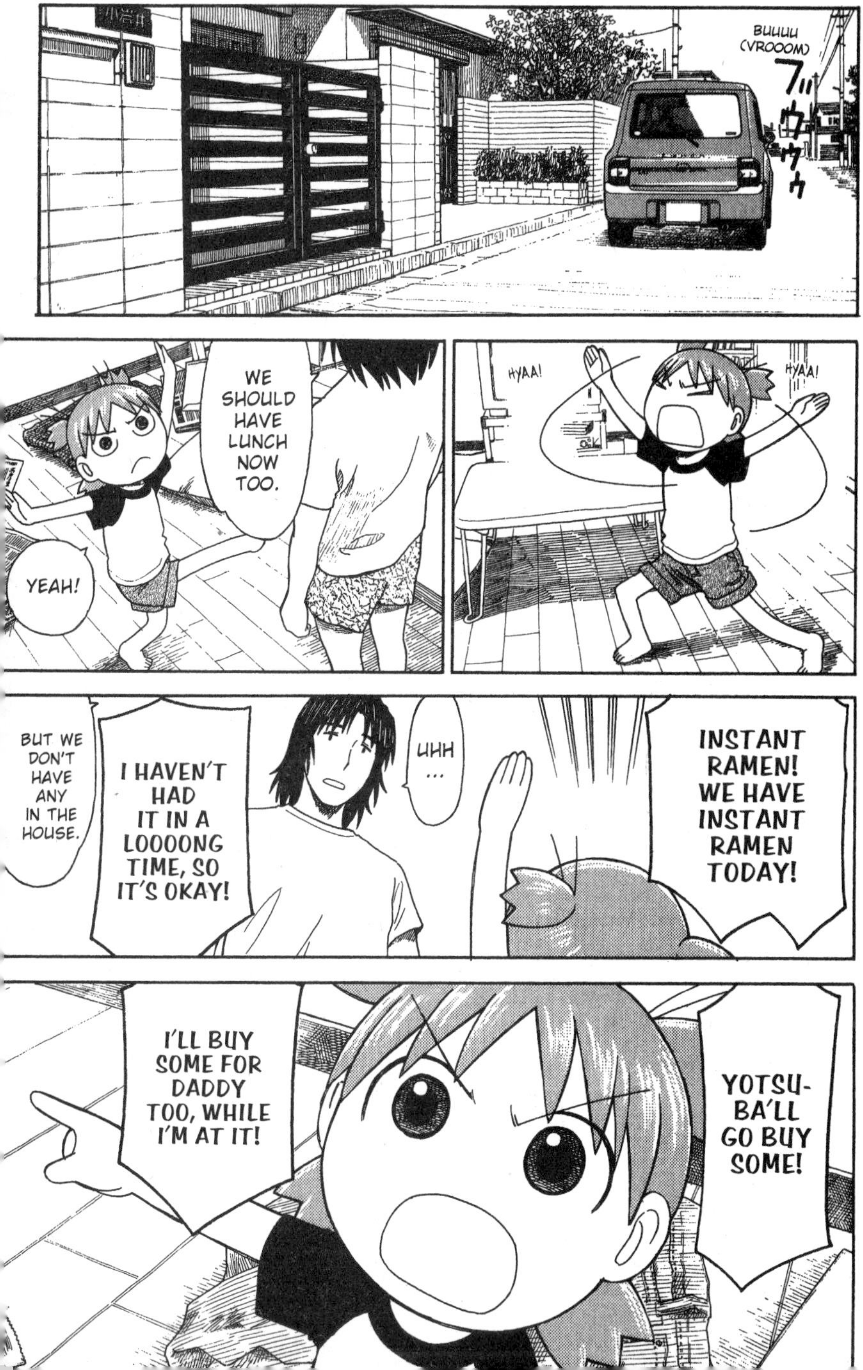
BUUUU (VROOOM)
HYAA!
HYAA!
WE SHOULD HAVE LUNCH NOW TOO.
YEAH!
INSTANT RAMEN! WE HAVE INSTANT RAMEN TODAY!
UHH ...
I HAVEN'T HAD IT IN A LOOOONG TIME, SO IT'S OKAY!
BUT WE DON'T HAVE ANY IN THE HOUSE.
YOTSU-BA'LL GO BUY SOME!
I'LL BUY SOME FOR DADDY TOO, WHILE I'M AT IT!

I'M NOT LIKE THAT KID!

AH HA HA!

YOU'LL GET LOST AND TRIP AND FALL AND CRY...

GOING ON AN ERRAND IS HARD! IT MIGHT TURN OUT LIKE THAT TV SHOW "MY FIRST ERRAND."

I KNOW.

I CAN GO.

CONVE- NIENCE STORE.

WELL, THE CONVE- NIENCE STORE IS CLOSE, AND THE WAY IS SAFE...

...OKAY THEN, MAYBE I'LL ASK YOU TO GO ON A LITTLE ERRAND.

YES, SIR!

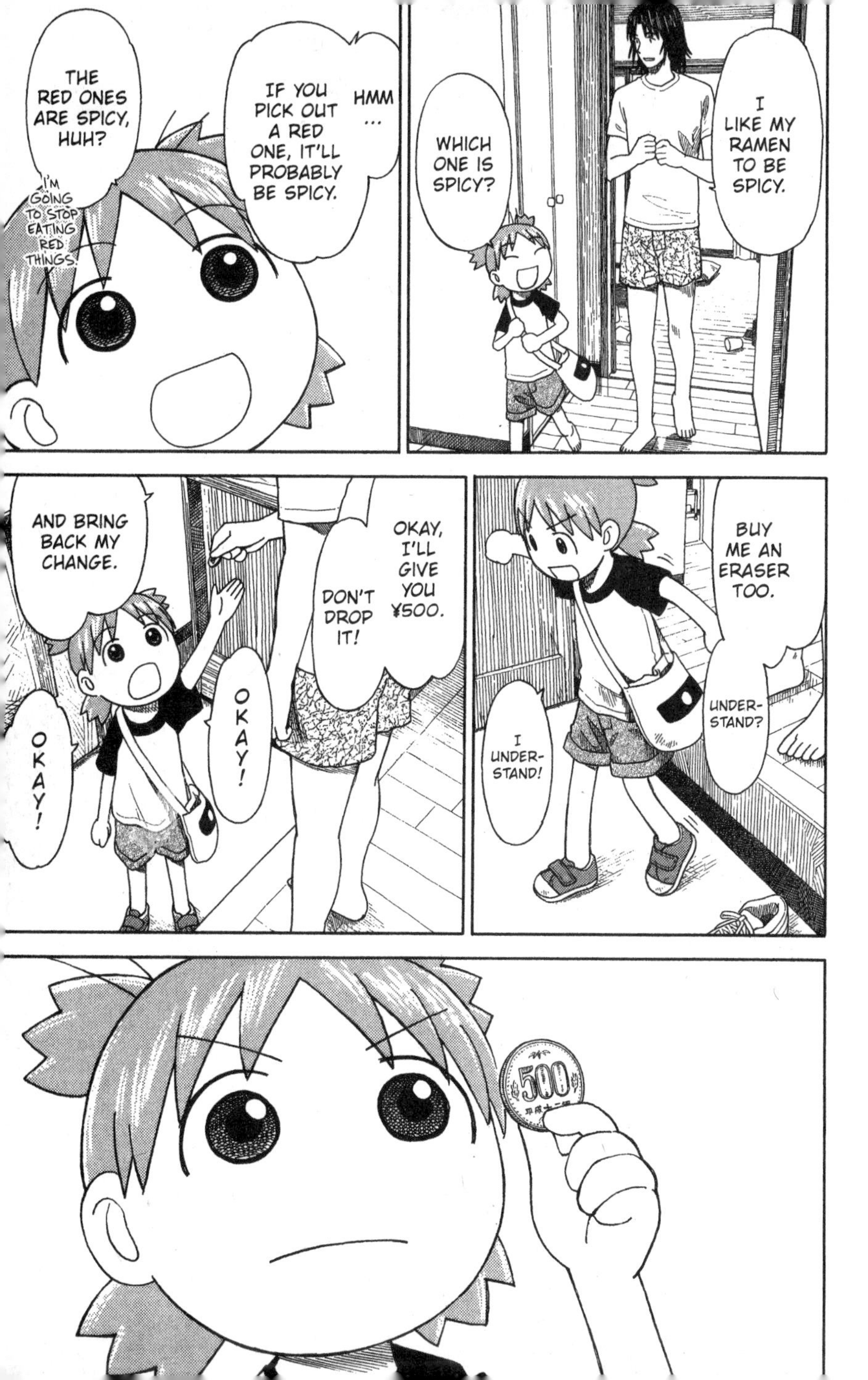
I LIKE MY RAMEN TO BE SPICY.
WHICH ONE IS SPICY?
HMM ...
IF YOU PICK OUT A RED ONE, IT'LL PROBABLY BE SPICY.
THE RED ONES ARE SPICY, HUH?
I'M GOING TO STOP EATING RED THINGS.
BUY ME AN ERASER TOO.
UNDER-STAND?
I UNDER-STAND!
OKAY, I'LL GIVE YOU ¥500.
DON'T DROP IT!
OKAY!
AND BRING BACK MY CHANGE.
OKAY!
500

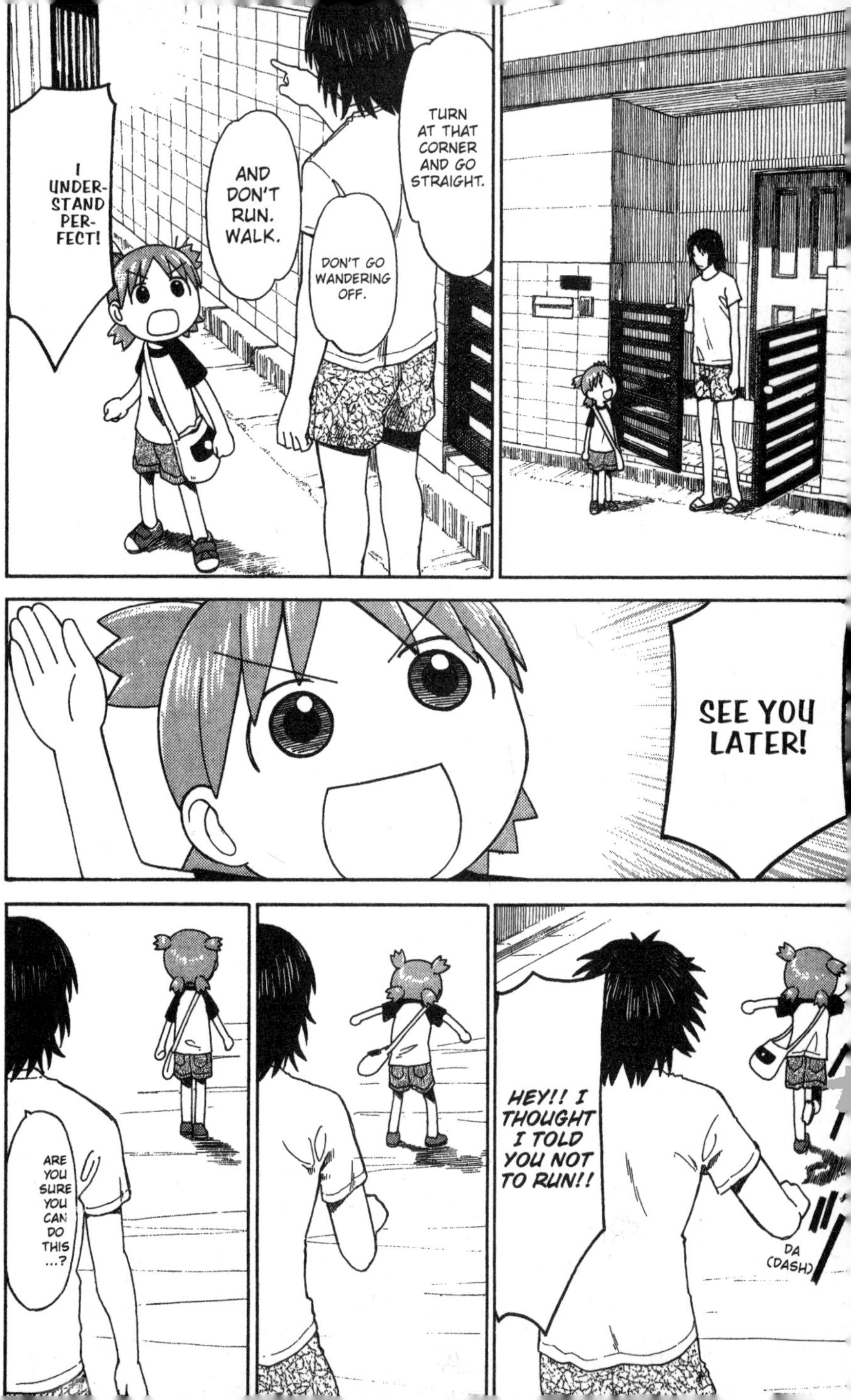
TURN AT THAT CORNER AND GO STRAIGHT.
DON'T GO WANDERING OFF.
AND DON'T RUN. WALK.
I UNDERSTAND PERFECT!
SEE YOU LATER!
HEY!! I THOUGHT I TOLD YOU NOT TO RUN!!
DA (DASH)
ARE YOU SURE YOU CAN DO THIS ...?

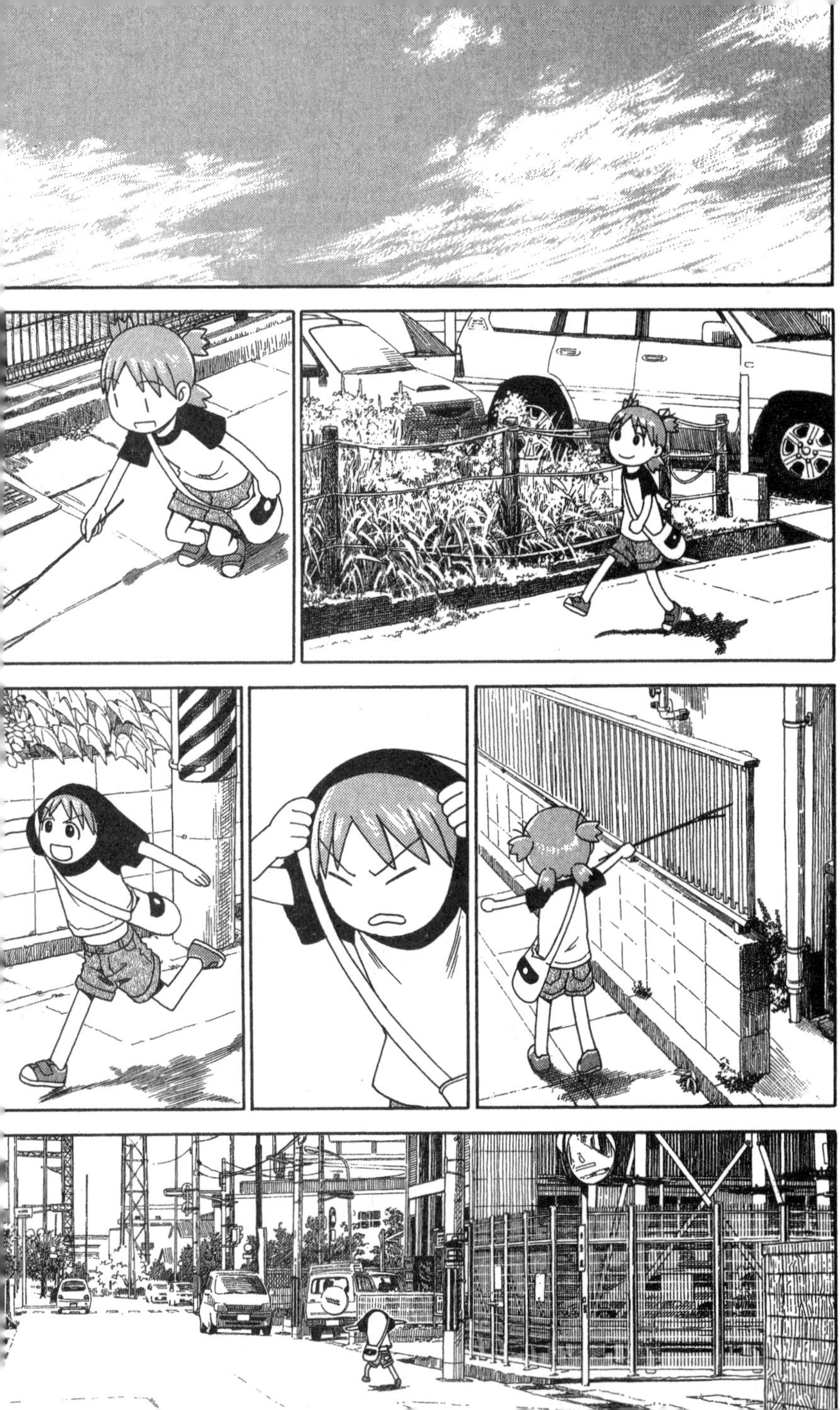

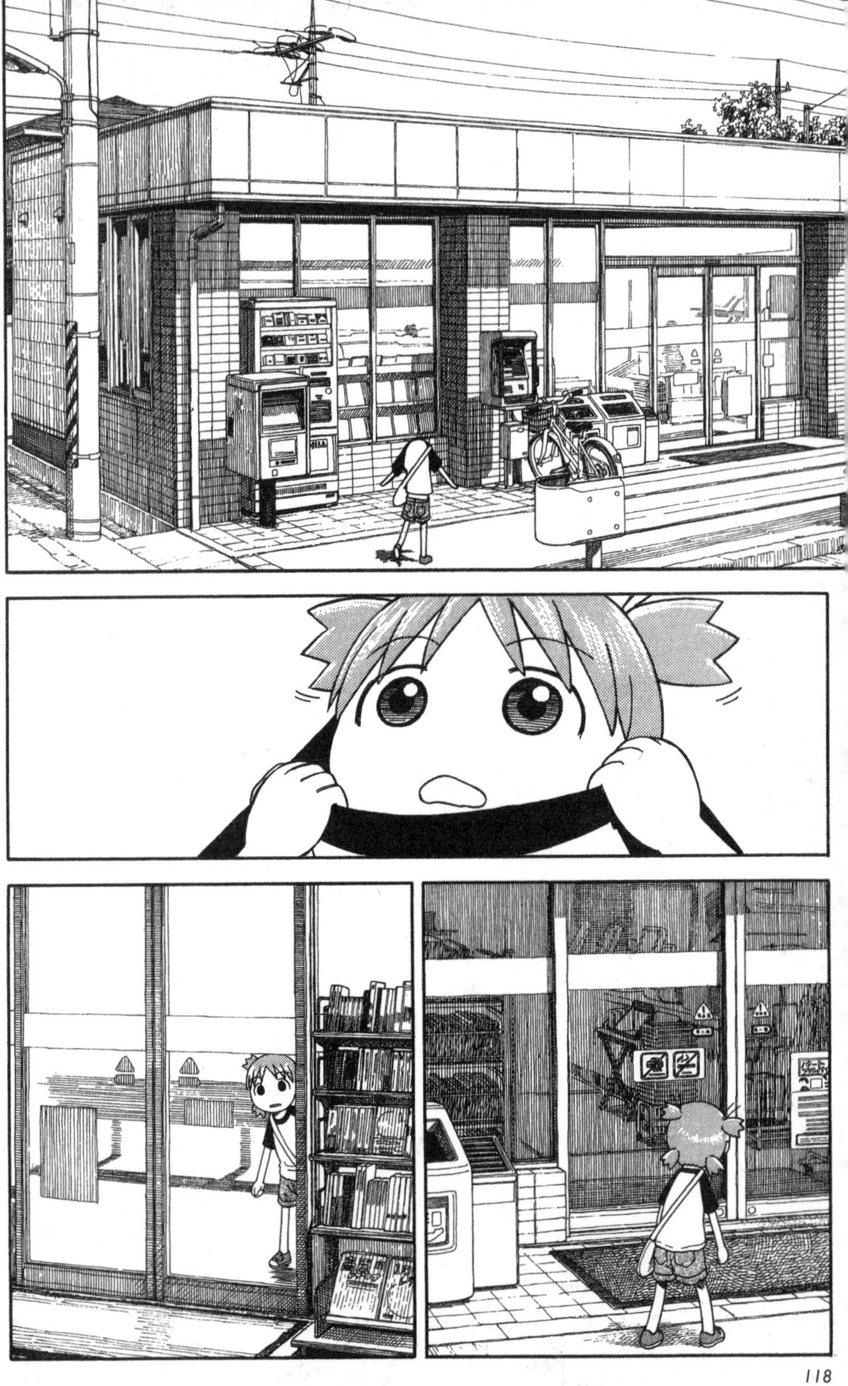

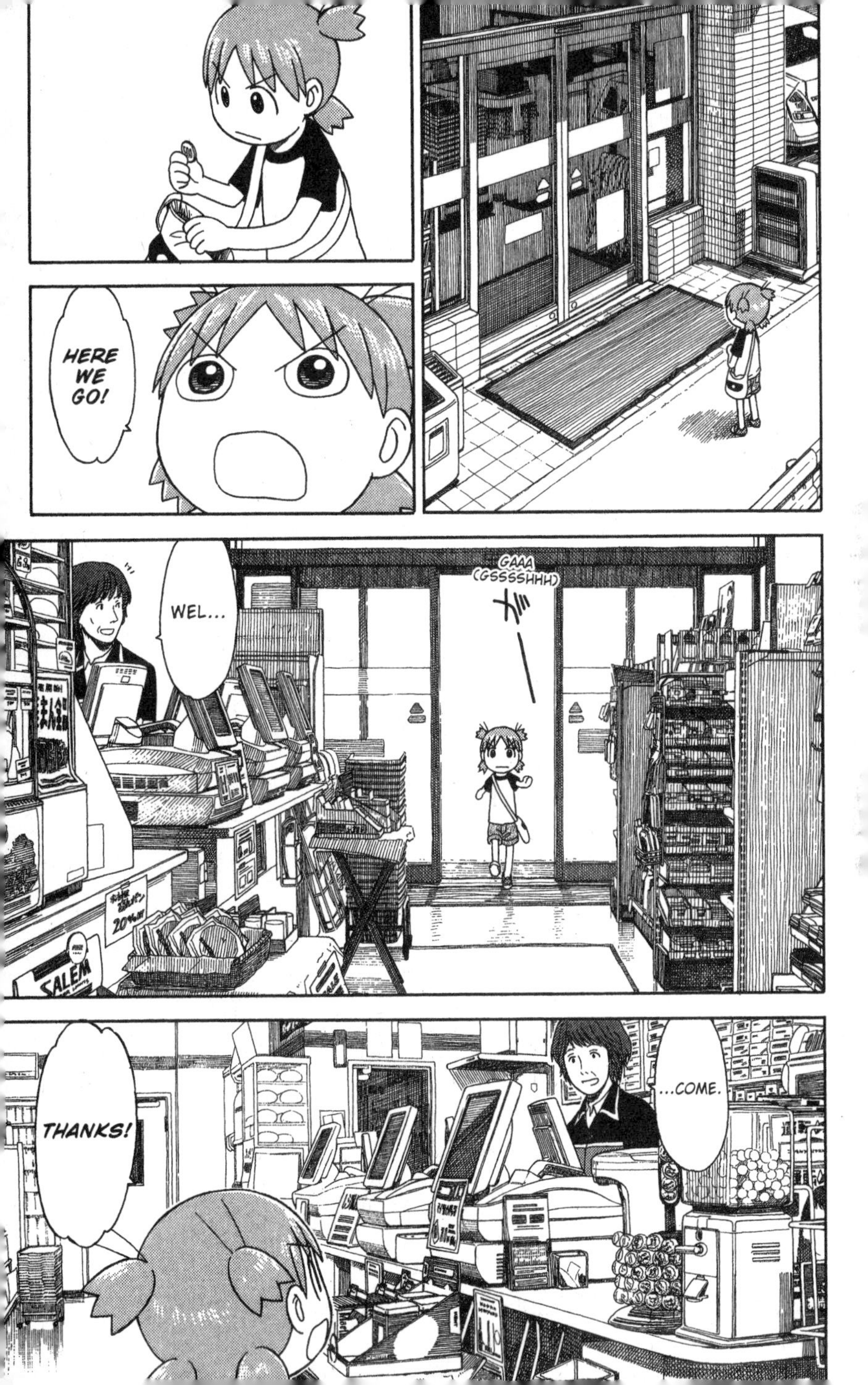
HERE WE GO!
GAAA (GSSSSHHH)
ガー
WEL...
SALEM
...COME.
THANKS!

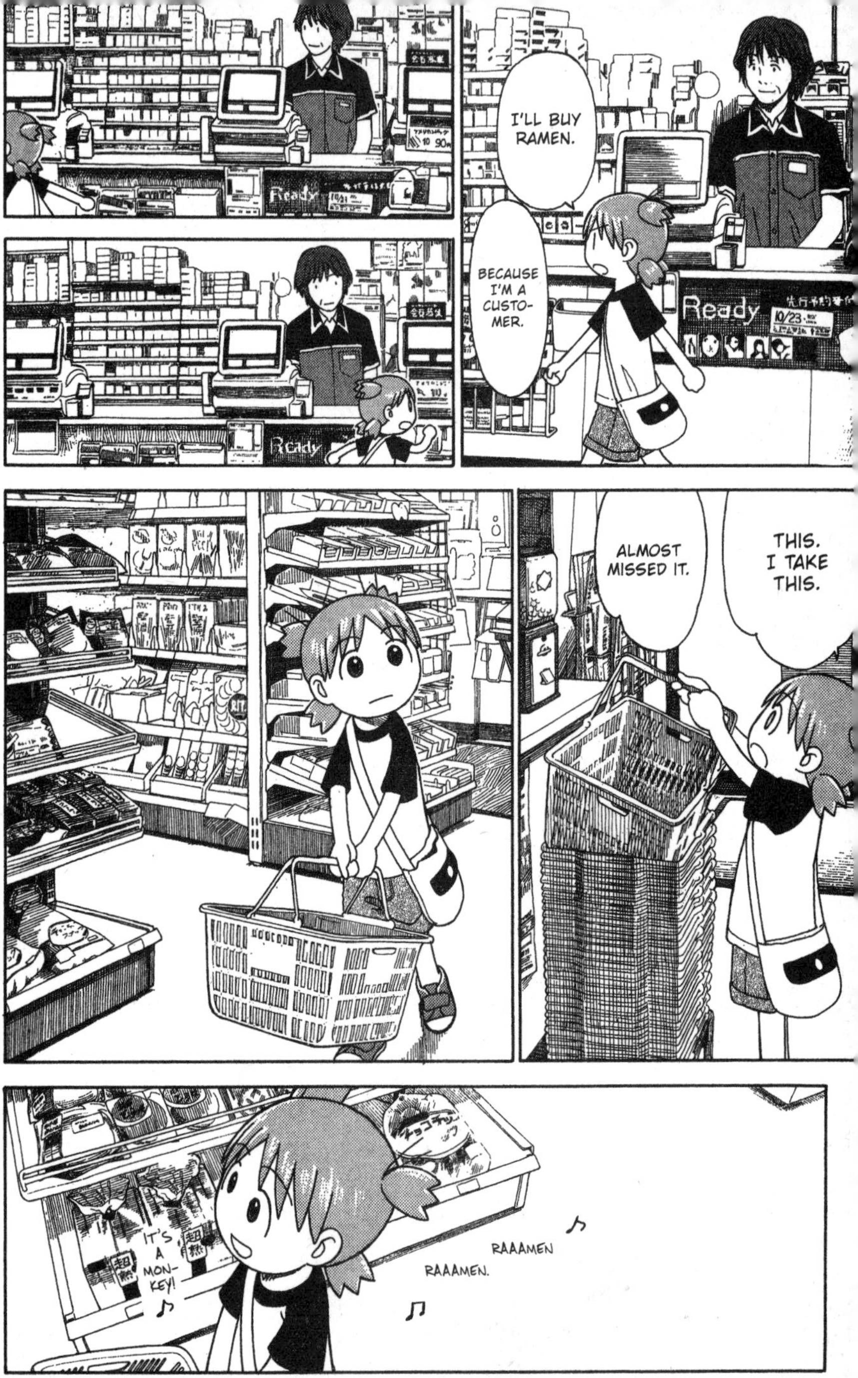
I'LL BUY RAMEN.
BECAUSE I'M A CUSTOMER.
THIS. I TAKE THIS.
ALMOST MISSED IT.
RAAAMEN
RAAAMEN.
IT'S A MONKEY!

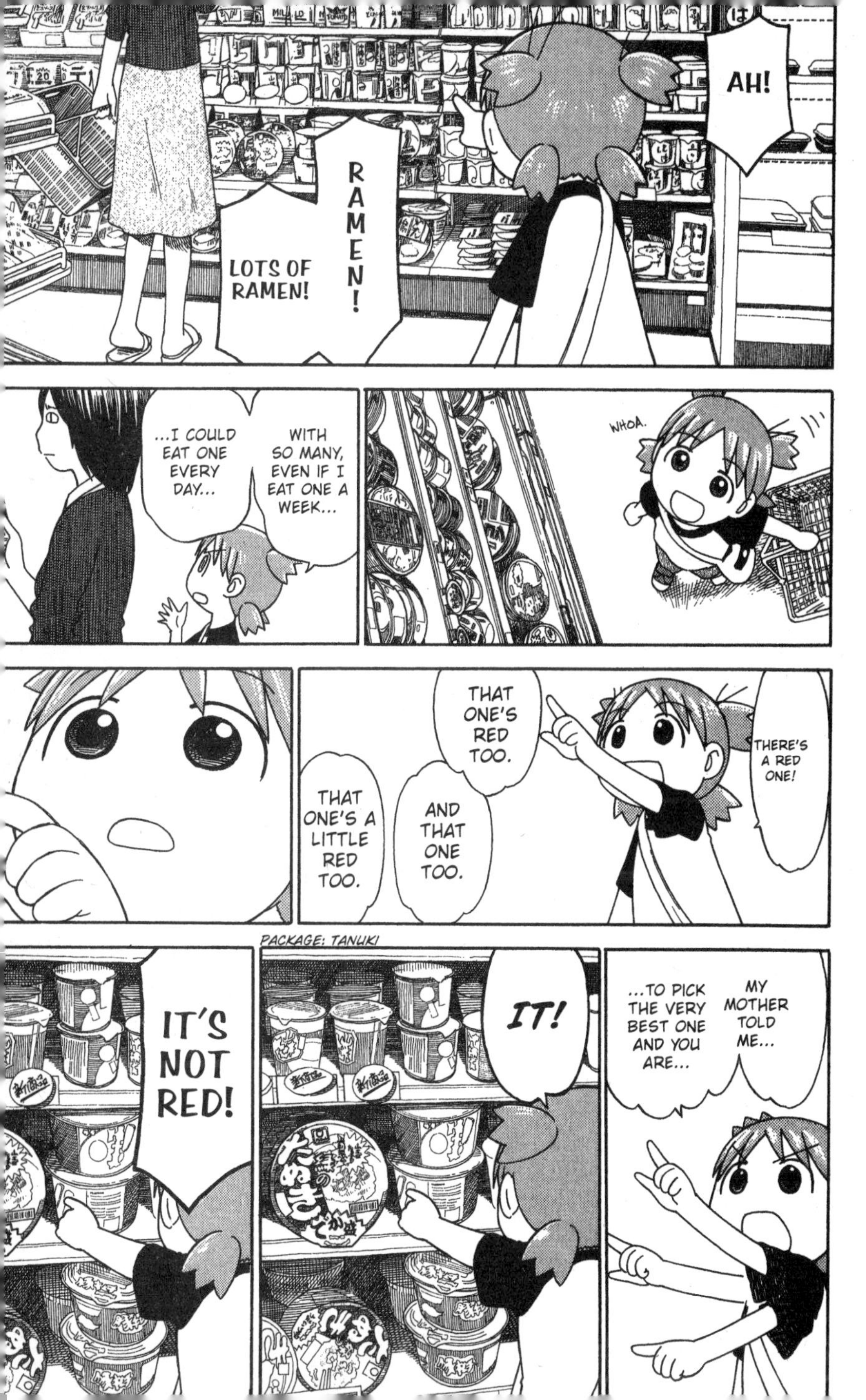
AH!
RAMEN!
LOTS OF RAMEN!
WHOA.
WITH SO MANY, EVEN IF I EAT ONE A WEEK...
...I COULD EAT ONE EVERY DAY...
THERE'S A RED ONE!
THAT ONE'S RED TOO.
AND THAT ONE TOO.
THAT ONE'S A LITTLE RED TOO.
MY MOTHER TOLD ME...
...TO PICK THE VERY BEST ONE AND YOU ARE...
IT!
PACKAGE: TANUKI
IT'S NOT RED!

CH-

PEP- -I-

-PER -LI

CHILI PEPPER!

THIS IS RED.

OH.

IT'S A GOOD RED.

PACKAGE: CHILI PEPPER NOODLES VERY SPICY

HUH!?

YES?

'SCUSE ME!

HMM.

UM...

IS THIS SPICY?

THIS IS FOR...

...DADDY.

THE SPICY ONES ARE RED.

YOTSUBA DOESN'T LIKE THE SPICY ONES.

THE RED ONES.

DADDY LIKES THE SPICY ONES.

FIVE?

ABOUT FIVE?

YEAH.

YES, I THINK THAT'S PRETTY SPICY.

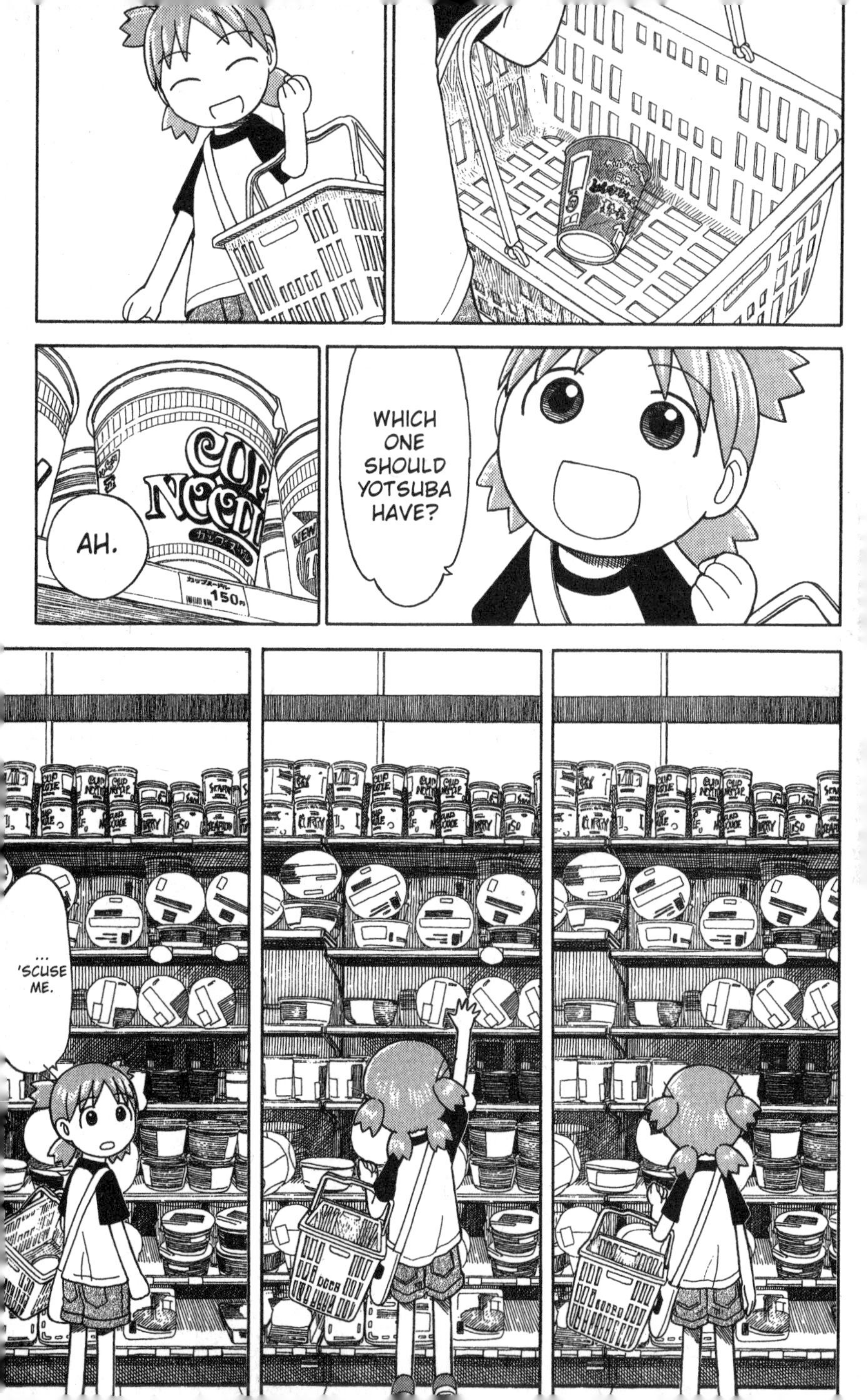
WHICH ONE SHOULD YOTSUBA HAVE?
AH.
... 'SCUSE ME.

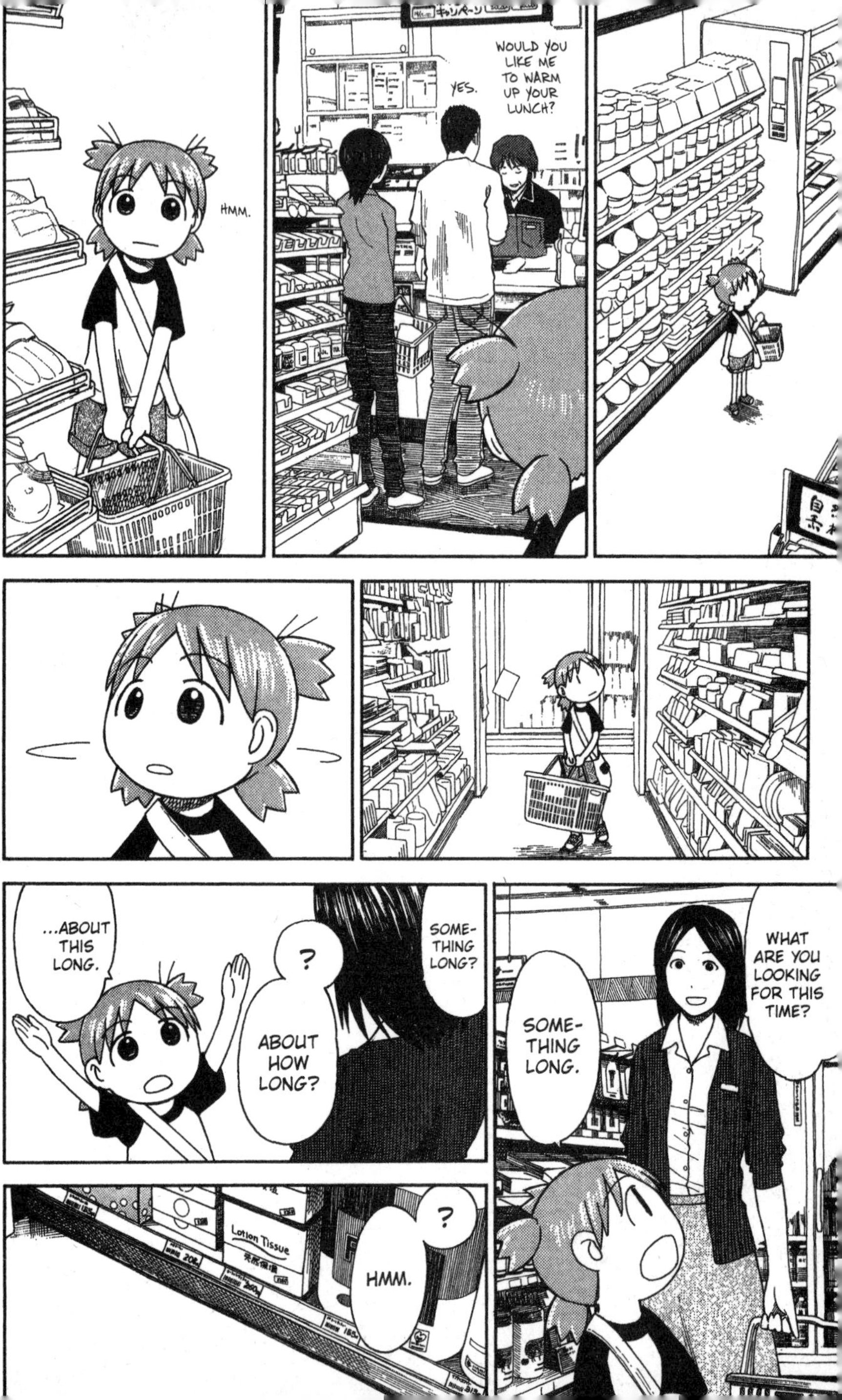

WOULD YOU LIKE ME TO WARM UP YOUR LUNCH?
YES.
HMM.
WHAT ARE YOU LOOKING FOR THIS TIME?
SOME-THING LONG.
SOME-THING LONG?
?
ABOUT HOW LONG?
...ABOUT THIS LONG.
?
HMM.
Lotion Tissue

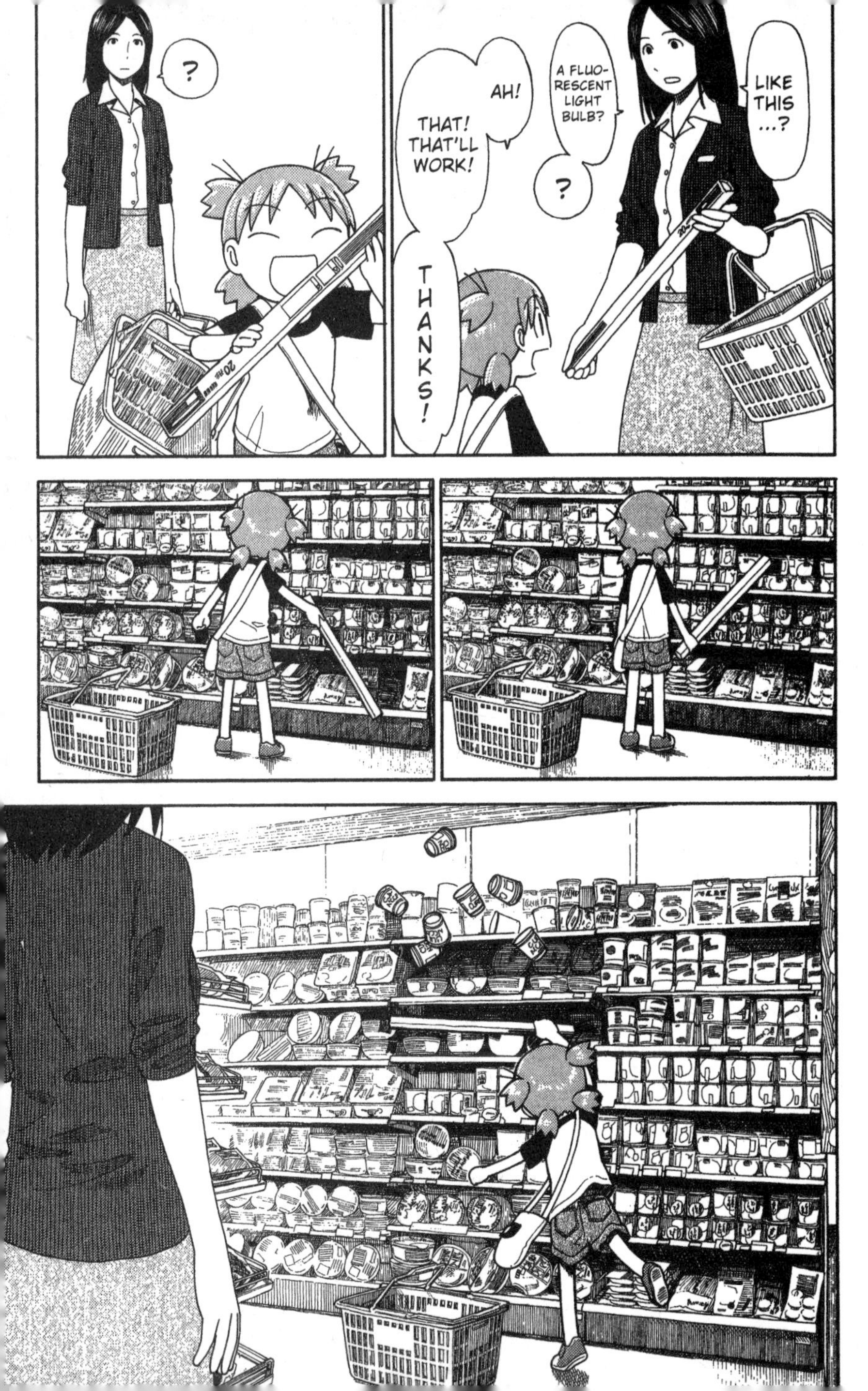
LIKE THIS ...?
A FLUO-RESCENT LIGHT BULB?
?
AH!
THAT! THAT'LL WORK!
THANKS!
?

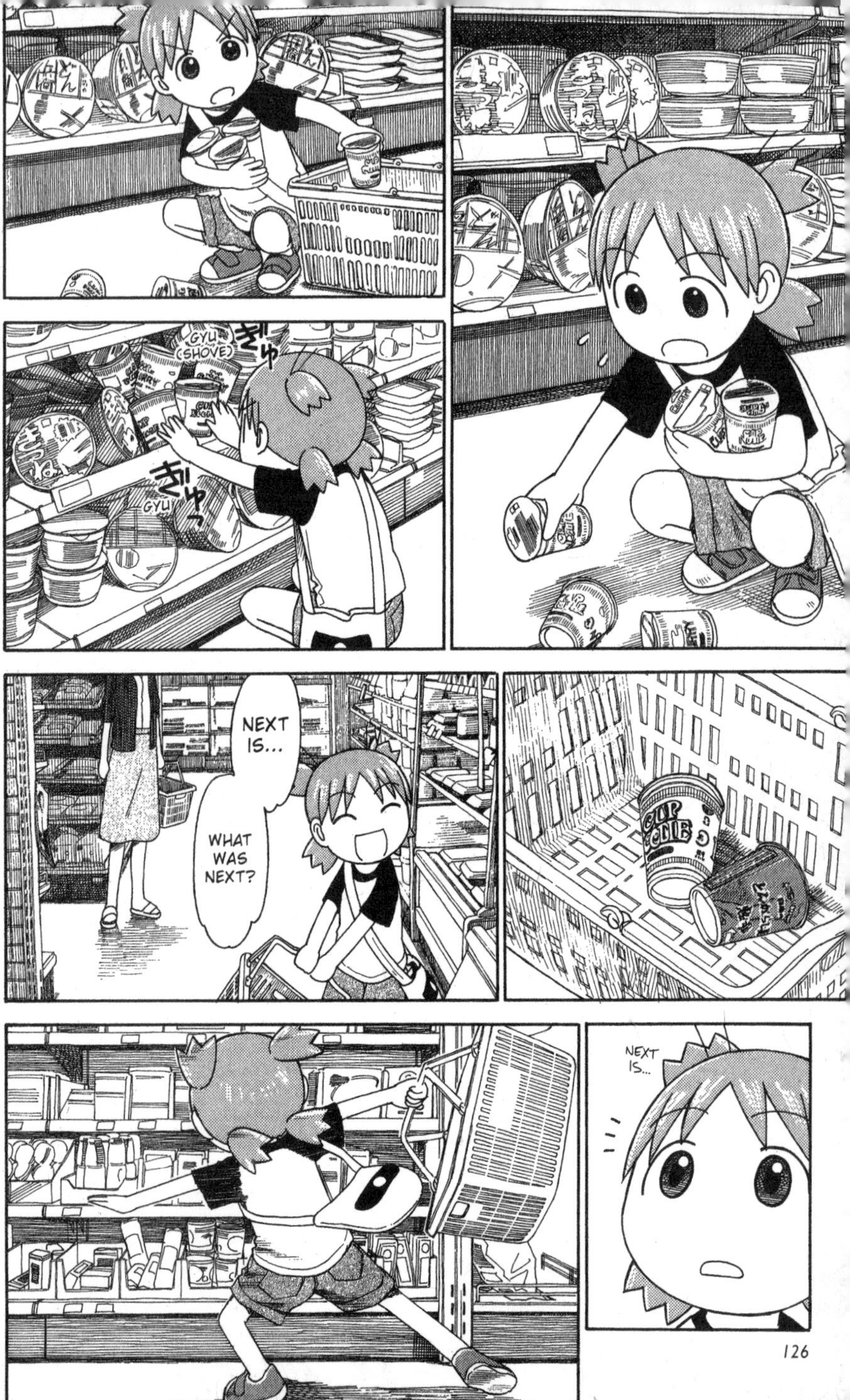
ぎゅ
GYU (SHOVE)
ぎゅっ
GYU
NEXT IS...
WHAT WAS NEXT?
NEXT IS...

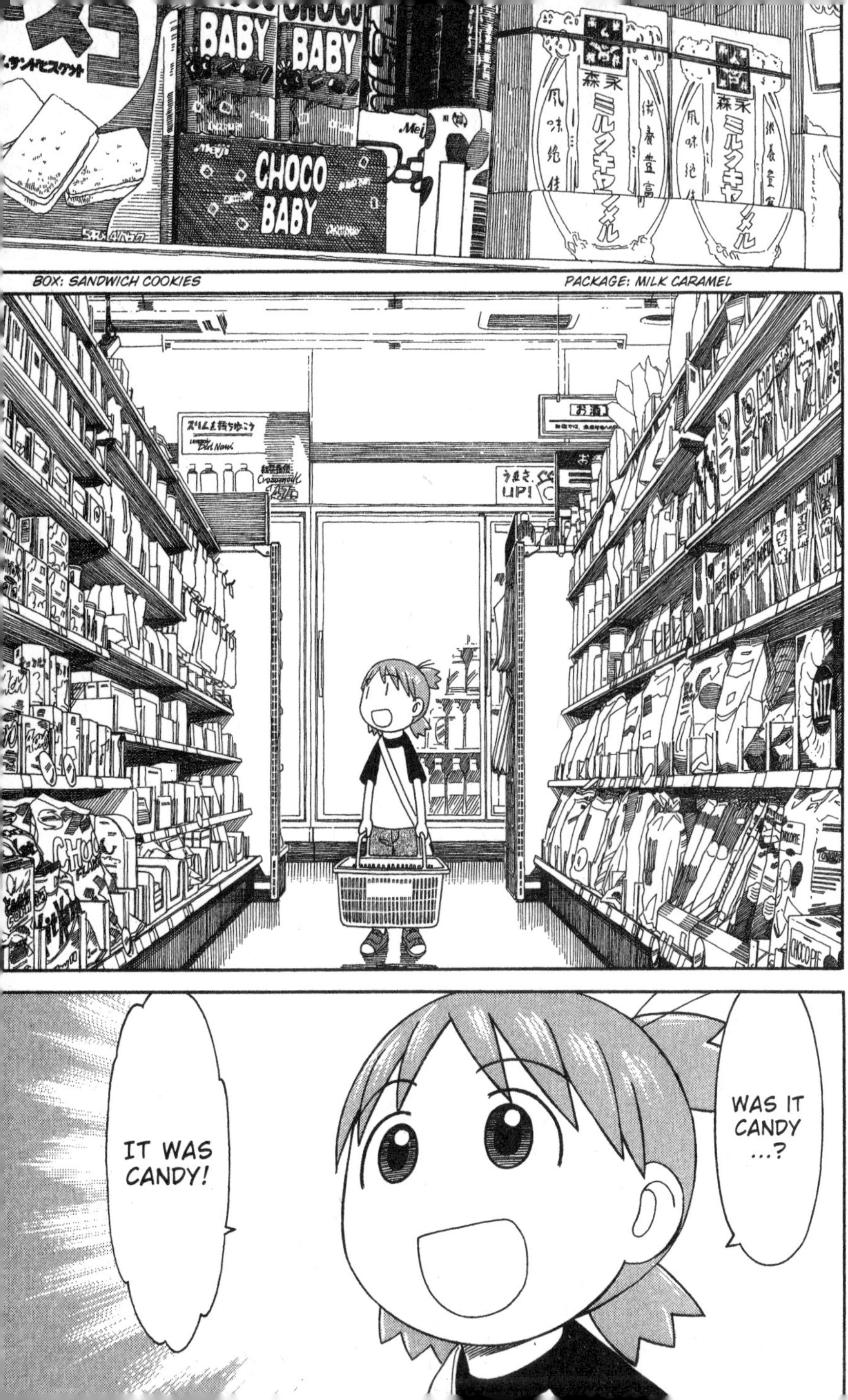
森永 ミルクキャラメル
CHOCO BABY
BOX: SANDWICH COOKIES
PACKAGE: MILK CARAMEL
WAS IT CANDY ...?
IT WAS CANDY!

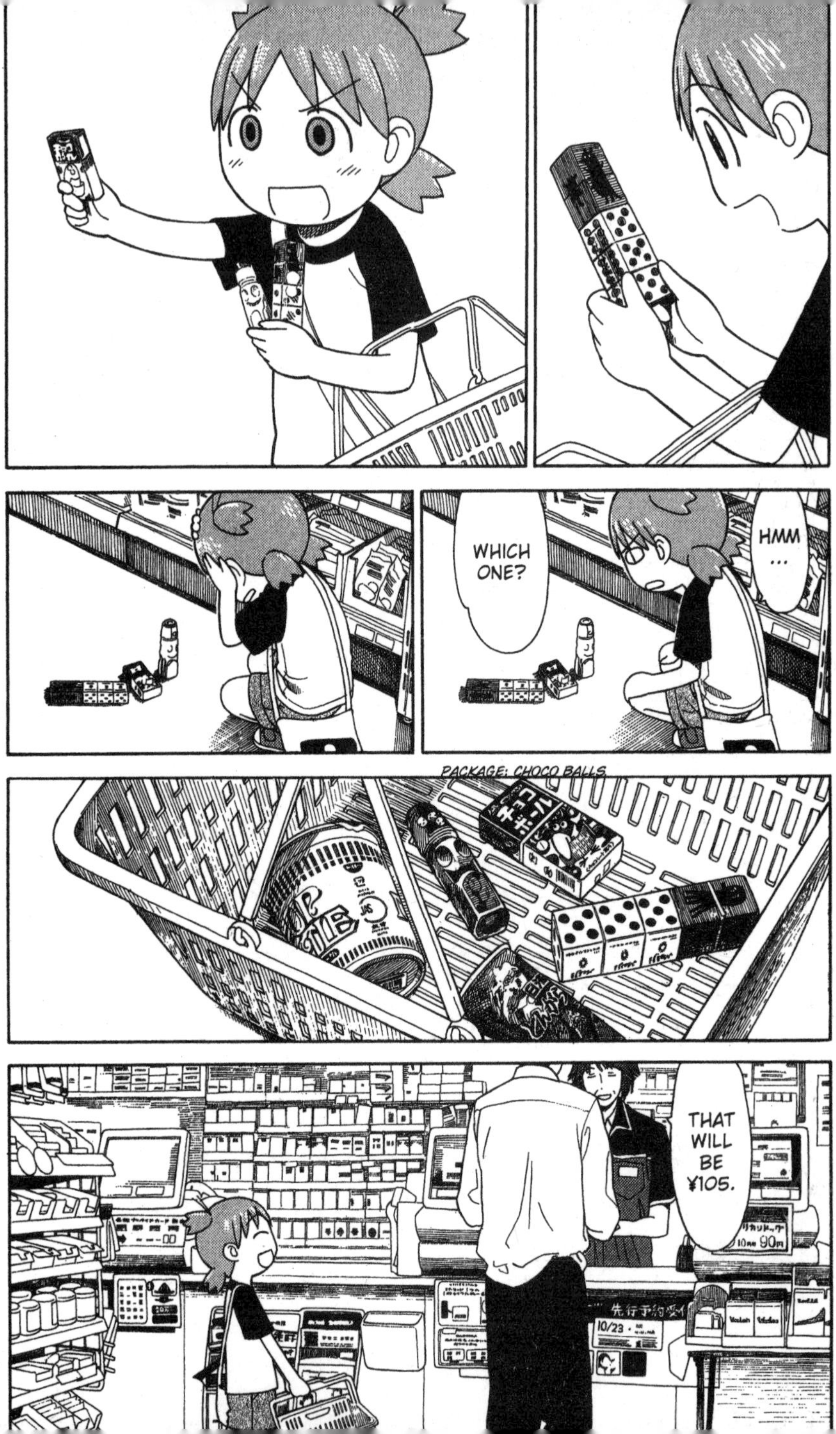
HMM ...
WHICH ONE?
PACKAGE: CHOCO BALLS
THAT WILL BE ¥105.

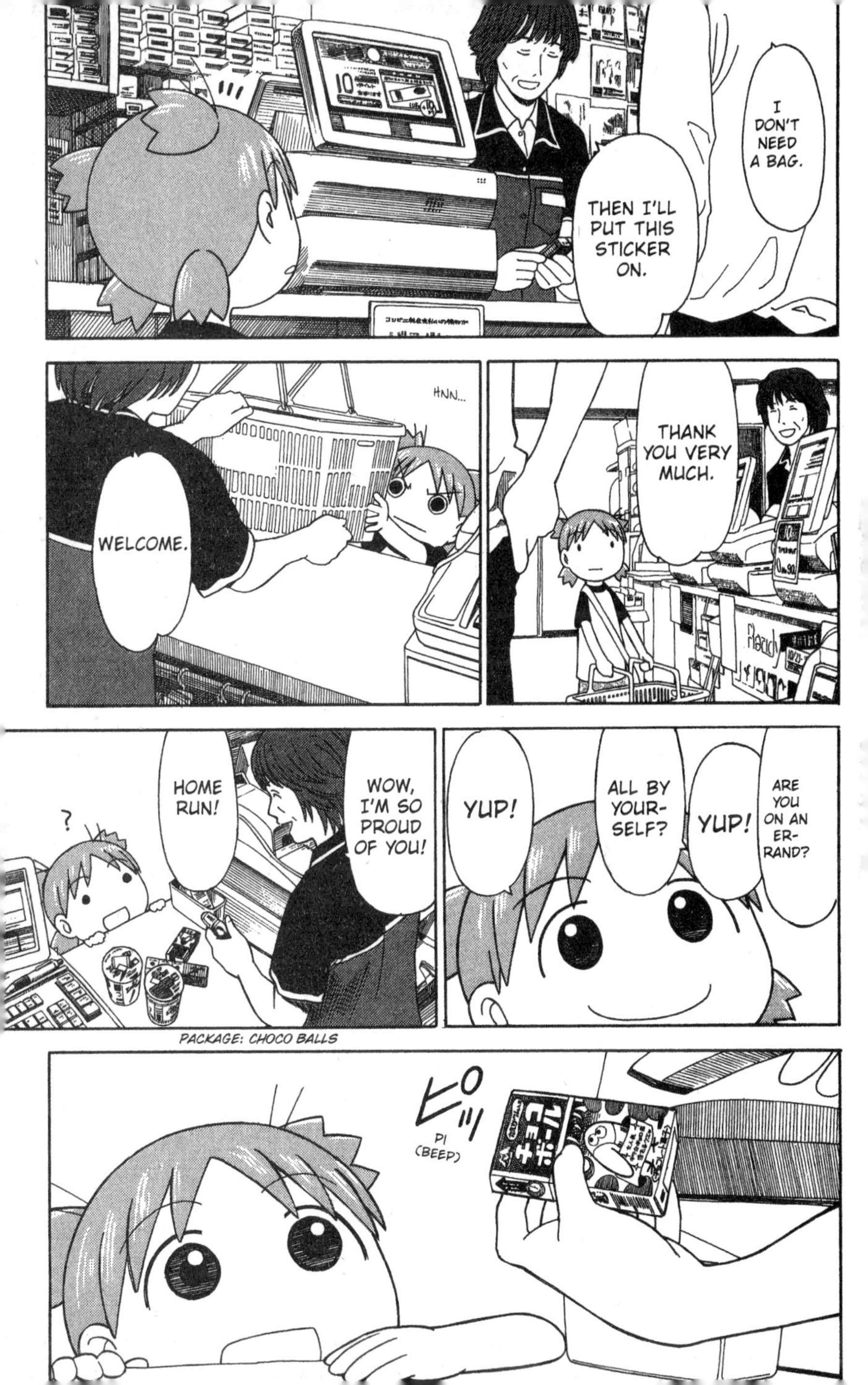
I DON'T NEED A BAG.
THEN I'LL PUT THIS STICKER ON.
THANK YOU VERY MUCH.
HNN...
WELCOME.
ARE YOU ON AN ERRAND?
YUP!
ALL BY YOURSELF?
YUP!
WOW, I'M SO PROUD OF YOU!
HOME RUN!
?
PACKAGE: CHOCO BALLS
PI (BEEP)

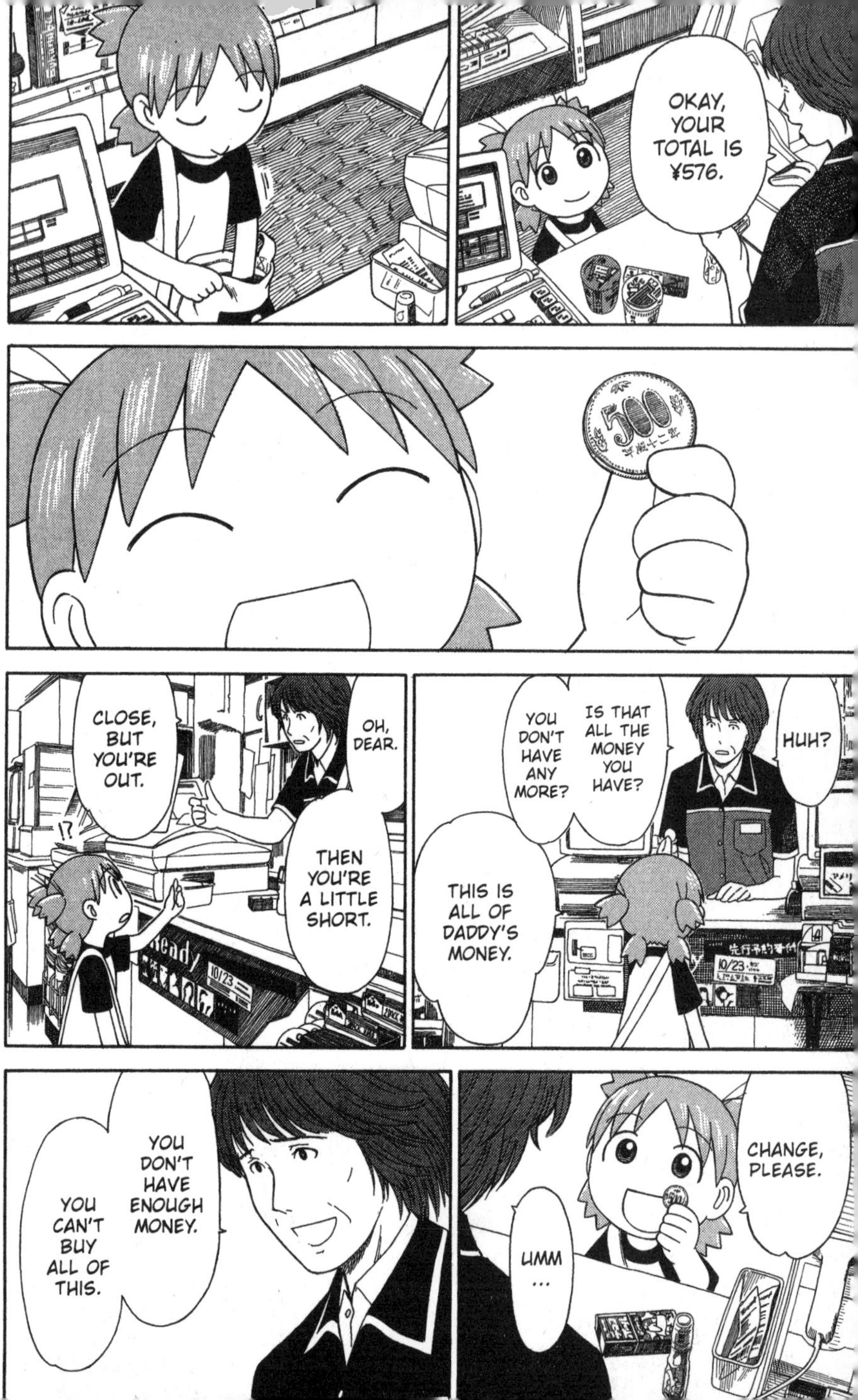

OKAY, YOUR TOTAL IS ¥576.
HUH?
IS THAT ALL THE MONEY YOU HAVE?
YOU DON'T HAVE ANY MORE?
THIS IS ALL OF DADDY'S MONEY.
OH, DEAR.
CLOSE, BUT YOU'RE OUT.
!?
THEN YOU'RE A LITTLE SHORT.
CHANGE, PLEASE.
UMM ...
YOU DON'T HAVE ENOUGH MONEY.
YOU CAN'T BUY ALL OF THIS.

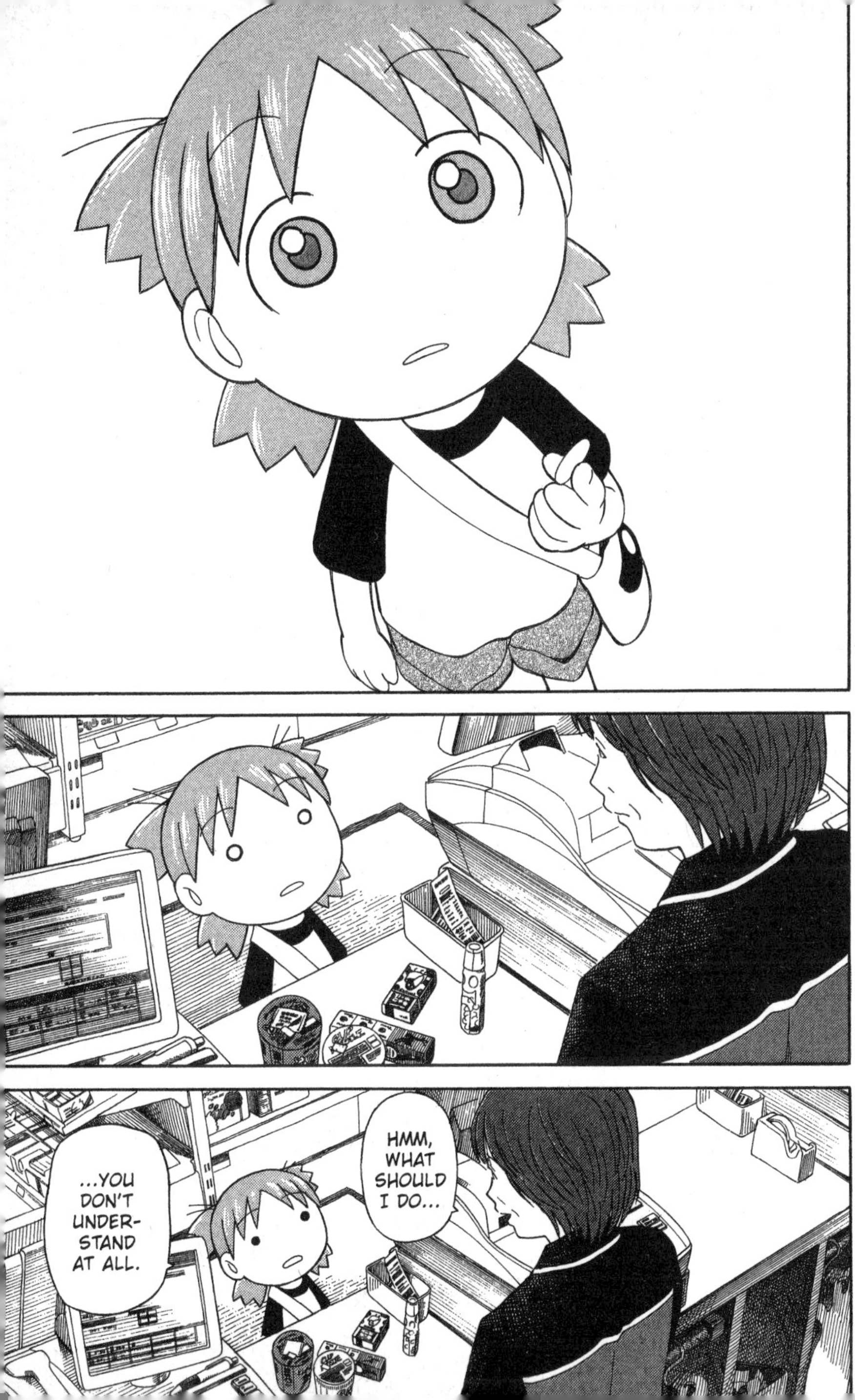
HMM, WHAT SHOULD I DO...
...YOU DON'T UNDER-STAND AT ALL.

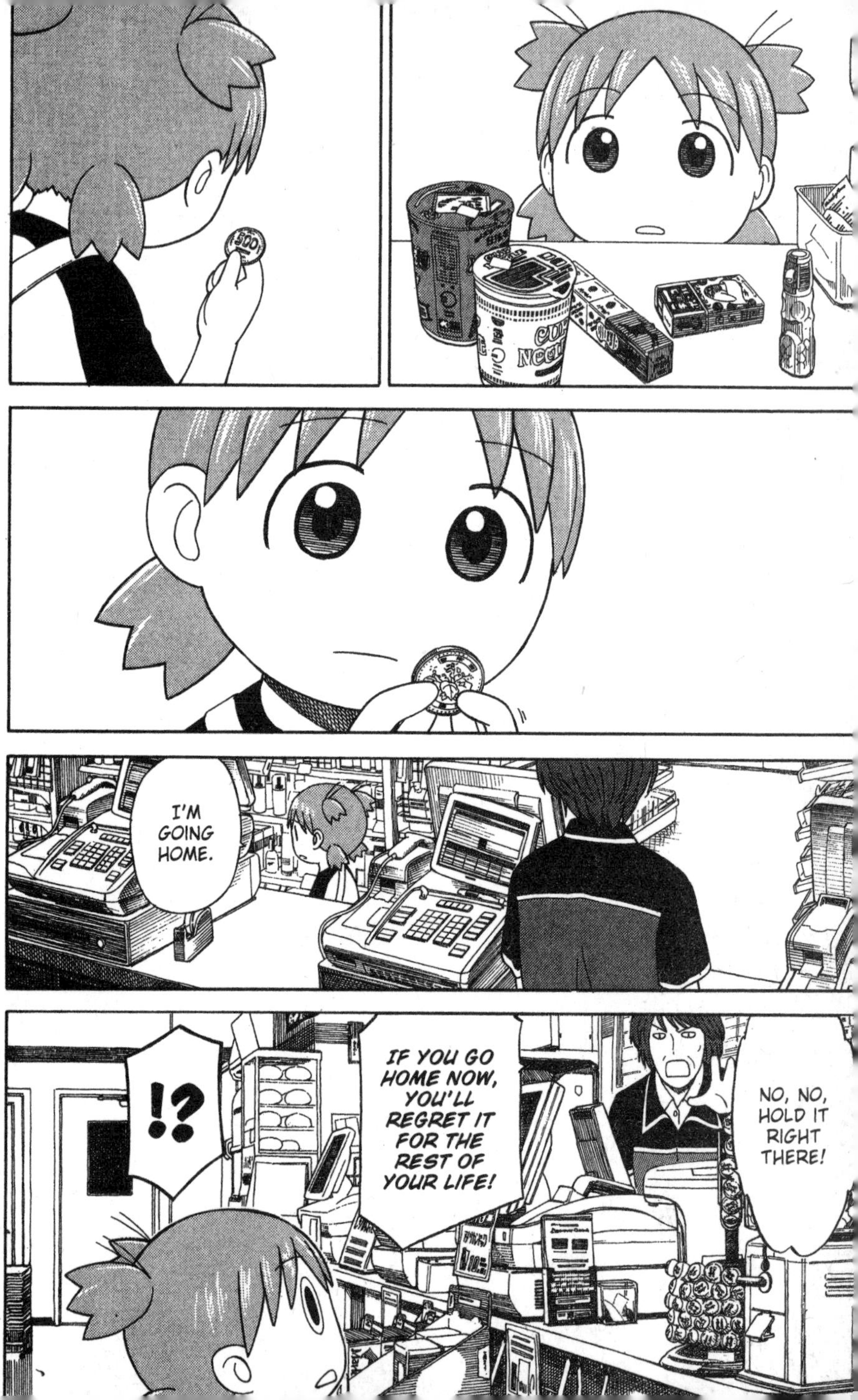
I'M GOING HOME.
NO, NO, HOLD IT RIGHT THERE!
IF YOU GO HOME NOW, YOU'LL REGRET IT FOR THE REST OF YOUR LIFE!
!?

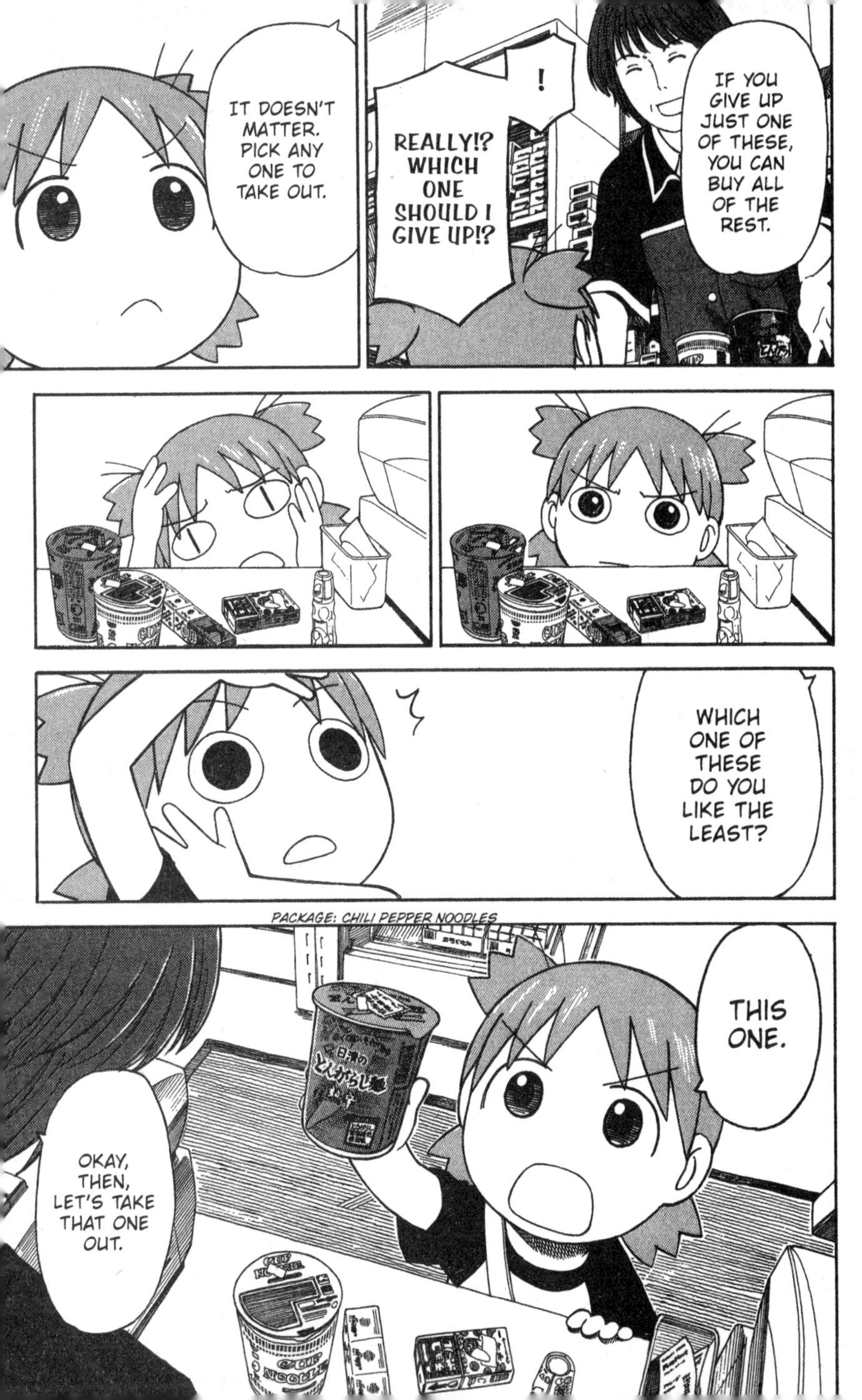
IF YOU GIVE UP JUST ONE OF THESE, YOU CAN BUY ALL OF THE REST.
!
REALLY!? WHICH ONE SHOULD I GIVE UP!?
IT DOESN'T MATTER. PICK ANY ONE TO TAKE OUT.
WHICH ONE OF THESE DO YOU LIKE THE LEAST?
PACKAGE: CHILI PEPPER NOODLES
THIS ONE.
OKAY, THEN, LET'S TAKE THAT ONE OUT.

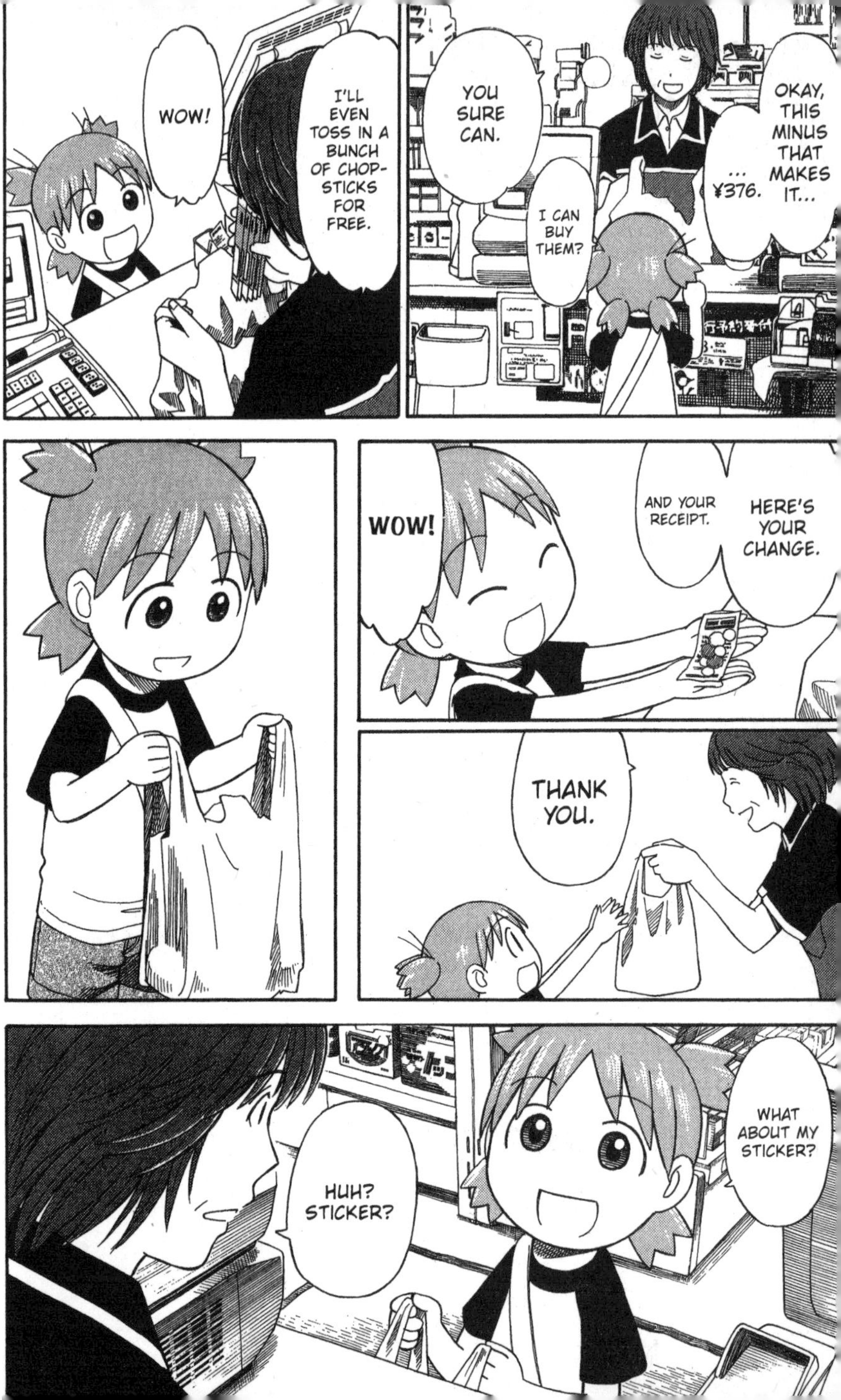
OKAY, THIS MINUS THAT MAKES IT...
...¥376.
I CAN BUY THEM?
YOU SURE CAN.
I'LL EVEN TOSS IN A BUNCH OF CHOP-STICKS FOR FREE.
WOW!
HERE'S YOUR CHANGE.
AND YOUR RECEIPT.
WOW!
THANK YOU.
WHAT ABOUT MY STICKER?
HUH? STICKER?

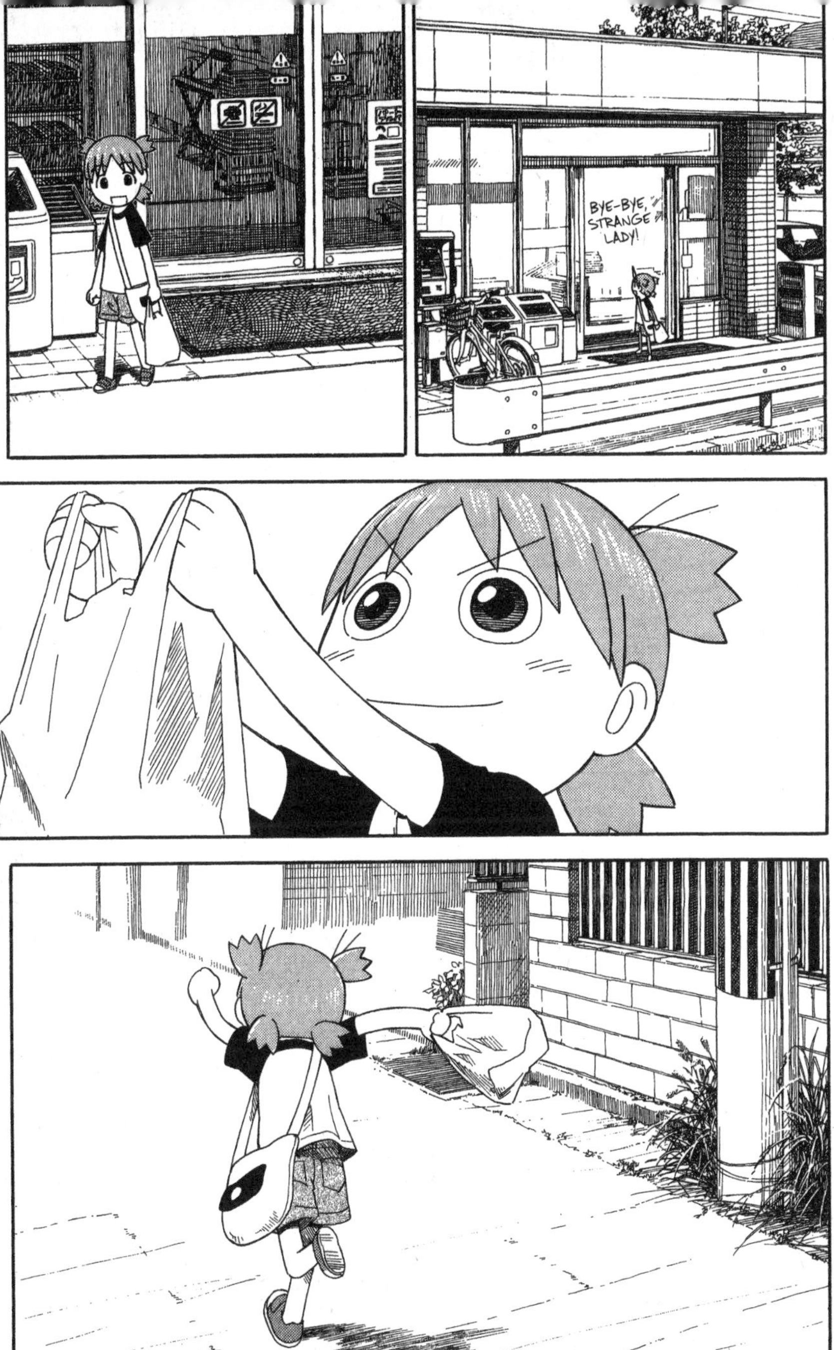
BYE-BYE, STRANGE LADY!

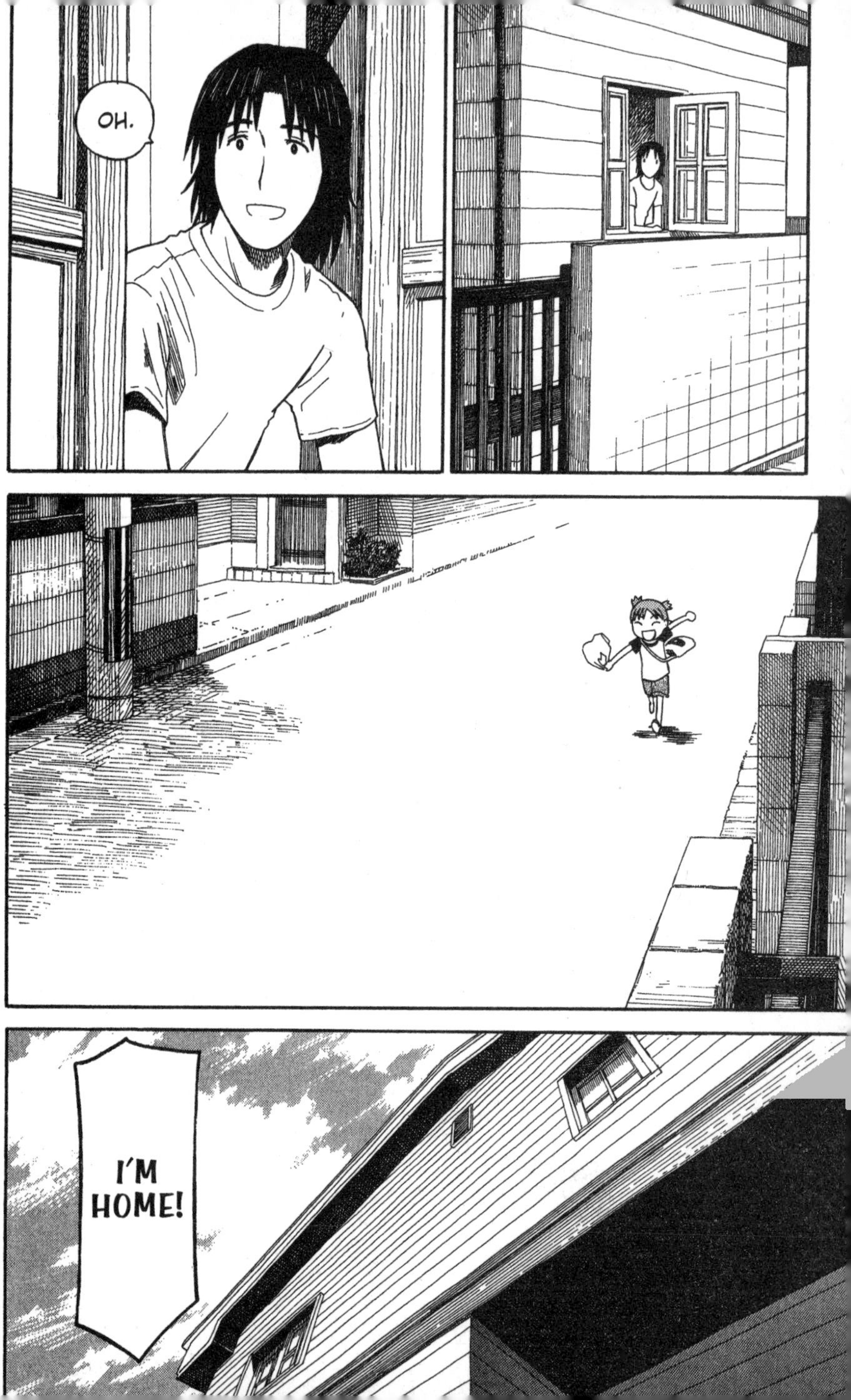
OH.
I'M HOME!

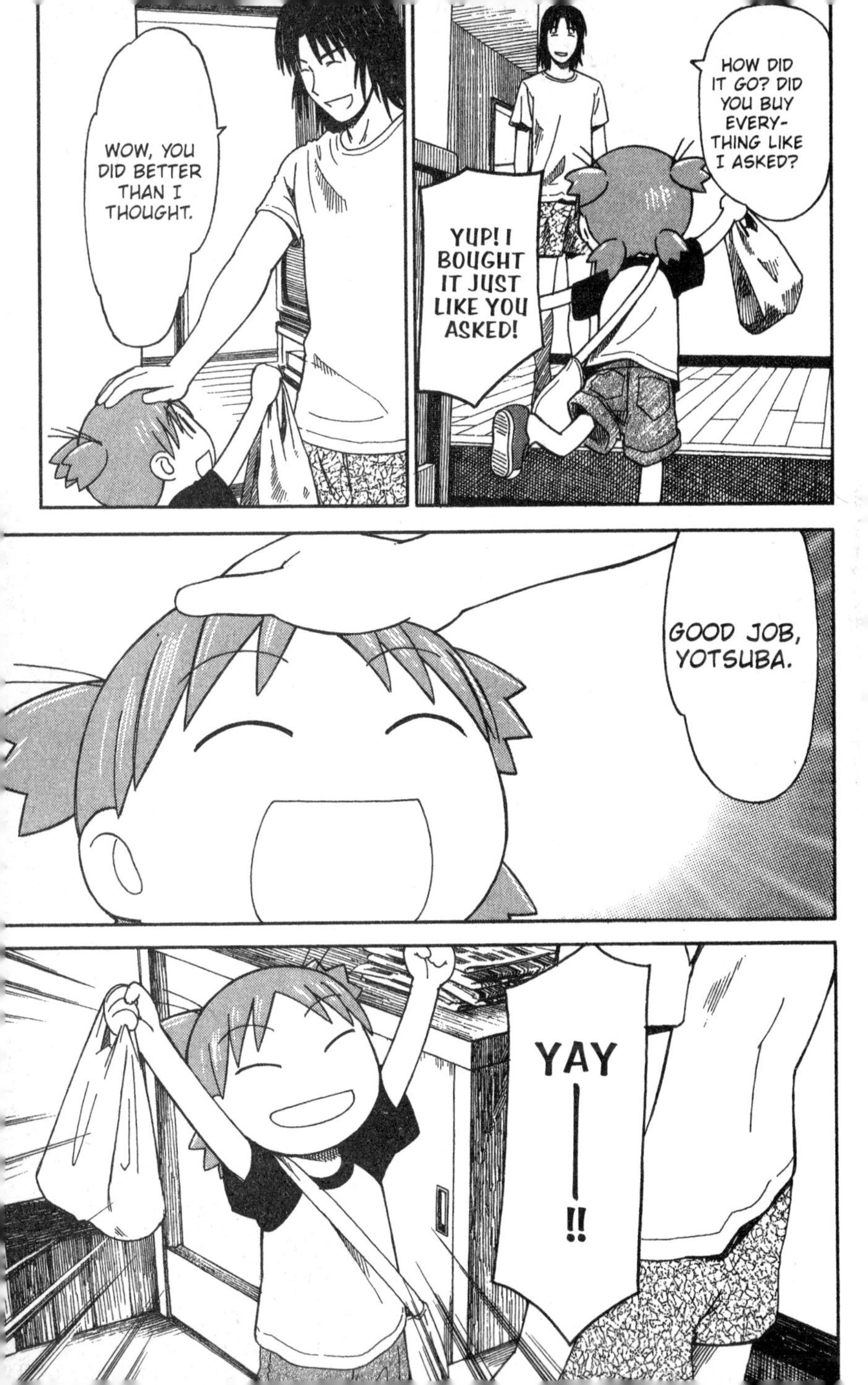
HOW DID IT GO? DID YOU BUY EVERY-THING LIKE I ASKED?
YUP! I BOUGHT IT JUST LIKE YOU ASKED!
WOW, YOU DID BETTER THAN I THOUGHT.
GOOD JOB, YOTSUBA.
YAY——!!

YOTSUBA&!

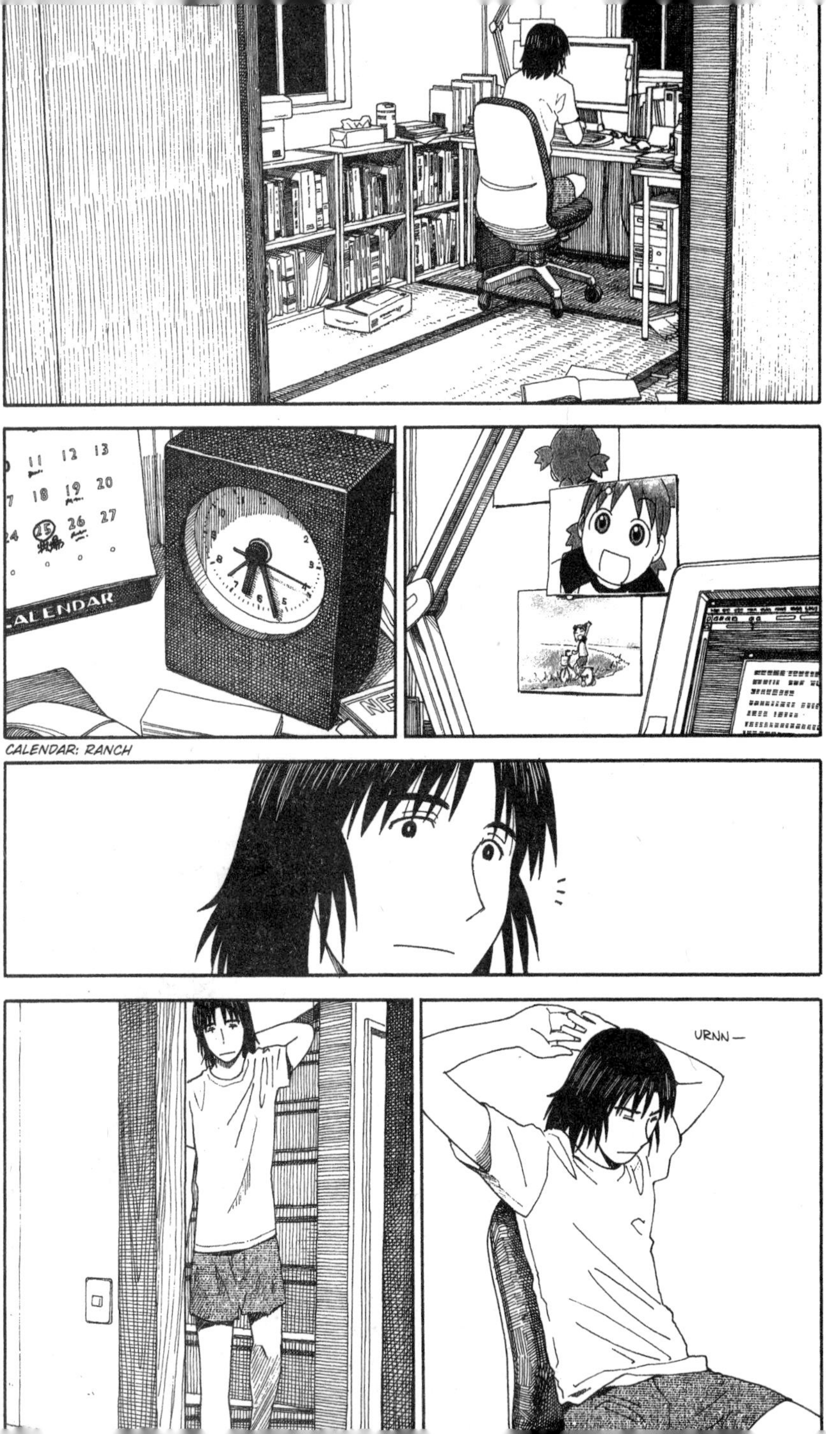
CALENDAR
CALENDAR: RANCH
URNN—

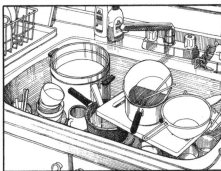

I WOULDN'T BE SURPRISED IF A NEW LIFE-FORM STARTED GROWING IN THERE.

YOTSUBA, ABOUT DINNER...

HEY!

I GUESS WE'LL ORDER TAKE-OUT.

......

GUUU (SNOOORE)

OH.

PACHI
(BLINK)

SHE'S SLEEPING ALREADY?

MUKU
(SHF.)

HEY, YOTSUBA...

LET'S TAKE OFF!

TIME TO GO TO THE RANCH!

WHAT!?

!?

WE'LL BE GOING TO THE RANCH TOMOR- ROW.

WE'RE NOT TAKING OFF ANYWHERE.

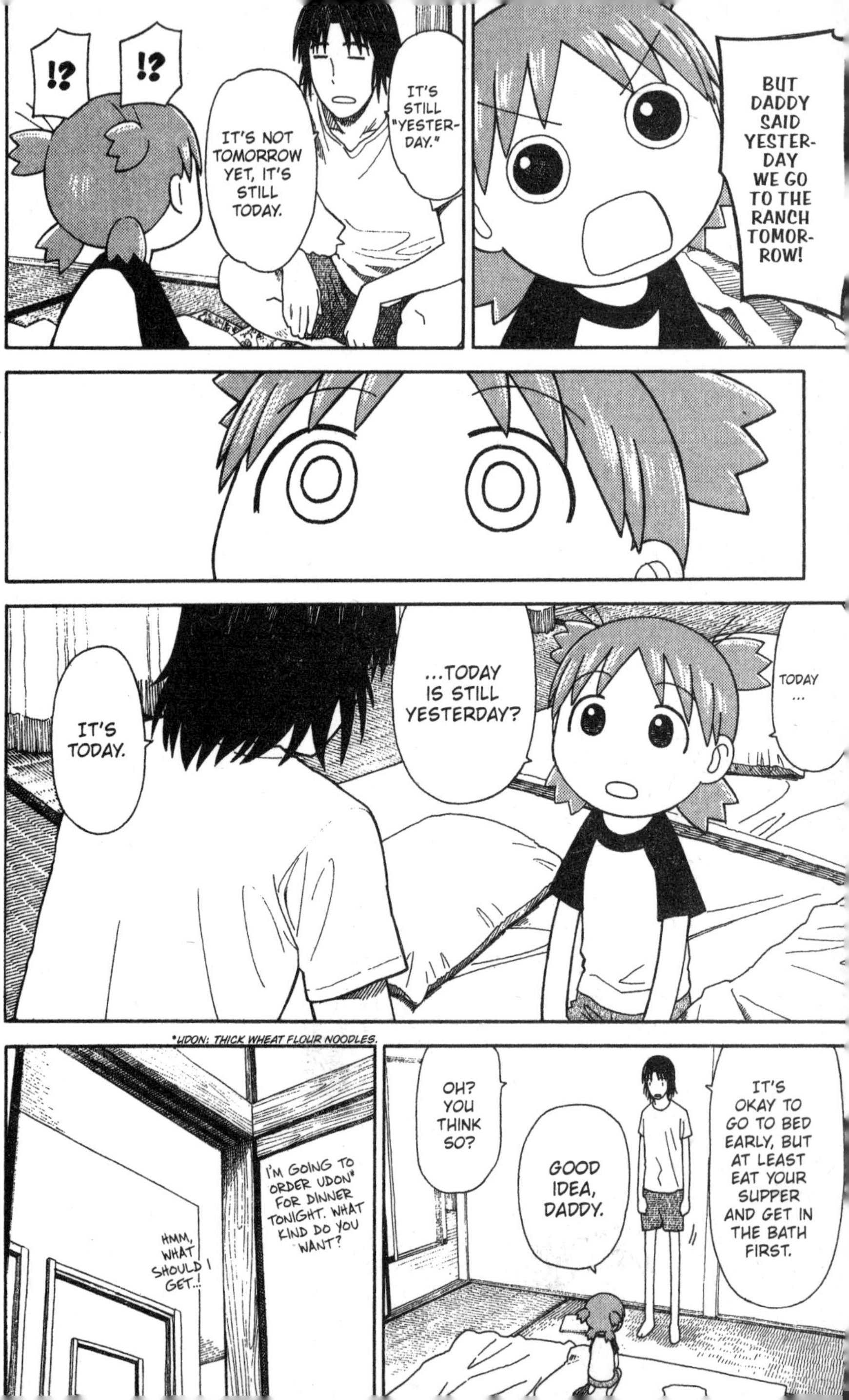
BUT DADDY SAID YESTERDAY WE GO TO THE RANCH TOMORROW!
IT'S STILL "YESTERDAY."
IT'S NOT TOMORROW YET, IT'S STILL TODAY.
!?
!?
TODAY ...
...TODAY IS STILL YESTERDAY?
IT'S TODAY.
IT'S OKAY TO GO TO BED EARLY, BUT AT LEAST EAT YOUR SUPPER AND GET IN THE BATH FIRST.
GOOD IDEA, DADDY.
OH? YOU THINK SO?
I'M GOING TO ORDER UDON* FOR DINNER TONIGHT. WHAT KIND DO YOU WANT?
HMM, WHAT SHOULD I GET...
*UDON: THICK WHEAT FLOUR NOODLES.

FIVE! SIX!
SEVEN!

YOU
SLEPT TOO
MUCH THIS
AFTERNOON.

CAN'T
SLEEP!

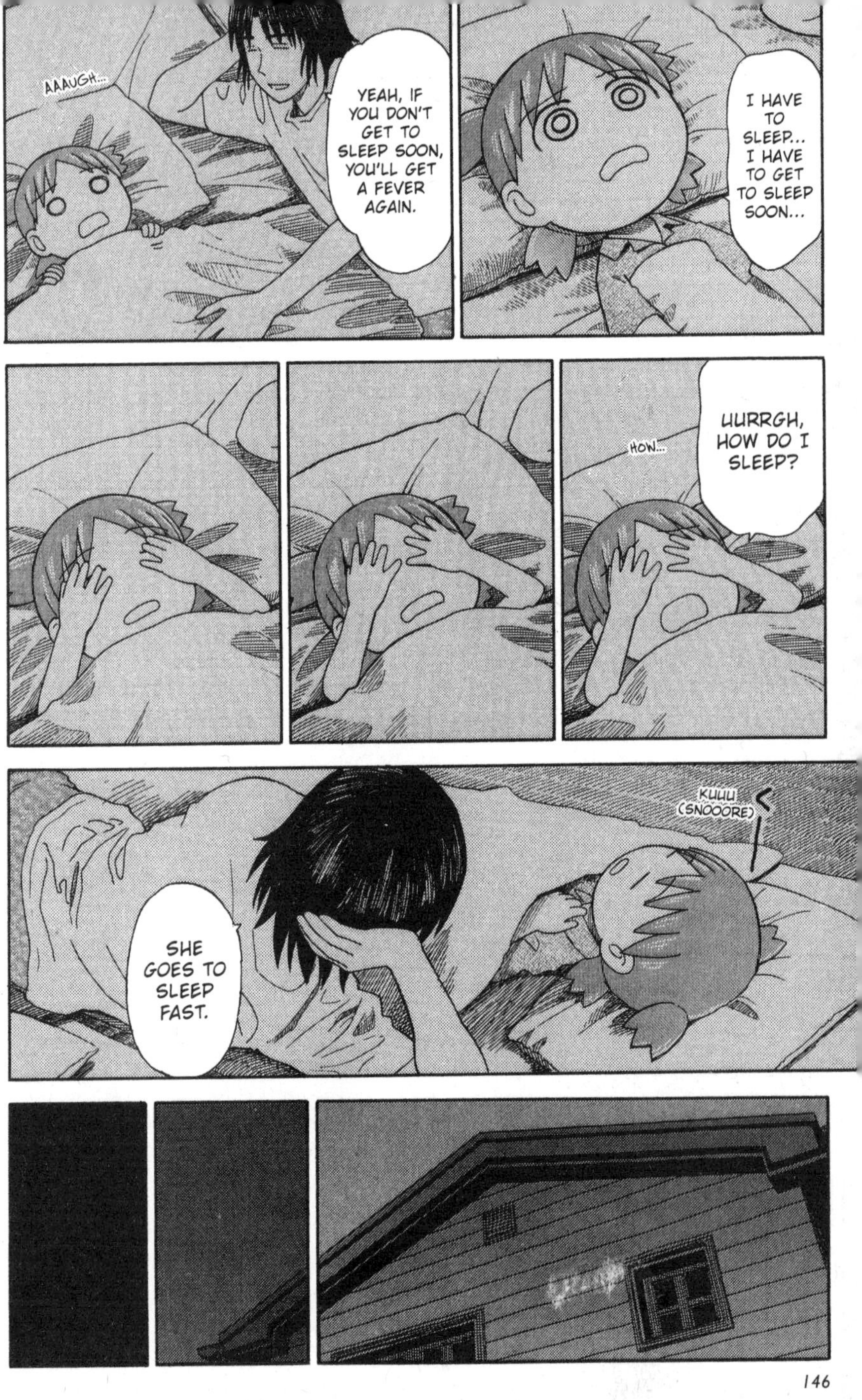
I HAVE TO SLEEP... I HAVE TO GET TO SLEEP SOON...
YEAH, IF YOU DON'T GET TO SLEEP SOON, YOU'LL GET A FEVER AGAIN.
AAAUGH...
UURRGH, HOW DO I SLEEP?
HOW...
KUUU (SNOOORE)
SHE GOES TO SLEEP FAST.

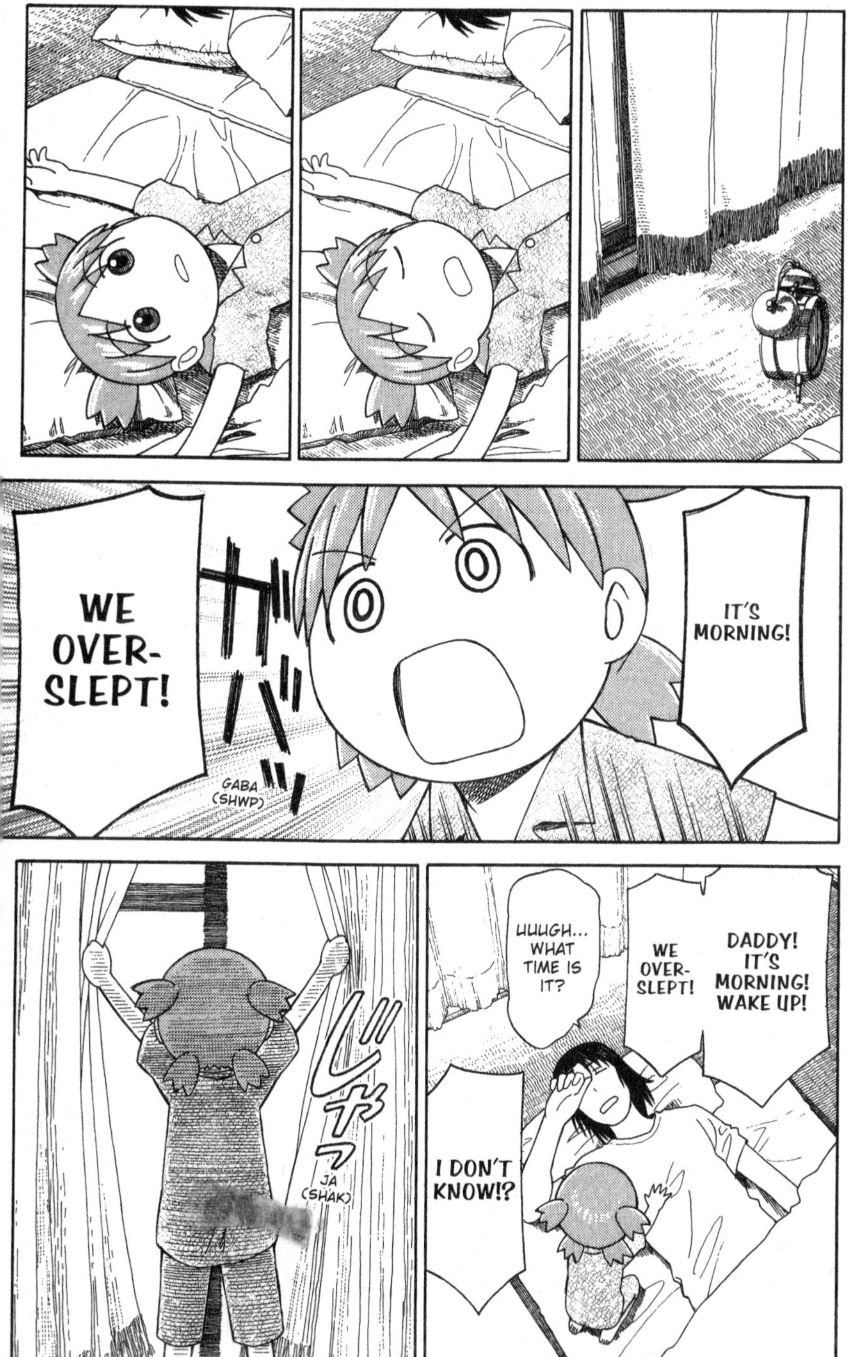
IT'S MORNING!
GABA (SHWP)
WE OVER-SLEPT!
DADDY! IT'S MORNING! WAKE UP!
WE OVER-SLEPT!
HUUGH... WHAT TIME IS IT?
I DON'T KNOW!?
JA (SHAK)

YOTSUBA& TAKING OFF

#47

SFX: GARA (CLATTER)

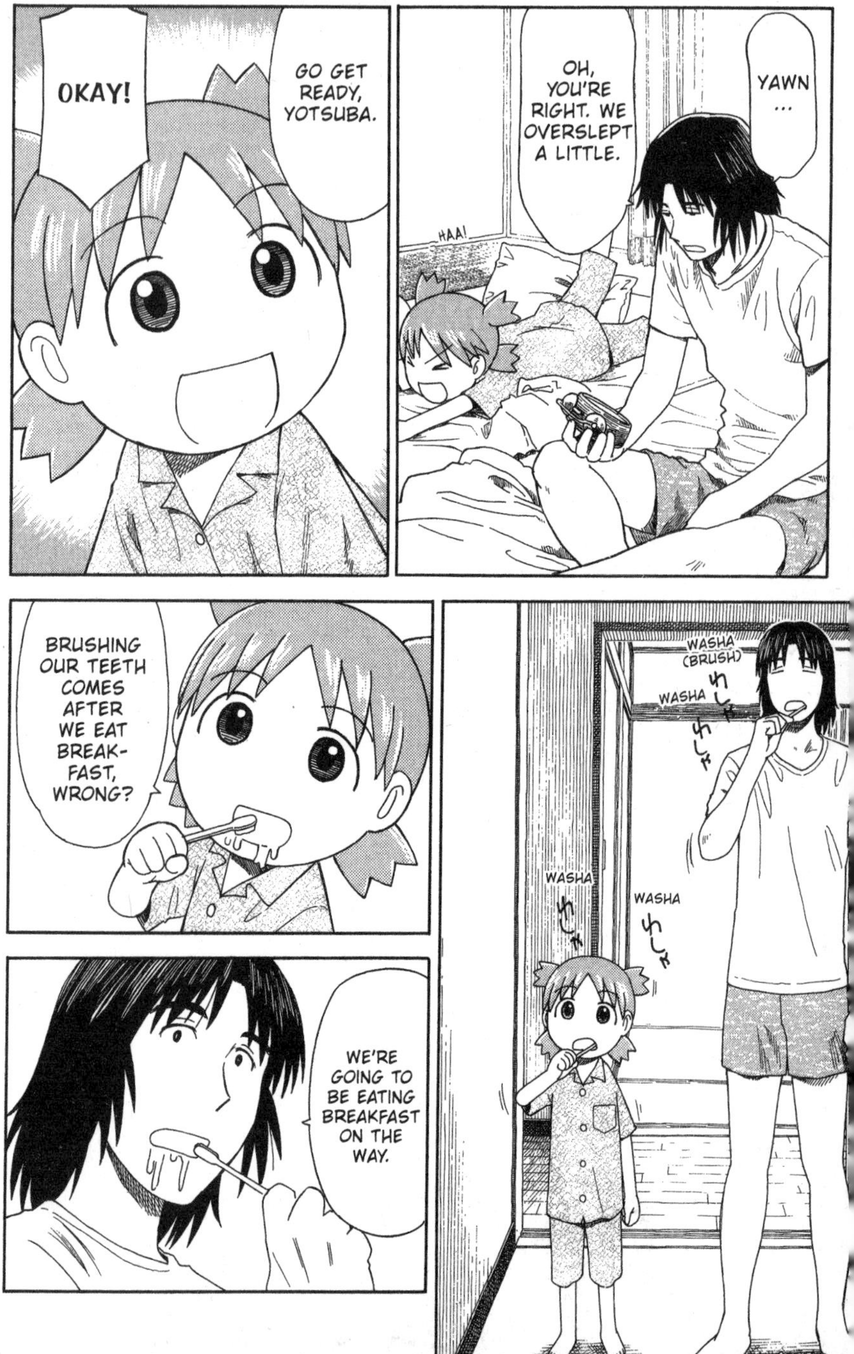
YAWN ...
OH, YOU'RE RIGHT. WE OVERSLEPT A LITTLE.
HAA!
GO GET READY, YOTSUBA.
OKAY!
WASHA (BRUSH)
わしゃ
WASHA
わしゃ
WASHA
わしゃ
WASHA
わしゃ
BRUSHING OUR TEETH COMES AFTER WE EAT BREAK-FAST, WRONG?
WE'RE GOING TO BE EATING BREAKFAST ON THE WAY.

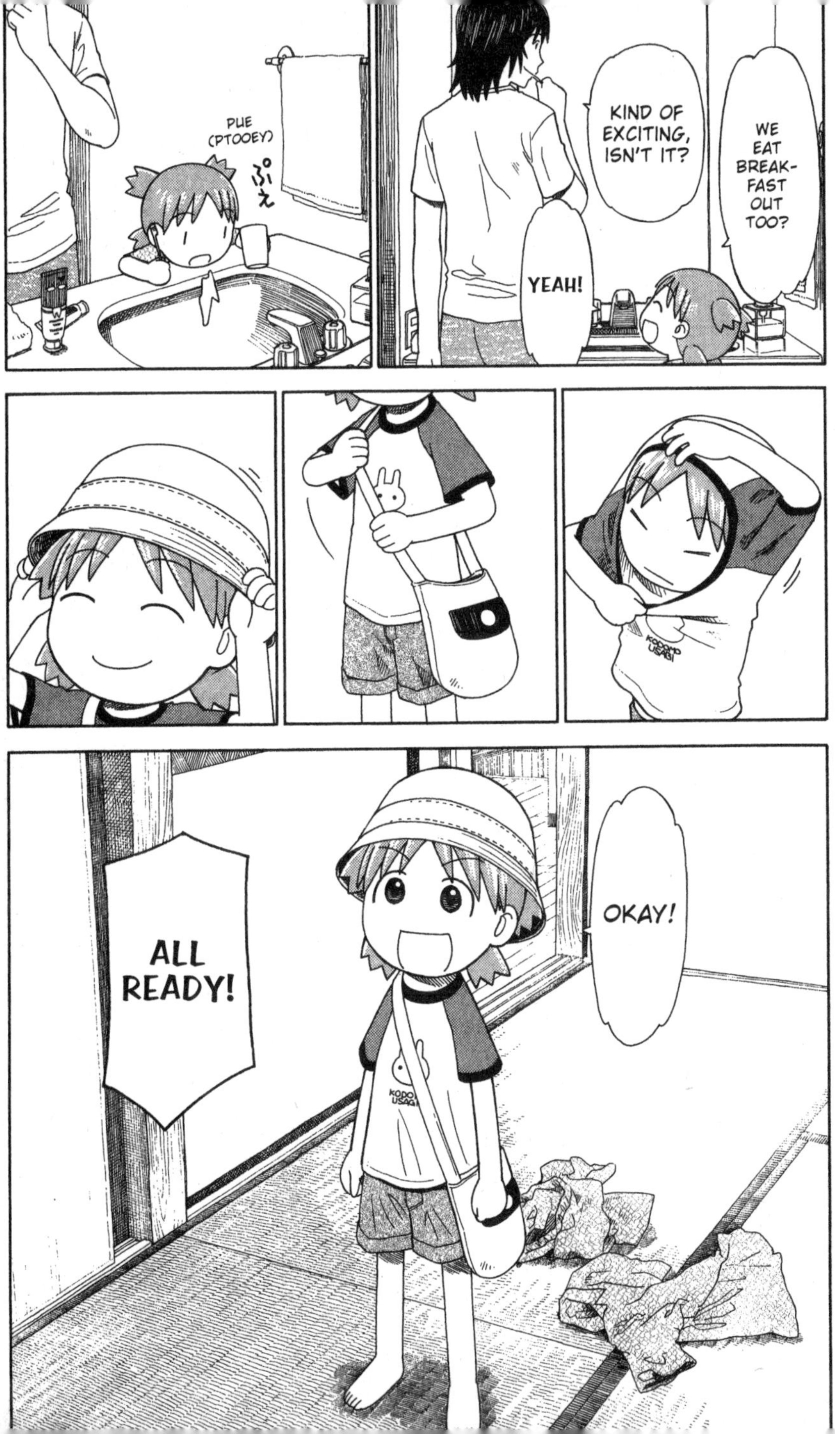
WE EAT BREAK-FAST OUT TOO?
KIND OF EXCITING, ISN'T IT?
YEAH!
PUE (PTOOEY)
ぷえ
KODOMO USAGI
KODOMO USAGI
OKAY!
ALL READY!

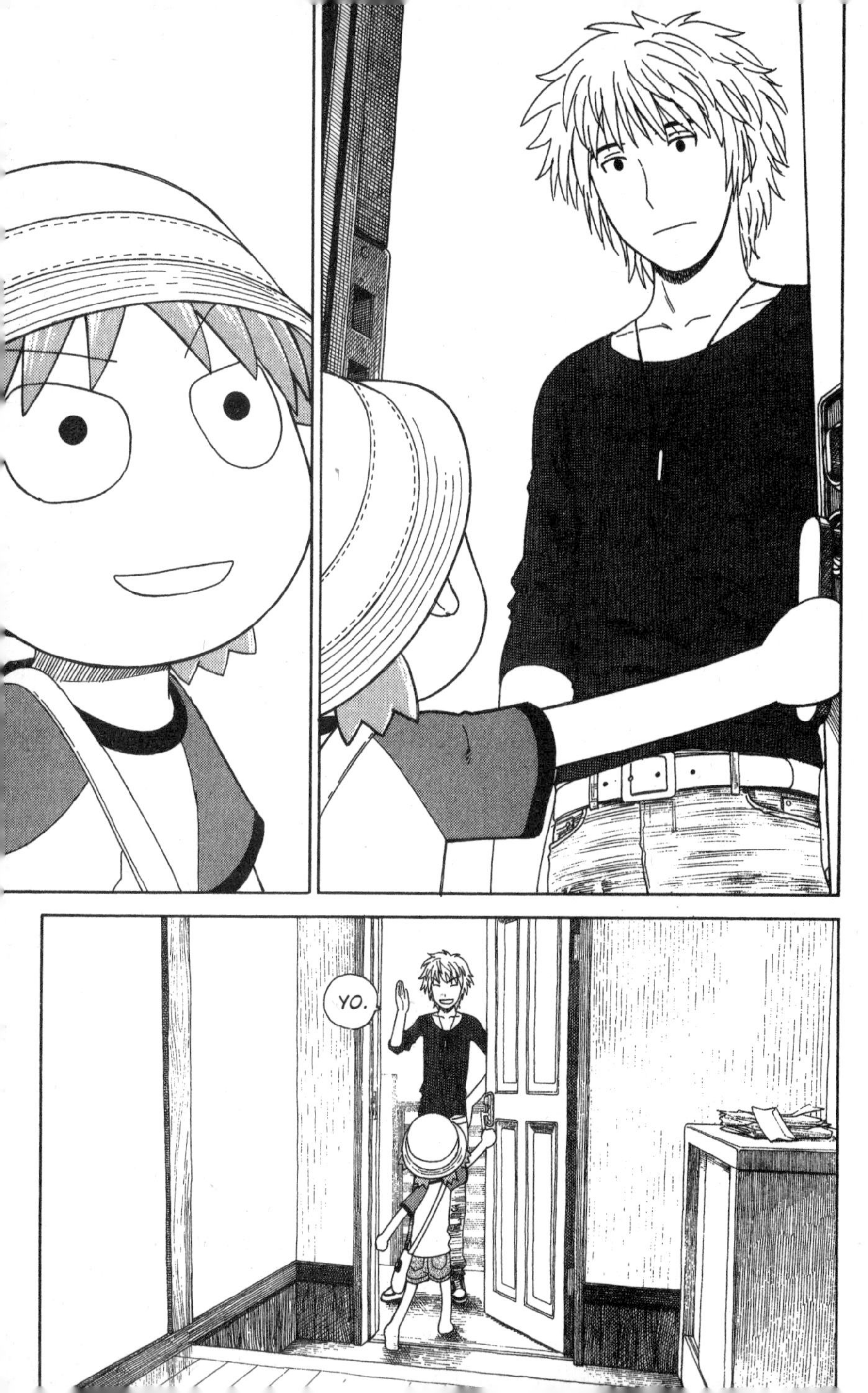
YO.

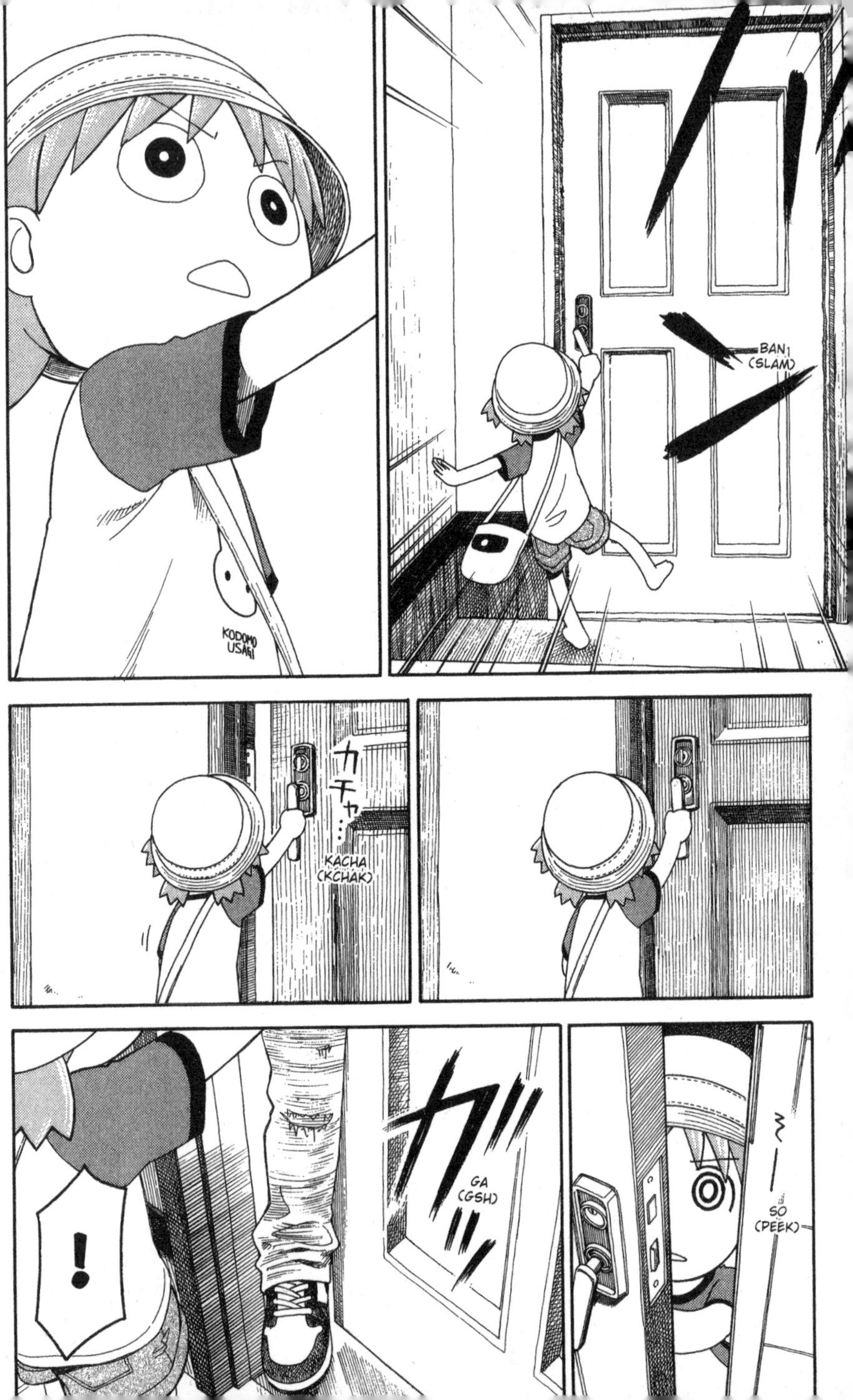
BAN (SLAM)
KODOMO USAGI
カチャ…
KACHA (KCHAK)
SO (PEEK)
GA (GSH)
!

155

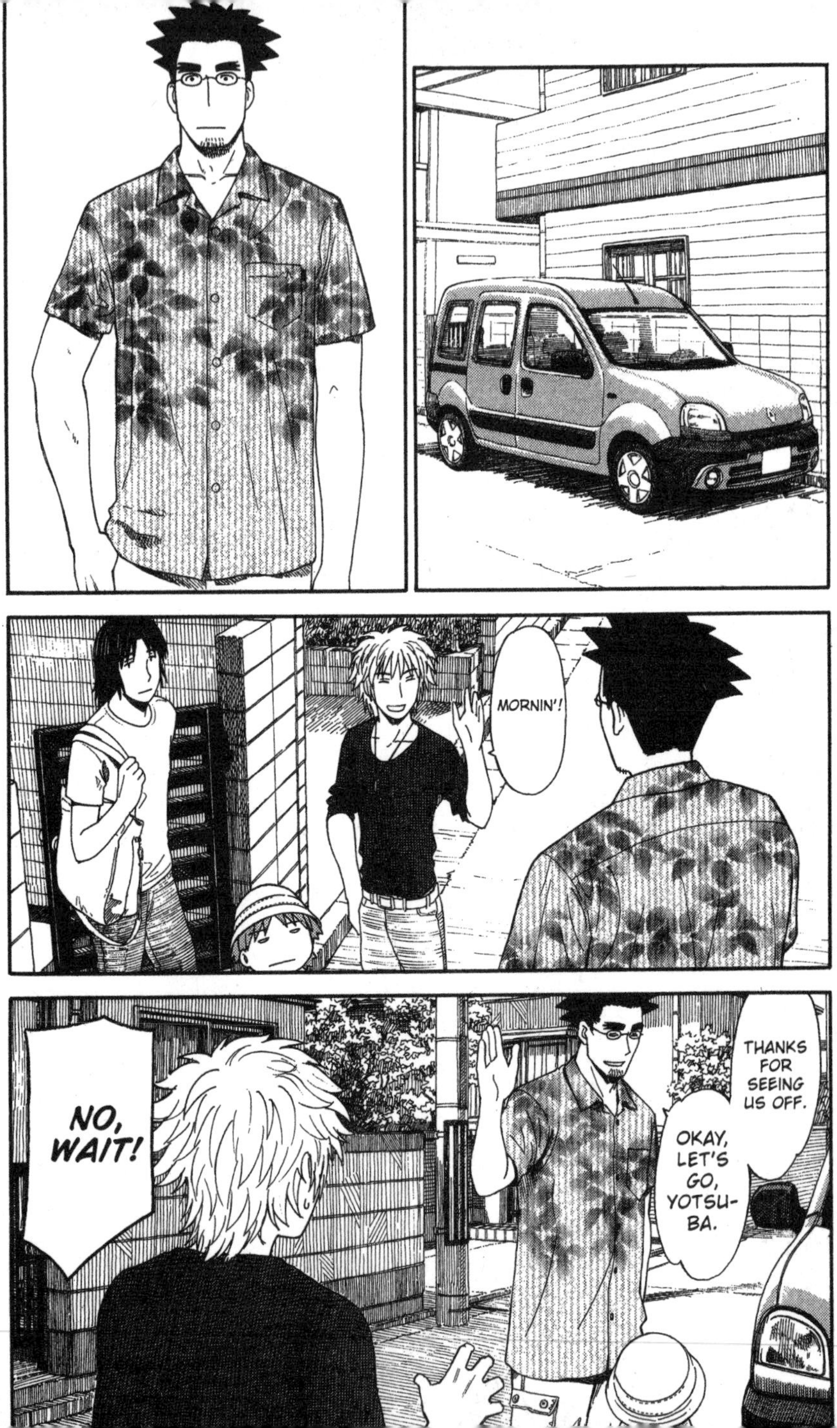
MORNIN'!
THANKS FOR SEEING US OFF.
OKAY, LET'S GO, YOTSU-BA.
NO, WAIT!

HMM.

I WORKED ON MY DAY OFF THE DAY BEFORE YESTERDAY TOO.

I TOOK A VACATION DAY.

I DON'T TAKE MANY DAYS OFF, SO I'VE GOT A BUNCH OF THEM NOW.

DON'T YOU HAVE TO WORK? PLAYING HOOKY?

NOBODY ASKED YOU.

I WANT TO GO TOO.

LET'S GO TO THE RANCH TOGETHER, YOTSUBA!

WHAT DO YOU THINK, YOTSUBA?

YOTSUBA, YANDA SAYS HE WANTS TO GO TOO.

N. O.

YEAH, HE'S RIGHT. THE MORE THE MERRIER.

COME ON, YOTSUBA. THE MORE THE MERRIER!

WHY'D YOU SPELL IT OUT?

HUH!?

WHY NOT!?

EVEN IF IT'S YANDA?

IT'LL BE FUN! CRAZY FUN!

ANSWER HER, ALREADY!

THE 'RULE,' HUH?

HUH? WHY?

THAT'S THE RULE!

YO-TSUBA SAYS "LET'S TAKE OFF"!

SORRY.

FOLLOW THE RULE, YANDA!

GOOD.

...TAKE OFF!

LET'S...

YAAAY!

YOTSUBA SITS IN FRONT!

YAAAY!

I LIKE THE FRONT TOO!

GU
(GLARE)

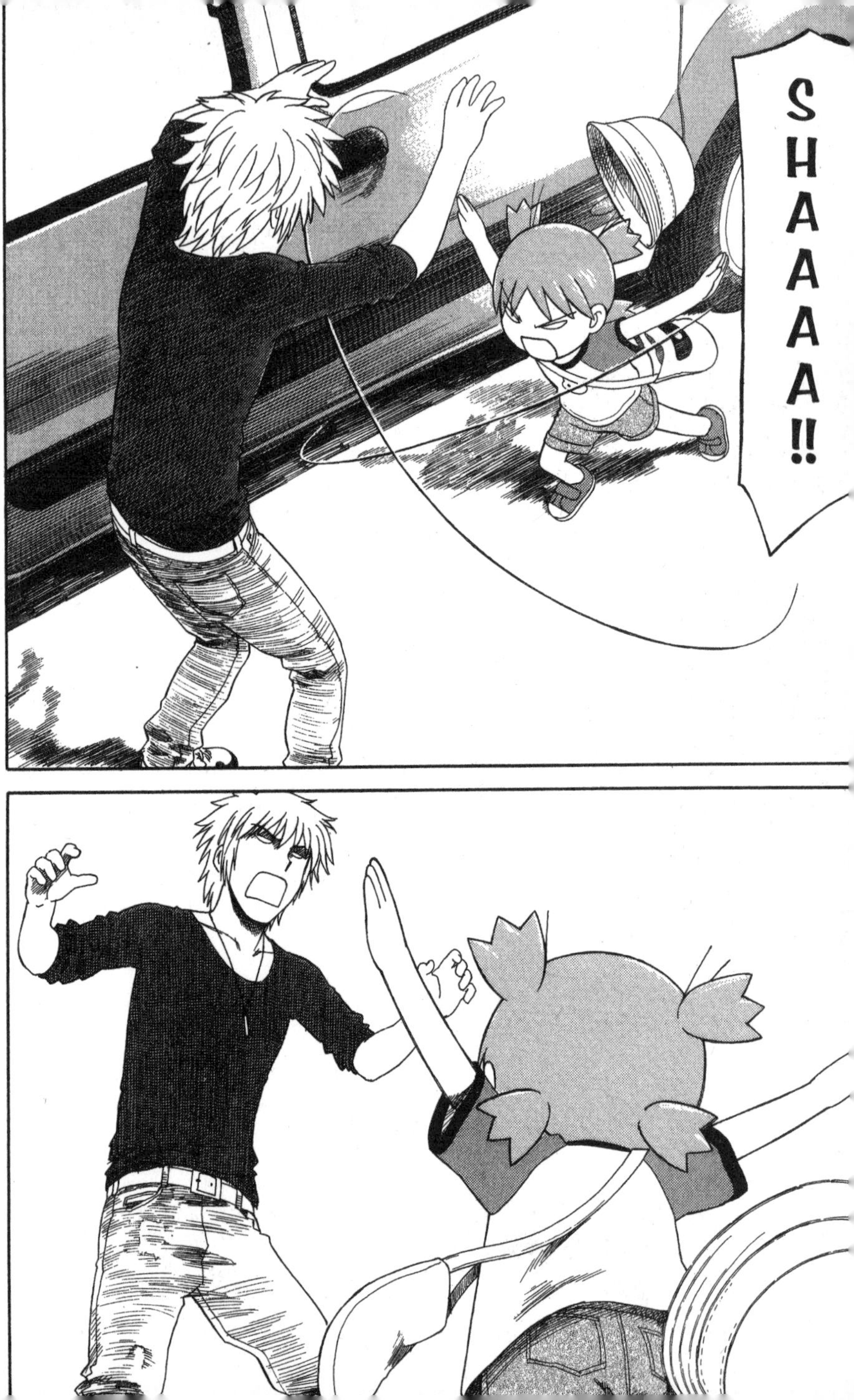
SHAAAAA!!

HUH!? DECIDES WHAT!?

YUP.

WELL, THAT DECIDES IT...

HUH!? WHY!?

HMPH

I'M GETTIN' IN!

I'M GETTIN' IN!

WE'LL LEAVE YOU BEHIND.

YOU GETTING IN OR NOT? WE'LL LEAVE YOU BEHIND.

WOW, THE STEERING WHEEL'S ON THE LEFT? THAT'S PRETTY BRASH FOR A FLORIST'S BRAT.

THIS IS THE FIRST TIME I'VE RIDDEN IN THIS CAR.

SHUT UP. THIS WAS ALL THEY HAD WHEN I BOUGHT IT.

I LIKE THE STEERING WHEEL ON THE RIGHT.

DADDY, I'M HUNGRY.

DID YOU DO SOMETHING BAD?

HUH? HE DIDN'T FEED YOU?

WE HAD NO BREAKFAST.

YOU'RE HUNGRY ALREADY? THAT CAME OUT OF NOWHERE.

HOLD ON A LITTLE LONGER.

WE'RE ALL GOING TO EAT AT A SERVICE AREA.

YOTSUBA HAD CROQUETTE UDON.

BUT HINODEYA'S HANDMADE, SO IT'S GOOD, ISN'T IT?

WHO ASKED YOU?

YOTSUBA HAD UDON FROM HINODEYA YESTERDAY.

WE'LL BE AT THE SERVICE AREA IN ABOUT THIRTY MINUTES.

HOW MUCH LONGER 'TIL WE CAN EAT?

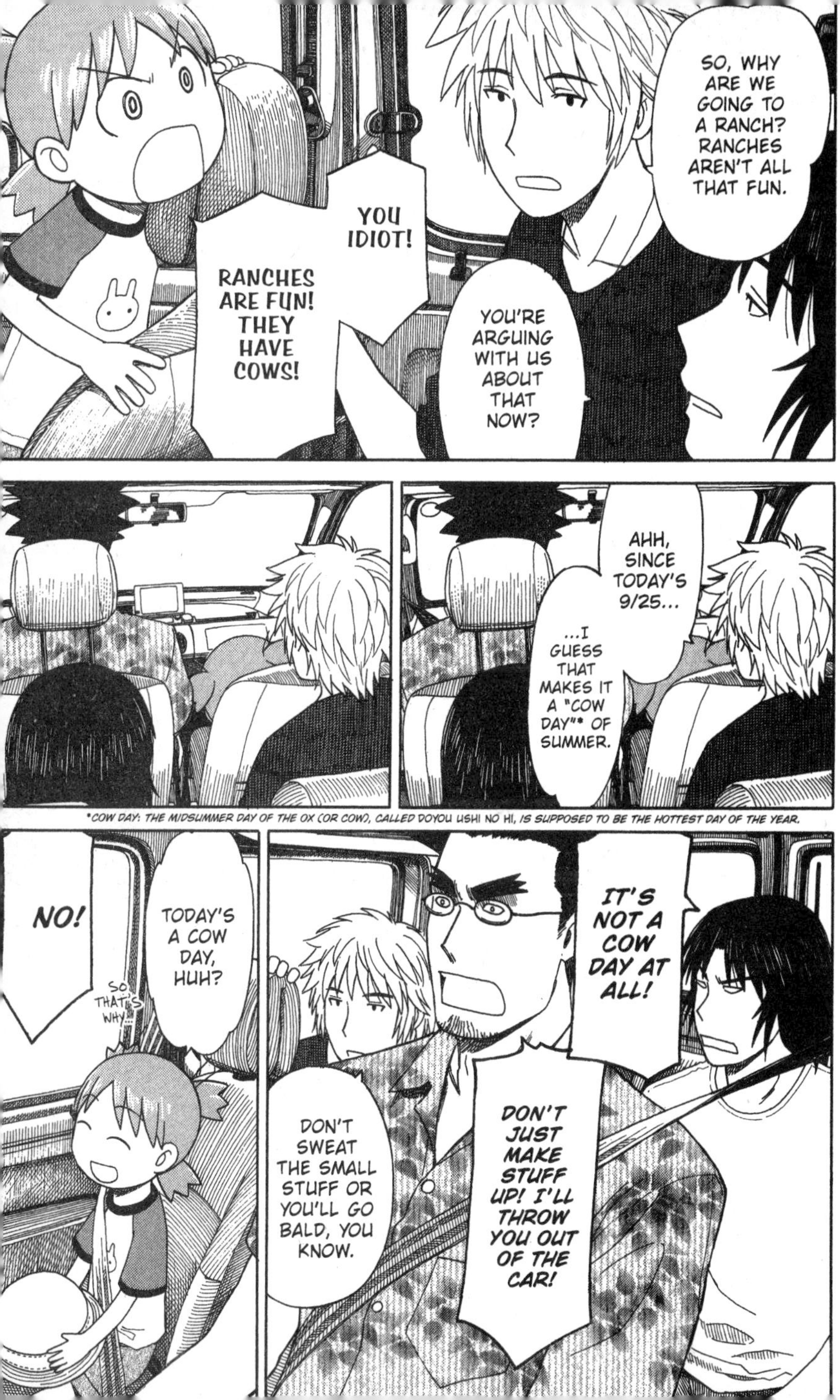
SO, WHY ARE WE GOING TO A RANCH? RANCHES AREN'T ALL THAT FUN.
YOU IDIOT!
RANCHES ARE FUN! THEY HAVE COWS!
YOU'RE ARGUING WITH US ABOUT THAT NOW?
AHH, SINCE TODAY'S 9/25...
...I GUESS THAT MAKES IT A "COW DAY"* OF SUMMER.
IT'S NOT A COW DAY AT ALL!
DON'T JUST MAKE STUFF UP! I'LL THROW YOU OUT OF THE CAR!
DON'T SWEAT THE SMALL STUFF OR YOU'LL GO BALD, YOU KNOW.
TODAY'S A COW DAY, HUH?
NO!
SO THAT'S WHY...

*COW DAY: THE MIDSUMMER DAY OF THE OX (OR COW), CALLED DOYOU USHI NO HI, IS SUPPOSED TO BE THE HOTTEST DAY OF THE YEAR.

JUMBO! IS THAT WHERE YOU PAY THE MONEY!?

YOU PAY THE MONEY WHEN YOU LEAVE. THIS IS WHERE YOU TAKE THE TICKET.

THE TICKET!

OHHH!

NO. OKAY, YOTSUBA. GO AHEAD AND TAKE IT FOR ME.

THIS BOOTH DOESN'T HAVE E.T.C.,* RIGHT?

YO-TSUBA WANTS TO TAKE IT!

SIGN: TAKE TICKET

*E.T.C.: ELECTRONIC TOLL COLLECTION

YEAH. TAKE IT FOR ME.

OH! PAPER CAME OUT!

通行券を お取り下さい
TAKE TICKET

通行券を お取り下さい

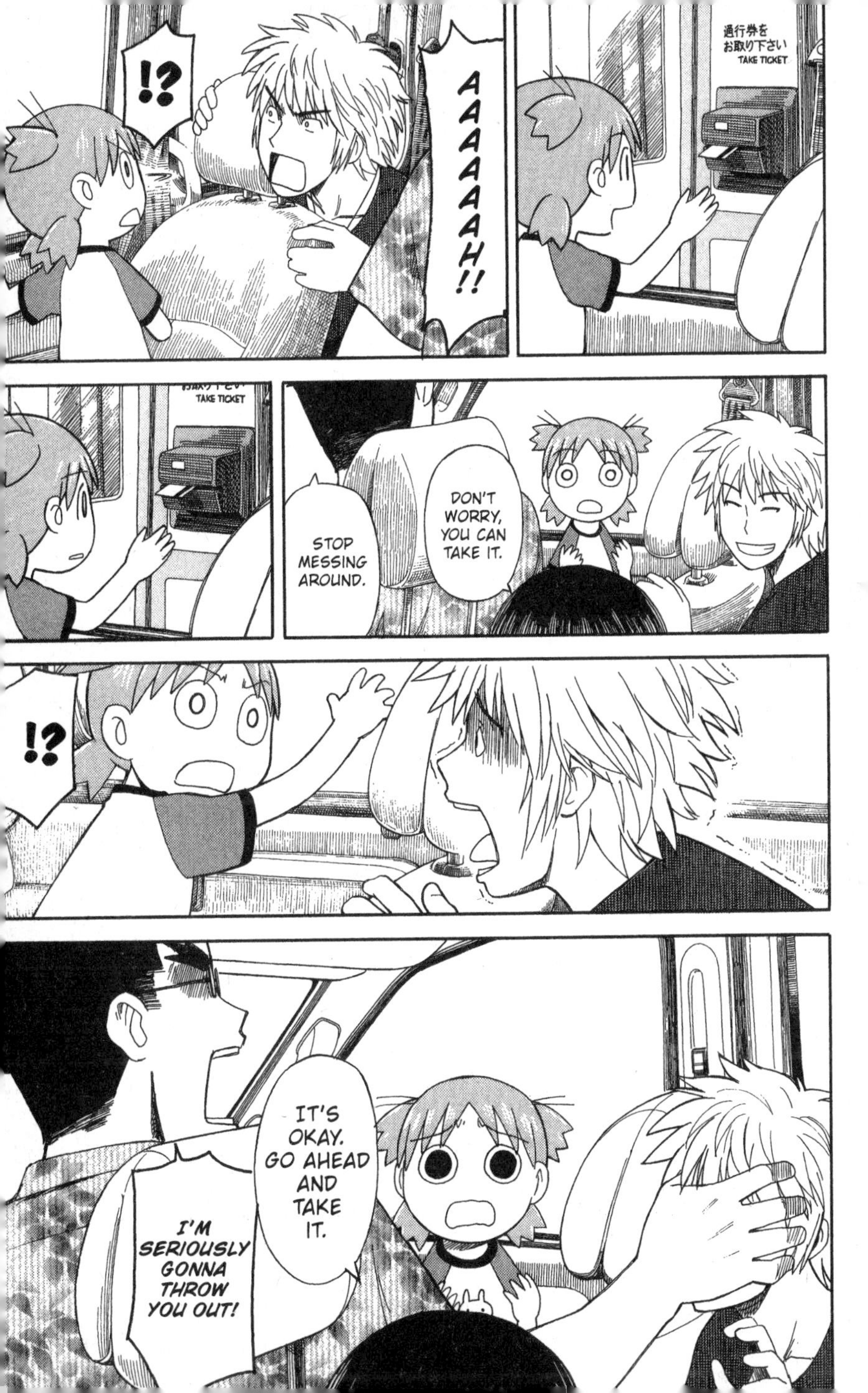
通行券を
お取り下さい
TAKE TICKET
AAAAAAAH!!
!?
DON'T WORRY, YOU CAN TAKE IT.
STOP MESSING AROUND.
TAKE TICKET
!?
IT'S OKAY. GO AHEAD AND TAKE IT.
I'M SERIOUSLY GONNA THROW YOU OUT!

YOTSUBA&! THE RANCH

#48

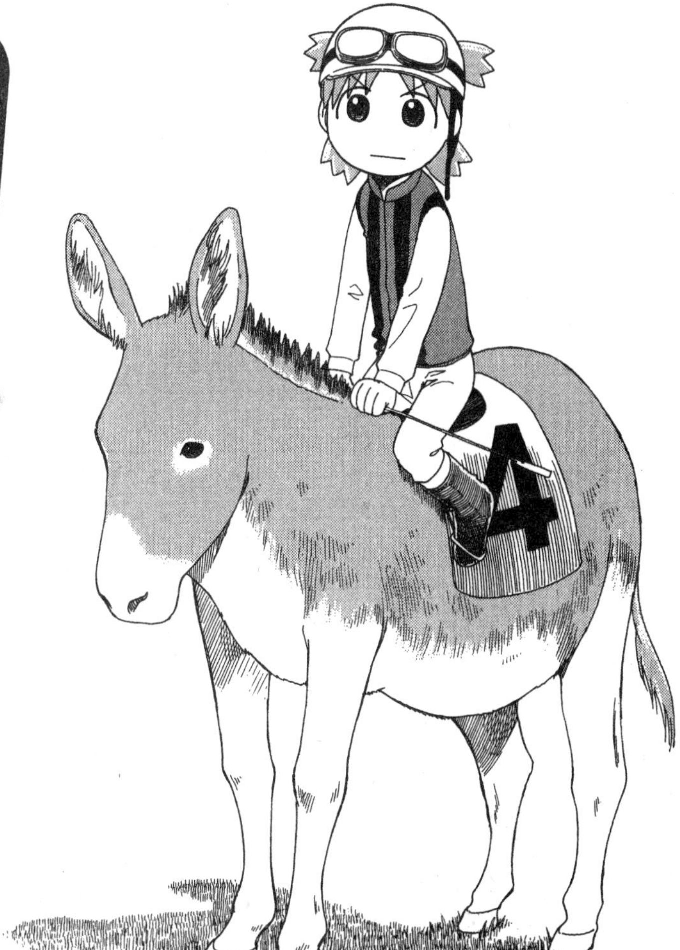
4

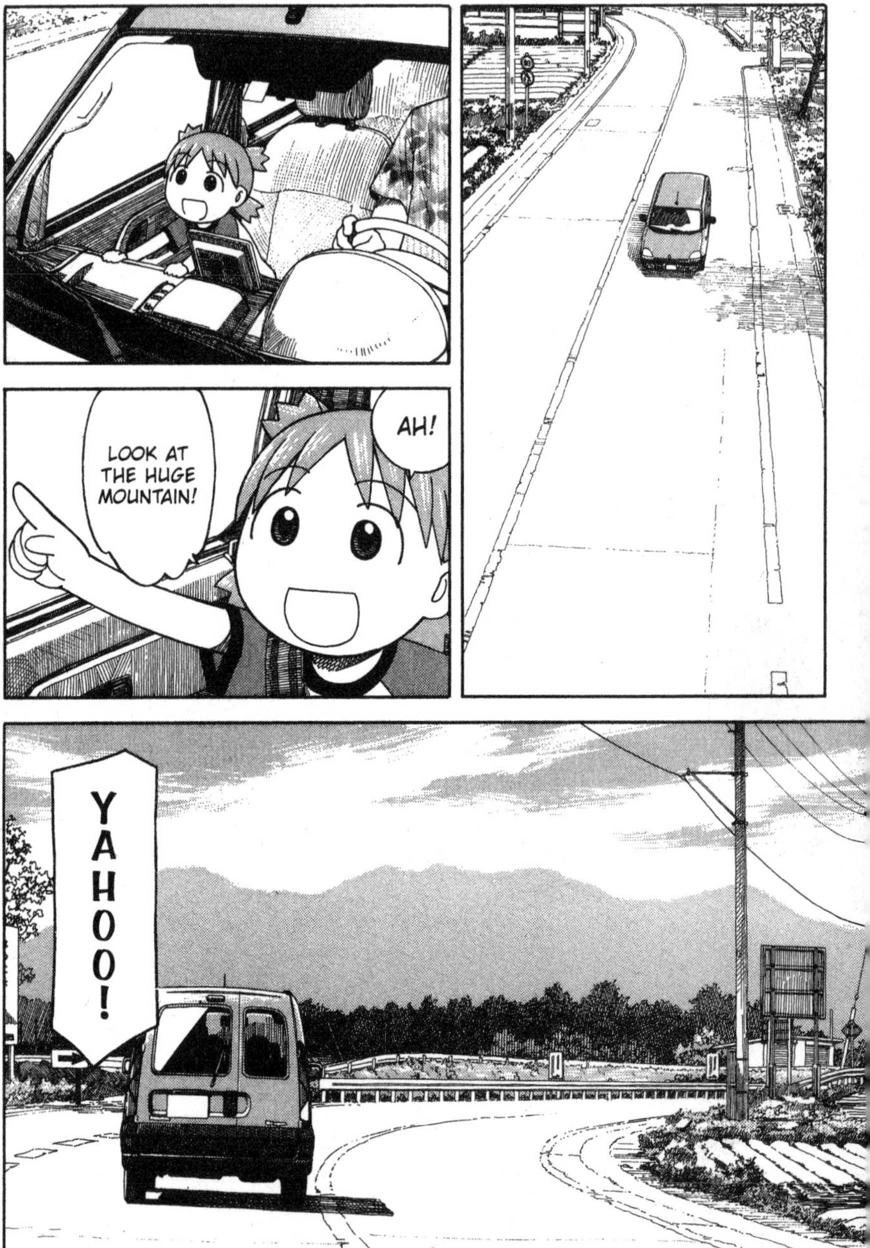
AH!
LOOK AT THE HUGE MOUNTAIN!
YAHOOO!

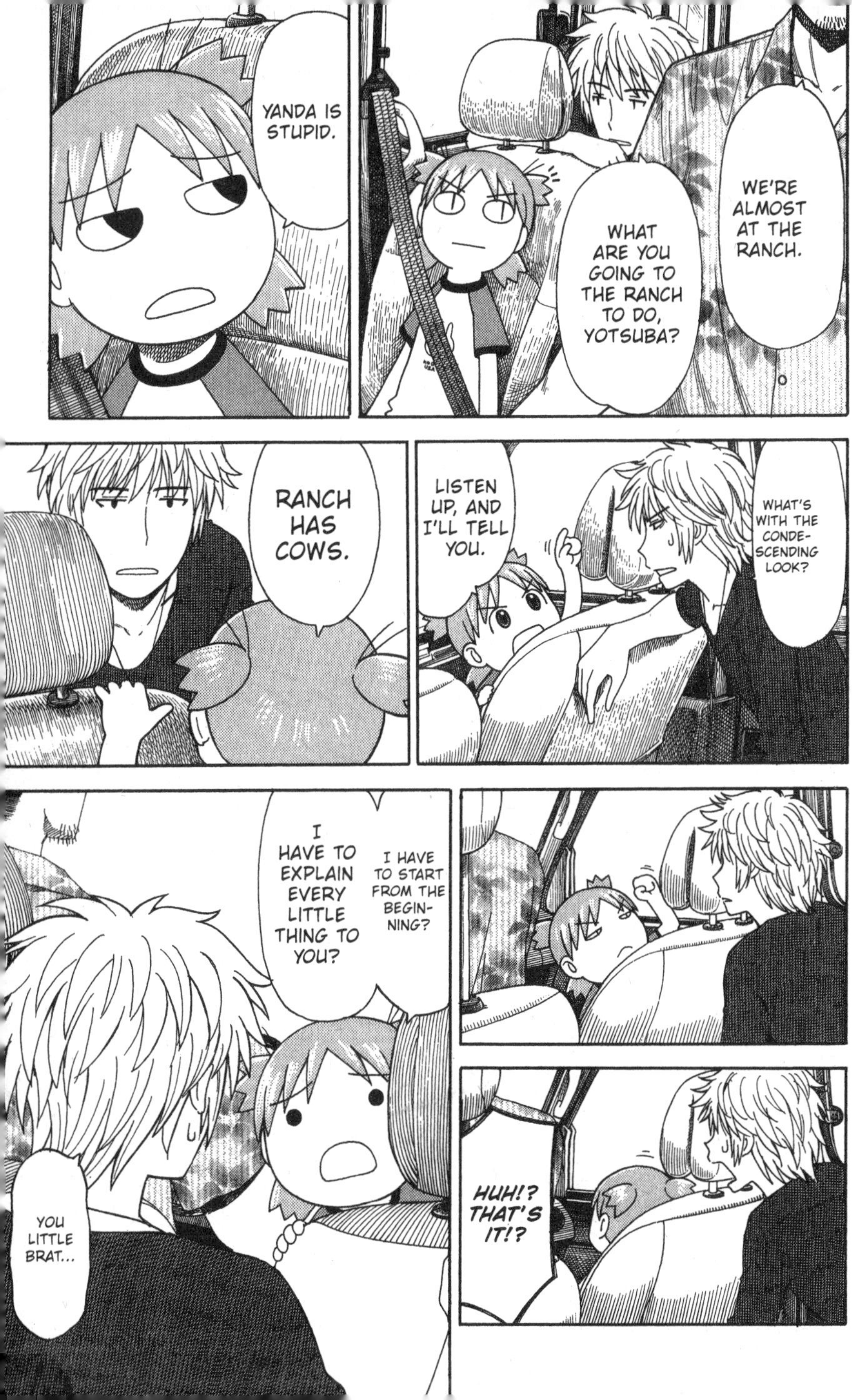
WE'RE ALMOST AT THE RANCH.
WHAT ARE YOU GOING TO THE RANCH TO DO, YOTSUBA?
YANDA IS STUPID.
WHAT'S WITH THE CONDE-SCENDING LOOK?
LISTEN UP, AND I'LL TELL YOU.
RANCH HAS COWS.
HUH!? THAT'S IT!?
I HAVE TO START FROM THE BEGIN-NING?
I HAVE TO EXPLAIN EVERY LITTLE THING TO YOU?
YOU LITTLE BRAT...

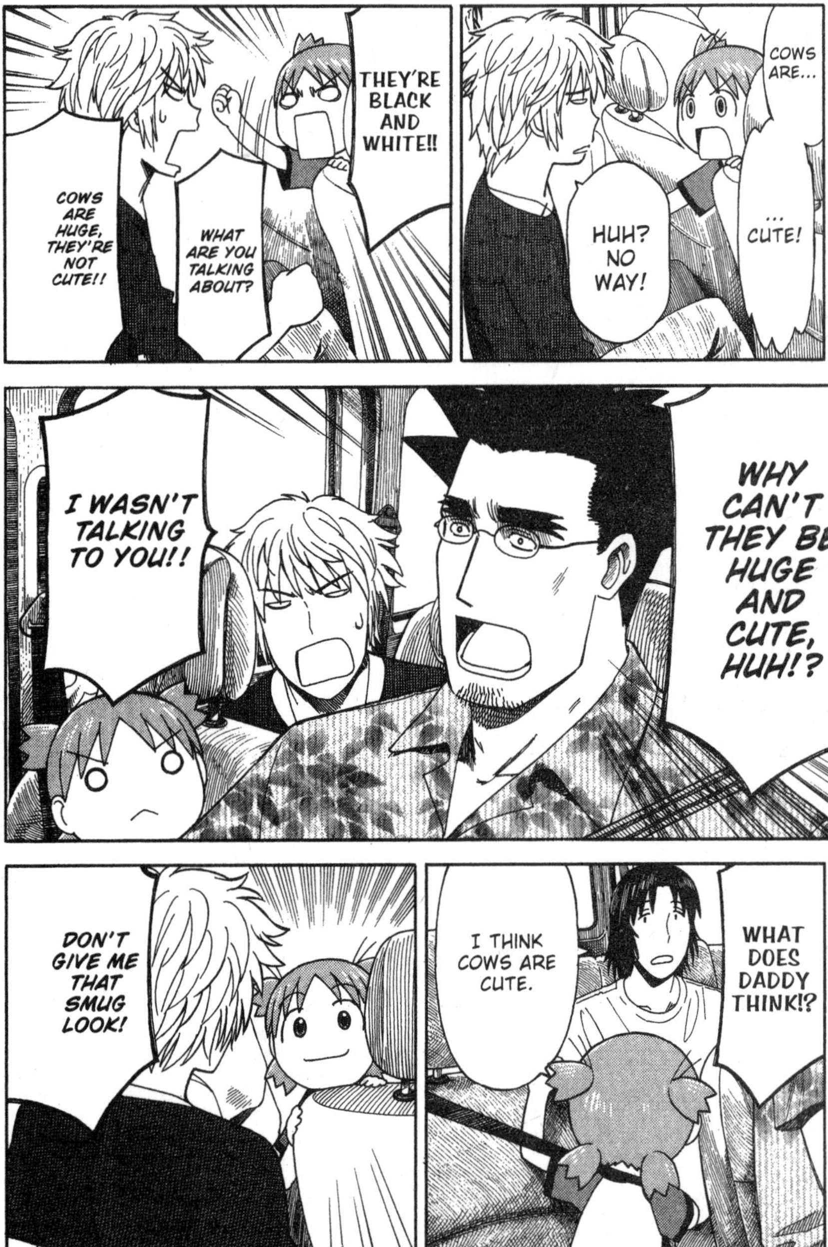
COWS ARE...
...CUTE!
HUH? NO WAY!
THEY'RE BLACK AND WHITE!!
WHAT ARE YOU TALKING ABOUT?
COWS ARE HUGE, THEY'RE NOT CUTE!!
WHY CAN'T THEY BE HUGE AND CUTE, HUH!?
I WASN'T TALKING TO YOU!!
WHAT DOES DADDY THINK!?
I THINK COWS ARE CUTE.
DON'T GIVE ME THAT SMUG LOOK!

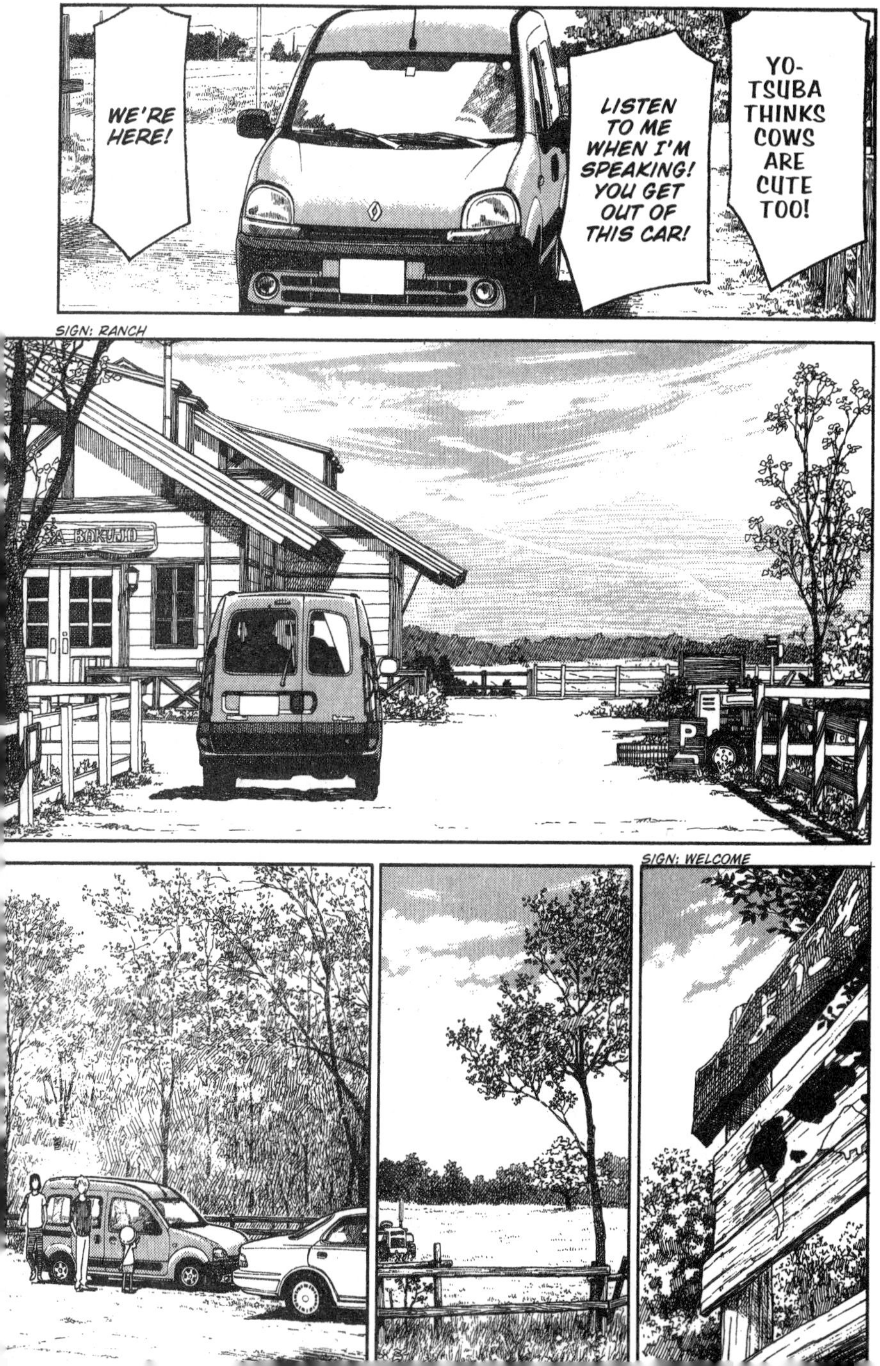
YO-TSUBA THINKS COWS ARE CUTE TOO!
LISTEN TO ME WHEN I'M SPEAKING! YOU GET OUT OF THIS CAR!
WE'RE HERE!
SIGN: RANCH
A BOKUJO
SIGN: WELCOME

NOT JUST THE HOUSE...

THERE'S COWS IN THERE?

THIS HOUSE IS THE RANCH!?

WOON...

SO THIS IS IT...

I THINK SO.

CAN WE JUST GO IN?

ALL OF IT!?

THE WHOLE THING!?

THIS WHOOOLE AREA IS THE RANCH.

YEAH!!

COME ON, GUYS!

AH!

THERE!

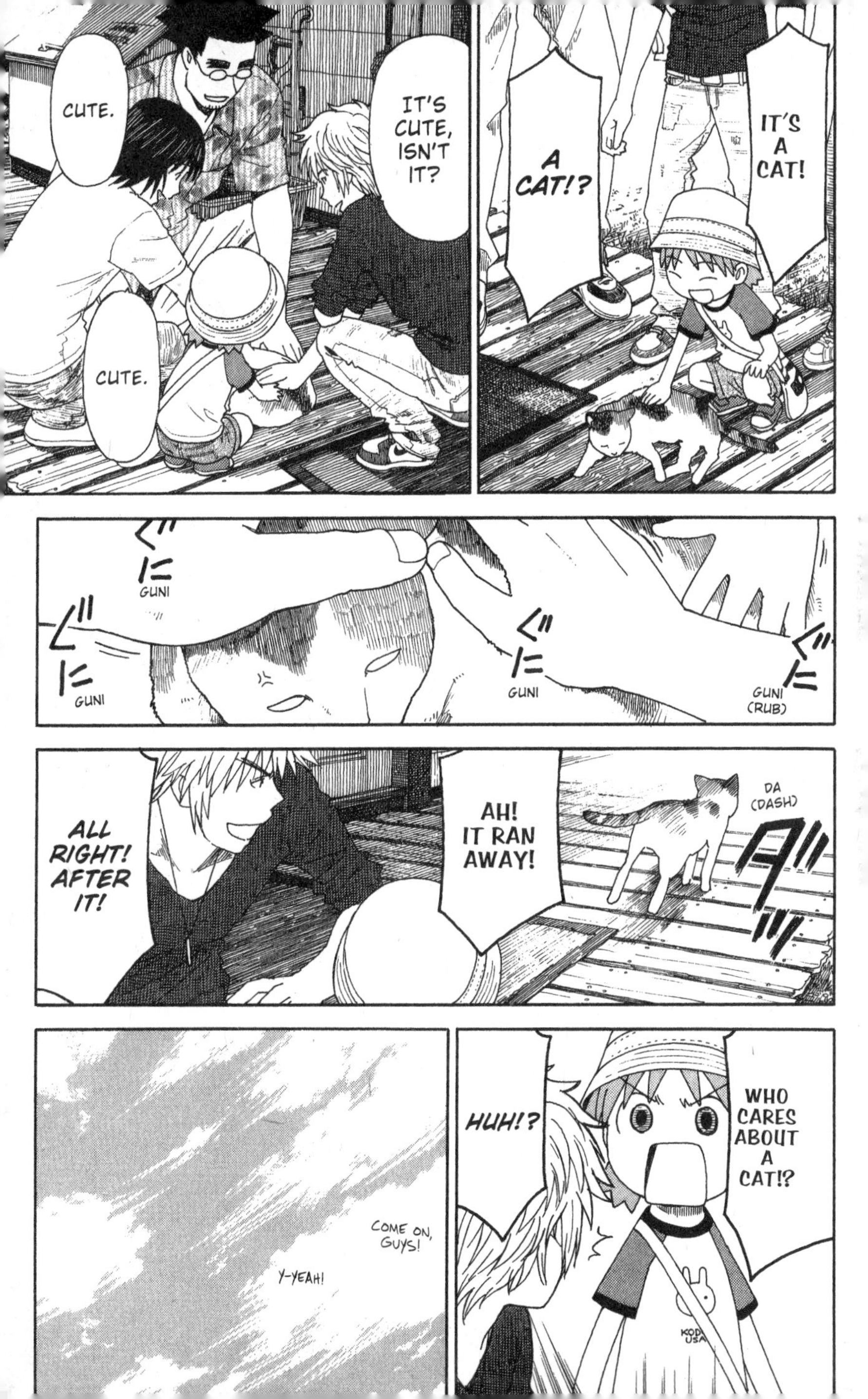
IT'S A CAT!
A CAT!?
IT'S CUTE, ISN'T IT?
CUTE.
CUTE.
ぐに
GUNI (RUB)
ぐに
GUNI
ぐに
GUNI
ぐに
GUNI
ダッ
DA (DASH)
AH! IT RAN AWAY!
ALL RIGHT! AFTER IT!
WHO CARES ABOUT A CAT!?
HUH!?
COME ON, GUYS!
Y-YEAH!

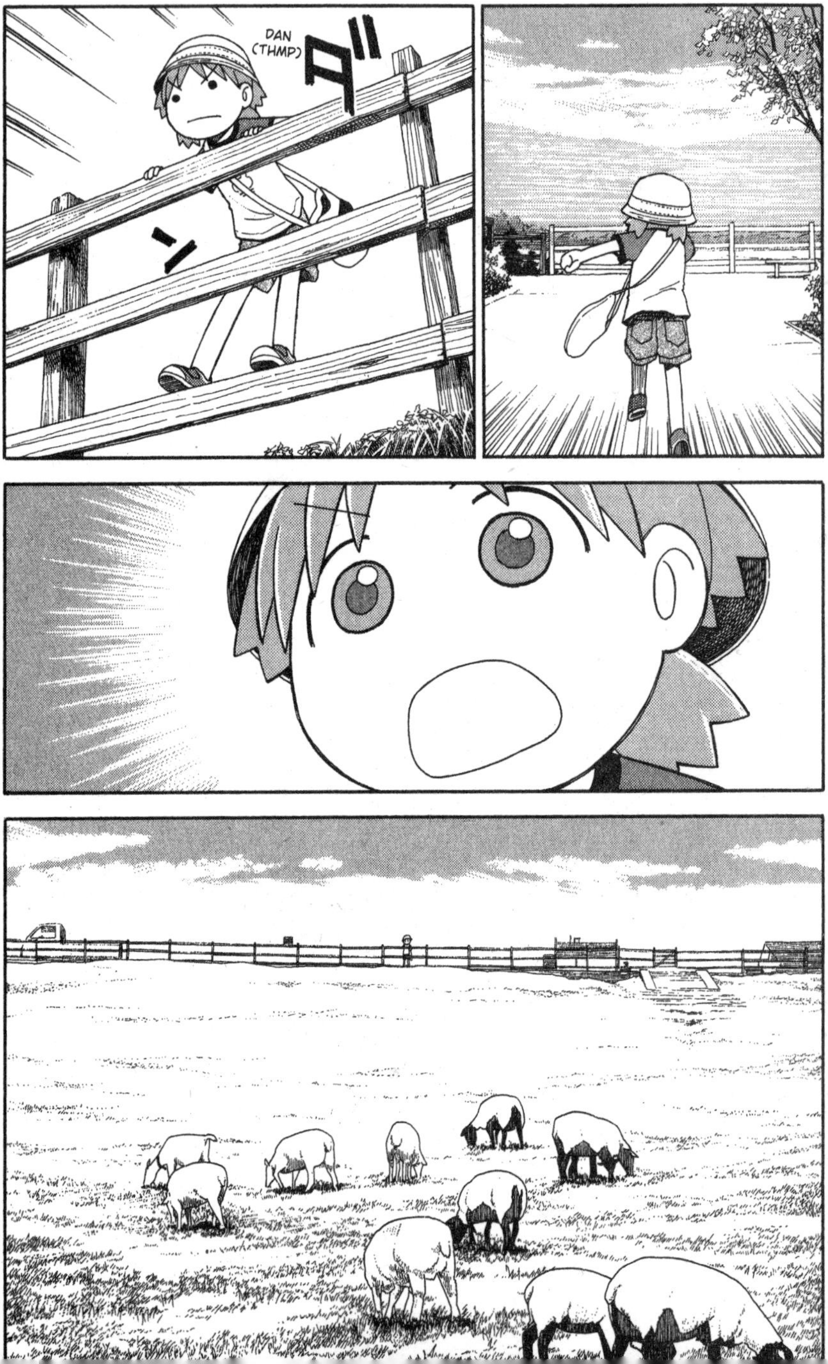
DAN (THMP)

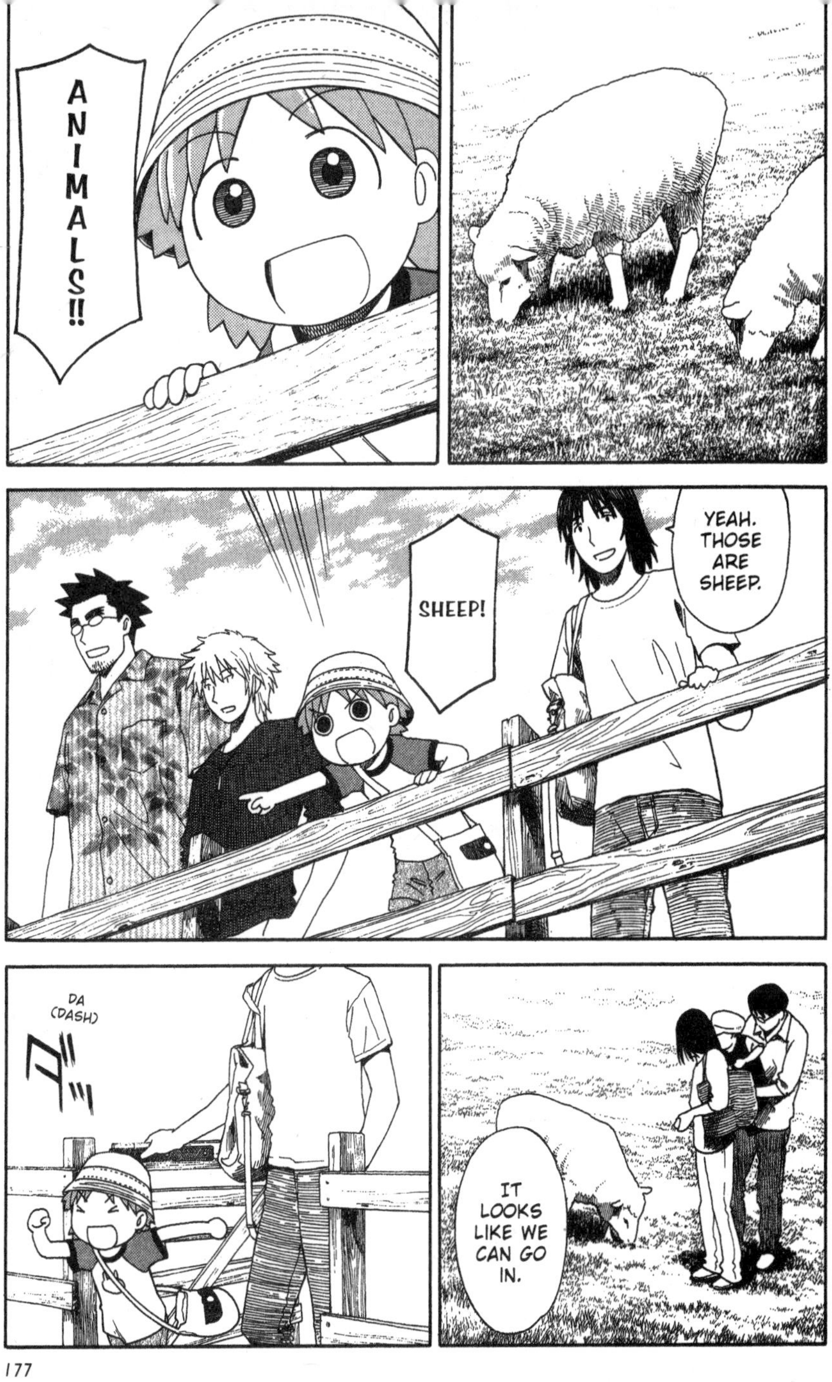
ANIMALS!!
YEAH. THOSE ARE SHEEP.
SHEEP!
IT LOOKS LIKE WE CAN GO IN.
DA (DASH)

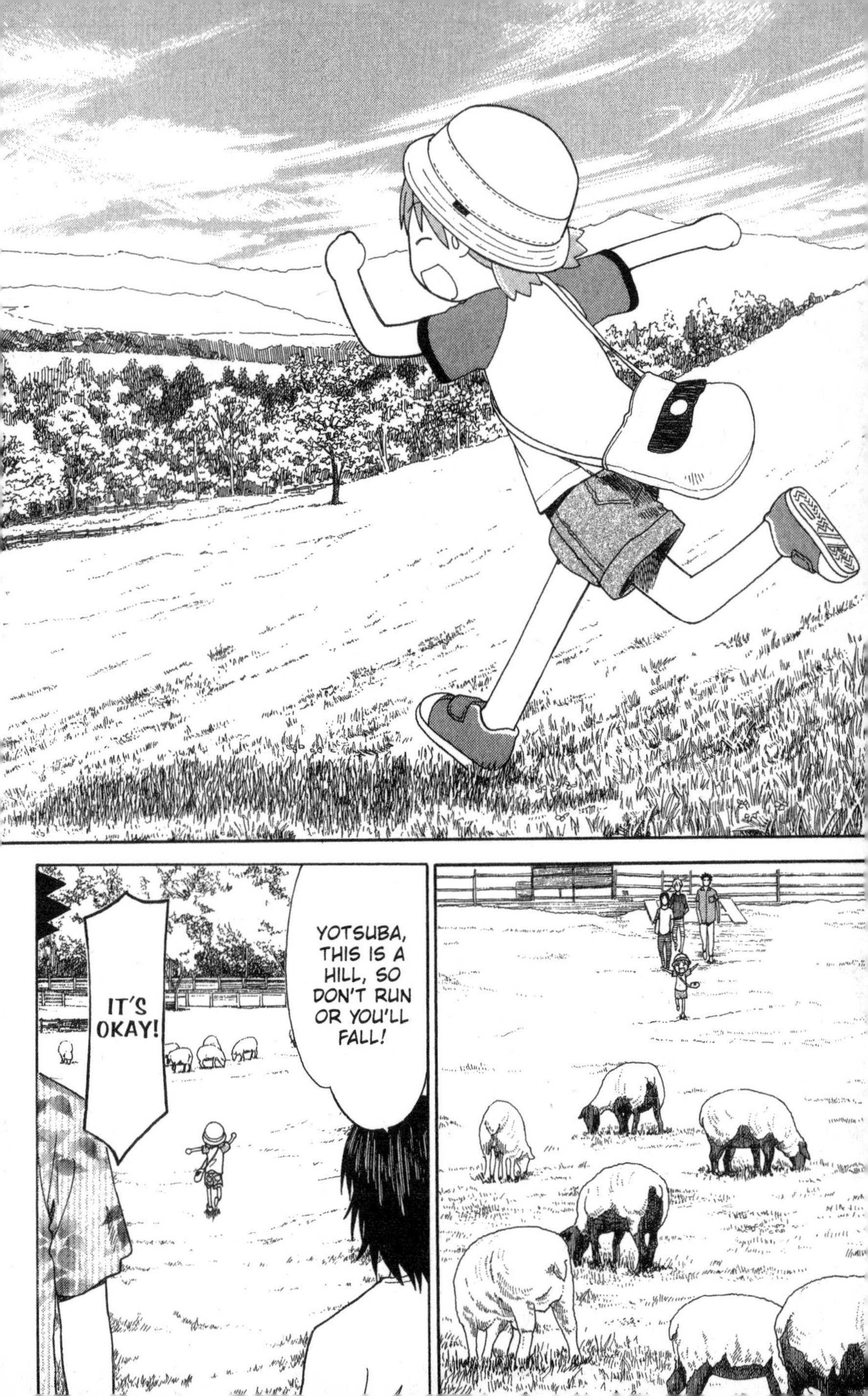
YOTSUBA, THIS IS A HILL, SO DON'T RUN OR YOU'LL FALL!
IT'S OKAY!

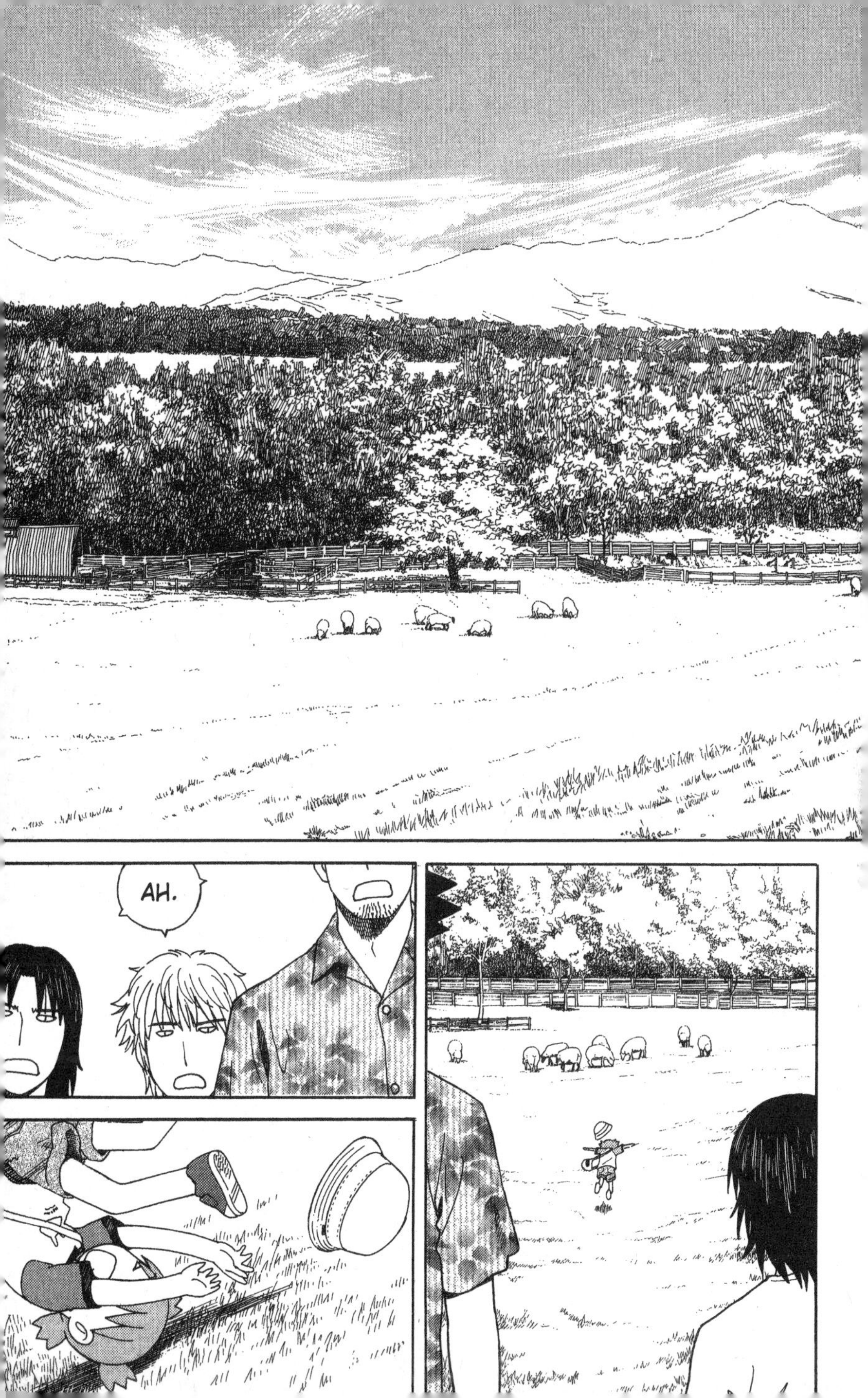
AH.

ROLL ROLL ROLL! AH-HA-HA-HA-HA!

MAN, SHE REALLY ROLLED!

AH HA HA HA!

SFX: GERA (CACKLE) GERA GERA

!?

YOU SCARED THEM, AND THEY RAN AWAY.

NOW LOOK.

AWWW...

YOU WILL? OKAY THEN, GO AHEAD.

YOTSUBA WILL APOLOGIZE TO THE SHEEP AND MAKE UP WITH THEM.

HEEEY! SHEEP!

DON'T BE SCARED ANY MORE, ALL RIGHT?

I FELL, SO I COULDN'T HELP IT.

DON
(THUD)

LET'S BE FRIENDS, OKAY?

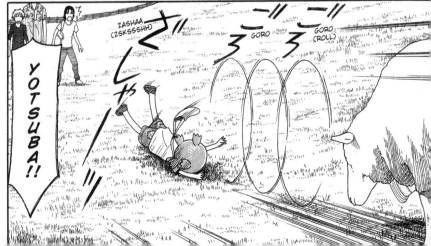

ZASHAA
(ZSKSSSHH)

GORO

GORO
(ROLL)

YOTSUBA!!

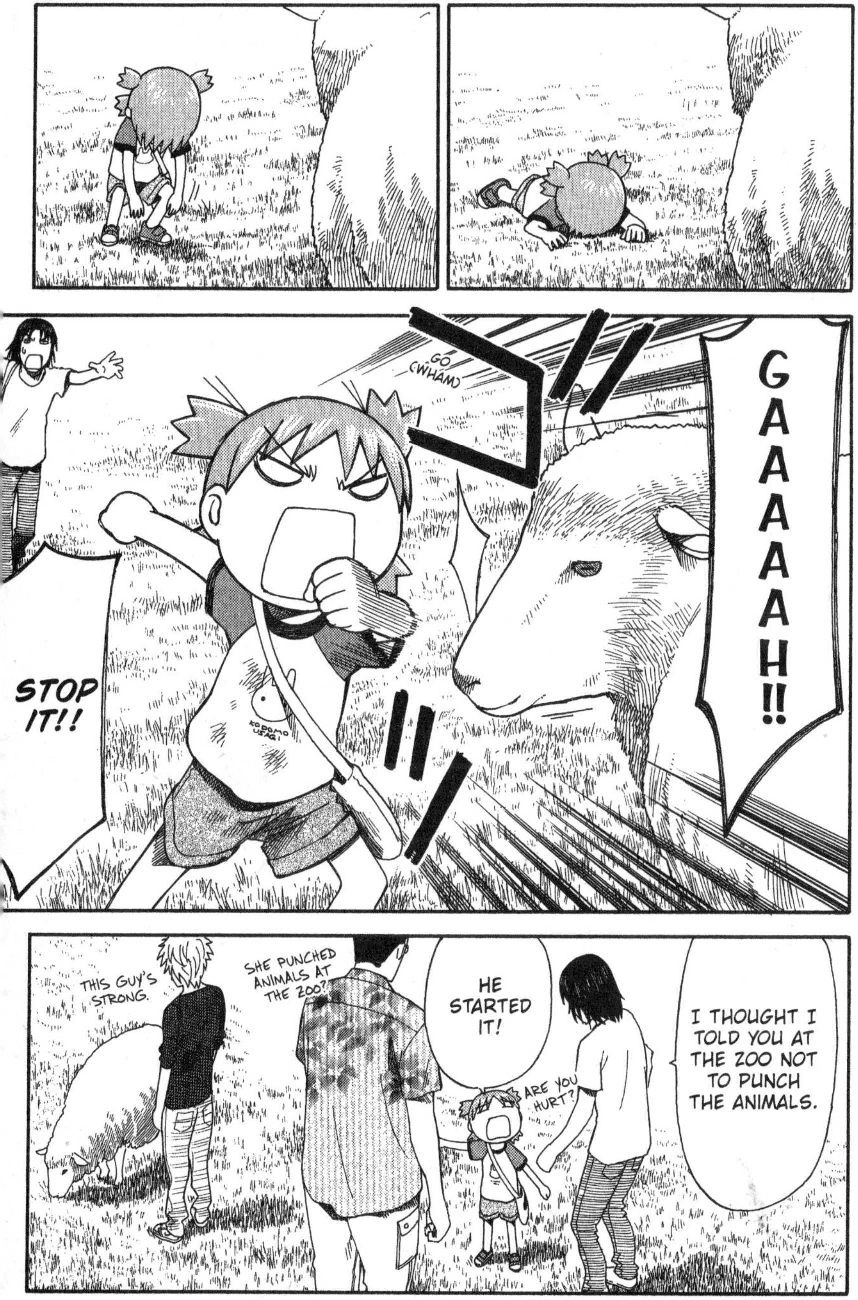
GAAAAAAH!!
GO (WHAM)
KODOMO USAGI
STOP IT!!
I THOUGHT I TOLD YOU AT THE ZOO NOT TO PUNCH THE ANIMALS.
ARE YOU HURT?
HE STARTED IT!
SHE PUNCHED ANIMALS AT THE ZOO?
THIS GUY'S STRONG.

HORSE-TAIL?

WHAT ARE THEY ALL EATING?

WELL, THAT'S JUST HOW THEY ARE.

HOW CAN THEY EAT GRASS?

...I DO WONDER HOW THEY CAN DO THAT, THOUGH...

THEY'RE EATING GRASS!

AH! GRASS!

SFX: ZUZUZU (SLIIDE)

WOW! THEY'RE USEFUL!

THIS WOOL IS USED TO MAKE THINGS LIKE SWEATERS AND CARPET.

OHHH!

THEY GO FAR IN!

YOTSUBA, DIG YOUR HANDS INTO THE SHEEP'S WOOL.

ズズズ

OOH!

THEY'RE ALWAYS EATING.

THESE ONES ARE GOATS.

THEY'RE CUTE.

I LIKE GOATS BETTER THAN SHEEP.

GOAT'S MILK?

FUR? MEAT?

HMM, I WONDER WHAT THEY USE THESE GOATS FOR...

GOATS ARE...

WHAT ARE GOATS USEFUL FOR?

BUT I HAVEN'T SEEN ANY BEING SOLD.

DON'T TEASE HIM! DON'T TEASE THE GOAT!

ARE YOU MAKING YOURSELF USEFUL AT THIS RANCH?

HEY, GOAT. WHAT ARE YOU USEFUL FOR?

GET TO WORK, GOAT.

SIGN: EXPERIENCE COW MILKING, EVERY DAY 11:00 A.M., EVERY DAY 1:00 P.M., PRICE PER PERSON ¥700

... MILKING ...?

OKAY, LET'S DO THIS.

乳しぼり体験
1回目 11時 00分
2回目 13時 00分
料金 お一人様 700円
※ソフトクリーム付き
お申込みのお客様は INFORMATION まで

SIGN (CONT.): *ICE CREAM INCLUDED, INTERESTED PERSONS SHOULD GO TO THE INFORMATION WINDOW

IT'S A DOG! THERE'S A DOG TOO!

WHAT ARE YOU TALKING ABOUT?

IT SAYS, "EXPERIENCE COW MILKING"! YOU GET TO DO WHAT THE RANCH HANDS DO AND MILK A COW!

EXCUSE COW MILKING!

EXCUSE ME.

THIS IS THE COWS' HOUSE.

WHOSE HOUSE IS THAT?

OHHH, THIS IS WHERE THEY LIVE...

CAN I GO INTO THE COWS' HOUSE?

UM, EXCUSE ME.

YOU'RE HERE FOR THE COW MILKING, RIGHT?

COULD YOU WAIT JUST A MOMENT? I'M GETTING EVERYTHING READY.

SURE. GO RIGHT AHEAD.

OH!

OH!

WHOA THERE.

WAAAH!

WHY, YOU LITTLE LIAR.

KYUU (PINCH)

DON'T GRAB MY NOSE!!

WHAT, YOU'RE NOT AFRAID OF COWS, ARE YOU?

WHAT ARE YOU DOING!?

THEY'RE CUTE, RIGHT?

YOU'RE SCARED.

I'M NOT AFRAID!!

I AM NOT SCARED!!

OKAY, IF YOU'RE NOT AFRAID, THEN PROVE IT.

I'LL PROVE IT!

YEAH, I GUESS IT WOULD...

AH-HA-HA-HA! HER VOICE SOUNDS SO NASAL!

I GOT THE POINT!! YOTSUBA, I GOT THE POINT!!

GU (CLENCH)

WAH!! DON'T PUNCH IT!!

THESE GUYS MIGHT LOOK LAID-BACK, BUT THEY'LL PUT UP A FIGHT, SO WATCH OUT.

I GOT YOUR POINT, YOTSUBA. YOU'RE NOT AFRAID.

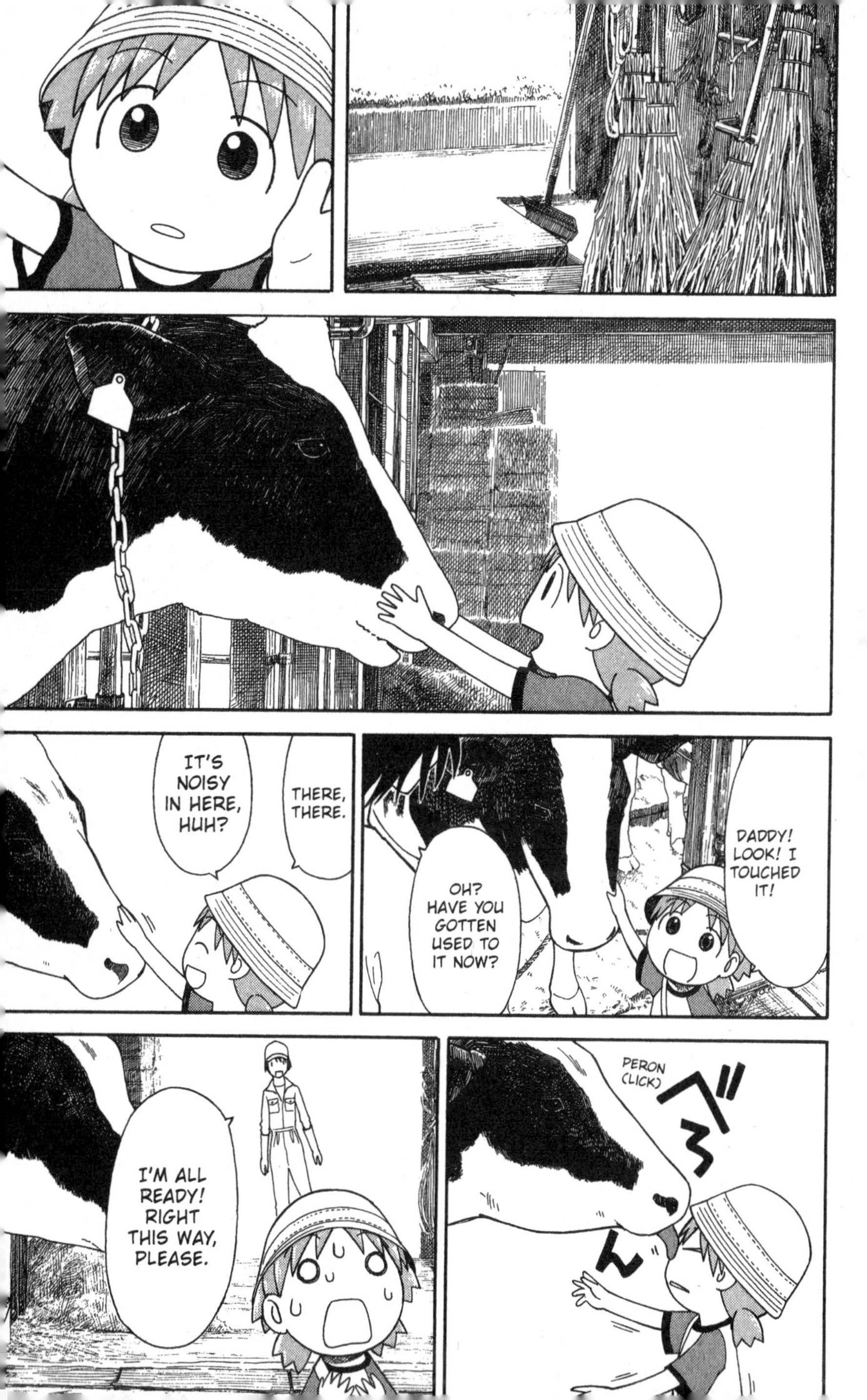
DADDY! LOOK! I TOUCHED IT!
OH? HAVE YOU GOTTEN USED TO IT NOW?
THERE, THERE.
IT'S NOISY IN HERE, HUH?
PERON (CLICK)
べろん
I'M ALL READY! RIGHT THIS WAY, PLEASE.

?

LINE UP, LINE UP!

FOUR PEOPLE, RIGHT?

THREE!

ONE!

FOUR!

TWO!

HUH? OH, YEAH...

DO IT! DO IT RIGHT!

ONE!

OOH.

IT'S WARM.

1, 2, 3, 4, 5...

HUH?

SFX: CHAAA (FSSSHHT)

SQUEEZE IT QUICKLY.

YOU CAN SQUEEZE IT HARDER.

SQUEEZE THE VERY TOP PART TIGHT.

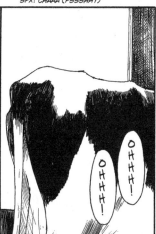

OHHH! OHHH!

DADDY, I DID IT!

IT CAME OUT!

YANDA, YOU BE QUIET!

WHAT ARE YOU TALKING ABOUT? THAT /S MILK.

IT'S JUST LIKE MILK.

AH HA HA HA!

THAT'S MILK.

WHAT DOES JUMBO THINK!?

!

WHAT? REALLY!?

THAT'S MILK.

YO-TSU-BA.

AH!

PERO (CLICK)

THE COW DID...?

THE COW MADE IT HERSELF. SHE SAVED IT UP IN THERE HERSELF.

UMM...

WHO MADE IT!? WHO PUT IT IN THERE!?

THERE'S MILK IN THERE!

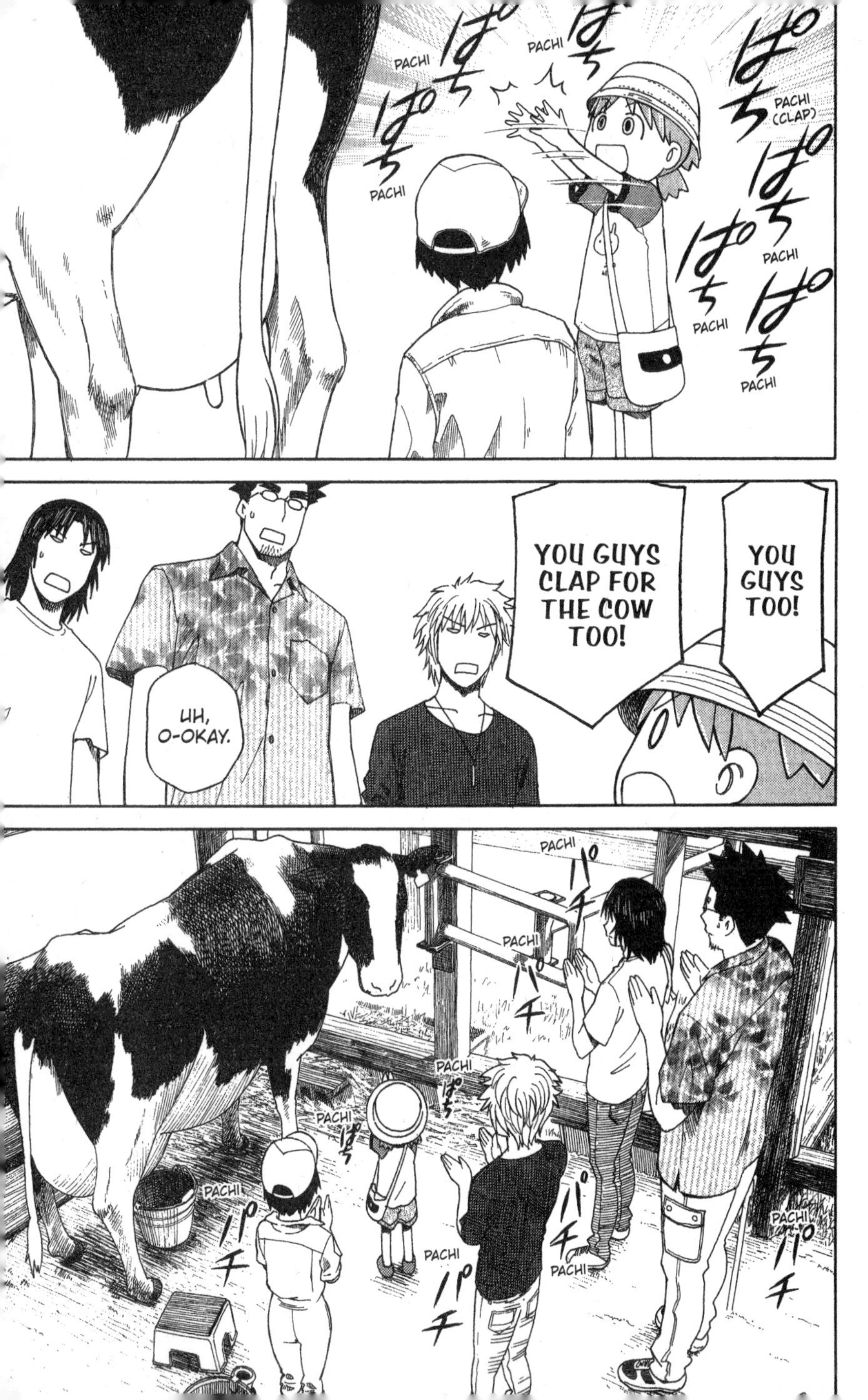
ぱち
PACHI (CLAP)
ぱち
PACHI
ぱち
PACHI
ぱち
PACHI
ぱち
PACHI
ぱち
PACHI
ぱち
PACHI
YOU GUYS TOO!
YOU GUYS CLAP FOR THE COW TOO!
UH, O-OKAY.
PACHI パチ
PACHI パチ
PACHI パチ
PACHI パチ
PACHI ぱち
PACHI ぱち
PACHI パチ
PACHI パチ

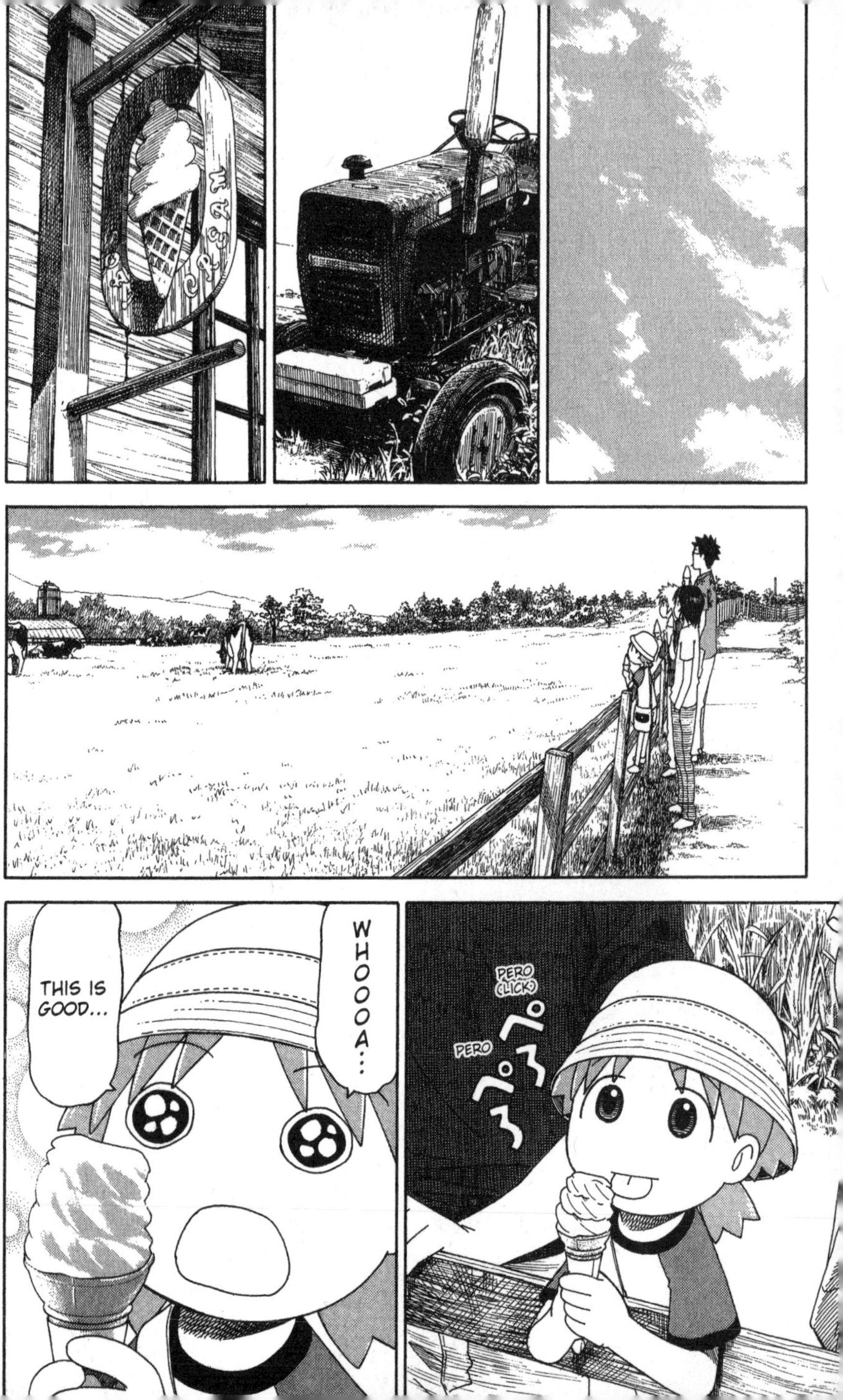
PERO (LICK)
PERO
ぺろぺろ
WHOOOA...
THIS IS GOOD...

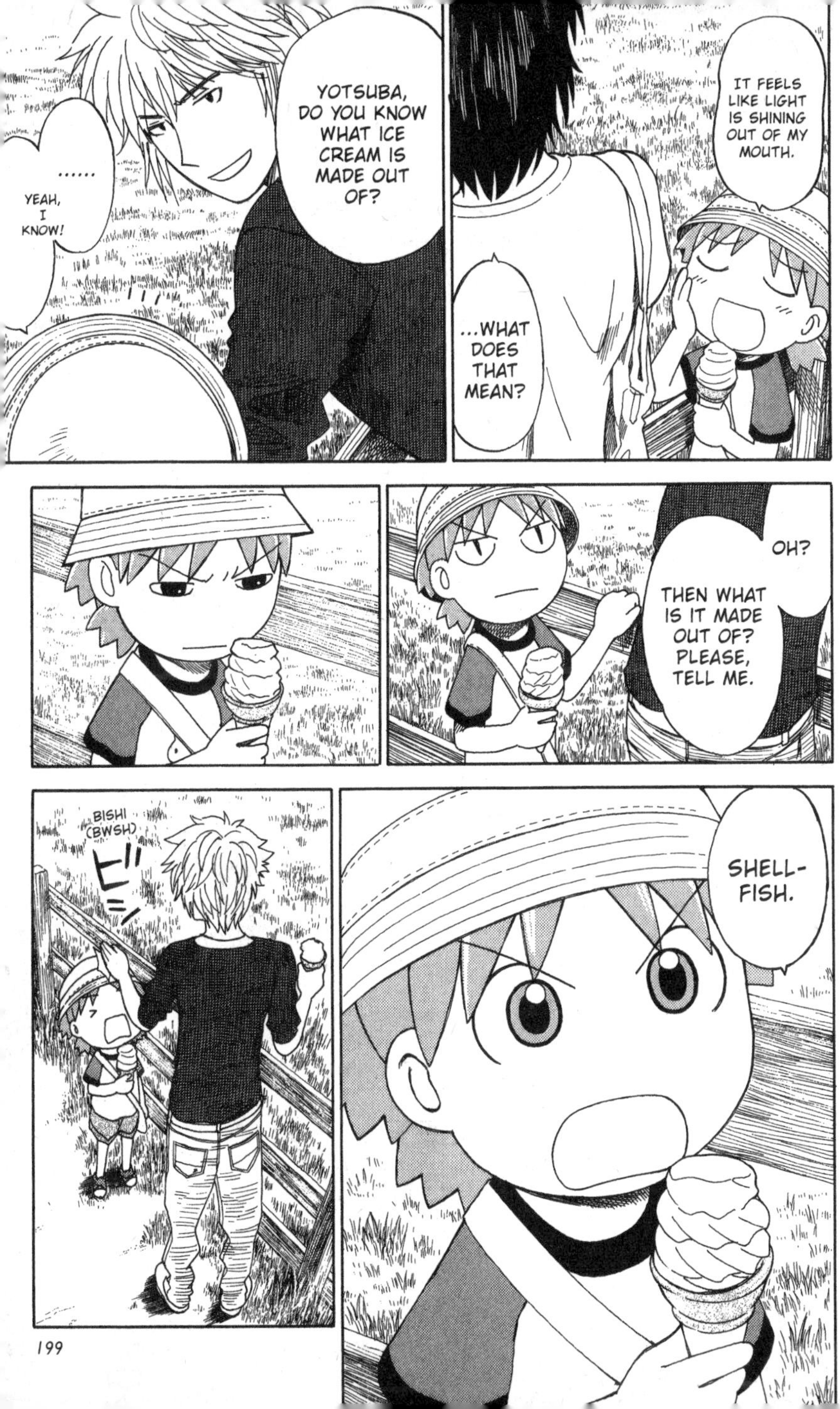
IT FEELS LIKE LIGHT IS SHINING OUT OF MY MOUTH.
...WHAT DOES THAT MEAN?
YOTSUBA, DO YOU KNOW WHAT ICE CREAM IS MADE OUT OF?
......
YEAH, I KNOW!
OH?
THEN WHAT IS IT MADE OUT OF? PLEASE, TELL ME.
SHELL-FISH.
BISHI (BWSH)
ビシ

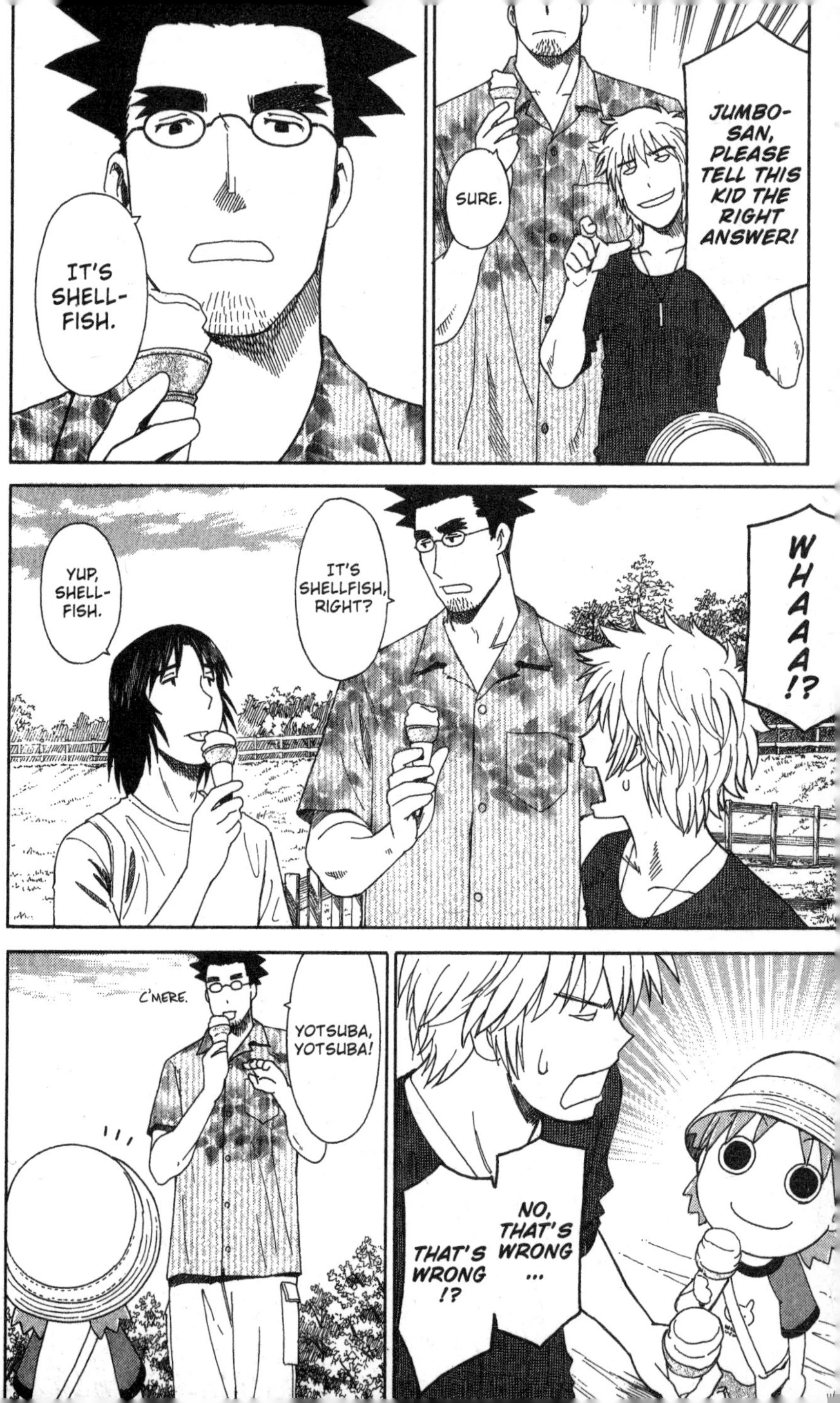
JUMBO-SAN, PLEASE TELL THIS KID THE RIGHT ANSWER!
SURE.
IT'S SHELL-FISH.
WHAAAA!?
IT'S SHELLFISH, RIGHT?
YUP, SHELL-FISH.
NO, THAT'S WRONG ...
THAT'S WRONG !?
YOTSUBA, YOTSUBA!
C'MERE.

······

WHA!?

······

THE SHELL-FISH WAS A LIE!

IT'S ACTUALLY MADE OUT OF MILK!

WHAAA!?

LIAR!

I DID NOT.

IN FACT, YOU'RE THE ONE WHO GOT TRICKED!

YOU DIDN'T TRICK ME AT ALL!!

NO!

HA-HA-HA-HA-HA!

TRICKED YOU!

HEY! LISTEN TO ME!

I HAVE TO GIVE THE COWS SOME GRASS.

AH.

OKAY THEN, WHAT'S BUTTER MADE OUT OF?

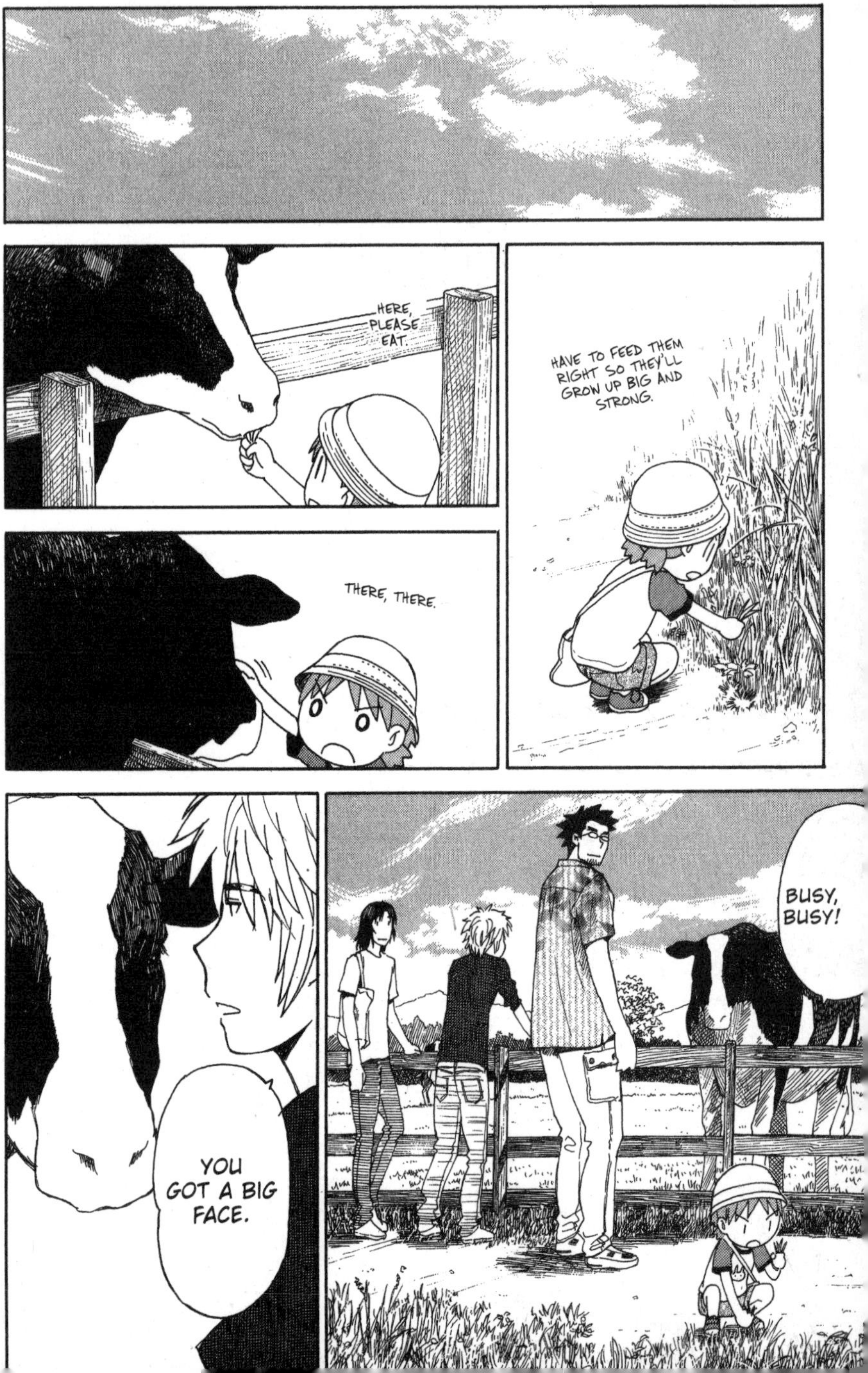
HAVE TO FEED THEM RIGHT SO THEY'LL GROW UP BIG AND STRONG.
HERE, PLEASE EAT.
THERE, THERE.
BUSY, BUSY!
YOU GOT A BIG FACE.

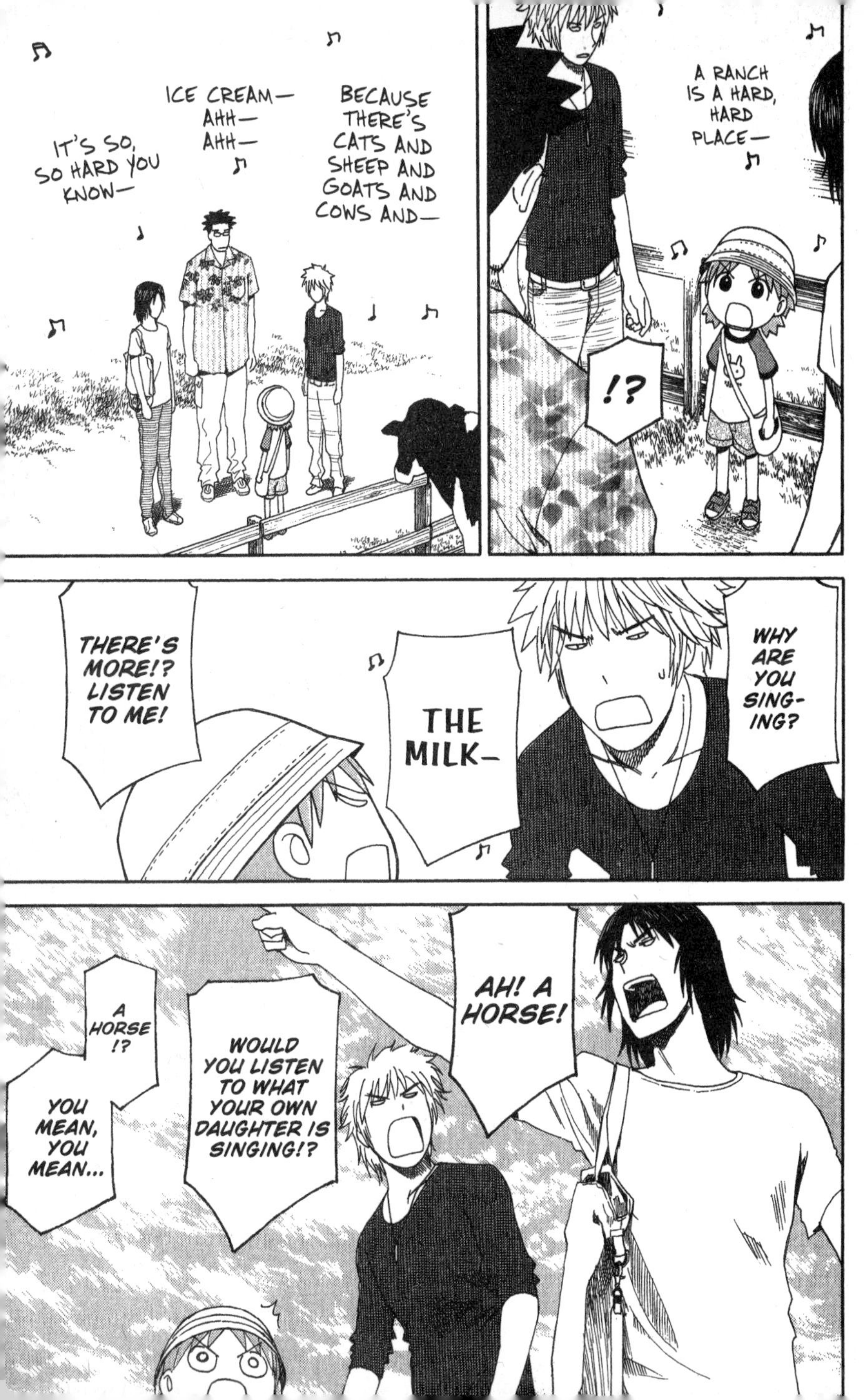
A RANCH IS A HARD, HARD PLACE—
!?
BECAUSE THERE'S CATS AND SHEEP AND GOATS AND COWS AND—
ICE CREAM— AHH— AHH—
IT'S SO, SO HARD YOU KNOW—
WHY ARE YOU SINGING?
THE MILK—
THERE'S MORE!? LISTEN TO ME!
AH! A HORSE!
WOULD YOU LISTEN TO WHAT YOUR OWN DAUGHTER IS SINGING!?
A HORSE!?
YOU MEAN, YOU MEAN...

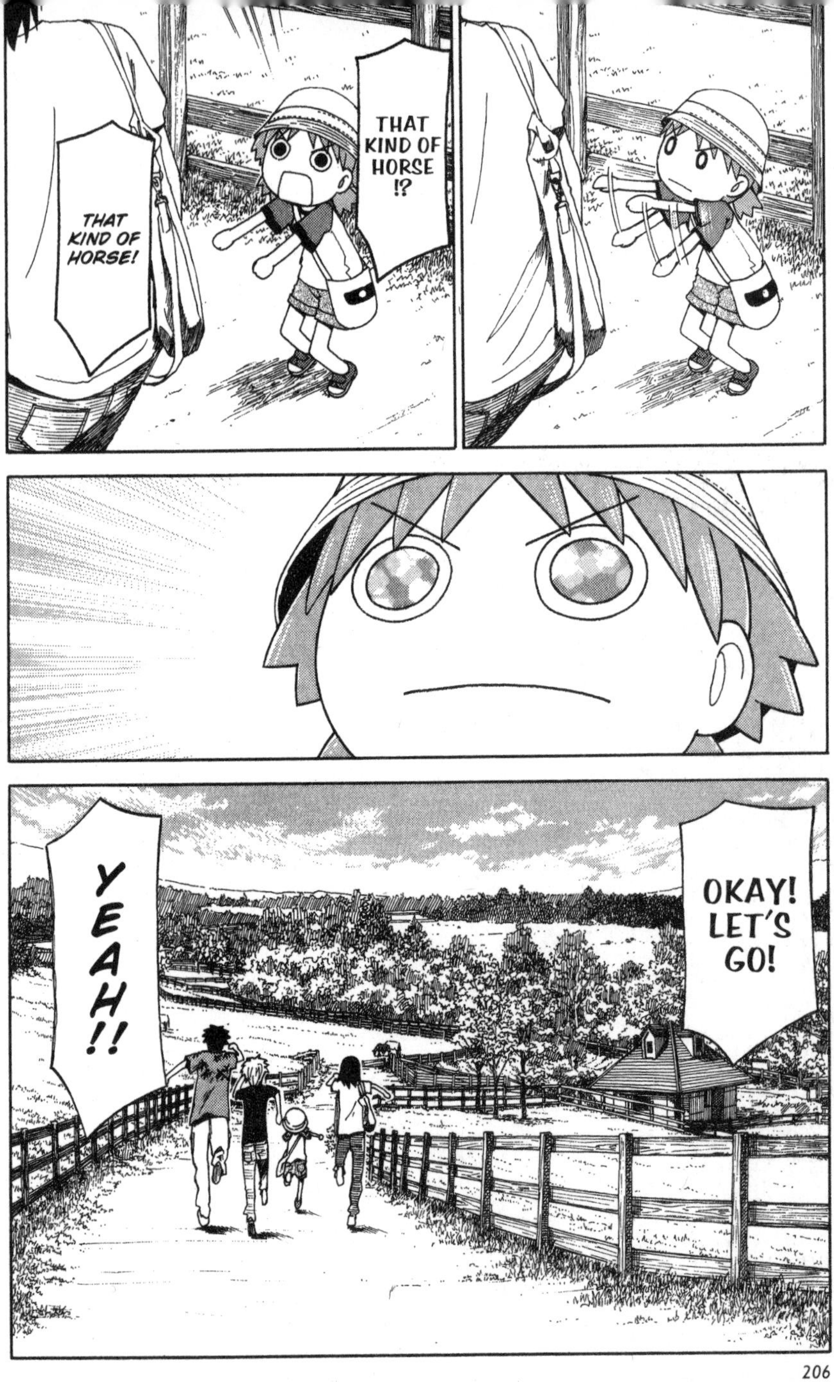
THAT KIND OF HORSE !?
THAT KIND OF HORSE!
OKAY! LET'S GO!
YEAH!!

YOTSUBA&! 7

KIYOHIKO AZUMA

Translation: Amy Forsyth
Lettering: Terri Delgado

YOTSUBA&! Vol. 7
© KIYOHIKO AZUMA / YOTUBA SUTAZIO 2007
Edited by ASCII MEDIA WORKS
First published in Japan in 2007 by
KADOKAWA CORPORATION, Tokyo.
English translation rights arranged with
KADOKAWA CORPORATION, Tokyo,
through Tuttle-Mori Agency, Inc., Tokyo.

English translation © 2009 by Yen Press, LLC

Yen Press
1290 Avenue of the Americas
New York, NY 10104

Visit us at yenpress.com
facebook.com/yenpress
twitter.com/yenpress
yenpress.tumblr.com
instagram.com/yenpress

First Yen Press Edition: December 2009

Yen Press is an imprint of Yen Press, LLC.
The Yen Press name and logo are trademarks of Yen Press, LLC.

ISBN: 978-0-316-07325-7

20 19 18 17 16 15

WOR

Printed in the United States of America

YOTSUBA&!

ENJOY EVERYTHING.

TO BE CONTINUED!

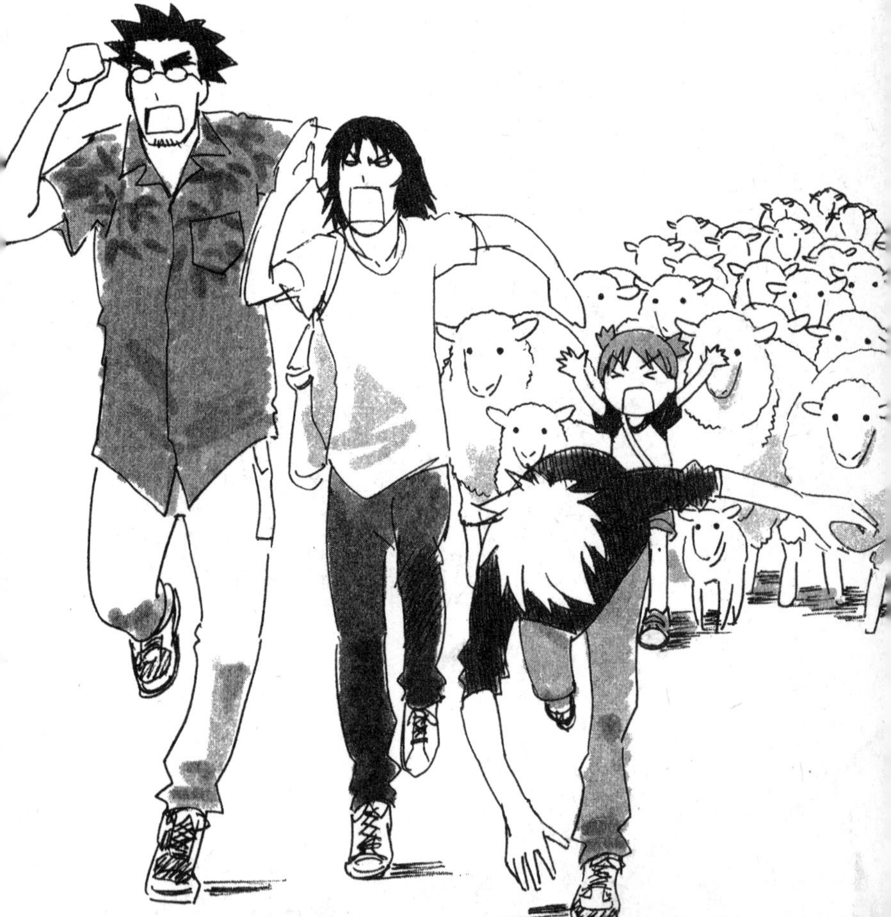